D1544869

"When I entered Babylon in peace, and took up my royal
abode in the palace of the princes amid acclamation and
shouts of joy, the mighty lord Marduk inclined the great
hearts of the Babylonians towards me . . . I liberated those
who dwelt in Babylon from the yoke that chafed them . . .
I am Cyrus, king of all things, the great king . . . king of all
the earth . . ." So runs the inscription in Babylonian
characters on the clay cylinder of Cyrus. The last words
might almost suggest that the biblical Chronicler had them
in mind: "Thus saith Cyrus king of Persia, All the kingdoms
of the earth hath the Lord God of heaven given me . . ."
(II Chronicles 36:23).
In 539 B. C.—a year after Cyrus had beaten the army
of Nabonidus, the Babylonian king—the occupation
of Babylon by the Persians settled the fate of the last
great empire of Mesopotamia. The time had come of which
it was said: ". . . after seventy years be accomplished
at Babylon I will visit you . . . in causing you to return to
this place" (Jeremiah 29:10).

DANIEL

Other Books in the
BIBLE STUDY TEXTBOOK SERIES

DANIEL

by

Paul T. Butler

College Press, Joplin, Missouri

CONTENTS

CONTENTS

DEDICATED TO

GALAND AND JYNNE KINNARD

father and mother of

GALE

my wife

and

sources of encouragement

help and wisdom

to

me

DANIEL

Daniel was a godly man
And thankful through his days . . .
He never failed to pray to God
And give Him all the praise.

His trials were so many,
And he was tempted sore . . .
But he was saved by righteousness,
And the godly cloak he wore.

Interpreting the royal dreams
Through wisdom from on high . . .
He ever gave the praise to God,
As his life did verify.

In the fiery furnace
And in the lions' den . . .
The flames were stayed, the jaws were set
Before oppressing men.

But he emerged triumphant,
For God was ever near . . .
He guards His children from all harm
When danger does appear.

Through our temptations and our trials,
On life's tempestous ways . . .
I thank Thee, God, for Daniel,
And for his life of praise.

Upon my knees, I pray that God,
Will make me thankful too . . .
And worthy of His love and care . . .
I know He'll see me through!

Author Unknown

DANIEL

INTRODUCTION

Author: Daniel, a Hebrew statesman. His name in Hebrew, *Daniyyel*, means "God is Judge" or "God is my Judge" or "judge who pronounces judgment in the name of God." We know very little of the person Daniel. He was probably of royal lineage (1:3). He was taken to Babylonia as a young man (just how old he was when this happened we do not know—probably 20 years of age or younger). He died probably soon after receiving and recording the closing series of his prophecies (chap. 10-12), which he himself places in the third year of the reign of Cyrus. But when, and under what circumstances, his death occurred is unknown. He apparently did not return to Palestine with his people but spent his last days in Babylon. If he was taken to Babylon "in the third year of Jehoiakim" (606 B.C.) and lived past the return of the Jews to Palestine (536 B.C.) it would mean he lived more than 70 years in Babylonia alone! Thus his death would come at the ripe old age of 80-90, depending upon his age when he was taken to Babylon.

Daniel was truly a man of God. He was a man of faith, courage and conviction. He was ready at all times to declare without fear or favor what he believed and to stand for his convictions regardless of the circumstances and consequences. There are marks of true nobility, gentleness, compassion and unreproachable integrity borne out in his dealings with his contemporaries. His personal integrity was so great that he could be heard and trusted even by those monarchs who did not believe in his God. As a consequence of his veracity and erudition, he was made ruler over the province of Babylon and chief of the governors over its wise men under two Babylonian emperors and under Darius the Mede he was one of the three presidents of the satraps.

Dean Farrar was impressed with the absence of Daniel's name from all ancient documents outside the Scriptures as a strong reason to question the actual, historic personage of Daniel. Robert Dick Wilson deals with this "argument from silence" in a very lucid way in his book *Studies in The Book of Daniel*, published by Putnam. Dr. Wilson points out that it is hardly fair, in the first place, to use silence to argue against Daniel's existence. Secondly, all the ancient Babylonian documents are silent about the numerous governors, judges, generals, priests, wise men, writers, sculptors, architects and all kinds of famous men who must have lived during that long period. But does the silence concerning such as these mean the emperor had not such judges, priests, etc.?

Edward J. Young in *The Prophecy of Daniel*, published by Eerdmans, gives five lines of evidence proving the Daniel of whom the book testifies is the author of the book:

1. In the second half of the book Daniel names himself (speaking in first person) as the one receiving the revelations, and he is ordered to preserve the book in which these words are found (12:4).

2. It should be obvious to any honest reader that the book is the work of one person throughout. The first part prepares for the second; all sections are mutually related to one another; the historical narratives are interdependent; the character of Daniel is always the same.

3. Jesus Christ validates its authorship by Daniel (Mt. 24:15). One should also compare Mt. 10:23; 16:27 ff; 19:28; 24:30; 25:31; 26:64.

4. The Septuagint and the books of Maccabees show definite influence by the book of Daniel. Jewish tradition attributes its authorship to this Daniel.

5. The book is saturated with historical nuances of Babylonian and Persian background. It had to be written by a person contemporary with the events.

Date: H. C. Leupold dates the writing of this book between 538-528 B.C. Merrill C. Tenney gives "shortly after his last vision, in 536 B.C." as the date. Keil and Delitzsch say it was written "during the exile" by Daniel. Edward J. Young agrees with the above statements. Practically all conservative scholars date the book somewhere near 536 B.C.. Porphyry, a neo-Platonic philosopher of the third century A.D. was probably the first significant unbelieving critic of the book of Daniel. He alleged it was written by someone who lived in Judea during the times of the Antiochus Epiphanes (175-163 B.C.). According to Prophyry predictive prophecy is impossible therefore the book could not have been written before the events so an imposter wrote the book and lied for the sake of reviving the hope of the Jews during the terrible times of Antiochus Epiphanes. The modern critical view, fathered by Leonhard Bertholdt (1806-08) is that the book was written by an unknown Jew in Palestine at the time of the Maccabees in the second century B.C. Our personal observation, after studying the arguments of the critics many years now, is that all those who insist the book was written after the events recorded therein, do so because of the same prejudgment and presupposition as Porphyry—that predictive prophecy is impossible.

The destructive critics argue for a late date on the basis of three alleged evidences: historical, linguistic and theological. It is not the purpose of this commentary to offer a technical study of all the critical problems of the book of Daniel. However, we feel we must deal with these problems as concisely as possible because their resolution has direct bearing on true and honest exposition of the text.

1. *Historical*: It is alleged that Daniel is of late date because it is placed in the *Kethubhim* or *Hagiographa* (writings) instead of the Prophets. However, some of the other documents of the Hagiographa are of great antiquity (Psalms, Job, Proverbs). Position in the Hagiographa is no proof of a late date of composition. It is further alleged that there are historical inaccuracies which make it likely that the author lived at a late date. In Daniel 1:1 it is stated that Nebuchadnezzar invaded Palestine in the third year of Jehoiakim, whereas Jeremiah 46:2 says that the first year of Nebuchadnezzar was the fourth year of Jehoiakim. Recent investigations show that the Jews reckoned their regnal year from the first month preceding the year of accession thus 605 B.C. would have been the fourth year of Jehoiakim who came to the throne in 608. The Babylonians, however, reckoned the first regnal year from

the next succeeding new year's day. Therefore, the year 605 would be only Jehoiakim's third year according to the Chaldean reckoning. Nebuchadnezzar's first regnal year began in April, 604, even though he had been crowned in September, 605. Daniel has written from the Chaldean viewpoint and Jeremiah from the Jewish. Both are correct, and the critics are wrong. Another historical discrepancy is alleged in that Daniel represents Belshazzar as the last king of Babylonia and as being slain when Babylon was taken by the Medes. Profane history seemed to indicate that Nabonidus was the last king of Babylon, and further that he was killed in the capture. Archaeologists have discovered clay tablets bearing inscriptions which prove that Belshazzar was Nabonidus' son and co-ruler with him, and that he was active as the ruler during any absence of Nabonidus. Why would Belshazzar promise to the interpreter of the inscription on the wall (chap. 5) promotion to the status of third ruler in the kingdom? Why not promise him promotion to second ruler? Obviously because Belshazzar himself was only the second ruler, inasmuch as Nabodidus his father was still alive. (cf. *Archaeology and Bible History*, by Joseph P. Free)

2. *Linguistic*: There are some Persian words in the text of the book. We admit that Daniel wrote the book (or at least a portion of the book) as late as the Persian dominion. He lived in it and it is not strange that some of the few political terms would be used. There are some Greek words (basically only three such words are used and they are of musical instruments) in the text. But Greek commercial and cultural activity and influence was already widespread before 600 B.C. As early as the reign of Sargon (722-705 B.C.) there were, according to the Assyrian records, Greek captives being sold into slavery from Cyprus, Ionia, Lydia and Cilicia. In the Neo-Babylonian ration tablets published by E. F. Weidner, Ionian carpenters and

shipbuilders are mentioned among the recipients of rations from Nebuchadnezzar's commissary—along with musicians from Ashkelon and elsewhere. Portions of Daniel written in Aramaic have several words spelled with a *d* which critics argued were spelled with a *z* in Daniel's time, the *d* being used much later. However, certain texts among the *Ras Shamra* (Ugaritic) *Texts*, which are dated as early as 1500-1400 B.C. prove that the words in Aramaic were spelled both ways even centuries before Daniel! As to the question of why half the book was written in Aramaic (first half) and half in Hebrew (last half), the reason for the choice is fairly obvious. Those portions of Daniel's prophecy which deal generally with Gentile affairs were put into a linguistic medium which all the public could appreciate whether Jew or Gentile. But those portions which were of particularly Jewish interest were put into Hebrew in order that they might be understood by the Jews alone.

3. *Theological*: Basically, the theological arguments for a late date for Daniel revolve around the unbelieving critic's presuppositions against the supernatural in miracle and prophecy. The critics lay customary emphasis upon the supposed evolutionary development of the Jewish religion. They point to motifs and emphases in Daniel which they insist evolved only during the intertestamental period. These emphases include prominence of angels, the stress upon the last judgment, the resurrection from the dead, the Messianic kingdom. Any reader of the Old Testament may quickly verify the fact that many prophets, long before Daniel's time, spoke of angels, judgment, the Messianic kingdom, and a few concerning the resurrection. On the other hand, works which are admittedly of the second century B.C., such as I Maccabees and the Greek additions to Daniel, Baruch and Judith, show none of the four elements (angelology, resurrection, last judgment, Messiah!)

Purpose: Leupold writes: ". . . a book of comfort, designed for evil days as well as for good days. By the help of it Israel could discern that its oppressions were, indeed going to be heavy, but, on the other hand, that they were foreknown by God and were therefore not to be dreaded too much. For if an all-knowing God had seen what would transpire He must at the same time be an omnipotent God who would be able to deliver His own, as well as a faithful God would would not suffer them to be tempted above what they were able."

Gleason Archer writes: ". . . the overruling sovereignty of the one true God, who condemns and destroys the rebellious world power and faithfully delivers His covenant people according to their steadfast faith in Him."

G. Campbell Morgan writes: "If I were to summarize the Book of Daniel I could do it in two sentences: first of all, the messages of Daniel, whether those delivered to pagan kings or those recorded that have been for the people of God, emphasize first the government of God over all kings and all nations; and secondly, they emphasize the fact of the continuity of that government until the consummation in which God's will shall be done, His throne recognized, and the victory be with Him." Dr. Morgan's paean of Daniel is well stated: "I am so glad in these days that I have my Old Testament still, and I am watching the goodness of God in human history over all the machinations of men."

The great lessons of Daniel are the general principles of other Old Testament prophets particularized! (cf. our commentary on Hosea, Joel, Amos, Obadiah and Jonah). God presides over the history of the world; the Gentile nations as well as the Jews have always been under His control; the succession of human empires is ordained by Him; He permits the pride and fury of oppressors for a time, but humbles them in the end, and saves His own; His kingdom will come in due time, and will endure forever; faithfulness and constancy to Him lead to a life beyond death, and to an eternal reward of glory.

Style: The revelations concerning the future given in Daniel are in the form of dreams and visions, highly symbolic and figurative. There is a reason for this. This book was written about and during a period of the deepest national misery of the people of God. In fact the period of the *Indignation* (8:19) had begun. There were undoubtedly many questions in the hearts of the pious Jews of the captivity such as: What does the future hold in store for God's people? Will He leave us here, dispersed, or will He send His redeemer? If the latter, how is this to be accomplished, and, when? What can be done by anyone about these great, powerful, absolute pagan emperors?

In the style of prophecy they were accustomed to, the "covenant people" usually occupied the center of the stage. The world-powers by which they were harassed or threatened usually were noticed only incidentally and then as sympolical representatives of the spirit of world-power that opposes God. *Daniel has a new point of reference!* He is in the very center of that world-power which had overthrown and subjugated all the nations of the East, including the covenant people. From this frame of reference he predicts the rise of a *succession* of world-kingdoms, which shall destroy one another until an eternal kingdom of truth and righteousness shall be established on their ruins by the direct interference in history, at a particular point, by the God of heaven. In all of this Daniel relies almost exclusively upon symbolic, apocalyptic language. It is contrary to the nature and genius of prophecy, especially to prophecy of such a broad eschatological scope as this, to reveal the future in prosaic forms. In all prophecy there is an element of obscurity and God decreed it to be so for He said He would not speak to other prophets face to face as He had to Moses (Num. 12:1-8), but to those following Moses He promised He would speak in dreams and visions. It is to be expected therefore that in revelations given in visions and dreams we would have a great deal of imagery and symbolism. When one considers the standpoint of Daniel such is to be expected. His circumstances were unique as were those of John, the author of the New Testament Apocalypse. Both were commissioned to relate unpalatable predictions of doom upon the pagan societies in which they lived. The style or form of Daniel is due to its subject matter. No other prophetical

9

book of the Old Testament speaks of the heathen nations and their relation to the people of God with the same fullness and definiteness as does Daniel.

The word apocalyptic comes from the Greek word *apokalypsis* which means "revelation" or "unveiling," and is applied to those writings which contain revelations of the secret purposes of God expressed by a high degree of symbolism. The development of world-power over a span of 600 years or more, the succession of judgments of God visited in history upon the enemies of God's people, closing with the establishment of God's kingdom on earth and the accomplishment of redemption through a Redeemer are the "secrets" of God Daniel is commissioned to "unveil." If the book is to retain any semblance of mystery at all (which by the very nature of the mysterious would excite people to read and long for fulfillment), it must make use of imagery and symbolism. Within the Old Testament, this form of prophetical writing is approached by the closing chapters of Ezekiel (40-48) and is directly represented in the first half of Zechariah (1:8). In the New Testament symbolico-apocalyptic writing is found only in the Revelation of John which is a *continuation and NT application of the prophetic principles of Daniel.*

Background: One must go back to the time of Hezekiah to appreciate the background of Daniel's experiences in Babylon. Hezekiah's glorious reform (II Chron. 29-31) was short lived. Manasseh, Hezekiah's son, set up idolatrous images all over the land of Judah (even in the Temple) (II Chron. 33:7). He slew those few devout Jews who refused to follow his wicked example of idolatry. His apostasy was the main cause for captivity (cf. Jer. 15:4).

Manasseh eventually repented but his change of heart was too late to undo the evil which had become a way of life for the nation and to avert the judgment of God. Manasseh's son Amon came to the throne but he was so wicked his servants assassinated him, and the people placed his God-fearing son, Josiah, on the throne (II Chron. 33:21-25). While workmen were restoring the Temple, the book of the law of Jehovah was found. Josiah attempted a reform but he met an untimely death in the battle of Megiddo (II

Chron. 35:20-37). His son, Jehoahaz, the people's choice, was quickly removed by Pharaoh-Necho, and replaced by the deposed king's brother, Jehoiakim.

In the battle of Carchemish (605 B.C.) (cf. II Chron. 35:20; Jer. 46:2) Nebuchadnezzar of Babylon defeated Pharaoh-Necho, and the 70 years of Babylonian captivity began (Jer. 25:1-12; Dan. 9:1-2). It was at this time that Daniel and his friends were carried away to Babylon. Habakkuk prophesied during the reign of the wicked Jehoiakim as well as Jeremiah (ministry during 626-586 B.C.). Jeremiah predicted Babylonian domination of Judah as a judgment of God to which the people were to submit but Jehoiakim, sitting in his winter palace and listening to the reading of Jeremiah's prophecies, burned the scroll on which they were recorded. These prophecies were immediately re-written by Jeremiah with the addition of a terrible judgment of God upon Jehoiakim. His son, Jehoiachin, reigned only three months and was deported to Babylon with a number of other important people of Judah (including Ezekiel).

Zedekiah, a third son of Josiah, was Judah's last king. Zedekiah's tragic end is vividly described in II Kings 25:4-7. The people, except the poorest, were carried away to Babylon (II Kings 25:11). The basic reason for the Babylonian captivity is given in II Chron. 36:14ff.

William Hendriksen characterizes the attitudes of the people in captivity very well. The first years were *years of false hopefulness*. The early exiles were confident that conditions would soon change and they would return to their land. Was not Jehovah's temple in Jerusalem still standing? Jeremiah writes and attempts to deter them from putting trust in their false prophets (Jer. 29; Ezek. 17:11-24). Secondly, there were *years of hopelessness*. When the temple was destroyed in 586 B.C. it seemed to many as if Jehovah had completely forsaken His people. Despair entered the hearts of the people and is expressed in one of the Captivity Psalms (Psa. 137). Ezekiel is God's chosen vessel in Babylon to comfort the exiles. Thirdly, there came a *season of revived hopefulness*. For those who availed themselves of the opportunity to return to their country (and those who did so in spirit but because of position or age were not able to [e.g. Daniel]), hope stirred anew in their hearts that God was faithful and had yet greater things in store for His people. For others the *time of indifference and assimilation* set in. Babylonia to the south, Media and Mesopotamia to the north had become "home" to them. They intermarried with the people of the land and adopted their religion (Ezek. 20:31-32 and cf. also Esther).

The Jews in Exile were permitted to form colonies in which their communal life could continue. For the most part they were permitted to gather in the homes of their elders and worship their God and read their holy scriptures. Life during the exile was highly diversified. Most Jews were probably agriculturists and earned their living by farming. Some ultimately entered business. Many became rich and influential. Other Jews became trusted men in government. An abundance of archaeological data now available describes in detail the types of houses, utensils, etc., used during the neo-Babylonian and Persian eras.

The captivity served a three-fold purpose. First it was God's method of punishment for their sins (II Chron. 36:15-17). Second, it was a means of purification and preparation of the remnant for God's Messianic purposes (Ezek. 36:22-31). Third, God used it to bless the Gentile nations in preparing them to be called into the Messianic kingdom (cf. Micah 5:7).

Outline: Some divide the book into two general divisions: (1) Daniel revealing God's purposes for the Gentile nations; (2) Daniel revealing God's plans for the covenant people. Hendriksen divides the book (1) God's Sovereignty in History; (2) God's Sovereignty in Prophecy.

We choose to divide the book into three parts thusly:

I   Daniel's Faith (chap. 1)   Dedication

II Daniel's Fortitude (chap. 2-6)   Determination

III Daniel's Foreknowledge (chap. 7-12)   Divination

We shall elaborate upon the above outline with more detail as we proceed in exegesis through the book.

SPECIAL STUDY ONE

NEBUCHADNEZZAR'S BABYLON

excerpt from

EXILE AND RETURN

by Charles F. Pfeiffer

Published by Baker Book House

A clay tablet which dates back to Persian times contains a map of the world. Various towns are marked, along with the canals and waterways which made them possible. Around the whole span of the earth's surface is an ocean which has the appearance of a tire on a wheel. Beyond are yet other regions, indicated by triangles which touch the outer rim of the ocean. The geographical center of this universe, however, was the city of Babylon.

Babylon was an ancient city. We are told that Nimrod began his ancient empire there (Gen. 10:10). About 1830 B.C. a dynasty of kings from Babylon began to annex surrounding city-states and the First Dynasty of Babylon began is quest for power. The famed Hammurabi codified Babylonian law (ca. 1700 B.C.) and ruled all of southern Mesopotamia, extending his conquests as far as Mari on the middle Euphrates.

The glory of Babylon declined and southern Mesopotamia was ruled for centuries by governors appointed by the Assyrians who ruled from Asshur and Nineveh. When, under Nabopolassar, the Babylonians rebelled against Assyria and, in 612 B.C., helped destroy Nineveh, the center of empire, if not the center of the universe, could be identified with the ancient Babylon.

Our knowledge of ancient Babylon comes from a variety of sources. It is described in the Bible as the capital city of the nation which took Judah into captivity. Daniel and his companions were trained as courtiers in the schools of Babylon. The Greek historian Herodotus, who wrote a century and a half after Nebuchadnezzar, described the city as a vast square, 480 stades (55¼ miles) in circumference, surrounded by a huge moat of running water, beyond which were ramparts two hundred cubits high and fifty cubits broad! Herodotus tells us that the streets were arranged at right angles, a fact later verified by Koldewey, the excavator of Babylon. The Euphrates was walled on both sides as it made its course through the city, a series of gates providing the inhabitants of Babylon access to the river. Diodorus Siculus and other Greeks spoke in admiration of Babylon, unquestionably the largest and most magnificent city of the ancient world.

The Book of Daniel records the boast of Nebuchadnezzar, "Is not this great Babylon that I have built?" (Dan. 4:30). The words are not without meaning. In addition to the walls which surrounded Babylon, Nebuchadnezzar was personally responsible for much that was within the city. He laid out and paved with bricks the great Procession Way which led to the temple of Marduk. The palace of his father Nabopolassar was completely rebuilt. Beams of cedar were imported from distant Lebanon for the project.

Nabopolassar had already begun the rebuilding of Babylon, but it was left to Nebuchadnezzar to pursue the work in earnest. Before the death of Nabopolassar about two-thirds of the work he had planned for the protection of Babylon had been completed. The inner wall of the city, known as Imgur-Bel, was finished. He also had built an outer wall, the Nimitti-Bel, and reconstructed the city gates with cedar wood covered with strips of bronze. Symbolic guardians of the city were the half-human, half-animal bronze colossi which stood at the threshold.

Nebuchadnezzar took up where his father left off. A third massive wall was built on the east side of the city at a distance of four thousand cubits from the outer wall. Before this was a moat, walled around with bricks. Similar defenses were built on the west, but they were not as strong because the desert formed a natural barrier.

To the north, the direction from which trouble might be expected, Nebuchadnezzar pursued a different plan. Between the two walls, and between the river and the Ishtar Gate he constructed an artificial platform of brick laid in bitumen. Upon this elevated platform he built a citadel which was connected with his royal palace. In this way he made the north wall so solid that it could be neither broken down nor breached. The citadel could be used as a watch-tower and, if need be, destructive missiles could be shot or thrown from it upon any enemy who might have reached the outside of the walls. Apart from the possibility of treachery within, Babylon appeared impregnable.

The Neo-Babylonian period is well documented, and Nebuchadnezzar has left us accounts of his building operation. In describing his work on the walls he declares:

> Nebuchadnezzar, king of Babylon, the restorer of Esaglia and Ezida, son of Nabopolassar am I. As a protection to Esagila, that no powerful enemy and destroyer might take Babylon, that the line of battle might not approach Imgur-Bel, the wall of Babylon, that which no former king had done, I did; at the enclosure of Babylon I made an enclosure of a strong wall on the east side. I dug a moat, I reached the level of the water. I then saw that the wall which my father had prepared was too small in its construction. I built with bitumen and brick a mighty wall which, like a mountain, could not be moved, and connected it with the wall of my father; I laid its foundations on the breast of the underworld; its top I raised up like a mountain. Along this wall to strengthen it I constructed a third, and as the base of a protecting wall I laid a foundation of bricks, and built it on the breast of the under-world, and laid its foundation. The fortifications of Esagila and Babylon I strengthened, and established the name of my reign forever.

Archaeology has provided us with the tools to evaluate the boasts of Nebuchadnezzar and the reports of Herodotus. In 1898 Robert Koldewey began the excavation of Babylon under the auspices of the *Deutsche Orientgesellschaft.* Work continued for more than eighteen years. Full reports of Koldewey's work appeared in his book, *Das wieder erstehende Babylon,* which contained photographs and plans of the city and its principal structures. The foreword to the first edition was dated, "Babylon, May 16, 1912." A fourth edition appeared in 1925.

Koldewey came upon the walls of Babylon during the early days of his dig. It took considerable time to excavate them, but the results were indeed impressive. Around the ruins of the city was a brick wall 22⅓ feet thick. Outside this wall was a space 38⅓ feet wide, then another brick wall, 25 feet thick. If the outer wall were breached the invader would find himself trapped between two walls. Lining the inner side of the citadel moat was still another wall, 12 feet thick. In times of danger the moat could be flooded.

The walls were surmounted every 160 feet by watch-towers. Koldewey suggests that there were 360 such towers on the inner wall (an estimate based upon the pattern of the ruins). Excavations indicate that the towers were 27 feet wide, and they probably were 90 feet high (much less than the 300 feet mentioned by Herodotus). Ancient historians tell us that two chariots could be driven abreast on the road which ran on top of the wall and completely surrounded the city. The walls were constantly patrolled by guards.

There were numerous gates in the walls, although Herodotus' reference to one hundred gates must be dismissed as hyperbole. The most famous entrance into the city was the Ishtar gate which led from the north of the city into the Procession Way. The gate was fifteen feet wide and its vaulted passageway was thirty-five feet above the street level. The bricks were so molded that they form bas-relief figures of bulls and dragons. Their surfaces were overlaid with thickly colored enamels. Nebuchadnezzar used properly fired bricks, and they have remained through the ages. The sun dried bricks used by his predecessors have disintegrated long ago.

The Procession Way was primarily used for the great annual occasion when king and people went to the temple of Marduk at the New Year's Festival. During the forty-three years of his reign, Nebuchadnezzar continued to beautify the Procession Way. He wrote:

Aibur-shabu, the street of Babylon, I filled with a high fill for the procession of the great lord Marduk, and with Turmina-banda stones and Shadu stones I make this Aibur-shabu fill for the procession of his godliness, and linked it with those parts which my father had built, and made the way a shining one.

The pavement of the Procession Way was built over a base of bricks covered with bitumen. It consisted of blocks of limestone with sides more than a yard wide, pointed with asphalt. Inscribed on the underside of each of the slabs were the words:

Nebuchadnezzar, King of Babylon, son of Nabopolassar, King of Babylon, am I. Of the streets of Babylon for the procession of the great lord Marduk, with slabs of limestone, I built the causeway. Oh, Marduk my lord, grant eternal life.

Along the walls of the Procession Way was a series of 120 lions in enameled relief. They were spaced at 64 foot intervals and gave a sense of awe to the street. The lions had hides of white or yellow, with manes of yellow or red. They were posed against a background of light or dark blue. The Procession Way was 73½ feet wide.

At the annual New Year's Festival, statues of the principal deities were assembled from all the provinces of the kingdom and solemnly carried through the Ishtar Gate out to the northern outskirts of the city. There they were transferred to boats and taken to the Garden Temple up the river. This was followed by the consummation of the sacred marriage of the principal god and goddess, which was presumed to guarantee the fertility and prosperity of the whole land. On the eleventh day of the month Nisan the procession joyously returned through the Ishtar Gate from the north. Marduk led the procession in his chariot-boat. Behind the chief god of Babylon rode the king in his chariot. Behind the king were carriage-boats containing the images of the other gods worshiped in Babylon.

Along the Procession Way was the famous staged-tower or ziggurat of Babylon known as E-temen-anki—"The House of the Foundation of Heaven and Earth"—which rose 300 feet into the air and could be seen from a distance by travelers approaching the city. Fifty-eight million bricks are said to have been used in its construction. Like Babylon itself, the ziggurat goes back to remote antiquity. On its top was a Temple to Marduk, the god of Babylon. Enemies of the state—such as Tukulti-Ninurta, Sargon, Sennacherib, and Ashurbanipal—devastated the city and destroyed the Marduk shrine. The tower was rebuilt by the Neo-Babylonian rulers Nabopolassar and Nebuchadnezzar. In a sense it pictured both the glories of Marduk, and of Marduk's city, Babylon. Nabopolassar declared:

> The lord Marduk commanded me concerning E-temen-anki, the staged tower of Babylon, which before my time had become dilapidated and ruinous, that I should make its foundations secure in the bosom of the nether world, and make its summit like the heavens.

The ziggurat consisted of seven terraces, on the top of which was a temple made of bricks enameled bright blue to

17

represent the heavens. The temple was approached by a triple staircase, at the middle of which there was a place where the visitor might rest. Within the temple was a couch and a golden table. This was regarded as the abode of Marduk. No one except a priestess, who served as the consort of the god, was to enter this shrine. The prosperity of the land was thought to depend upon this sacred marriage ritual.

Across the street from the ziggurat was the temple area known as E-sag-ila ("The house which lifts up the head"). Herodotus visited the E-sag-ila and was much impressed by its golden figure of "Zeus" (Babylonian Bel-Marduk) seated in the shrine beside a golden table. According to the statistics which Herodotus gives (which may be exaggerated) the gold of these objects weighed about 890 talents, or 4800 pounds with a current value of $24,000,000. "Zeus" appeared as a half-animal, half-human creature. Outside the sanctuary were a number of other altars and statues including a standing figure of Marduk, twelve cubits (twenty feet) high, of solid gold. The complex of buildings occupied sixty acres, bounded on the west by the Euphrates and on the east by the Procession Way. Towering 470 feet above the ground was the shrine known as the E-kur ("Temple mountain") built on a terrace of asphalted bricks like the nearby ziggurat.

The total number of shrines in ancient Babylon, as recorded in contemporary inscriptions, appears incredible. We read that,

> There are altogether in Babylon fifty-three temples of the great gods, fifty-five shrines dedicated to Marduk, three hundred shrines belonging to earth divinities, six hundred shrines for celesital divinities, one hundred and eighty altars to the goddess Ishtar, one hundred and eighty to the gods Nergal and Adad, and twelve other altars to various deities.

North of the ziggurat was a mound called Kasr on which Nebuchadnezzar built the most imposing of his palaces. The palace walls were of finely made yellow brick, and floors were of white and mottled sandstone. The palace was adorned with reliefs in blue glaze. Its gates were guarded by gigantic basalt lions.

18

Near the palace were the famed Hanging Gardens, considered to be one of the Seven Wonders of the Ancient World. Nebuchadnezzar built the gardens for his wife who missed the hills of her Median homeland. The gardens appear to have been terraced and set on a small hill beside the palace, flanked by the Procession Way and the Ishtar Gate.

Josephus quotes from Berossus, *History of Chaldea*, an account of the building of Nebuchadnezzar's palace and the hanging gardens,

> In this palace he erected retaining walls of stone to which he gave an appearance very like that of mountains and, by planting on them trees of all kinds, he achieved this effect and built the so-called hanging garden because his wife, who had been brought up in the region of Media, had a desire for her native environment.

The gardens were irrigated by means of an endless chain of buckets which raised water to the highest point of the terrace. The gardens were impressive when viewed from a distance from the city. The visitor to Babylon could see the tops of the trees towering above the city walls.

Nebuchadnezzar's Babylon was an excellent example of early city planning. The city was divided into a number of rectangles by wide roads which were named after the gods of the Babylonian pantheon. On the left bank of the Euphrates we find the streets of Marduk and Zababa intersecting at right angles with the streets of Sin and Enlil. On the right bank we find an intersection of the streets of Adad and Shamash. Except for the famed Procession Way, Babylon's streets were not paved.

A bridge connecting the eastern or New City with the western city of Babylon had stone piers and a timber foot path which could be withdrawn in times of emergency. Permanent bridges were rare in the ancient East, and the one across the Euphrates was a source of wonder to travelers.

The business life of the city centered in the wharves which flanked the Euphrates. Business offices were located along the river bank. The market sector of ancient Babylon has not been identified, but it was probably located in the *Merkes* quarter.

19

The houses of the city were frequently three or four stories high, being built according to a pattern which has been familiar in the East from ancient times to the present. Each home would be built around a central courtyard. There would be no windows facing the street, but all light would come through the courtyard. Access to the rooms of the second story was by a wooden balcony which extended around the entire inner courtyard. A narrow door in one of the first floor rooms opened into the street.

Ancient Babylon required a system of canals if the best use was to made of the waters of the Tigris and the Euphrates. Hammurabi, the famed king of the Old Babylonian Empire had been a canal builder, and his successors needed to be careful to insure proper irrigation of the fields. When Nebuchadnezzar came to the throne of Babylon, its eastern canal had so deteriorated that there were places where its channel could not be traced. Nebuchadnezzar had it redug, and then walled up from the bottom. Because the canal passed through Babylon, it was necessary to build a bridge across it.

Although most of his energy was spent on Babylon itself, Nebuchadnezzar did not completely neglect the other cities of Mesopotamia. He rebuilt the walls of Borsippa and restored the temples of the city to a good state of repair.

Nebuchadnezzar was an able and an energetic sovereign. He was in all respects the most able as well as the most ambitious ruler of his day. In him the Neo-Babylonian Empire reached its zenith. Great as were his accomplishments both on the field of battle and in building the cities of his kingdom, Nebuchadnezzar left an empire that had no political stability. His own personality held it together, and when that was gone it was not long before his dynasty came to an end.

EXILIC TIMES

	JUDAH	BABYLON	MEDIO-PERSIA	EGYPT
639	Josiah			
626		Nabopolassar		
609	Jehoahaz Jehoiakim Jeremiah			Necho
605		Nebuchadnezzar		
597	Jehoiachin Zedekiah Ezekiel			Psammetichus
594	Daniel			
588				Apries
586	Jerusalem destroyed			
568				Amasis
562		Awel-Marduk (Evil-Merodach)		
560		Neriglissar (Nergal-sharezer)		
559			Cyrus	
556		Nabonidus and Belshazzar		
539	Edict— return of the Jews	Fall of Babylon		
530			Cambyses	
522	Zerubbabel Haggai, Zechariah		Darius	
515	Temple completed			
485			Xerxes	
479			(Esther)	
464			Artaxerxes I	
457	Ezra			
444	Nehemiah			
423			Darius II	
404			Artaxerxes II	

from *The Old Testament Speaks*
by Samuel J. Schultz,
pub. by Harper & Bros. Publishing Co.

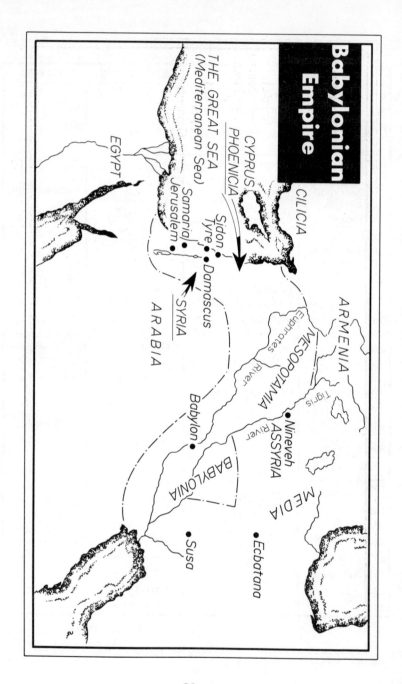

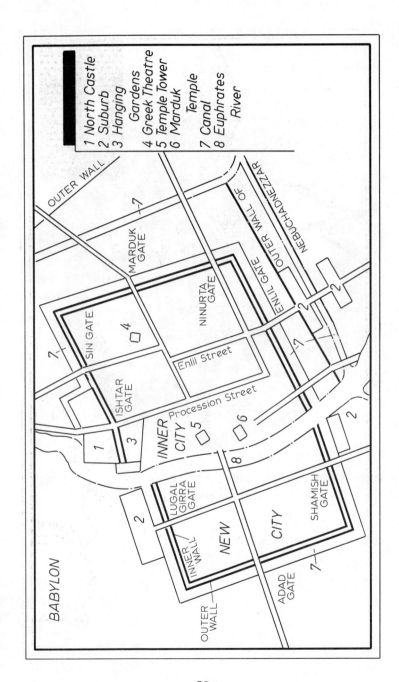

BABYLON

1 North Castle
2 Suburb
3 Hanging Gardens
4 Greek Theatre
5 Temple Tower
6 Marduk Temple
7 Canal
8 Euphrates River

OUTER WALL

MARDUK GATE

SIN GATE

ISHTAR GATE

Enlil Street

NINURTA GATE

Procession Street

INNER CITY

ENLIL GATE

OUTER WALL OF NEBUCHADNEZZAR

LUGAL GIRRA GATE

INNER WALL

NEW CITY

OUTER WALL

ADAD GATE

SHAMISH GATE

CAMEO OF NEBUCHADNEZZAR NOW IN THE MUSEUM
AT FLORENCE

CHAPTER ONE

I. DANIEL'S FAITH—1:1-21

I. PAGANIZATION ATTEMPTED

TEXT: 1:1-7

1 In the third year of the reign of Jehoiakim king of Judah came Nebuchadnezzar king of Babylon unto Jerusalem, and besieged it.

2 And the Lord gave Jehoiakim king of Judah into his hand, with part of the vessels of the house of God; and he carried them into the land of Shinar to the house of his god: and he brought the vessels into the treasure-house of his god.

3. And the king spake unto Ashpenaz the master of his eunuchs, that he should bring in certain of the children of Israel, even of the seed royal and of the nobles;

4 youths in whom was no blemish, but well-favored, and skilful in all wisdom, and endued with knowledge, and understanding science, and such as had ability to stand in the king's palace; and that he should teach them the learning and the tongue of the Chaldeans.

5 And the king appointed for them a daily portion of the king's dainties, and of the wine which he drank, and that they should be nourished three years; that at the end thereof they should stand before the king.

6 Now among these were, of the children of Judah, Daniel, Hananiah, Mishael, and Azariah.

7 And the prince of the eunuchs gave names unto them: unto Daniel he gave the name of Belteshazzar; and to Hananiah, of Shadrach; and to Mishael, of Meshach; and to Azariah, of Abed-nego.

QUERIES

a. When did this seige of Jerusalem by Nebuchadnezzar occur?

b. Why attempt to nourish the Hebrew lads on Babylonian "dainties?"
c. Why were the Hebrew lads given Babylonian names?

PARAPHRASE

In the third year of the reign of Jehoiakim, king of Judah, Nebuchadnezzar, king of Babylon came to Jerusalem and encircled the city with his army and beseiged it. And the Lord permitted Nebuchadnezzar to capture Jehoiakim along with some of the sacred vessels of worship from the temple of God. Nebuchadnezzar took all his plunder along with his prisoners back to his own land of Babylon and he put the sacred vessels on display in the treasury of his own pagan temple. Then Nebuchadnezzar ordered Ashpenaz, the chief of his servants, to select some of the young Jewish nobles and to train them in Babylonian language, sciences and culture. Ashpenaz was instructed to select young, strong, healthy, good-looking men who were well informed, widely read in many fields, alert and sensible and possessed of poise and self-confidence sufficiently to make a good appearance in the court of the king. And the king took special occasion to command that they should receive a daily serving of the richest and most desirable food and wine from his own table for a three-year training period. He planned to develop these young men physically, mentally and socially in order that they might become his advisors. Daniel, Hananiah, Mishael and Azariah were four of the young men chosen, all from the tribe of Judah. And as a part of their naturalization into Babylonian life, the king's chief servant gave them Babylonian names. Daniel was called Belteshazzar; Hananiah was called Shadrach; Mishael was called Meshach; Azariah was called Abed-nego.

COMMENT

v. 1 IN THE THIRD YEAR . . . OF JEHOIAKIM . . . Immediately the problem of an apparent discrepancy between Daniel and Jeremiah confronts us. (1) Jeremiah 25:1 says that the *fourth* year of Jehoiakim and the *first* year of Nebuchadnezzar were the same; (2) Jeremiah 46:2 has Nebuchadnezzar defeating the army of Pharaoh-Necho at

Carchemish in the *fourth* year of Jehoiakim; (3) and, finally, Jeremiah 25:8-14 seems to imply that Nebuchadnezzar had *not yet* come against Jerusalem (at all?) in the *fourth* year of Jehoiakim. Yet, Daniel says not only that Nebuchadnezzar did come against Jehoiakim in Jehoiakim's *third* year, but that Nebuchadnezzar was *king* when he came in this *third* year, while Jeremiah specifically states that the *first* year of Nebuchadnezzar was not until the *fourth* year of Jehoiakim.

Historical research offers two possible solutions one of which is undoubtedly the correct answer: (1) According to the Babylonian way of designating time of regnal activity, only the *first full year* of reign was called the first year of a king's reign. The year in which the king ascended the throne, whether at the first of the year or later, was *not* designated his first year, but "the year of accession to the kingdom." Daniel, writing in Babylon, many years after the event, would undoubtedly use Babylonian terminology, especially in such a technical matter, speaks of Jehoiakim's *third* year but means the same year as does Jeremiah in mentioning the *fourth* year (Jeremiah writing in Judah, using Jewish terminology). Edward J. Young points to a biblical example of such a difference between Babylonian and Jewish methods of reckoning regnal activity. There is a passage in II Kings 24:12 through 25:30 where the *eighth* and *nineteenth* years of a reign are spoken of; the parallel passage to this in Jeremiah 52:28-30 speaks of the same reign as in the *seventh* and *eighteenth* years. The following table will help to clarify this point:

Babylonian	*Jewish*
Accession	First Year
First Year	Second Year
Second Year	Third Year
Third Year (Daniel 1:1)	Fourth Year (Jer. 25:1)

(2) There is a passage in Josephus (cf. Antiquities X:II:I and Contra Apion 1:19) which he copied from Berossus, the Chaldean historian, which relates that Nabopolassar, Nebuchadnezzar's father, had heard that a governor whom he had not set over Egypt had revolted. Being himself old,

27

Nabopolassar dispatched his son leading the massive Babylonian army to take the rebel in hand. This Nebuchadnezzar set out to do; but while engaged in the task, his father took sick and died. Whereupon Nebuchadnezzar turned over his captives to his subordinates, selected a small band of the most courageous of his soldiers set out immediately for the capitol city of Babylon to take over the reigns of government. Among the captives Nebuchadnezzar left with his subordinates were "Jews, Phoenicians and Syrians, and of the nations belonging to Egypt." This would imply that Nebuchadnezzar had been engaged in an expedition against Jerusalem prior to the battle at Carchemish. Notice that Daniel 1:1 does not state that Nebuchadnezzar conquered and destroyed the city of Jerusalem in the third year of Jehoiakim! only that he "came and besieged it." But, if Nebuchadnezzar besieged Jerusalem *before* he went home at the death of his father to take the reins of government, why does Daniel say *king* Nebuchadnezzar besieged the city? Daniel, writing long after the event, is using the *proleptic* form in applying the title *king*. We sometimes say, "In the childhood of President Lincoln," or "when President Teddy Roosevelt charged up San Juan hill."

The two foregoing positions are outlined here for sake of clarity. It would seem that either position is entirely credible. Which of the two is most probable, the reader must decide for himself:

(1)	(2)
1. Early 606 B.C. Jer. delivers the address recorded in Jer. 25	Early in 605 B.C. Jer. delivers the address recorded in Jer. 25
2. 606 B.C. Neb. besieges Jerusalem; carries off Jehoiakim, temple vessels, Daniel and friends	Early in 605 Neb. defeats the Egyptians at Carchemish (Jer. 46:2)
3. Nebuchadnezzar h a s t e n s home at death of his father	Nebuchadnezzar then appears in Palestine
4. Early 605 B.C. Neb. defeats Egyptians at Carchemish	Then occurs the siege of Dan. 1:1; also recorded in II Ki. 24:1; II Chron. 36:6-7

5. Nebuchadnezzar comes a-   Neb. hastens to Babylon at
gainst Jerusalem t w i c e   death of his father
more, 597 B.C. and 586 B.C.

v. 2 AND THE LORD GAVE . . . INTO HIS HAND . . . AND
HE CARRIED THEM . . . TO THE HOUSE OF HIS GOD . . . Although Nebuchadnezzar was unaware of it, and probably
would not have admitted it at the time (however, he was
later to change his mind), he became an instrument of the
Divine will. God permitted Nebuchadnezzar to exercise his
fury against Jerusalem and to take the covenant people into
captivity for the good of God's people (cf. Jer. 25:1ff; Jer.
27:5-7, etc.). Please refer also to *Minor Prophets*, by Paul
T. Butler, published College Press, Special Studies on Philosophy of History.

Nebuchadnezzar is spelled Nebuchadrezzar in Babylonian and means "Nebo protect the boundary," or "Nebo
protect the crown." Jehoiakim was not deported, (cf. II
Chron. 36:5) therefore all that Nebuchadnezzar "brought
to the treasure house of his god" were some of the sacred
vessels from the temple in Jerusalem. The suffix "them"
can only refer gramatically to the vessels. Some of these
vessels Belshazzar (Nebuchadnezzar's grandson) desecrated
by using them in a drunken, riotous feast (Dan. 5:2-4). It
was customary in those days for conquerors to commandeer
and plunder thoroughly the treasuries of the vanquished.
The rapine of defeated foes is still practiced by ungodly
nations today—Russia robbed Europe of some of its most
priceless treasures during World War II. The Babylonian
prince took his booty home and put it in safe deposit in the
treasure-house of the temple to his pagan gods.

v. 3 . . . THE KING SPAKE UNTO ASHPENAZ . . . THAT
HE SHOULD BRING CERTAIN OF THE CHILDREN OF ISRAEL . . .
Lange points out that it is possible that Ashpenaz himself
might not have been a literal eunuch since Joseph's master
at the court of Pharaoh is called by the same Hebrew word
and yet was married (cf. Gen. 37:36; 38:1-7). It is highly
probable though that Ashpenaz and all his subordinates were
eunuchs in the literal sense. However, it is not necessary
to assume that Daniel and his Hebrew friends were made to

become literal eunuchs. In fact, Ezekiel 14:20 seems to imply that Daniel had sons and daughters. It may also be assumed that Daniel would resist being made a eunuch with as much forcefulness as he did the "king's dainties" since the law of Moses prohibited a eunuch to enter the congregation of Israel, (Deut. 23:1).

Ashpenaz, major-domo, was commanded by the king to select only the most eminent of the captives—those of royal stock. By this means he could gather, from every subjugated nation, a select body of talented young diplomats. The value of such a heterogeneous group to a pagan court, representing an amalgamation of many different political, cultural and intellectual ideas and secrets, is at once evident. Daniel was from the tribe of Judah, the royal tribe of Israel.

v. 4 . . . NO BLEMISH . . . WELL-FAVORED . . . SKILFUL IN ALL WISDOM . . . ENDUED WITH KNOWLEDGE . . . UNDERSTANDING . . . SCIENCE . . . AS HAD ABILITY TO STAND IN THE KING'S PALACE . . . TEACH THEM . . . LEARNING AND . . . TONGUE OF THE CHALDEANS . . . These are the king's own specifications. He is first of all interested that these young men who will grace his court have no physical infirmity or blemish. They must be physically handsome. Beauty was regarded almost as a virtue among the ancients. The king would not permit an ugly, misshapen, stooped, or scarred courtier. But more important, they were to be mentally alert and capable of analytical understanding. They were to be more than mere philosophers and theorists— they were to be apt at making practical applications of what was learned and known. As the Hebrew puts it— they were to have a "knowing knowledge." They were to be possessed already of a great amount of contemporary "science" and "knowledge." Nebuchadnezzer had in mind the extra-ordinary young man. He desired only the brilliant, the scholarly.

His purpose in being so selective was to gather a group of young men eager to learn and easy to teach the sciences and culture of the Babylonians. The king's theory was that if he could provide himself with a retinue of widely diversified sources of knowledge and wisdom and at the same time

Babylonianize them or bind them to loyalty to Babylon, he would be that much more able to conquer and rule.

Daniel and the other three lads were enrolled in a "crash" course in Babylonian culture and for three years were given the ancient equivalent of a liberal education. We gain some idea of the literary resources of the seventh century before Christ when we are introduced through archaeology to the vast library of Ashurbanipal (704-681 B.C. just prior to Daniel's day) which contained 22,0000 volumes of cuneiform (i.e. "wedge-shaped" writing) clay tablets. These tablets contain religious, literary, and scientific works among which were the Babylonian creation and flood tablets. These tablets came from a variety of sources. Many were copied from originals by his own scribes. He dispatched officials to the cities of his Empire with orders to gather all texts of importance. One of his extant discoveries ends with the words, "If you hear of any tablet or ritualistic text that is suitable for the palace, seek it out, secure it, and send it here.'"

The Babylonians inherited the sexagesimal system from the ancient Sumerians. This system of numbering by sixties is still in use. We reckon sixty seconds to the minute, and sixty minutes to the hour. The system is also used in the division of the circle into three hundred and sixty degrees. Clay tablets have been found showing common familiarity with measurement of the area of rectangles and of right and isoceles triangles. An amazing knowledge of algebra is also shown in the Babylonian literature—tablets of squares, square roots, cubes, and cube roots. The Pythagorean theorem was known by the Babylonians more than a thousand years before Pythagoras!

Closely related to their knowledge of mathematics was their science of astronomy. By 800 B.C. Babylonian astronomers had attained sufficient accuracy to assign positions to the stars and note their heliacal settings. An attempt was made to determine cause and effect relationships between the motions of the heavenly bodies and purely human events and this is known as astrology and is definitely not scientific. A cuneiform tablet from about 700 B.C. classifies the fixed stars. Lengths of daylight and darkness at a given time could be predicted by the Babylonians.

In the field of medicine certain scientific advances were made. Their attempt to learn the will of the gods by an examination of animal entrails furnished, by way of analogy, some idea of human anatomy. As early as the Code of Hammurabi (1700 B.C.) physicians performed delicate operations on the human eye.

Babylonian science was the result of observation and classification and they used it to serve many practical purposes. Taxonomy in plant, animal and mineral kingdoms was practiced. Chemistry and metallurgy were everyday sciences in Daniel's day.

And, of course, there was an extremely complicated theology or philosophy of Babylonian religion. We will deal with this aspect of Daniel's education in a later section of the text.

v. 5 . . . A DAILY PORTION OF THE KING'S DAINTIES, AND OF THE WINE WHICH HE DRANK . . . The king commanded that these young men enrolled in instruction in Babylonian culture should also learn to live (especially to eat indulgently) like Babylonian men of eminence. He ordered that they learn the social graces of the Babylonian royal table by eating from the king's kitchen. "Dainties" probably refer to foods in which only the king could afford to indulge—luxurious, costly, rare, delicate—food that is associated with the lives of those who are lovers of pleasure and luxury. By association with this type of food they would be exposed to a subtle moral softening and weakening process. Godly people are warned to abstain from indulging in such eating of the flesh (cf. Psa. 141:4; Prov. 23:1-3; Rev. 18:14).

The king's purpose in this was certainly pragmatic and perhaps psychological. It is clear from the phrase, "that at the end thereof they should stand before the king," the practical end the king sought was training in social graces befitting men of the court. And, it may be, Nebuchadnezzar was attempting a psychological "brainwashing" through such a thorough introduction into Babylonian table manners. The next verses suggest this.

v. 6-7 . . . THE PRINCE OF THE EUNUCHS GAVE NAMES UNTO THEM . . . In olden days most names were theophoric. That is, they had the name of the deity incorporated. Daniel means "my judge is God;" Hananiah means "gracious is Jehovah;" Mishael means "who is He that is God?" and Azariah means "Jehovah hath helped." When the Babylonians changed their names it meant they intended to honor their gods for victory over the Hebrews whose God the Babylonians believed they had vanquished. A parallel for such action is found in II Kings 23:34; 24:17; Esther 2:7.

Beltheshazzar means "protect his life;" Shadrach means "command of Aku (the moon god);" Mesach means "who is what Aku (the moon god) is?" and Abednego means "servant of Nebo." No doubt the purpose of the Babylonian king was to so assimilate these young men into the Babylonian culture they would become, for all practical purposes, Babylonians and dissociate themselves completely from the Hebrew ways; even from their God. Although these lads did accommodate themselves readily to new knowledge and new culture, they remained true to their knowledge of and daily walk with the Living God. The rest of their story is yet to be learned.

QUIZ

1. What evidence is there that Daniel (606-536 B.C.) wrote this book and not some pesudo-Daniel of 200-1000 B.C.?
2. What is the purpose of the book of Daniel?
3. What is apocalyptic literature?
4. Describe the city of Babylon in Daniel's day—give its location, etc.
5. Show how the apparent discrepancy between Jeremiah's account of Jehoiakim and Nebuchadnezzar and Daniel's account do not contradict.
6. How extensive was the knowledge and wisdom of the Babylonians at this time?
7. Why did the king insist on these young men eating food from his table?

II. PERSEVERANCE ACTUATED

TEXT: 1:8-16

8 But Daniel purposed in his heart that he would not defile himself with the king's dainties, nor with the wine

which he drank; therefore he requested of the prince of the eunuchs that he might not defile himself.

9 Now God made Daniel to find kindness and compassion in the sight of the prince of the eunuchs.

10 And the prince of the eunuchs said unto Daniel, I fear my lord the king, who hath appointed your food and your drink: for why should he see your faces worse looking than the youths that are of your own age? so would ye endanger my head with the king.

11 Then said Daniel to the steward whom the prince of the enuchs had appointed over Daniel, Hananhia, Mishael, and Azariah:

12 Prove thy servants, I beseech thee, ten days; and let them give us pulse to eat, and water to drink.

13 Then let our countenances be looked upon before thee, and the countenance of the youths that eat of the king's dainties; and as thou seest, deal with thy servants.

14 So he hearkened unto them in this matter, and proved them ten days.

15 And at the end of ten days their countenances appeared fairer, and they were fatter in flesh, than all the youths that did eat of the king's dainties.

16 So the steward took away their dainties, and the wine they should drink, and gave them pulse.

QUERIES

a. What sort of "defilement" was Daniel anxious to avoid?
b. Was the physical development natural or miraculous?
c. What is "pulse?"

PARAPHRASE

Daniel solemnly resolved that he would not deny the God of Israel by eating food and drinking wine from the king's table which had been dedicated to the worship of idols. He courteously requested from the king's chief servant that he not be forced to participate in the worship of idols by partaking of this food. Now Daniel allowed God to live in and through him to such an extent that the chief servant of the king was inclined toward Daniel with kindness and compassion. Yet, as kindly disposed as he was to Daniel's regard for principle, he explained his own predicament, saying, I dare not grant your request because my king shows no mercy to those who disobey him. He has ordered this food for you, and if you do not eat it and your physical development deteriorates, he will execute me without mercy. Afterward Daniel politely asked the understeward assigned to serve them their food if he would be willing to perform a simple test which would involve no personal danger to himself—Give us a simple vegetable and water diet for just ten days. Then, at the end of this short period, compare our physical development with that of those young men who eat the king's rich delicacies and decide upon our request according to what you see. So the servant agreed to Daniel's proposition and fed them vegetables and water for ten days, and at the end of ten days he saw that their physical development was even more what the king desired than those who had been eating the king's food and the steward did not bring them food from the king's table any more but continued to give them vegetables to eat.

COMMENT

v. 8 DANIEL PURPOSED IN HIS HEART THAT HE WOULD NOT DEFILE HIMSELF . . . The godly parents of this young Hebrew must have been of the same caliber as the parents of John the Baptist, "righteous before God, walking in all the commandments and ordinances of the Lord blameless" (Luke 1:6): They had done a superb job of rearing their son in the admonition and nurture of the Lord. Daniel was possessed of the great principles of righteousness and holiness and faith. He was not one who sought to be justified by a righteousness which is of law-keeping but by a righteousness which is by faith.

Leupold points out that there are three aspects of Daniel's heathen environment about which he had to make moral decisions as affecting his relationship to the Living God: (1) the acquistion of heathen wisdom; (2) the bearing of heathen names; (3) the eating of heathen food sacrificed to idols. Daniel knew that in studying heathen sciences he could not be compelled against his conscience to believe those elements of that science that were false. He may have taken

Moses and Joseph as his examples of guidance. Their exposure to heathen sciences and myths did not destroy their faith. Daniel's second experience, that of being given a heathen name, he simply had to endure as something he could do nothing about. It had no bearing on his relationship to God any more than children today who are given "heathen" names deliberately or unconsciously by their parents.

The matter of eating from the king's table was much more serious. It was a matter which would involve his relationship with God. All meals served at the king's table were of foods (especially wine and meats) which had been used in worship ceremonies dedicated to heathen idols. To share in such a feast was, according to an eternal principle, the same as worshipping the idol (cf. I Cor. 10:20ff). The significance of Daniel's act does not, as Lange comments, consist in a legalistic asceticism but in the proof of resolute faith and obedient devotion to the Living God rather than giving the slightest respect to a pagan idolatry.

But notice the courteous and amiable manner Daniel displayed in expressing his faith and devotion to righteous principle. He displays no fanaticism or rudeness, but honestly and frankly states his intention to the chief servant and asks his help.

v. 9 . . . GOD MADE DANIEL TO FIND KINDNESS AND COMPASSION . . . Most commentators speak as if God worked a miracle of "irresistible grace" upon the heart of the chief eunuch so that he could not help himself but to show kindness and compassion toward Daniel. We prefer to presume, in the light of biblical teaching that man is a free moral agent, that the Spirit of God working in the heart of Daniel and subsequently in his actions toward this chief eunuch moved the eunuch to kindness and compassion. All the glory is to be given to God. For it is God who works in Daniel to strengthen him that he should not yield in devotion to hold principle while at the same time being respectful and kind to the chief servant. "Blessed are the merciful, for they shall obtain mercy" (Matt. 5:7). The chief eunuch recognized that Daniel's request was made upon the basis of principle and he respected the request. The response of this pagan was, in the ultimate sense, to the grace of God manifested in the life of Daniel.

v. 10 . . . I FEAR MY LORD THE KING . . . SO WOULD YE ENDANGER MY HEAD WITH THE KING . . . The chief eunuch was under great psychological stress and, had not Daniel displayed the grace of God in his request, probably would have responded very inconsiderately with so unimportant a character as this Hebrew captive. He could very well have considered Daniel's request as insubordination and impudence. This chief steward was a trusted servant of an absolute monarch. Failure to carry out his emperor's wishes meant, if discovered, immediate death.

Yes, the chief steward sympathized with Daniel's principles, but it meant almost certain execution for him and so he was about to deny Daniel's request. Surely, he reasoned with Daniel, you young men would not want to be responsible for me losing my head to the king's executioner!

v. 11-13 . . . PROVE THY SERVANTS . . . TEN DAYS . . . GIVE US PULSE TO EAT . . . AND AS THOU SEEST, DEAL WITH THY SERVANTS . . . Daniel now proposes to one of the underservants appointed by the chief servant to serve Daniel and the three lads their fare, a very simple, reasonable and relatively safe experiment. For ten days Daniel suggests, they be fed "pulse" and water. *Zero'im* literally means, "things sowed." Things sowed were not customarily offered by pagans as food to their gods. This Hebrew word could be translated in a general sense as *vegetables*. It involves more than legumes (peas and beans) and would include wheat and other grains so that bread would be in their diet. Wine was not, of course, foreign to the Hebrew diet, except in this case the wine would have been associated with pagan worship ritual.

Ten days is reasonably short enough not to arouse the suspicion of the king and yet long enough to test the merits of the case. There are probably two elements involved in Daniel's proposal—his faith that God will provide and his common sense that overrich fare such as the luxurious table of the king, offered in unlimited amounts, is not as conducive to good health as is plain, substantial food. The Mosaic law implies this in its prohibition of eating fat (Lev. 7:22-24; 3:17; cf. also Titus 1:12-13).

Young argues that Daniel "received a special revelation from the Spirit of God and . . . in speaking he was acting in accord with that revelation." He says that if Daniel had made this offer merely upon his own initiative he would have been guilty of presumption. He asks, "What warrant could faith have that at the expiration of a short period of time such a change would be apparent in the physical appearance of the youths as is suggested here?" This in turn would imply that the resultant physiological excellence of the Hebrew youths over their contemporaries was miraculous. Such a miracle is not, of course, out of harmony with the historical record of the Old Testament—many such miracles are recorded, and did occur. We simply do not have a sufficient amount of testimony from Daniel to make a final decision in the matter of *how* it occurred. It would seem that a combination of three elements may be involved: (a) a direct revelation to Daniel plus (b) Daniel's common sense based on past experience and (c) faith in the directions of God as revealed in the Mosaic law concerning the eating of certain foods. Whatever the case, we consider Daniel's proposal a direct expression of his trust and devotion to the Living God.

v. 14-16 . . . AND AT THE END OF TEN DAYS THEIR COUNTENANCES APPEARED FAIRER . . . SO THE STEWARD TOOK AWAY THEIR DAINTIES . . . AND GAVE THEM PULSE . . . The remarks of Leupold are appropriate here: "It may seem that a disproportionate amount of emphasis is being given to a secondary matter. But the meticulous care exercised by these young men in doing the will of their God is perhaps the strongest indication that could be found of their complete allegiance to their God. Their determination shows how clearly they discerned what issues were at stake, and how correctly they were getting their bearings in the matter of making an adjustment in reference to daily contact with heathen life. The issues involved were not trifles. In this matter they had to take a stand."

For the believer in God there are three areas of morality: (a) that which is always right; (b) that which is always wrong; (c) that which is a matter of opinion (which the believer is at liberty to choose, guided by love for God and fellow-man). Daniel was called upon to act in all three realms. It is always right to be kind and courteous to one's fellow man—Daniel did so. It is a matter of opinion about learning from the literature and culture of the world—Daniel did so and used it to serve God and man. It is always wrong to blaspheme God by worshipping idols—Daniel refused. The believer's liberty is bounded by Divine authority as revealed in a propositional revelation and is also bounded by the principle of love—love for God and His will first, and love for man second. The only way the believer knows a proper action or expression of love is by direction of the revealed will of God. A believer does not live by practising any ethic or moulding himself on any ideal, but by a faith in God which finally ascribes all good to Him and seeks His will as it has been revealed through His prophets and His Son and recorded inerrantly in the Bible.

QUIZ

1. What were the three aspects of Daniel's heathen environment about which he had to make moral decisions?
2. Why was the matter of eating the king's dainties more serious than the other?
3. How does Daniel behave toward his captors in resisting defiling of himself?
4. How did Daniel find favor in the eyes of the chief eunuch?
5. What are the three areas of morality for the believer in God?
6. How did Daniel behave in these three areas?
7. What is the believer's ultimate source of knowing what is right and wrong?

III. PROSPERITY AWARDED

TEXT: 1:17-21

17 Now as for these four youths, God gave them knowledge and skill in all learning and wisdom: and Daniel had understanding in all visions and dreams.

18 And at the end of the days which the king had appointed for bringing them in, the prince of the eunuchs brought them in before Nebuchadnezzar.

19 And the king communed with them; and among them all was found none like Daniel, Hananiah, Mishael, and Azariah: therefore stood they before the king.

20 And in every matter of wisdom and understanding, concerning which the king inquired of them, he found them ten times better than all the magicians and enchanters that were in all his realm.

21 And Daniel continued even unto the first year of king Cyrus.

QUERIES

a. How did God give these youths knowledge, learning and wisdom?

b. Who were the magicians and enchanters in Babylon?

c. Who is king Cyrus?

PARAPHRASE

God gave these four youths supernatural ability to learn and they soon mastered all the literature and science of the time; and God gave to Daniel special ability in understanding the meanings of dreams and visions when they are given as divine messages. And when the three-year training period was completed, the chief of the eunuchs brought all the young men in this training program to the king for interview and examination. King Nebuchadnezzar interviewed each one at length and found that none of them impressed him as much as Daniel, Hananiah, Mishael and Azariah. So they were appointed to his regular staff of advisors. And in all matters requiring information and reasoned judgment the king found these young men's advice ten times better than that of all the skilled wise men and prognosticators in his realm. And Daniel held this appointment as the king's counsellor for some twenty-four years and through five or six emperors, until sometime in the first year of the reign of Cyrus the Persian.

COMMENT

v. 17 . . . GOD GAVE THEM KNOWLEDGE AND SKILL IN ALL LEARNING AND WISDOM . . . The only conclusion to reach from the statement in verse 17 is that the ability to gain knowledge and have learning and wisdom was a direct and supernatural gift of God to the four young lads. The gift of God was received, of course, willingly and we may safely presume they applied themselves diligently to their task. The phrase "skill in all learning and wisdom" indicates God gave them a power to perceive, distinguish and judge everything they learned whether it was to be accepted and practiced and taught as truth or to be rejected as false. They had inerrant insight into all the knowledge and learning of Babylonians. Leupold says, ". . . a discernment that enabled these four to sit in judgment on all secular learning that was offered them and to evaluate it according to the estimate of all-wise God." They were also given "wisdom" which is the ability to rightly apply the knowledge acquired as God would have it applied. Daniel was given an additional gift that the other three did not have— understanding in all visions and dreams.

Visions and dreams were often used by God in the Old Testament to reveal special missions or messages to certain men (cf. Jacob, Joseph, etc.). Inasmuch as these dreams and visions were usually in extended symbolism they required special, divine interpretation, directly from God or through one of God's appointed messengers. This would be especially necessary when such dreams and visions were given to pagan rulers. Daniel's gift was extraordinary. See our introductory study entitled "Interpreting The Prophets," in *The Minor Prophets*, by Paul T. Butler, pub. College Press, for information on dreams and visions. Daniel was not unique in this gift of interpreting dreams and visions (Joseph had the gift and exercised it extensively).

v. 18-19 . . . AND AMONG THEM ALL WAS FOUND NONE LIKE DANIEL, ETC. . . . It is still amazing to some people, but true in most cases, that firm but courteous propagation of principle and truth will be appreciated and rewarded even by pagans who themselves are prone to follow false-

41

hood and myth. Joseph, Moses, Peter and John and Paul are prime examples as they stood before pagan rulers and princes. This is true because truth is always wise! What is true may not be immediately and physically pleasurable, but it is always wise. And only the degraded reprobate will fail to recognize that. It did not take Nebuchadnezzar long to recognize the contrast between the wisdom of these four youths and the foolishness of the mythology and mysticism of the enchanters and magicians.

v. 20-21 . . . HE FOUND THEM TEN TIMES BETTER THAN ALL THE MAGICIANS AND ENCHANTERS . . . The word "ten" is, of course, hyperbolic and simply means Daniel and his three companions were found exceedingly wise and perceptive. They were much more learned and discerning than the young men who had been born and reared in Babylon— in fact more than all the trained wise men of Babylon!

It would be well to give a brief resume of Babylonian religion here. The religion which the Jews of the Exile found in Babylon had roots which went back over two thousand years. The ancient Sumerian religion was highly polytheistic and made a practice of absorbing or incorporating every religion or god it contacted. The god of a victorious state was considered to be the most powerful deity, for warfare was always waged on two levels. The earthly states were championed by their celestial deities, and the battles in the sky were accounted as real as the battles on earth (cf. Daniel chap. 10). In very ancient Sumerian times (2000 years before the Jewish captivity) the chief god was known as Anu, the sky god who was regarded as father of the great gods. The second great god was Bel (the Semitic Baal) which means "Lord," and he was ruler of earth. The third of the great Sumerian gods was known as Enki who ruled the waters upon which the Babylonians believed the terrestial world floated. Then there was a pantheon of some 4000 gods which included Sin the moongod, Shamash, the sun-god, and Adad the storm god. Fertility and reproduction in the Tigris-Euphrates valley were associated with Ishtar also the goddess of war. There was Ninurta, fertility god who was responsible for the annual flooding of the rivers; Gibil the god of fire who was invoked by magicians in their tasks of exorcism—he was called upon to burn to death evil spirits and sorcerers; Nergal, destroyer of life, the god of pestilence and death, god of the land of no return; Nabu (Nebo) god of the scribes who was keeper of the Table of Fate with power to prolong or shorten life (Nebuchadnezzar's name expresses faith in Nebo).

During the First Dynasty of Neo-Babylon an important revolution took place in the religion of the country. A minor deity named *Marduk* was chosen as the principal god of the whole of Babylonia and was placed at the head of the pantheon. The mythological story of how he rescued all the gods and goddesses from the monster Tiamat and was acknowledged by all he rescued as chief god is too long to recount here. Tammuz, son of Ishtar, was a god of vegetation who disappeared each year in the late summer and returned (i.e. was resurrected) the following spring (cf. Ezek. 8:14). In the Greco-Roman world Tammuz was worshiped as Adonis (a name which is a variant of the Semitic *Adon*, lord, or master).

The Babylonians of Daniel's day had an elaborate system of good genies or spirits and evil genies. Evil genies were believed to enter houses even when doors were bolted and if they found men or women in sin without the protection of their personal god they entered that man or woman and possessed them. The Babylonian felt himself surrounded by ghosts, or spirits of men whose lives had proved unhappy on earth. The ghosts had been cheated out of happiness in this life and, nursing their grief, they were determined to torment the living.

This is the kind of "learning and wisdom" Daniel and his three friends, and especially Daniel, would later renounce in favor of being true to Jehovah God and would, indirectly at least, expose as mythological and false. We shall deal with the magicians and enchanters in chapter two.

QUIZ

1. What was the knowledge and skill in learning and wisdom given these youths?
2. Why did God use visions and dreams to communicate to man?

3. Why is truth usually rewarded with respect even by heathen?
4. What was the character of Babylonian religion?
5. Who was the chief god of the Babylonians in Daniel's day?

SERMON NUMBER ONE

DARE TO BE A DANIEL . . .

Text: Daniel 1:8

INTRODUCTION

I. WHY WAS DANIEL IN BABYLON?

A. He was one of the first groups of captives carried away from Jerusalem to Babylon during the period of Judah's downfall and the Captivity of the entire nation of Judah

The captivity of the Jews was prophesied by Jeremiah

B. Daniel's subsequent life indicates that he could not have been one of the many reprobates who brought God's wrath upon the nation of Judah causing the captivity

We assume therefore that God had special need of Daniel and allowed him to be taken to Babylon to serve Him and those who would repent while in captivity

C. John Noble came to this conclusion concerning his imprisonment in Communist Russian prison camps for some 12-13 years

". . . there were those cynics and skeptics among my fellow prisoners who asked how anyone could give thanks to a God who was permitting us to suffer as we did . . . I always answered to such criticism that while I did not know what purpose was being served by the suffering we were enduring, I was sure that there was a reason. I felt that God would deal in due time with the atheists of Russia and that meanwhile the world must see by the suffering of the victims of communist tyranny what an evil system it is."

II. WHAT WAS BABYLON LIKE?

A. The city was surrounded by 60 miles of wall, 300 ft. high, 80 ft. thick, submerged underground 35 ft. (in order to keep enemies from tunnelling under). The Euphrates river split the city in the middle. The temple of Bel contained a golden image and golden table which weighed more than 25 tons. It had 53 temples and 180 altars and some 4000 gods.

B. The king's palace was perhaps the most magnificent building ever erected in antiquity. It was protected itself by 4 succeeding walls plus moats and other defense mechanisms.

C. The hanging gardens, built by Nebuchadnezzar for one of his homesick queens, consisted of several tiers of arches, each holding up a solid platform 400 ft. sq. upon which would be planted trees, shrubs, flowers, gardens of all kinds. These platform gardens were watered by hydraulic pumps pumping water upward from one level to another.

D. Their society and culture was what would be expected from a pagan empire—sensual, luxurious, indulgent, cruel, proud and powerful.

E. In such a land and amongst such a people was the young man Daniel.

DISCUSSION

I. DARE TO BE A DANIEL, DARE TO STAND ALONE

A. He had his friends with him; he was not all alone

1. They stood many of the tests of loyalty to God with Daniel

2. What a blessing believing and faithful friends can be

3. The great apostle Paul was blessed with a few faithful friends Luke, Barnabas, John Mark, Silas, Titus

    4. It is a great consolation to a believer who has to suffer to know there are other believers sharing in the same experiences and remaining faithful

    5. As Christians we are one body of believers and when one member suffers we all suffer (cf. Rom. 12:15; I Cor. 12:25-26)

    6. Yet, each believer must ultimately stand alone when his faith is tested

B. He had his God; he was not all alone

    1. He undoubtedly was reared in a God-fearing, God-worshipping Jewish home and knew by the experience of faith that God was with him

    2. He knew by God's supernatural manifestation of Himself in miraculous deeds that God was with him; physical development on a diet of vegetables; supernatural learning and wisdom and ability to interpret dreams

    3. His providential reception by this pagan court should indicate to him that God was protecting him

    4. Yet, God could not make Daniel's choices for him
. . . SO DANIEL WAS, IN A VERY REAL SENSE, STANDING ALONE

    5. Daniel, all alone, had to CHOOSE whether to self-righteously refuse training in the wisdom of the Chaldeans or to recognize there was nothing basically immoral in studying in a selective way and making the most of every opportunity to glorify God among the heathen.

C. Daniel had choices to make and so he was all alone

    1. His friends could not decide for him; HE MUST STAND ALONE

    2. God will not choose for him; HE MUST DECIDE FOR HIMSELF

    3. Daniel and his three friends STOOD PRACTICALLY ALL ALONE AS THEY CHOSE TO REFUSE PARTICIPATION IN IDOL WORSHIP

    4. Every believer must make personal choices which no one else can make for him

    5. Every believer must realize that those who truly trust the Lord are in the minority and often times

it will appear as if no one but themselves are standing up for righteousness and truth

6. The Bible teaches that believers are to be set apart from the world (II Cor. 6:14—7:1; Jn. 17:14-17; Matt. 7:13-14, etc.)

D. Examples of those who have stood alone (except that God was with them):
1. Noah (preached 120 years only 8 were saved)
2. Abraham (left his own country and wandered)
3. Moses (stood against Egypt and Pharaoh)
4. David (stood alone against Goliath, then against Saul)
5. Paul (stood against the heathen world; against Judaizers)
6. Martin Luther (stood against powerful world church)
7. Alexander Campbell (stood against denominationalism)
8. PERFECT EXAMPLE: JESUS CHRIST, even His friends deserted Him; was forsaken by God in order to suffer our eternal punishment for us
9. John Noble, "I was increasingly certain that many of these Russians respected the courage with which prisoners held to their faith in God and that they would have liked to join us if they could."

II. DARE TO HAVE A PURPOSE FIRM

A. Definition of Dare: "resolution; bravery, courage; backbone; venturous; challenging; unflinching."
1. Standing alone without a godly purpose is vanity and pride; such are rebels without causes for any cause that is not godly is a losing cause!
2. Daniel had purpose because he had conviction. He was fully persuaded that God exists and that He is a jealous and loving God

B. Daniel's Purpose
1. To glorify God. This was Daniel's target—his main concern in every experience that life brought him.
2. He refused to eat from the king's table because in so doing he would be participating in the wor-

ship of idols. Practically all the rich and luxurious food and wine the king and his court ate had been devoted as sacrifices to pagan idols. To eat this food Daniel would give the king the impression that he was willing to worship idols. Daniel's purpose was just the opposite.

3. It may also be that some of the food from the king's table was "unclean" according to Mosaic law. Daniel's purpose was to uphold the law of God in every instance possible.

4. Daniel knew that if he trusted God, God would manifest His power and it was Daniel's purpose to let his life and his mouth be a testimony to the True and Living God.

5. In doing this Daniel would become a source of light to the darkened pagan society dwelling in ignorance and sin. He would at the same time become a source of encouragement and strength to his Jewish brethren in captivity.

C. Every believer needs to have a purpose firm

1. I have a sermon entitled "A Life Worth Living" with three main points: (a) Have a Belief Worth Trusting; (b) Have a Job Worth Doing; (c) Get a Reward Worth Having.

2. Daniel could have rationalized like so many of us do today and said, "When in Babylon, do as the Babylonians do." BUT HE KNEW HOW TO SAY "NO!" AND MEAN IT! It was not easy for him. Consider all the pressures he had to endure.

3. Self-control is the mark of real man-hood. Strong men, cruel men, shrewd men may control nations and empires but if they cannot control self they are the weakest of all men: cf. Alexander the Great; Hitler, etc.

4. The world, for the most part, respects purity, courage, honesty, conviction.

5. The people who have done the most for mankind and in a lasting nature are men who have had the one purpose which counts the most—TO GLORIFY GOD! Think of Joseph, Esther, Francis

Bacon, Micheangelo, Handel, Lincoln, David Lloyd George, Pascal, Michael Faraday, etc.

6. Such a purpose will come only with persuasion that God is, that Jesus Christ is the living, reigning, returning Lord, and that the Bible is the Word of the Spirit. SUCH A PURPOSE WILL COME ONLY WITH DAILY, SWEET COMMUNION WITH GOD THROUGH HIS WORD AND PRAYER! This is where Daniel's purpose came from.

7. John Noble, "This I found that honesty paid even in a Russian concentration camp where it might seem that only a fool would try to hold to a conventional moral standard. I had resolved to try to show . . . by example, what the faith of a Christian could do. Many times thereafter I discovered that no matter where I was, honesty got me further."

III. DARE TO MAKE IT KNOWN

A. Daniel had conviction and purpose and was not afraid to make it known

1. There were plenty of excuses Daniel might have had to keep silent about his faith in God
2. To the contrary, Daniel took every opportunity to testify concerning the True and Living God
3. There was the time he prayed to Jehovah with his windows open in defiance to the king's edict
4. There was the time he delivered the true message of God to Nebuchadnezzar about his insanity
5. There was the time he delivered the true message of God to Belshazzar
6. And, of course, there were many other occasions

B. This world needs people, Christian people, who will dare to make their purpose known—to glorify God.

1. Our heathen world needs believers with conviction. About the only conviction most people have today is that it's wrong to have convictions.
2. Dare to proclaim the counsel of God—the *whole* counsel of God
3. Dare to make the most for God of every situation

49

4. Dare to be honest with self, with God, with associates in every situation—Daniel did not give up, but neither did he cause undue alarm or antagonism in the heart of his pagan ruler. Joseph and Moses and Paul are prime examples.

5. Believers will never be encouraged and strengthened unless there be those who have purpose who will dare to make it known

6. Unbelievers will never become believers unless believers dare to make the gospel known (Rom. 10:17)

C. Examples of those who dared to make it known

1. All the Old Testament prophets; Isaiah (ch. 6); Jeremiah (ch. 1 and 20:9); Jonah, Ezekiel, Amos, Hosea, etc.

2. John the Baptist: one of the loneliest men who ever walked the earth was fearless in making the glory of God known

3. Paul the apostle—preached from house to house, night and day, with tears; preached to kings and authorities

4. Jesus Christ—this was His "food" (Jn. 4); Zeal for the house of God consumed Him (Jn. 2). Jesus dared to "tell it like it is" (cf. Jn. 7-8-9; Matt. 23, etc.)

D. How may every believer "dare" to make his purpose known?

1. By personal evangelism with his neighbors, friends and relatives

2. By teaching a Bible School class (elders are to be "apt to teach")

3. By supporting various arms of evangelism with financial means: Bible Colleges; T.V. Programs; Missionaries; Printing Efforts

4. By writing letters to unconverted friends and relatives

5. By living lives that do not compromise with worldliness but yet do not withdraw into a monastic life and dissociate from the daily affairs of needy men.

CONCLUSION

I. HERE IN THE FIRST REAL TEST OF DANIEL'S FAITH WE SEE VICTORY

A. God providentially cared for them in the matter of food and they developed physically to a state more to be desired than their heathen contemporaries

B. God providentially supplied greater knowledge, learning, wisdom than all their contemporaries

C. Notice: these providential blessings were not afforded for Daniel to indulge himself but to give him greater opportunity to serve the Lord

D. God has promised to give every believer such an abundance of *opportunity* to serve the Lord (cf. Eph. 3:20; II Cor. 9:6-15) Joseph recognized this, Gen. 50:20

II. AT THE END OF DANIEL'S LIFE AND BOOK (ch. 12 WE SEE VICTORY

A. It is significant that of all the Old Testament books, Daniel is the one which deals most of moral courage and faith—and it is the one which deals the most with the resurrection

B. Daniel is given a vision of victory like the aged John in Revelation. Daniel's curiosity almost gets the best of him—he wants to know the why and wherefore of all that he had seen in vision but God knows that what he needs most is assurance of victory.

C. "They that be wise, shall shine like the brightness of the firmament; and those who turn many to righteousness, like the stars for ever and ever."

D. "But go your way till the end; and you shall rest, and shall stand in your allotted place at the end of the days."

E. DANIEL, WHO HAD WITNESSED SO COURAGEOUSLY AND FAITHFULLY TO HIS LAST DAYS IS TOLD, "YOU SHALL REST."

DANIEL, WHO DARED TO STAND ALONE, DARED TO HAVE A PURPOSE FIRM, DARED TO MAKE IT KNOWN . . . SHINES AS THE BRIGHTNESS OF THE FIRMAMENT, ONE

OF THE BRIGHTEST OF THOSE STARS WHICH HAVE
TURNED MANY TO GOD AND RIGHTEOUSNESS

III. WILL YOU DARE TO BE A DANIEL . . . A JOSEPH
. . . A MOSES . . . A PAUL?

EXAMINATION ONE

REFUTATIONS

(Answer the following by giving the argument which will
correct the statement)

1. The Book of Daniel was written in the 2nd century
B.C. by an unknown author. Refute!
2. We know very little about the Babylon of Daniel's time.
Refute!
3. There is a contradiction between Daniel and Jeremiah
about the dates of Nebuchadnezzar's attack upon Jerusalem. Refute!

ASSOCIATIONS

(Associate the persons or events of column one with the
correct person or event of column two.)

1	2
Jehoiakim	king of Persia
Belteshazzar	king of Babylon
Cyrus	river in Babylon
steward	mountain in Palestine
Ashpenaz	king of Judah
Nebuchadnezzar	Daniel
Babylon	Meshach
Abednego	Mesopotamia
Hananiah	Shadrach
Chaldeans	chief of eunuchs
Jerusalem	servant
Shinar	capitol of Judah
Mishael	Babylonian people
	Azariah
	Euphrates
	territory in Babylon
	Mishael

MEMORIZATIONS

(Fill in the blanks:)

But Daniel _____ in his heart that he would not _____ himself with the king's _____, nor with the wine which he drank; therefore he requested of the prince of the _____ that he might not _____ himself. Now God made Daniel to find _____ and compassion in the sight of the prince of the _____.

EXPLANATIONS

1. Explain why the king of Babylon took these young men and fed them and trained them in Chaldean wisdom.
2. Explain why Daniel could permit himself to be trained in Chaldean (pagan) sciences, literature, etc., and still be faithful to God.
3. Explain how the Hebrew youths could subsist in this meager diet and still be healthier than their contemporaries.
4. Explain how Daniel and the other three could be ten times wiser than other Babylonian enchanters.

SPECIAL STUDY TWO

THE BABYLONIAN PRIESTHOOD

In ancient Babylon the king served as both High Priest and civil ruler. He performed sacrifices and determined the religious life of his subjects. Since the king could not personally officiate in each of the temples in his realm, he appointed substitute priests to perform the routine priestly labors. Each temple would have a high priest, appointed by the king, and a number of lesser priests, known as *shangu,* who were also responsible to the king. The temple affairs were administered by these men who were chosen because of their fitness for the work.

There were other priestly functions of a specialized nature which presupposed specific training. The task of divination, the interpreting of dreams, and otherwise determining the will of the gods, was entrusted to the *buru* priests. The interpretation of oracles and dreams was on the basis of a long tradition of divination which the *buru* priests was expected to master. Hepatoscopy, or divination by the liver, was an ancient method of divination used by Hittites and Etruscans as well as by the Babylonians. The liver was regarded as the seat of the mental life. At the time of sacrifice, a god was thought to take hold of the victim, and the god's thoughts were presumed to enter the animal's liver. After a kid or sheep was slaughtered sacrificially, the victim's body was opened and preliminary conclusions drawn. Then the liver was removed and subjected to careful examination. Actual livers were compared with terra-cotta models and abnormalities were noted. We do not know how various configurations were interpreted but we know that ancient kings and their officers had a high regard for divination by the liver.[1]

Hittites and Etruscans, in common with Babylonians, also studied the flight patterns of birds as a means of divination. We do not know exactly what they looked for, but diviners skilled in this type of divination regularly accompanied the armies of Babylon.

1. Divination by liver was one means used by Nebuchadnezzar in determining whether to attack Jerusalem or Rabbath Ammon (Ezek. 21:18-23).

Babylon was noted for its astrology, but this differed in important particulars from the astrology which developed in medieval times, based on Greek antecedents. Babylonian astrologers noted the direction of the winds, the color of the stars, and the occulation of planets and eclipses. The information provided by Babylonian astrologers was used in agriculture as well as in matters of national policy.

The Babylonian priests were constantly on the lookout for the abnormal. Any unusual circumstance attending a birth, human or animal, would be considered a sign which needed interpretation. If an exorcist were called to the home of an invalid, everything which he encountered along the way would be considered significant. If water were spilled on the road, its pattern might contain a message. The shape of oil which had formed on the surface of water would be duly noted. If an animal or plant were encountered, its significance would require interpretation.

To the Babylonian with his world of gods and demons it was particularly important to have means of frustrating the forces of evil. A class of priests known as *ashipu* specialized in counteracting the work of demons. A formula used in one of their spells runs:

> Thou are not to come near to my body,
> Thou art not to go before me,
> Thou art not to follow after me,
> Where I stop thou art not to stop,
> Where I am thou art not to sit,
> My house thou art not to enter,
> My roof thou art not to haunt,
> Thou art not to put thy foot in my foot's imprint,
> Where I go thou art not to go,
> Where I enter thou art not to enter.

The purpose of the *ashipu* was always benevolent. He sought to help the sufferer who was physically ill, and in this sense his work anticipates the physician. All sickness was associated with sin in Babylonian thought, so the *ashipu* sought to discover what sin had been committed by his "patient." A list of possible sins would be read with the thought that one of them might have been committed unconsciously. Only when the proper sin had been identified could the *ashipu* overcome the demon that had controlled the individual.

Sometimes demons were induced to leave their victims on the basis of a promise that the *ashipu* would give. A substitute habitation (such as a pig) was sometimes offered. At other times the demon might be bribed with a list of gifts that would be his as a reward for leaving his victim.

Another technique was to drive the demon from his victim. This might be done by preparing medicines of nauseous and putrid substances which the victim was required to eat. Presumably, if they were vile enough, the demon himself would not wish to remain. Eventually, by the process of trial and error, some substances were employed which had genuine medicinal value. Thus medicine, although mixed with magic, became a genuine science.

Sometimes demons could be fooled. One recognized means of doing this was by placing an animal on top of a sick man. By following a prescribed ritual, the demon might be persuaded to enter the animal instead of the human. One such prescription reads:

> Take a suckling-pig and set it level with the head of the sick man. Take out its heart and put it over the sick man's heart. Sprinkle the sides of the bed with its blood. Dismember the suckling-pig and lay the parts in the sick man's members. Then purify this man with pure water . . . Offer the suckling-pig in his place. Let its flesh be as the flesh of the sick man, his blood as the blood of the sick man.

The *ashipu* priest was clothed in red when performing his functions. Red was deemed particularly potent in warding off evil spirits. He might also be dressed in a fish-like skin to emphasize his relationship to the wise god, Ea. Traditional formulae were uttered verbatim. The priest would call upon the demon by name, demanding that he cease tormenting his victim and depart. Calling upon the good gods to aid the sufferer, the *ashipu* priest would exorcise the demon.

Another specialized function was the chanter who, by his songs, was supposed to "soften the heart of the gods." Prayers were intoned by the chanters, who were accompanied by large drums or lyres. The lyre was usually decorated with a bull's head, and the tone itself was likened to the bellow of a bull. Of the ancient Babylonian chants which we possess, fifty-seven require the accompaniment of a drum, forty require a flute, and forty-seven involve the "lifting of hands" in the attitude of prayer.

The Book of Daniel gives us a Biblical picture of the Babylonian priests and wise men at work. Diviners claimed to have existed as a separate order from remote antiquity, and it was required that they be physically sound. Daniel and his companions are described as "children in whom was no blemish" (Dan. 1:4). The Babylonian texts insist: "the diviner whose father is impure and who himself has any imperfection of limb or countenance, whose eyes are not sound, who has any teeth missing, who has lost a finger, whose countenance has a sickly look or who is pimpled, cannot be the keeper of the decrees of Shamash and Adad."

Those who purpose to be Babylonian diviners were required to take a long course of study before they could serve at the Babylonian court. The Hebrew captives were subjected to a three year training program in "the learning and the tongue of the Chaldeans" (Dan. 1:4-5) after which they were given court appointments. It is evident that Babylonians were receiving the same schooling, for we are told that Daniel and his friends were "ten times better than all the magicians and astrologers" (Dan. 1:20). When the wise men of Babylon were unable to interpret the dream of Nebuchadnezzar we are told that Daniel did so, after which the king placed him "over all the wise men of Babylon" (Dan. 2:48).

The Book of Daniel makes it clear that diviners were expected to be able to interpret anything, and that they formed an important element in the king's court. The godly Daniel, however, humbly trusting his God, showed Nebuchadnezzar that the magic and sorcery of Babylon could not be trusted to meet the basic problems of men or nations.

CHAPTER TWO

I. DESPOT'S DREAM—2:1-16

a. CHALLENGE TO CHALDEANS

TEXT: 2:1-6

1 And in the second year of the reign of Nebuchadnezzar, Nebuchadnezzar dreamed dreams; and his spirit was troubled, and his sleep went from him.

2 Then the king commanded to call the magicians, and the enchanters, and the sorcerers, and the Chaldeans, to tell the king his dreams. So they came in and stood before the king.

3 And the king said unto them, I have dreamed a dream, and my spirit is troubled to know the dream.

4 Then spake the Chaldeans to the king in the Syrian language, O king, live for ever: tell thy servants the dream, and we will show the interpretation.

5 The king answered and said to the Chaldeans, The thing is gone from me: if ye make not known unto me the dream and the interpretation thereof, ye shall be cut in pieces, and your houses shall be made a dunghill.

6 But if ye show the dream and the interpretation thereof, ye shall receive of me gifts and rewards and great honor; therefore show me the dream and the interpretation thereof.

QUERIES

a. Why is Nebuchadnezzar concerned with this particular dream?

b. Why does the text mention the Syrian (Aramaic) language?

c. Why did Nebuchadnezzar forget the dream?

PARAPHRASE

One night in the second year of his reign, Nebuchadnezzar had a very vivid and graphic dream. He was unable to sleep because he was deeply agitated in his mind and

58

soul to know if the dream had some meaning for his life.
So he immediately called in all his magicians, enchanters
and sorcerers and wise men and demanded that they tell
him what his dream had been.   When they had come into
his presence, the king said to them, I have had a terrifying
and mystifying dream and my very soul is in great anxiety
to know what it means.   Then the king's wise men, speaking in the Aramaic language, which was the language of
common discourse then, said to the king, O king, may you
live forever: if you will tell your humble servants the
details of your dream we will begin at once to use all our
knowledge and mystic powers to discern the interpretation
of your dream.   But the king replied, You are supposed to
know every hidden thing: the details of the dream are
thoroughly and indelibly set in my mind and now I am
testing your claims.   If you do not tell me exactly both the
details of the dream itself and the interpretation of the
dream, I will have you literally cut to pieces and dis-
membered and your homes destroyed and publicly disgraced.
But, if you tell me both the dream and its interpretation
I will give you many wonderful gifts and honors.   So, begin!

COMMENT

v. 1 . . . NEBUCHADNEZZAR DREAMED DREAMS; AND HIS
SPIRIT WAS TROUBLED. . . .   According to Babylonian reckoning, the second year of the reign of Nebuchadnezzar would
be the third year of Daniel's training.   First year of reign
for a Babylonian emperor was called The Year of Accession;
his first year of reign would really be his second year; and
his second year of reign would really be his third year on
the throne.   Even at that, this very graphic dream, sent
by God, occurred at a very early period of this heathen
emperor's reign.

Young seems to think the force of the plural should be
translated "Nebuchadnezzar was in a state in which a dream
came to him."   Leupold believes the king dreamed several
dreams, one of which finally roused and disturbed him.
Whatever the case, the significant dream was the one of
the great image.   And it was no ordinary dream, but one
which Jehovah God sent directly to this pagan ruler.   It was

59

such an arresting dream he could not sleep for anxiety of
spirit and soul, deeply troubled as to its meaning. The
dream must have been so vivid as to seem to be actually
happening right then—the king was terrified.

v. 2-3 . . . THE KING . . . COMMANDED . . . THE CHAL-
DEANS, TO TELL HIS DREAMS . . . Four classes of dream
interpreters or wise men are summoned to appear before
the king. Leupold translates "magicians" as *scholars;* "enchanters" as *astrologers.* From other listings of such wise
men in Daniel it does not seem any technical sense is intended here. The fourfold mention here is evidently designed
to include all the classes of wise men and priests of Babylonian religion (see our Special Study on *Babylonian Priesthood* at the end of this chapter). "Chaldeans" constitute
the most important group in the entire assembly. They
seem to be regarded in their day as the very *elite* of Babylonian society, men in whose ranks the emperor himself
appears to have been enrolled. A people by the name of
"Chaldean" lived in southern Babylonia in the days of the
early patriarchs (cf. Gen. 11:28). They were a warlike
group who in the course of time caused the Assyrians much
trouble and finally overcame them in the person of Nabopolassar, Nebuchadnezzar's father. These "Chaldeans" of
Daniel's time were, therefore, probably men of great learning who could trace their ancestry back to families of the
original conquerors of Babylon. They made themselves
masters of that group of wise men who exercised the strongest influence in the political and religious affairs of the state.

The Babylonians, as did other ancients, put much stock
in a philosophy that the movements of the stars and
heavenly bodies determined the events of history and destinies of men on the earth. Astrology, the casting of horoscopes and other predictions based on observations of the
stars was used to determine political, religious and moral
meaning to mystical experiences such as dreams. Nebuchadnezzar undoubtedly had some strange, inexplicable foreboding concerning the dream that kept him awake.

v. 4 . . . TELL THY SERVANTS THE DREAM, AND WE
WILL SHOW THE INTERPRETATION . . . Xenophon relates that
the Babylonians spoke a form of Aramaic and it is not

unlikely that this would be the language of common discourse. The covenant people of the exile returned to their homeland speaking Aramaic which they learned in captivity. Just why the fact is deemed necessary to mention in v. 4 that the Chaldeans spoke to the king in the Syrian (Aramaic) language is unkonwn.

The Chaldeans made the only request they could, being finite creatures with no knowledge of the secrets of men's hearts unless they are told those secrets. There was no possibility of anyone telling the king what he had dreamed unless he tell them the dream or unless God, who knows all the secrets of men's minds, tell it. God did eventually tell it through Daniel. If the king had related the facts of his dream to the Chaldeans, they could have set about at once to compare the details with their astrological charts, cast their horoscopes, made their incantations, submitted the dream to their magic and have come up with an interpretation (which, by the way, would probably have been flattering to the king's ego and favorable to his whims of government and indulgence).

v. 5-6 . . . IF YE MAKE NOT KNOWN . . . THE DREAM AND THE INTERPRETATION . . . YE SHALL BE CUT IN PIECES . . . BUT IF YE SHOW THE DREAM AND THE INTERPRETATION, YE SHALL RECEIVE . . . GIFTS . . . REWARDS . . . GREAT HONOR . . . Why did Nebuchadnezzar insist that the Chaldeans tell him the details of the actual dream as well as the interpretation? It is not because he had forgotten the dream. Our English translation is misleading here. Leupold, Young and many others agree that the proper rendering of the original here should read "the matter has been fully determined by me." The king was sure and certain of the details of the dream itself. Now he was testing his "wise men" to see, in such a significant experience, if they really had access to the deepest and most completely hidden things. It may very well be that Nebuchadnezzar, deep within himself, knew that most of the religion of Babylon was mere superstition and not the truth—he must have been skeptical of a great part of it. There is a record of a king of Yemen, Rabia by name, who saw a vision and was terrified by it. He assembled all the priests and magicians and star-gazers of his kingdom and said to them, "Verily, I have seen a vision and was frightened by it. Tell it to me and its interpretation." They said, "Relate it to us, and we shall inform thee of its interpretation." So he replied, "If I tell you it, I shall have no certainty as to what you tell me of its interpretation. Verily, no one knows the interpretation unless he knows it before I tell him (the dream)." So, Nebuchadnezzar was putting his wise men to the test to determine once and for all if they could divine the secret things of men and nature or not.

The despotic nature of the punishment pronounced should the Chaldeans fail is in character for an Eastern monarch of that day. Assyrians and Persians were especially notorious for the barbarity of their punishments. Even today in Arabia cruel punishments for misdemeanors are meted out even to the severing of members of the body for certain crimes. These Chaldeans faced certain dismemberment since they had no power to tell Nebuchadnezzar his dream. They would be hacked to pieces and their homes razed. And as a final indignity the ruins of their homes would be made public toilets.

It is plain that God is active in this matter to demonstrate to Nebuchadnezzar, to Daniel, to all the heathen who will learn and to all the covenant people who will learn, that there is only One, True God, who knows the secrets of men and Jehovah is His Name; there is only one true prophet of God, Daniel is his name. God sent the dream; now He, through His prophet, will demonstrate that the interpretation His prophet places on the dream is true because His prophet will tell the king what he dreamed.

QUIZ

1. How many years had Nebuchadnezzar actually been on the throne now?
2. Who are the "Chaldeans" and where did they come from?
3. Why did the Chaldeans speak to the king in Syriac (Aramaic)?
4. Why did Nebuchadnezzar insist that they tell him his dream?

5. How was God at work in this event in Nebuchadnezzar's life?

b. DILEMMA OF THE DIVINERS

TEXT: 2:7-11

7 They answered the second time and said, Let the king tell his servants the dream, and we will show the interpretation.

8 The king answered and said, I know of a certainty that ye would gain time, because ye see the thing is gone from me.

9 But if ye make not known unto me the dream, there is but one law for you; for ye have prepared lying and corrupt words to speak before me, till the time be changed: therefore tell me the dream, and I shall know that ye can show me the interpretation thereof.

10 The Chaldeans answered before the king, and said, There is not a man upon the earth that can show the king's matter, forasmuch as no king, lord, or ruler, hath asked such a thing of any magician, or enchanter, or Chaldean.

11 And it is a rare thing that the king requireth, and there is no other than can show it before the king, except the gods, whose dwelling is not with flesh.

QUERIES

a. Why was Nebuchadnezzar suspicious of their "stalling?"

b. Why was the king's demand such a "rare" thing?

c. Which "gods" did the Chaldeans have in mind?

PARAPHRASE

The Chaldeans replied again, If the king please, only tell his humble servants what he dreamed and we will most gladly show him its interpretation. But the king retorted, I can see very plainly that you are only stalling for time, because you are aware that my mind is made up to punish you severely if you do not tell me the dream. And, you are correct, for if you do not tell me what I dreamed there is only one consequence you may expect—the punishment which I have decreed. I know what you are up to—you have agreed with one another to try to deceive me with words hoping that the passing of time will bring a change in my demands. I am wise to your scheme. Tell me the dream—only then will I believe that you can show me the true interpretation. The Chaldeans pleaded with the king, saying, You are asking the impossible—there is not a man on the earth who can tell the king what he has dreamed. No great king, lord or ruler such as yourself has ever asked such an impossible thing of any mortal magician, enchanter or Chaldean such as we. What you have asked is so difficult there is no human being who could ever reveal to the king what he dreamed. Only the gods could do this and they do not dwell on earth with mortals.

COMMENT

v. 7 . . . LET THE KING TELL HIS SERVANTS THE DREAM . . . Notice the subtle flattery here. The Chaldeans berate themselves as "servants." They must find out what the dream was and so they insist—but they insist politely.

v. 8 . . . I KNOW . . . THAT YE WOULD GAIN TIME, BECAUSE . . . THE THING IS GONE FROM ME . . . They are not fooling the king. He knows they are stalling for time and he knows why—they are aware of his resolute determination that they shall either tell him what he dreamed or they shall be punished severely. It is the immutability of the king's decree that is meant by the phrase "because ye see the thing is gone from me."

v. 9 . . . YE HAVE PREPARED LYING AND CORRUPT WORDS TO SPEAK BEFORE ME, TILL THE TIME BE CHANGED . . . Nebuchadnezzar seems to be fully cognizant of their scheme to hide their insufficiency. He senses that there is some kind of collaboration between them to speak words of deception and legerdemain until, they hoped, circumstances would change; perhaps the king's ugly mood will change with time

64

if they can only stall the matter by talk. But the king sees through their scheme. If they do not with haste make known to the king what he dreamed as well as the interpretation, he has determined their fate by royal decree and that decree cannot be changed.

v. 10-11 . . . THERE IS NOT A MAN UPON THE EARTH THAT CAN SHOW THE KING'S MATTER . . . EXCEPT THE GODS, WHOSE DWELLING IS NOT WITH FLESH . . . These Chaldeans face a terrifying dilemma. On the one hand there is a desperate attempt not to say anything that might further irritate or offend the despot; on the other hand they must convey to the king the idea that his demand is unreasonable and impossible. Their first statement is a frank admission of their impotency in the matter demanded. Then they hastily add another subtle innuendo of flattery, "No great king or ruler has ever asked such an impossible thing from such lowly magicians and enchanters as we." They are trying to convey to the king that the gods have not given these priests of the national religion the power to reveal the dream—they have power only to interpret the dream. Their statement is that only the gods could produce what the king has demanded and the gods do not dwell among men. There seems to be in their consciousness an admission of higher, superhuman beings, but their concepts are so saturated with ignorance and moral depravity they are thoroughly polytheistic. The enchanters specify that the gods do not dwell with men in order to specify that they have no way of being instructed with the superior knowledge of the gods.

QUIZ

1. How do the Chaldeans use flattery to try to learn the king's dream?
2. What does the king accuse them of attempting to do?
3. What advantage did the Chaldeans think time would bring them?
4. How did the Chaldeans frankly declare their inability to tell his dream?

c. SAVED BY THE SUBJUGATED

TEXT: 2:12-16

12 For this cause the king was angry and very furious, and commanded to destroy all the wise men of Babylon.

13 So the decree went forth, and the wise men were to be slain; and they sought Daniel and his companions to be slain.

14 Then Daniel returned answer with counsel and prudence to Arioch the captain of the king's guard, who was gone forth to slay the wise men of Babylon;

15 he answered and said to Arioch the king's captain, Wherefore is the decree so urgent from the king? Then Arioch made the thing known to Daniel.

16 And Daniel went in, and desired of the king that he would appoint him a time, and he would show the king the interpretation.

QUERIES

a. Why destroy all the wise men of Babylon?
b. Why did Daniel think he could do what the others could not?

PARAPHRASE

The admitted inability of the Chaldean wise-men to be able to tell Nebuchadnezar his secret dream and its interpretation made the king's anger grow exceeding furious. He commanded that all the wise-men of the city of Babylon should be executed. The decree of the arrest and execution of all the wise-men was made official and as it was being carried out they eventually came to arrest Daniel and his three Hebrew companions. When Arioch, the captain of the king's guard, came to arrest Daniel, Daniel reasoned with him with great discretion and prudence. Among other things, Daniel asked Arioch why the decision of the king was so severe. Arioch answered Daniel and told him all about the wise-men's failure and the king's decree. It was then that Daniel, observing all the proper protocol, gained audience with the king and asked for a personal appointment affirm-

66

ing that he would be able to show both the dream and the
interpretation.

COMMENT

v. 12-13 . . . THE KING WAS ANGRY AND VERY FURIOUS
. . . The verb used here indicates a growing mounting anger
until it reaches the point of violence. He commanded that
all the wise-men of Babylon be put to death. The king is
enraged at these who have gained fame and fortune and
power by claiming to know the deepest secrets of man and
the gods—and they cannot even tell him what he has
dreamed.

After the king issued his personal command it would
have to be transmitted in formal publication throughout the
capitol city. His guards would have to go in search of many
of the wise-men not present at the royal court that particular day. It would be some time before the actual execution could take place. Finally, the captain of the king's
guard, Arioch, came to take Daniel and his three Hebrew
companions into custody.

v. 14-16 THEN DANIEL RETURNED ANSWER WITH COUN-
SEL AND PRUDENCE . . . The first thing to realize about this
account is that it is very abbreviated—we do not have a
record of all that Daniel must have said to Arioch. As
Leupold says, "The very audacity of Daniel's plan" must
have impressed Arioch. Besides, the king would still be
perplexed as to the interpretation of his dream and knowing
of the exceptional wisdom and capabilities of Daniel (Arioch
had undoubtedly heard of Daniel's fame also), it would be
very prudent for Daniel to talk with Arioch and persuade
him that he could interpret the king's dream. Daniel was
acting on the basis of his faith in God and without doubt
on the basis of a revelation from God that he should do so.

Daniel speaks to Arioch as if they were already well
acquainted—perhaps even good friends—when he asks, "Why
is the decree of the king so severe?" Arioch feels impelled
to answer Daniel's question and probably relates the entire
incident to him.

Leupold points out that when Daniel "went in, and
desired of the king . . ." we must presume that Daniel went

through the proper channels and observed the correct proto-col in approaching the king. We know from the book of Esther that unless one were bidden properly to approach an Eastern potentate to do so presumptuously meant certain death. All that Daniel asks is "time." This will postpone the execution until he could commune with his God, and give the desired interpretation to the king.

It is most interesting to note that Daniel was sure he could give the king the interpretation of the dream before he had even received the knowledge of what the dream was from God (cf. 2:19). Daniel had such faith in God that he believed the will of God would be done before it was actually done! This same "great" faith the Lord expects of all His children. Only the "interpretation" is mentioned and not the dream itself. However the conciseness of the narrative explains this omission. If Daniel knows the in-terpretation, he most certainly must first know the dream and he is not asking the king what the dream was, as did the Chaldeans.

QUIZ

1. Why seek out Daniel to be slain?
2. How did Daniel answer with "counsel and prudence?"
3. Why did Daniel ask for an appointment to the presence of the king?
4. How would one have made such an appointment in those days?

II. DANIEL'S DECLARATION—2:17-35

a. PRAYER

TEXT: 2:17-24

17 Then Daniel went to his house, and made the thing known to Hananiah, Mishael, and Azariah, his com-panions:

18 that they would desire mercies of the God of heaven concerning this secret; that Daniel and his companions

should not perish with the rest of the wise men of Babylon.

19 Then was the secret revealed unto Daniel in a vision of the night. Then Daniel blessed the God of heaven.

20 Daniel answered and said, Blessed be the name of God for ever and ever; for wisdom and might are his.

21 And he changeth the times and the seasons; he removeth kings, and setteth up kings; he giveth wisdom unto the wise, and knowledge to them that have understanding;

22 he revealeth the deep and secret things; he knoweth what is in the darkness, and the light dwelleth with him.

23 I thank thee, and praise thee, O thou God of my fathers, who hast given me wisdom and might, and hast now made known unto me what we desire of thee; for thou hast made known unto us the king's matter.

24 Therefore Daniel went in unto Arioch, whom the king had appointed to destroy the wise men of Babylon; he went and said thus unto him: Destroy not the wise men of Babylon; bring me in before the king, and I will show unto the king the interpretation.

QUERIES

a. Was Daniel selfish in praying for his own safety?
b. Does God really have a hand in putting rulers in rule?
c. Why does Daniel pray for the safety of the Chaldean wise men?

PARAPHRASE

Then Daniel went home and told the whole matter to Hananiah, Mishael, and Azariah, his companions, and having confided in them he asked them to pray to the God of the heavens to grant them His mercy and reveal to them this secret mystery in order that Daniel and his companions would not be executed together with the rest of the wise men of Babylon. And that very night the secret of the king's dream was revealed unto Daniel in a vision. Then, in prayer, Daniel praised the God of heaven, saying, Blessed be the name of God forever and ever, for He alone has all wisdom and all power. World events are under His control and are used for His purpose. He removes kings and rulers and sets others on their thrones according to His sovereign purpose. All true wisdom, knowledge and understanding comes from Him. All His plans that are not yet known to man He reveals in His own good time and His own way because He knows all things that are hidden. He is all-wise and there is no ignorance in Him at all. I think and praise You, oh God of my fathers, for You have given me wisdom and ability to solve the problem at hand. You have revealed to me all that we desired concerning the king's perplexity. Then Daniel went in to see Arioch, who had been ordered to execute the wise men of Babylon, and said, Do not slay the wise men of Babylon. Take me in to the king and I will reveal to him the interpretation of his puzzling dream.

COMMENT

v. 17-18   THEN DANIEL WENT TO HIS HOUSE, AND MADE THE THING KNOWN . . . Daniel's associates are so thoroughly one with him in faith in God and in purpose to glorify God that he can immediately confide in them and seek their assistance. Daniel asks their counsel and consent, and believes that their fellowship in intercessory prayer will please the Lord and accomplish His will for their lives in this particular circumstance. The chief object of the intercession is not selfish. This is evident when in verse 24 Daniel interceeds on behalf of the pagan wise men of Babylon that they might not be slain. Daniel's purpose in praying for salvation from the executioner's sword was because he was fully persuaded God had put him in Babylon "for just such a time as this." Daniel simply wanted to be allowed to be God's "living sacrifice" to bring the revelation of God to this pagan emperor and to God's own covenant people who so desperately needed strengthening now. He was praying for a higher purpose than mere physical existence, but physical existence was a necessity that the higher purpose be served.

v. 19-22 . . . THE SECRET REVEALED UNTO DANIEL . . . THEN DANIEL BLESSED . . . GOD . . . WISDOM AND MIGHT ARE HIS . . . AND HE CHANGETH THE TIMES AND THE SEASONS . . .

HE REMOVETH KINGS, AND SETTETH UP KINGS . . . This is
one of those most arresting passages of O.T. scripture speaking of the divine sovereignty and immutability of the purposes of God in the events of earth's history. It does not
teach "predestination" or "irresistible grace" in the strict
Calvinistic sense. However, it is a fact of scripture, too
often ignored by Restoration preachers and writers, that the
prophets and apostles speak of God as doing things which He
permits, without distinguishing verbally between His direct
action and His permissive action. If we are going to speak
where the Bible speaks we must insist upon preaching the
Living God of intimate, actual relationships in every-day
history. Our God is God of the "now." In II Sam. 24:1
and I Chron. 21:1ff we read, respectively, that David was
moved by the Lord to number Israel and Judah, and that
Satan provoked David to number Israel. Taking these two
passages of Scripture together, there is no contradiction but
simply a lesson that God acts in what He permits. God
permitted Satan to provoke David to number Israel. Whatever God permits, He permits for His own good purpose.
Just as in the case of Joseph and his brethren, Joseph was
able to say, "you intended it for evil but God intended it
for good . . ." (Gen. 50:20). So we are to understand that
whatever evil God may permit in allowing despotic rulers
to reign He permits as a part of His disciplinary or sanctifying providence.

We quote here from Charles Hodge: "The decrees of God
are free in the sense of being absolute or sovereign. The
meaning of this proposition is expressed negatively by saying
that the decrees of God are in no case conditional. The
event decreed is suspended on a condition, but the purpose
of God is not. It is inconsistent with the nature of God to
assume suspense or indecision on his part . . . whatever
God foreordains must certainly come to pass. The distinction between the efficient (efficacious) and the permissive
decree of God, although important, has no relation to the
certainty of the event. All events embraced in the purpose
of God are equally certain, whether he has determined to
bring them to pass by his own power, or simply to permit
their occurrence through the agency of (the free will of)
his own creatures . . . some things he purposes to do, others

71

he decrees to permit to be done. He effects good, he permits evil. He is the author of the one, but not of the other.

"The universality of the decrees follows from the universal dominion of God. Whatever he does, he certainly purposes to do. Whatever he permits to occur, he certainly purposes to permit. Nothing can occur that was not forseen, and if foreseen, it must have been intended. As the Scriptures teach that the providential control of God extends to all events, even the most minute, they do thereby teach that his decrees are equally comprehensive." (cf. all of the following scriptures: Heb. 1:3; Col. 1:17; Neh. 9:6-7; Job 9:12; 12:7-10; Psa. 104:27-32; 135:6; I Chron. 29:12; Dan. 4:35; Jer. 27:5-7; Isa. 10:5ff; 45:5-7; and cf. also our commentary *Minor Prophets*, pages 93-111, "Theo-ramic Philosophy of History.")

Leupold notices how fluent Daniel was in Scripture in his prayer according to the quotations (on v. 20a see Psa. 103:1-2; Psa. 113:1-2 on v. 20b see I Chron. 29:11-12; Job 12:13; 16-22. on v. 21a see Psa. 31:15; on v. 21b see Job 12:18; Psa. 75:6-7 on v. 21c see I Ki. 3:9-10; 4:29; on v. 22r see Job 12:22; on v. 22b see Job 26:6; Psa. 139:12; Isa. 45:7; on v. 22c see Psa. 36:9 on v. 23a see Gen. 31:42; Ex. 3:15).

The phrase "changeth the times and the seasons" reminds us that God determines how long one culture or influence shall prevail and when another shall become operative. One dynasty influences world culture and wanes and disappears at the directing influence of God's immutable moral laws governing the universe, and another comes to the fore (cf. Jer. 27:5ff). God creates both "weal and woe" (cf. Isa. 45:5-7). God is able and does this because He has all wisdom and understanding and knowledge. He is able to reveal the future—the deep and secret things—because all time and space and mass are within His knowledge and control at all times—all at once. Nothing can be hidden from Him and if He hides anything man can know it only if He reveals it to man. "God is light and in him is no darkness at all . . ." (I Jn. 1:5). This entire passage (v. 20-22) has to do with God's special revelations to prophets (and later to apostles) concerning His scheme of redemption.

v. 23-24 I THANK THEE . . . THOU HAST MADE KNOWN
. . . THE KING'S MATTER . . . DANIEL WENT . . . UNTO ARIOCH
. . . DESTROY NOT THE WISE MEN OF BABYLON . . . I WILL
SHOW . . . THE KING THE INTERPRETATION. The original language here is emphatic . . . "THEE, praising am I." God is
placed first. It is interesting to note that Daniel, in his
prayer of praise, includes his companions as equally important in this matter. He does not forget them, thinking
that God is interested only in him. Having glorified the
name of God and being satisfied that he is carrying out the
will of God in this matter, Daniel seeks the emperor's
presence through Arioch, one of the chief guards of the
palace. He persuades Arioch not to destroy the wise men of
Babylon because he will be able to make known to Nebuchadnezzar both the dream and its interpretation. So
Daniel the captive, the foreigner, intercedes on behalf of
the Babylonian wise men and saves their lives through the
revelation God graciously provided. It is difficult for us,
inasmuch as we are so familiar with this account and removed from it some 2600 years, to realize that it was an
actual, historical event—it really happened. When we do
realize its actuality, we stand amazed at the working of God
in carrying out His purposes!

QUIZ

1. Why did Daniel immediately make known to his companions the matter?
2. Why did Daniel pray for salvation from the executioner's
   sword?
3. What does the phrase "he changeth the times and . . .
   seasons" mean?
4. How does God remove kings and set up kings?
5. What does the fact that this was an actual event mean
   to you?

b. PROFESSION

TEXT: 2:25-30

25 Then Arioch brought in Daniel before the king in haste,
    and said thus unto him, I have found a man of the

children of the captivity of Judah, that will make
known unto the king the interpretation.

26 The king answered and said to Daniel, whose name was
Belteshazzar, Art thou able to make known unto me
the dream which I have seen, and the interpretation
thereof?

27 Daniel answered before the king, and said, The secret
which the king hath demanded can neither wise men,
enchanters, magicians, nor soothsayers, show unto the
king;

28 but there is a God in heaven that revealeth secrets, and
he hath made known to the king Nebuchadnezzar what
shall be in the latter days. Thy dream, and the visions
of thy head upon thy bed, are these:

29 as for thee, O king, thy thoughts came into thy mind
upon thy bed, what should come to pass hereafter; and
he that revealeth secrets hath made known to thee
what shall come to pass.

30 But as for me, this secret is not revealed to me for any
wisdom that I have more than any living, but to the
intent that the interpretation may be made known to
the king, and that thou mayest know the thoughts of
thy heart.

QUERIES

a. Had Arioch "found" Daniel or had Daniel sought Arioch?
b. How did Daniel have the courage to talk about his God
   to king Nebuchadnezzar?
c. Does Daniel mean in v. 30 that God's immediate purpose
   was to reveal something to a pagan king?

PARAPHRASE

Then Arioch, in great excitement, brought Daniel into
the presence of the king, and said to him, O King, Behold,
I have found one of the captives from Judea who claims he
is able to tell you your dream and its interpretation. The
king said, Belteshazzar, is this true? Are you able to make
known to me both what I dreamed and its interpretation?
Daniel replied, As far as my revealing to you myself what
your dream was—I could not do it any more than your own

wise men. No mortal could do such a thing! But there is a God of heaven who reveals secrets. And He has seen fit in His own purpose to reveal to you, king Nebuchadnezzar, in your dream, what is going to happen in the future. Yes, your dream was this: You dreamed of coming events. He who reveals secrets was speaking to you. But, it is as I said before, it is not because I am wiser than any other living person that I know this secret of your dream, but because God has chosen me to be His instrument to make known to you what your secret thoughts mean.

COMMENT

v. 25-26 . . . ARIOCH BROUGHT IN DANIEL . . . I HAVE FOUND A MAN . . . ART THOU ABLE? Notice the precociousness of Arioch! He seizes the opportunity to feather his cap by claiming to "have found" an answer to the most perplexing problem Nebuchadnezar has ever had in all his life. In fact, Daniel had found Arioch! How could Arioch make such an incongruous statement seeing that he had just a few hours before this gained an audience before the king for this same Hebrew lad? Arioch is doing what is incongruous but normal for practically all underlings of some great monarch—making the most of any occasion to put himself in favorable estimation by his superior.

The king, greatly vexed of soul, and constantly plagued by such machinations of his underlings, probably did not give Arioch's attempt at politicking a second thought. He was intent upon finding someone who could set his mind at rest concerning this troubling dream. The king, skeptical that anyone could do what he asked, makes a special point of asking Daniel if he is able to tell both the dream and its interpretation. The king calls Daniel by his Babylonian name, Belteshazzar.

v. 27 . . . THE SECRET . . . THE KING . . . DEMANDED CAN NEITHER WISE MEN . . . ETC. . . . Daniel quickly disavows any human ability to tell secrets. He wants the king to be prepared for his next statement which will be a testimony to the One True God. Daniel's words are also a mild rebuke to the king for expecting so much from any human "wise man."

v. 28 . . . BUT THERE IS A GOD IN HEAVEN THAT RE-
VEALETH SECRETS . . . What a wonderful opportunity for
Daniel to plant the seed of Truth in the mind of a pagan
monarch. What courage it took to stand in the presence of
such an absolute despot who considered himself a god and
speak of The Living God. Daniel's courage was born of his
faith in God and his knowledge of the situation—the ex-
tremity of Nebuchadnezzar's anxiety.

The phrase "latter days" can mean only one thing in
its context! It refers to the days which follow from that
present time unto the coming of the Messianic kingdom
which occurred, of course, when the church was established
on Pentecost, Acts 2. We shall treat this subject thoroughly
in the remainder of the chapter.

v. 29 . . . THY THOUGHTS CAME . . . WHAT SHOULD
COME TO PASS HEREAFTER . . . Evidently the king had gone
to bed thinking about the future—what is going to happen
in my future. Nebuchadnezzar was somewhat of an "Alexander the Great." He had conquered the civilized world of
his day; he had done just about everything a monarch of
that day could do in conquests, building, etc. With such
personal glory already his he might well wonder what the
future had in store. He was at the top of the ladder already!
He lay down to dream because there were no more worlds
to conquer! And what a dream!

Daniel describes his God as The Revealer of secrets and
distinctly states that Jehovah has sent this dream to Nebuchadnezzar in order to tell him what shall happen in the
future.

v. 30 . . . AS FOR ME . . . NOT REVEALED . . . FOR ANY
WISDOM THAT I HAVE . . . Again Daniel disavows any personal, meritorious claim upon the gift of God to interpret
dreams. He makes it plain that he is being used only as
an instrument through which God is making known to the
king what all these secret thoughts and dreams mean.

We admire Daniel's courage before a great monarch
such as this. We would also do well to reflect on the trust
in God necessary for Daniel not to presumptuously claim for
himself these powers to reveal secrets! What a temptation

it would be for most of us to take to ourselves this glory rather than give it to God. Looked at from an immediate and physical or selfish perspective it could have been exceedingly profitable for Daniel to have claimed these powers all on his own. But, like Joseph, he said, "It is not in me; God will give Pharaoh an answer . . ." (Gen. 41:16).

QUIZ

1. Why did Arioch claim to have found Daniel when in the king's presence?
2. Why did the king ask Daniel if he were able to tell the dream?
3. How did Daniel rebuke the king's decree to kill all the wise-men?
4. What had the king probably gone to bed thinking about before his dream?
5. What does "the latter days" refer to?
6. What is especially significant of Daniel's disavowal to any personal merit?

c. PUBLICATION

TEXT: 2:31-35

31 Thou, O king, sawest, and, behold, a great image. This image, which was mighty, and whose brightness was excellent, stood before thee; and the aspect thereof was terrible.

32 As for this image, its head was of fine gold, its breast and its arms of silver, its belly and its thighs of brass,

33 its legs of iron, its feet part of iron, and part of clay.

34 Thou sawest till that a stone was cut out without hands, which smote the image upon its feet that were of iron and clay, and brake them in pieces.

35 Then was the iron, the clay, the brass, the silver, and the gold, broken in pieces together, and became like the chaff of the summer threshing-floors; and the wind carried them away, so that no place was found for them: and the stone that smote the image became a great mountain, and filled the whole earth.

QUERIES

a. Exactly what does the word "image" mean?
b. Why all the different metals in one image?
c. What is the significance of the grinding to dust of the image?

PARAPHRASE

Oh king, you saw in your dream a huge and powerful statue of a man shining brilliantly, frightening and terrible, so fascinating you were unable to take your eyes off what you saw. The head of this statue was made of purest gold, its chest and arms were of silver, its belly and thighs were of bronze, and it had legs of iron with feet part iron and part clay. Then as you watched, a stone was cut out by supernatural means. It came hurtling towards the statue and crushed the feet of iron and clay, grinding them into dust. Then the whole statue collapsed into a heap and the iron, clay, bronze, silver and gold were all ground into dust by the stone and the dust was blown away forever. The stone that struck down the great statue became a great mountain that covered the whole earth.

COMMENT

v. 31 . . . A GREAT IMAGE . . . THE ASPECT THEREOF WAS TERRIBLE . . . The image was a huge statue bearing the resemblance of a man. This dream-statue would undoubtedly appear to Nebuchadnezzar exactly like the statues of Assyrian-Babylonian men discovered by archaeologists. The original language indicates that Nebuchadnezzar was "continually staring" at this statue, as if transfixed by it. It was brilliant and terrifying.

v. 32-33 . . . HEAD OF GOLD . . . BREAST OF SILVER . . . BELLY . . . OF BRASS . . . LEGS OF IRON . . . FEET . . . OF IRON AND CLAY . . . Why all the different meals in one image? We suppose the scarcity of the metals would tend to give the image greater significance. We note the steady descending scale in preciousness of the metals from the head of the image down to its feet. The word translated brass means bronze or copper. One of the things which transfixed the king was the size of this statue. Another fascinating thing about it was its extraordinary splendor. It must have been an imposing sight indeed. As far as can be determined there is no precedent concerning such symbolism—therefore God has given a unique vision to the king—its origin is in divine revelation. We must look for a revealed interpretation, guided by common sense and hermeneutical principals that are in accord with other accepted interpretative principles.

v. 34-35 . . . A STONE . . . CUT OUT WITHOUT HANDS . . . SMOTE THE IMAGE . . . The dream now becomes a "moving picture." Action takes place. A stone (we would suppose a large stone) is "detached" or cut loose from, we assume, a mountain, and it is cut loose without natural or human aid—it must therefore have been cut loose by supernatural aid. We note that "stone" is an appropriate symbol here for the kingdom of God in both Old and New Testaments. In the Old Testament God refers to Himself as the Rock (cf. Deut. 32:15; Psa. 18:2; 31:2; 62:2; Isa. 44:8; 51:1) and Christ's diety is referred to as the "rock" upon which the church is built (Mt. 16:18; cf. also I Cor. 10:4).

The great statue lay directly in the path of the moving stone. The stone struck the statue specifically at the feet which was the most vulnerable part of the whole because they were part iron and part clay. The remainder of the statue was demolished so that the whole thing was utterly destroyed, ground to dust, and blown away with the wind. One might expect the statue to be broken into large portions with such a blow from a large stone, but a very unexpected thing happens—it is ground to dust in its entirely and the original language indicates the blowing away was so complete that the dust found no visible resting place. It is important to remember, when we come to the interpretation of the dream, that the *entire* statue was obliterated when the stone struck it.

The climax is the unusual, supernatural growth of the stone which had struck the image. It grew to such gigantic proportions that it became a huge mountain and filled the whole earth.

Leupold observes: "So the vision begins with a huge statue; it ends with the largest possible mountain. There is not a superfluous word in Daniel's entire description and account. It is a masterpiece of pithy word painting." This is indeed one of the finest examples of symbolism in Old Testament literature. It is a great aid in understanding the symbolism in other places in the scriptures (Ezekiel, Zechariah, Revelation).

QUIZ

1. What resemblance would this "great image" probably bear?
2. Why an image of different kinds of metals?
3. What caused the king to be so transfixed by this image?
4. Why is "stone" so appropriate here?
5. What is important about the stone striking the image in its interpretation?
6. How significant is the symbolism of this dream?

III.   DICTATORSHIP'S DESTINY—2:36-49

a.   FIRST THREE KINGDOMS

TEXT: 2:36-39

36 This is the dream; and we will tell the interpretation thereof before the king.

37 Thou, O king, art king of kings, unto whom the God of heaven hath given the kingdom, the power, and the strength, and the glory;

38 and wheresoever the children of men dwell, the beasts of the field and the birds of the heavens hath he given into thy hand, and hath made thee to rule over them all: thou art the head of gold.

39 And after thee shall arise another kingdom inferior to thee; and another third kingdom of brass, which shall bear rule over all the earth.

QUERIES

a. How could God give "the kingdom" to Nebuchadnezzar?
b. Who are the other two kingdoms?
c. Did they rule the entire earth?

PARAPHRASE

That was the dream you dreamed; now we shall tell you exactly what it means. You, O king Nebuchadnezzar, are a king over many lesser kings, for the God of heaven has given you rule over all the known civilized world and all the power, strength and glory you enjoy has been given you by Him. You are absolute monarch over all the inhabitants of the earth because God has given them into your hand. You and your glorious kingdom are represented on this great image you dreamed about by the head of gold. And after your kingdom has come to an end, another world ruler (Medo-Persian) will arise to take your place. This empire will be inferior in many ways to your empire. And after that kingdom has fallen, yet a third great empire (Greek) represented by the bronze belly of the statue, will rise to rule the world.

COMMENT

v. 36-38 . . . THOU, O KING, . . . ART THE HEAD OF GOLD . . . Having told Nebuchadnezzar exactly all the details of what he had dreamed, Daniel now prepares to give the king the divine interpretation of the dream. As may be seen from the succeeding verses, the main thrust of the whole dream is to predict the eventual, historical victory of God over "principalities and powers" and the establishment of God's kingdom here on earth, at a particular time in the history of the earth. Daniel was to tell the king that someday pagan domination of the civilized world would be overcome by a supernatural kingdom.

Daniel designates Nebuchadnezzar as the first representative of absolute world domination. Other prophets speak of the king of Babylon in the same manner (cf. Jer. 27:5-7; Ezek. 26:7). The king of Assyria, Sennacherib, made claim to universal domination, but Assyria was never the absolute ruler of the world in the same sense that Babylon and her successors were.

There can be no argument whatsoever with the designation of the first kingdom! Daniel explicitly states the head of gold represents Nebuchadnezzar's Babylon. Gold was a fitting symbol for it too! Herodotus, who was at Babylon

81

some ninety years after the era of Nebuchadnezzar, was amazed at the amount of gold which he found within the precincts of the sanctuary of Bel. In the smallest temple, which stood on the top of the tower of Babylon, was a table of gold. In the second temple below was an image of the god "all of gold," seated on a golden throne with a golden base and in front of "a large golden table." Outside the temple there was also an altar of "solid gold." All the gold used to form these sacred objects amounted—it is estimated —to eight hundred talents (a talent of gold would be worth approximately $100,000 in our inflationary society). From archaeological inscriptions left by Nebuchadnezzar we get the impression that his consuming interest was to build, beautify and glorify his beloved city Babylon. Nothing was too precious to be bestowed on his city. Herodotus records these instructions from Nebuchadnezzar's inscriptions: ". . . the walls of the cell of Merodach must be made to glisten like suns, the hall of his temple must be overlaid with shining gold, . . . and alabaster; and the chapel of his lord-ship which a former king had fabricated in silver, Nebu-chadnezzar declares that he overlaid with bright gold" (Herod. iii:1-7). The roofing of E-kua, the cell of Mero-dach, is also overlaid with bright gold; and the cell of Nebo at Borsippa is treated in the same manner.

The reference, while made to the Babylonian kingdom, is made in personal form for it is in the person of the emperor himself that the empire is embodied. It is perfectly true that Nebuchadnezzar's kingdom did not hold sway over the entire earth, but in the sense that it did hold dominion over the known, influential and powerful-enough-to-be-reckoned-with portions of the world it could be properly designated in the hyperbolical way Daniel did.

v. 39 . . . AFTER . . . ANOTHER KINGDOM INFERIOR TO THEE . . . AND ANOTHER THIRD KINGDOM . . . WHICH SHALL BEAR RULE OVER ALL THE EARTH . . . Now Daniel does not specify the second great world empire by name but there is enough symbolism and other details mentioned in Daniel chapter 7 and in history subsequent to these predictions of Daniel to make the task of discovering it rather simple.

With the coming of the Medo-Persian empire (the only true universal empire to follow the Babylonian) all the concentration of building simply for magnificence sake changed. The Semitic *keseph, kaspu* (silver) also means "money" since silver was the criterion of value and the medium of exchange then. When Daniel speaks of the *gold* giving place to the *silver*, he must mean that with the coming of the second kingdom, magnificence and outward show were exchanged for treasure, diligently collected by taxation and carefully hoarded up to form the muscles of war when needed. In Daniel, chapter 6, we read that an attempt was made by Darius, in the first year of the downfall of Babylon, to organize the finances of the empire. Herodotus shows that under Cambyses there was a system of taxation throughout the empire. However, it was under the second Darius, (Darius Hystaspes) that this system was brought to perfection. Herodotus furnishes us with a long and exact account of the 20 satrapies established by Darius and the yearly amount at which each was assessed. The tribute was paid in silver talents, except that of the Indians. The Indian satrapy was the richest of all, and yielded 360 talents of gold-dust, which the historian reckons as equivalent to 4,680 talents of silver, thus showing that silver was the standard of value. The Medo-Persian empire kept its eye steadily fixed on this main object and this is substantiated by the Old Testament (cf. Ezra. 4:13; Neh. 9:37). In consequence of this policy of the silver kingdom these kings became rich, and it is foretold in Daniel 11:2 that the fourth king, Xerxes, "Shall be far richer than they all; and that when he is waxed strong through his riches he shall stir up all against the realm of Greece." The vast army which Xerxes collected for the invasion of Greece, and with which he crossed over into Europe, would have been an impossibility but for the system of finance perfected by his father Darius. So keen was Darius in amassing wealth that, according to Herodotus, he appeared to his subjects as a huckster, "one who looked to making a gain in everything." The silver kingdom was stronger than the golden kingdom, and consequently it lasted very much longer. Babylon was master of the ancient world for only 70 years; Medo-Persia for over 200 years.

Silver was stronger than gold; but, as the Persian kings were soon to learn, brass was stronger than silver. The third kingdom of brass was that of the Greek empire which ruled over the world to a greater extent than either of the previous two. This was the empire built and ruled over such a short time by Alexander the Great. The power of the Medo-Persian empire built upon wealth was overcome by the force of arms wielded by a brave, idealistic and free people—the Greeks. Josephus saw in the mention of a brazen kingdom an unmistakeable prediction of the victorious arms of Alexander and his brazen-clad Greeks. Herodotus describes the striking difference between the brazen-clad Greek warriors and the Persians clad in soft hats, tunics with sleeves, and trousers. The fame of Greek battle armor was making itself known earlier than Nebuchadnezzar's time! Ezekiel speaks of the wares brought to the famous port of Tyre as including vessels of brass from Javan, Tubal and Heshech (Javan is simply another form of Ionian). The assumption that Alexander the Great's empire is the third is confirmed by the symbolism of Daniel chapter 7—we shall deal with this symbolism in our comments there.

In one sense there is progressive inferiority in the symbolism from one world power to the next. But in another sense there is progressive symbolism of superiority. The former is progression downward in outward magnificence while the latter is progression upward in power and extension. Keil thinks the progression toward inferiority is symbolic of the downward trend of inner unity and cohesion of the successive empires. Calvin thought the devolution was in the moral sphere. The bronze part of the great statue was that of the abdomen and the thighs which symbolically may point to that which began as a unit (the Greek empire) and divided itself into two separate parts (Syria and Egypt) which were not reunited when the last empire (Rome) appeared on the scene.

QUIZ

1. What is the main thrust of the whole dream of Nebuchadnezzar?

2. Where are we to begin in designating which part of the great statue symbolizes which world empire?
3. Why does the Babylonian empire so fittingly lend itself to being symbolized by gold?
4. Why the Medo-Persian empire symbolized by silver?
5. Why the Greek by bronze?
6. Is there any significance to the progression of inferior metals?

b. FOURTH KINGDOM

TEXT: 2:40-43

40 And the fourth kingdom shall be strong as iron, forasmuch as iron breaketh in pieces and subdueth all things; and as iron that crusheth all these, shall it break in pieces and crush.
41 And whereas thou sawest the feet and toes, part of potters' clay, and part of iron, it shall be a divided kingdom; but there shall be in it of the strength of the iron, forasmuch as thou sawest the iron mixed with miry clay.
42 And as the toes of the feet were part of iron, and part of clay, so the kingdom shall be partly strong, and partly broken.
43 And whereas thou sawest the iron mixed with miry clay, they shall mingle themselves with the seed of men; but they shall not cleave one to another, even as iron doth not mingle with clay.

QUERIES

a. What is the significance of the fourth kingdom subduing all?
b. Why is the emphasis so pointed on its weakness?
c. How will they "mingle themselves with the seed of men?"

PARAPHRASE

And the fourth kingdom shall have destructive power as strong as iron. Just like iron crushes and smashes all things, so shall this fourth kingdom crush and demolish all other kingdoms. The feet and toes you saw composed of two diverse elements symbolizes the fact that this kingdom shall be a divided kingdom. It will have in it the element of strength as is represented by the iron and it will have in it the element of weakness represented by the clay. This mixture of iron with clay also shows that these kingdoms will try to strengthen themselves by forming alliances with each other through intermarriage of their rulers; but this will not succeed any more than mixing iron with clay will not succeed.

COMMENT

v. 40 . . . THE FOURTH . . . STRONG AS IRON . . . BREAK IN PIECES AND CRUSH . . . Iron is a very appropriate symbol to describe the Roman empire. And, as a matter of fact, we are passing, generally speaking, from the bronze age to the iron age when we pass from the third kingdom (Greece) to the fourth kingdom (Rome). To the Roman poets, Virgil and Lucretius, bronze weapons spoke of olden time. Actually, iron was used long before the coming of the Roman empire, but it was not in wide-spread use before Rome. Iron swords and armor took the place of bronze weapons. The Roman infantry soldier of that era carried with him that distinctively Roman weapon the *pilum*, a sort of spear or javelin with a long iron neck fitted to a wooden shaft, the metal extending for about a third of its entire length. The feature Daniel emphasizes in his interpretation of this fourth empire is the strength of the iron kingdom. The Roman war machine was many times more destructive than any of its predecessors. The special feature of Alexander's career was its amazing swiftness (pictured by the four-winged leopard in Daniel chapter 7). But the special feature of Rome's empire was its total destructive power (depicted by the intensely ferocious beast in Dan. 7). Rome's ruthless severity is exemplified by her destruction of Carthage, the War against the slaves (Spartacus) when the Appian Way was lined with six thousand crosses bearing aloft as many bodies, and the siege and destruction of Jerusalem and the extinction of the Jewish nation.

One characteristic of the fourth kingdom (in Daniel 7, at least) was its diversity from all the kingdoms (beasts) before it. Boutflower illustrates this with a passage from I Maccabees 8:13-14 which relates the impression the Roman system of government made on the Jews. The whole passage emphasizes how very much the Oriental mind was impressed by this strange and novel form of government which was not inclined to dress and act with all the pomposity and subtleties of Eastern potentates. The Romans acted with brashness and nothing was sacred to them.

The strongest claim of the Roman empire to be the iron kingdom is found first in the length of its duration—the best proof of its strength. Babylon lasted only 70 years— Medo-Persian empire lasted 200 years—the Greek 130 years —while the Roman empire in its undivided state lasted some 500 years, and in its divided state as the ten kingdoms, continues in succession down to the present time. See comments on next verse.

v. 41-43 . . . FEET AND TOES . . . OF CLAY . . . OF IRON . . . DIVIDED . . . PARTLY STRONG . . . PARTLY BROKEN . . . MINGLE THEMSELVES . . . BUT . . . NOT CLEAVE ONE TO ANOTHER . . . Note: A fuller explanation of the relationship of the Roman empire to present day world powers will be made in chapter 7. Note: nowhere are "ten" toes specifically mentioned. We assume the statue had ten toes and not 6 or 15. The main emphasis of this passage is the eventual divided and weakened nature of this ferocious kingdom. There is no symbolic interpretation of the "ten" toes whatsoever. We agree with Leupold: ". . . the toes, generally speaking, represent the kingdoms into which the Roman Empire broke up when the disintegration set in . . . ten is the number of completeness or totality . . . the toes represent the sum total of these kingdoms. All attempts to name the resultant kingdoms of an earlier or a latter date prove abortive and unreliable. For the number ten is definitely a symbolic number as are numbers generally in visions or dreams of this type. There might in reality be nine or eleven or nineteen or twenty (divisions of the Roman kingdom). Ten represents the totality of whatever number there is." These divisions all arise, in one sense or another, historically from the ancient Roman Empire. This does not mean that each one of the empires must be able to trace its origin immediately to Rome. The kingdoms of modern Europe, for example, might be said to have come from the Roman Empire, but certainly not directly.

The lack of inner unity of this fourth empire and the tendency to fragment or splinter is described. Iron and clay will not fuse. There will always be something of the firmness of iron in this fourth empire, but there shall always be present a lack of cohesion. Never again will a world empire dominate the entire population of the earth in a universal way like the Babylonian, Medo-Persian, Greek, or early Roman empires.

The phrase "they shall mingle themselves with the seed of men; but they shall not cleave one to another," probably refers to the migration of barbarian hordes who came in countless myriads from the Germanic forests and central Europe and intermarried with Roman peoples (especially in the royal and ruling families) as a sort of melting-pot experiment to attempt to bring some inner unity to the expansive Roman empire. But the resultant stock was not of which enduring empires are made.

The important thing to remember about this whole image is that all together it represents symbolically pagan, heathen, carnal world-power in opposition to the kingdom of God. It is man's rule over man opposed to God's rule over man. Not that worldly governments are not necessary as temporary expedients due to man's sinful condition—indeed carnal government is necessary to restrain the lawless (cf. I Tim. 1:8-9; Rom. 13:1-7; I Pet. 2:13-17). But all carnal government is at best totally inadequate and at worst in direct opposition to what God has purposed for man through regeneration, repentance and renewed communion with Him in His new kingdom! So the fourth empire represents the early ferocious Roman empire, later divided into many successive kingdoms yet unable to ever again regain that inner unity necessary to dominate the whole world. Then we see the whole image which represents carnal government dealt a fatal blow by the kingdom of

God (the stone) beginning in the days of the kings of the fourth empire and eventually grinding the whole image into a dust which is blown away.

QUIZ

1. What is the fourth kingdom?
2. What is the first characteristic mentioned of this kingdom?
3. What characteristic of this kingdom is symbolized by feet and toes of iron and clay?
4. What is meant by "they shall mingle themselves with the seed of men?"
5. What is the important thing to remember about the whole image?
6. Why are carnal governments necessary?
7. Why is carnal government inadequate and opposed to God's ultimate purpose for man?

c. FINAL KINGDOM

TEXT: 2:44-45

44 And in the days of those kings shall the God of heaven set up a kingdom which shall never be destroyed, or shall the sovereignty thereof be left to another people; but it shall break in pieces and consume all these kingdoms, and it shall stand forever.

45 Forasmuch as thou sawest that a stone was cut out of the mountain without hands, and that it brake in pieces the iron, the brass, the clay, the sliver, and the gold; the great God hath made known to the king what shall come to pass hereafter: that the dream is certain, and the interpretation thereof sure.

QUERIES

a. In the days of which kings will God's kingdom be set up?
b. When will it break in pieces and consume all the kingdoms?
c. Why tell Nebuchadnezzar of things far in the future?

NEBUCHADNEZZAR'S DREAM
Daniel, Chapter Two

REPRESENTS IN ITS TOTALITY ALL HUMAN GOVERNMENT

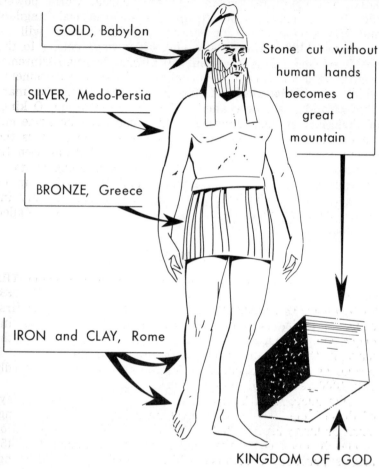

GOLD, Babylon

SILVER, Medo-Persia

BRONZE, Greece

IRON and CLAY, Rome

Stone cut without human hands becomes a great mountain

KINGDOM OF GOD

The kingdom of God, the Church, conquers and supplants all human government and eventually destroys all other sovereignty and becomes the only government in the new earth. Human governments are inadequate to bring about man's regeneration and are, for the most part, opposed to God's purposes, although they are necessary for restraining unregenerate and lawless men. All this is the symbolical meaning of Nebuchadnezzar's dream and is the teaching of the Scriptures, especially the New Testament.

PARAPHRASE

And in the days of the fourth empire, the last of the great world empires which represent carnal world power, the God of heaven will set up His supernatural kingdom and His kingdom will be eternal. This kingdom will be unconquerable by anyone else and will always belong to the people of God. This kingdom will ultimately reign supreme, eventually destroying and consuming all carnal governments which are inadequate and opposed to God's rule of man. This kingdom will be eternal. This is the meaning, O king, of that part of your dream in which you saw the stone cut out of the mountain without hands breaking into pieces the image of iron, brass, clay, silver and gold. God has seen fit to reveal to you, Nebuchadnezzar what He is going to do in the future with carnal government and the setting up of His own rule in the hearts of men—His kingdom. My interpretation of your dream is as certain as my detailed revelation of what it was.

COMMENT

v. 44-45　AND IN THE DAYS OF THOSE KINGS SHALL THE GOD OF HEAVEN SET UP A KINGDOM . . . THE DREAM IS CERTAIN, AND THE INTERPRETATION THEREOF SURE . . . The first thing to notice is that the kingdom of God is of Divine *origin* and eternal *duration*. If it is to be established in the days of the Roman empire and be of eternal duration it *cannot be a millenial kingdom* for the millennium is allegedly only 1000 years of literal duration!

We quote from Young here: ". . . the words, in the days of those kings, would refer most naturally to the four kingdoms or kings represented by the image. This interpretation is clearly involved in the symbolism of the image (vs. 45) and is permissible because, while distinct, these four kingdoms were also in a sense one. Medo-Persia conquered and incorporated Babylon. Greece did the same to Medo-Persia . . . the extent of the Roman Empire was far greater and more world-wide than any of the others. It was while the image was still standing that the blow was struck. So we may say that it was in the period of those four empires as together representing Gentile world dominion *but in the days of the last of the four* that the kingdom of Messiah was set up."

The whole picture then is that of God establishing His kingdom (the sovereignty or rule of God in the hearts of men through man's faithful response to the grace of Jesus Christ) and destroying the inadequate and opposing carnal worldly power which can never save or reunite man with God. And it all begins to happen during the days of the fourth world empire, Rome. All of this began, of course, when Christ was born, reached its climax when He was crucified when God "despoiled the principalities and the powers . . . and made a show of them openly, triumphing over them in Him" (Col. 2:15). It began receiving citizens on the day of Pentecost (Acts 2) when the first gospel invitation was given and obeyed. That the church is God's kingdom cannot be denied by careful and unbiased students of the New Testament. That the church was established and that Christ was born and died and raised from the dead in the days of the Roman empire cannot be denied by anyone who has the slightest inkling of history. So the kingdom of God was begun in the days of the Roman empire and now wherever the gentle gospel is preached it has victory and is continuing to overthrow the kingdom of the god of this world. But it shall not reach its culmination until the second coming of Christ and the end of time (cf. I Cor. 15:20ff). "Then comes the end, when he delivers the kingdom to God the Father after destroying every rule and every authority and power."

Certain "dispensational" teachers today would interpret this passage to the effect that the fourth empire represents a *revived* Roman empire of the future which will come to an end by a sudden catastrophic judgment, after which the kingdom of God (an alleged millenial kingdom of Rev. 20:1-6) will be set up. The destruction of the Gentile world power, according to this view, occurs not at the first coming of Christ, but at the second. The New Testament plainly teaches that God has destroyed the power not only of the devil but all rule and authority previously able to hold the spirit of man in bondage and ignorance—if man will hear believe and heed God's message.

A few quotations from a dispensational teacher will suffice as documentation. Gaebelein writes: "He (Christ at His first coming) did not smite the image; the image, so to speak, smote Him." "The stone strikes the image, when the ten toes, the final ten kingdom division of the Roman Empire, are in existence." "The stone which falls from above is the Second Coming of our Lord Jesus Christ, His coming in great power and glory."

Another dispensationalist, G. H. Lang, rejects the idea of a revived Roman empire but substitutes what might be called a revived Babylonian kingdom, with Babylon as the capital of Antichrist, for the fourth empire at which time God is supposed to set up a kingdom of a literal 1000 year duration.

One writer who calls himself a "premillennialist", Robert D. Culver, in *Daniel And the Latter Days*, writes, "The discerning reader will readily observe that . . . these systems (i.e. the interpretations of Allis, Leupold and Young) rest on a theory of church-kingdom identity—that the kingdom of God and the church are precisely identical. This is a position which cannot be sustained by Scripture, despite valliant attempts to make the Bible support it." It is inconceivable to us how any "discerning reader" of the New Testament can fail to observe that both Christ and the apostles clearly equated the kingdom of God and the church as one and the same. It seems clear that the "dispensational" and "premillenial" views of the kingdom of God miss completely the fact that the true significance of the kingdom of God is its spiritual nature.

Leupold sums up the meaning of the dream thusly: "Heretofore all that history seemed to amount to was: kingdom conquering and replacing kingdom. That however, is not an inevitable, unalterable cycle. For a new power, not conditioned by man's control, shall come into operation and shall break the old order of things and establish a lasting and definite victory . . . On this victorious note the interpretation ends."

Thus the dream sketched the course of the history of the world in bold strokes. Ever since the kingdom of God was established and its power to change men into the image of God was demonstrated, men have still blundered along trying to establish a lasting world power. But each product of human effort shall go the way of all flesh including republics, democracies, united nations, etc., for none of them are sufficient for man's dilemma—sin.

One of the arguments appealed to most by the dispensationalists is that the stone smashing the great image to dust speaks of violence and catastrophic overthrow of Gentile power—this cannot be the gospel. But the main emphasis is not on violence but power. Certainly the gospel has power (cf. II Cor. 10:3-5) and furthermore the christian or citizen of the heavenly kingdom is not to use carnal warfare in destroying strongholds. Thus the dispensational view that at the second coming of Christ a great, catastrophic, violent battle at Armeggedon, with carnal weapons of warfare will be fought and that this is the stone smashing the image to dust, has substituted the physical for the spiritual and has missed the entire spirit of the New Testament revelation of the kingdom of God! Please read the special studies of the *Minor Prophets*, College Press, on the subject of interpreting the prophets and premillennialism.

QUIZ

1. What is the first thing to notice concerning the kingdom which God would set up?
2. When, exactly, does this interpretation of Daniel say the kingdom of God would be set up?
3. What is the whole picture of the dream and its interpretation?
4. What significant aspect of the kingdom of God is neglected by the dispensational view of the dream?
5. Why is it not necessary to think that the kingdom of God's destruction of world-power must be violent and catastrophic?

d. FELICITOUS KING

TEXT: 2:46-49

46 Then the king Nebuchadnezzar fell upon his face, and worshipped Daniel, and commanded that they should offer an oblation and sweet odors unto him.

47   The king answered unto Daniel, and said, Of a truth your God is the God of gods, and the Lord of kings, and a revealer of secrets, seeing thou hast been able to reveal this secret.

48   Then the king made Daniel great, and gave him many gifts, and made him to rule over the whole province of Babylon, and to be chief governor over all the wise men of Babylon.

49   And Daniel requested of the king, and he appointed Shadrach, Meshach, and Abed-nego over the affairs of the province of Babylon: but Daniel was in the gate of the king.

QUERIES

a. Why did the king worship Daniel?
b. Was the kings' profession one of a true believer in God?
c. Where is "the gate of the king?

PARAPHRASE

Suddenly the king fell upon his face and did obeisance to Daniel as an act of respect to Daniel, a representative of the God who had revealed the king's dream, and the king commanded that tributes of offerings and incense be made in honor of Daniel. And the king said to Daniel, It is true! Your God is the God of all the gods. He is Ruler of kings. He is Revealer of secrets. I am convinced of this because you were able to reveal my secret dream. Then the king declared that Daniel should have great honor and position. He gave Daniel many rich gifts and appointed him to be the second in command over the province of Babylon and chief over all the Babylonian wise men. And Daniel requested favors for his Hebrew companions. So Nebuchadnezzar appointed Shadrach, Meshach and Abednego as Daniel's assistants, to be in charge of official affairs of the province of Babylon. Daniel served as chief magistrate in the king's court.

COMMENT

v. 46-47 . . . NEBUCHADNEZZAR . . . WORSHIPPED DANIEL . . . AND SAID, OF A TRUTH YOUR GOD IS THE GOD OF GODS . . .

The word "worship" does not always, in the Bible, mean religious worship. First, Daniel would not have permitted such a thing without some verbal correction, at least. Second, it was a common practice for pagan rulers to bow before those whom they thought were representatives of gods. Josephus records that Alexander the Great bowed before the high priest of the Jews, and when asked by his general, Parmenio, as to the meaning of his action, replied, "I do not worship the high-priest, but the God with whose high-priesthood he has been honored." We believe Nebuchadnezzar was simply showing his respect for Daniel and at the same time doing obeisance through Daniel as the accredited representative of the God who had the power to reveal secrets. Notice that Nebuchadnezzar does not in any way call Daniel a god. It is evident, therefore, that the king is worshipping and sacrificing to Daniel's God through Daniel as an intermediary.

It is further evident that Nebuchadnezzar is not making a profession or confession of Jehovah-God as a monotheist. His concept of deity is still one of polytheism. What he does recognize is the superiority of Daniel's God over all the other gods of his pantheon, for Daniel's God is able to do what the gods of the Chaldean wise men could not do— reveal his secret dream.

v. 48-49 . . . MADE DANIEL GREAT . . . GAVE HIM MANY GIFTS . . . MADE HIM TO RULE . . . AND BE CHIEF GOVERNOR OVER . . . WISE MEN . . . AND . . . SHADRACH, MESHACH, AND ABED-NEGO . . . The king's mood changed from one of rage to pleasantness. He seems greatly relieved to know the interpretation of his dream. Perhaps he was relieved to know there was nothing immediately foreboding toward him personally in this dream. Perhaps he is excited to learn there is some Power or some One who is able to know the secrets of men and he has this One's representative in his own court. Whatever the immediate reason we know that God was the giver of grace to Daniel in order that he should not perish but would be used by God as a vessel to serve His purpose.

The king now keeps his promise to reward richly anyone who could tell him his dream and its interpretation.

There is no way to know just how great was Daniel's reward. He was made "great" which probably means given social and political status next to the king himself. He was undoubtedly given a spacious home or palace with a retinue of servants, perhaps jewels and splendid robes. Daniel's official position was ruler of the province of Babylon. The word describing his office is *rab signin*, chief overseer. He certainly was not ruler over all the empire of Babylon. He was subordinate to the king for he had to make request to the king to get appointments for his three Hebrew companions to official position even in the province of Babylon. The king retained final authority in all matters in all provinces! It is not often that such recognition comes to a man who is so young! One note of interest concerning the date of writing of this book—if these words were written at the time of the Maccabees or at any other period of strict Judaism, it is difficult to understand why the author, supposedly a strict Jew with an abhorence of everything pagan, would represent his Jewish hero as receiving such honors from a pagan king.

Daniel is not ungrateful to forget his Hebrew companions and their courage and assistance in his confrontation with the king—they prayed with Daniel, and gave him encouragement. He made request to the king and Shadrach, Meshach and Abednego were appointed to official positions in the affairs of government in the province of Babylon, probably as Daniel's assistants. But Daniel was elevated to the position equivalent to cabinet office in the king's court. He was immediately responsible to the king as ruler over Babylon.

So Daniel's first confrontation with pagan dictatorship comes to a successful conclusion. But behind the scenes we see the providential, supernatural working of Jehovah-God in order that His purposes may be served. The carrying out of God's purpose through particular men (i.e. Daniel) is, of course conditioned upon the surrendered will of such persons. God could not work through Daniel if Daniel refuses to allow God to do so. But God does not need Daniel— He could find someone else through whom to work. Daniel needs God! God's purposes will conquer, one way or another, through one person or another—He is immutable, He does not change. But if man would wish to receive the rewards of God's purposes, man must submit to be used for God's purposes.

It is the lesson of this chapter of Daniel, and all succeeding chapters of Daniel (and all the Old Testament prophets), that the schemes, political kingdoms and religious philosophies of men will go the way of all flesh. One kingdom arises, proves to be inadequate for man's spiritual renewal, and collapses. Each new political or social structure invariably meets with the same overthrow simply because man is incapable of bringing about his own rebirth. This has to have a supernatural source. So history is one defeat after another. Our contemporary society with its philosophy of existential despair and desperation is simply another testimony to this reality of history. Man cannot find God—but MAN CAN KNOW THE GOD WHO HAS FOUND MAN BY REVEALING HIMSELF! The one who knows the Almighty God is delivered from the futility of hopelessness and despair. The one who knows God learns that history has a purpose because history is being used by the Supernatural God whose plan and power is to regenerate and renew all who will allow Him to do so. The kingdom, the spiritual brotherhood, of this God is man's only hope. This is the lesson of the great image Nebuchadnezzar saw in his dream. Daniel revealed God's message concerning this image. See our chart at the end of this chapter.

QUIZ

1. Give two reasons why we do not need to assume Daniel accepted the "worship" of king Nebuchadnezzar.
2. Why do we believe Nebuchadnezzar has not yet come to a monotheistic concept of God?
3. Why was the king's mood so radically changed from rage to pleasantness?
4. What was Daniel's official position after the king promoted him?
5. What positions did the Hebrew companions of Daniel likely receive?
6. What is the lesson of this chapter?

SERMON NUMBER TWO
DESPOTS, DREAMS AND DESTINIES
Text: Daniel 2

INTRODUCTION

I. DANIEL HAD BECOME ONE OF THE WISE MEN OF BABYLON, A "CHALDEAN"
   A. He had gone through a period of training
      1. Involving learning Babylonian history and culture
      2. Involving learning certain sciences
      3. This does not mean, of course, that he practiced all the false, pagan superstitious divinations, etc.
   B. He had made friends in influential places
      1. He had been accompanied in his training by the other three Hebrew youths
      2. The four together had found favor in the eyes of their teachers and were trusted

II. BACKGROUND OF CHALDEANS
   A. They were a group of pagan priests who used mysticism and superstition to practice their religion and science
      1. In ancient Babylon even the king served as the High Priest
      2. He performed sacrifices and determined the religious life of subjects
      3. He appointed substitute priests to perform the routine priestly labors
      4. Each temple had a high priest and a number of lesser priests
   B. They used various methods of attempting to know the messages or oracles of their gods and to foretell the future
      1. Astrology—the stars exerted a supposed influence over the fates of men and events; by observing their positions, conjunctions and oppositions, it might be ascertained what would be the destiny of individuals and nations

2. Necromancy—consisted in the belief that the dead must be acquainted with the world where they now dwell, so dark to the living, and that it might be possible to make a covenant or compact with the dead, by which they would be induced to disclose what they knew.

3. Divination—interpreting dreams and determining oracles from the gods; one method used was Hepatoscopy, divination by the liver—at the time of sacrifice a god was supposed to take hold of the victim and to enter the animal's liver because the liver was the seat of the mental life. After a kid or sheep was slaughtered sacrificially, the victim's body was opened and preliminary conclusions drawn . . . then it was removed from the body and examined more thoroughly, compared with models and abnormalities noted. They also studied flight patterns of birds for divining purposes.

4. Exorcism—a class of priests known as ashipu specialized in counteracting the work of demons; one method was to promise the demon a gift and entice him to come out—another was to give the victim nauseous and putrid substances as medicines to drive the demon out—sometimes they tried to fool the demons by placing animals on top of the sick people—they tried to scare them away by wearing red—then there were the chanters who tried to croon them out singing soothingly

C. The Babylonians placed a great emphasis on DREAMS

1. They believed that through the medium of dreams the Divine will might be made known and that the secrets of the future disclosed.

2. The theory was that during sleep the ordinary laws of the mind are suspended; the soul is abstracted from the visible world; the thoughts must then be originated by higher beings; in this state the dreamer has converse with an invisible world and sees much of what is future.

100

DISCUSSION

I. DESPOT'S DREAM

A. Challenge to the Chaldeans 2:1-6

1. God sent Nebuchadnezzar this dream directly "A great God has made known to the king what shall be hereafter" 2:45

2. The dream "shook him up"—he was in deep anxiety of spirit and soul. It was so vivid as to seem to be actually happening right then; IT WAS TERRIFYING!

3. He undoubtedly had some strange, inexplicable foreboding concerning the meaning of this dream and its symbolism

4. He called in his doctors of psychology; theology; etc.

5. He commanded, "What have I dreamed?" They replied, "Tell us the dream and we will tell you what it means!"

6. Now the king had not forgotten the dream, but he was probably tired of their hocus pocus and actually did not believe much of it; it may be that deep down inside himself, the king knew that most of the religion of Babylon was mere superstition and not truth HE WAS GOING TO FIND OUT ONCE AND FOR ALL IF THESE WISE MEN REALLY KNEW THE SECRETS OF THE GODS . . . IF THEY COULD TELL HIM WHAT HE DREAMED INSTEAD OF MAKING UP SOME EGO-FLATTERING INTERPRETATION, HE WOULD KNOW!

7. So this mighty, absolute, cold-blooded despot declared, "If you do not tell me my dream AND its interpretation, I will have you hacked limb from limb, and your homes publicly desecrated."

B. Dilemma of the Diviners 2:7-11

1. The Chaldeans begin by stalling for time

2. The king recognized this and senses some sort of collaboration amongst them to speak words of deception, hoping to "put him on" until times and circumstances change. They are hoping the king's ugly mood will change.

3. They face a terrible dilemma. They must not say anything that might further irritate the king; on the other hand they must convey to the king that what he asks is totally unreasonable and impossible.
4. They know they cannot do what the king demands but they do not want the king to know it

C. Saved by the Subjugated 2:12-16
1. Well, the king was not amused, and he did not cool down
2. He took all their stalling he could and in a furious rage ordered that all the wise men be arrested and slain
3. It took a little while to round them all up
4. In the meantime Daniel and his three companions took steps to save themselves and the other wise men
5. Daniel, by faith in God's word to him, told the king's servant that he could reveal the king's dream and its interpreation
6. As a last resort he was allowed to approach the king and ask for an appointment

II. DANIEL'S DECLARATION

A. Prayer 2:17-24
1. Daniel and his three companions ask God's blessing on their opportunity to witness to king Nebuchadnezzar the power of Jehovah
2. Daniel's prayer contains one of the most arresting passages of the O.T. speaking of the divine sovereignty and immutability of the purpose of God in the events of earth's history (v. 20-23)
3. Our God is the God of the Now! He determines rulers and seasons and the habitations of men. One dynasty influences world culture and wanes and disappears at the directing influence of God's immutable moral laws governing the universe, and another civilization comes to the fore (cf. Jer. 27:5ff).
4. God creates both weal and woe (Isa. 45:5-7)

    5. God is able to reveal the future—the deep and secret things—because all time and space and mass are within His knowledge and control at all times —all at once. He knows what is in man's mind and thought and heart because He, Himself, made man.

    6. And Daniel's prayer was answered, Daniel persuades Arioch not to destroy the wise men, and asks to be taken to the king to tell the dream and its interpretation

B. Profession 2:25-30

    1. What courage; what faith; WHO WOULD DARE TO STAND BEFORE THIS MIGHTY DESPOT UNLESS HE WERE ABSOLUTELY CERTAIN HE COULD PRODUCE WHAT THE DESPOT WANTED!

    2. But is this all Daniel did? Just tell the king his dream? Was Daniel only interested in telling the king in order that he not be slain with the other wise men?

    3. No. Daniel had another purpose, higher than escape from death—He purposed to witness to the king concerning His God, Jehovah

    4. How easy it would have been—how convenient— how practical—for Daniel to claim all the credit for being able to tell the king his dream—BUT HE GAVE ALL THE CREDIT AND GLORY TO GOD

C. Publication 2:31-35

    1. Notice how Arioch got in a little apple polishing on the side. He said he had found a Hebrew who could tell the king his dream—all the while it was Daniel who had found Arioch and asked to be taken to the king

    2. He intimates to Nebuchadnezzar that what God sent to him in dream form was a prediction of future events of history—"what should come to pass hereafter."

    3. So Daniel relates exactly what the dream was in detail—a huge statue, like unto a man, head of gold, breast of silver, belly of brass (bronze) legs and feet of iron and clay.

4. Then he saw a stone, cut out without hands, and it smote the image, ground it to dust and it was all blown away; while the stone grew into a huge mountain, covering the earth.

III. DICTATORSHIP'S DESTINY

A. First Three Kingdoms 2:36-39

1. Nebuchadnezzar, or more exactly, Babylon is the head of gold—the first representative of absolute world domination (cf. Jer. 27:5-7; Ezek. 26:7)
2. Herodotus, at Babylon 90 years after the era of Neb., was amazed at all the gold there. Golden tables, statues, thrones, walls overlaid, some $100,000 worth just in the temples . . . SYMBOLIZING GLORY, SHOW!
3. Medo-Persian empire is next. It is the next great world empire. There was no empire of the Medes alone. All the concentration on building simply for magnificence changed to a desire for silver (money) for power's sake. As a consequence of hoarding silver this empire became rich as was prophecied in Dan. 11:2. The silver kingdom was stronger than the gold, Babylon lasted 70 years; Medo-Persia lasted over 200 years
4. But bronze was stronger than silver. This is the Greek empire. Ruled over the world to greater extent than any of the previous. The power of the Medo-Persian empire built upon wealth was overcome by the force of arms wielded by, brave, idealistic, free people—the Greeks. Josephus saw in the mention of a brazen kingdom an unmistakabue prediction of the victorious arms of Alexander and his brazen-clad Greeks. Herodotus describes the striking difference between the brazen-clad Greek warriors and the Persians clad in soft hats, tunics with sleeves, and trousers.
5. In one sense we have in the symbolism a progressive inferiority in the metals from one world power to the next. But in another sense there is progressive symbolism of superiority. Progres-

sion downward in outward magnificence; progression upward in power and extension.

B. The Fourth Kingdom 2:40-43

1. Iron is very appropriate symbol to describe the Roman empire. We pass, generally speaking, from the bronze age to the iron age when we pass from Greece to Rome

2. The Roman infantry soldier of that era carried with him that distinctively Roman weapon the pilum, a sort of spear or javelin with a long iron neck fitted with a wooden shaft, the metal extending for about a third of its entire length.

3. The feature Daniel emphasizes in this empire is its strength. The Roman war machine was many times more destructive than any of its predecessors. Rome's ruthless severity is exemplified by the destruction of Carthage; the War against the Slaves; (when the Appian way was lined with 6000 crosses; and the siege and destruction of Jerusalem.)

4. Rome was not impressed by the pomposity and sublieties of the Eastern potentates—the Romans acted with brashness and boldness.

5. The Roman empire lasted in its undivided state some 500 years.

6. But this kingdom was to become divided and weak

7. There is no mention of ten toes, so we are not forced to find ten specific succeeding emperors or empires coming from the Roman Ten. If we must place some assumed significance on the toes, would be symbolic of completeness. Ten represents the totality of however many successive kings or emperors there might be.

8. The phrase "They shall mingle themselves with the seed of men" refers to the attempts of the Roman empire to intermarry with the barbarian princes and princesses of the Germanic forests and central Europe in order to bring solidarity to the Roman empire. But it failed.

9. There will always be something of the firmness of iron in this fourth empire, but there shall

always be present a lack of cohesion. NEVER
AGAIN WILL A WORLD EMPIRE DOMINATE THE ENTIRE
POPULATION OF THE EARTH IN A UNIVERSAL WAY
LIKE THE BABYLONIAN, PERSIAN, GREEK OR EARLY
ROMAN EMPIRE! World governments continue and
all of them, more or less, come from Rome, but
never again a universal one except the FIFTH!

THE IMPORTANT THING TO REMEMBER ABOUT THIS WHOLE
IMAGE IS THAT ALL TOGETHER IT REPRESENTS SYMBOLICALLY
PAGAN, HEATHEN, CARNAL WORLD-POWER IN OPPOSITION TO
THE KINGDOM OF GOD. IT IS MAN'S RULE OVER MAN OPPOSED
TO GOD'S RULE OVER MAN.

NOT THAT WORLDLY GOVERNMENTS ARE NOT NECESSARY AS
TEMPORARY EXPEDIENTS DUE TO MAN'S SINFUL CONDITION—
INDEED CARNAL GOVERNMENT IS NECESSARY TO RESTRAIN THE
LAWLESS (I Tim. 1:8-9; Rom. 13:1-7; I Pet. 2:13-17). BUT
ALL CARNAL GOVERNMENT IS, AT BEST TOTALLY INADEQUATE,
AND AT WORST IN DIRECT OPPOSITION TO WHAT GOD HAS
PURPOSED FOR MAN THROUGH REGENERATION, REPENTANCE
AND RENEWED COMMUNION WITH HIM IN HIS NEW KINGDOM.

SO THE FOURTH EMPIRE REPRESENTS THE EARLY FEROCIOUS
ROMAN EMPIRE, LATER DIVIDED INTO MANY SUCCESSIVE KING-
DOMS YET UNABLE TO EVER AGAIN REGAIN THAT INNER UNITY
NECESSARY TO DOMINATE THE WHOLE WORLD. THEN WE SEE
THE WHOLE IMAGE WHICH REPRESENTS CARNAL GOVERNMENT
DEALT A FATAL BLOW BY THE KINGDOM OF GOD (THE STONE)
BEGINNING THE DAYS OF THE KINGS OF THE FOURTH EMPIRE
AND EVENTUAL GRINDING THE WHOLE IMAGE INTO A DUST
WHICH IS BLOWN AWAY!

C. The Final Kingdom (The Fifth Kingdom Universal)
   2:44-45
   1. Notice: It is of Divine origin; it is eternal in
      duration. IT CANNOT BE THE SO-CALLED MILLENIAL
      KINGDOM OF THE DISPENSATIONALISTS FOR THAT IS
      SUPPOSED TO LAST ONLY FOR A LITERAL 1000 Years.
   2. In the days of those kings means that it was in
      the period of those four empires as together repre-
      senting Gentile world domination, BUT IN THE

DAYS OF THE LAST OF THE FOUR that the kingdom of Messiah was set up.

3. The whole picture is that of God establishing His kingdom (see sovereignty or rule of God in the hearts of men through man's faithful response to the grace of Jesus Christ) and destroying the inadequate and opposing carnal worldly power (ideas of men for man's salvation), which can never save or reunite man with God. And it all begins to happen during the days of the fourth world empire, Rome.

4. All of this began, of course, when Christ was born, reached its climax when He was crucified when God "Despoiled the principalities and the powers . . . and made a show of them openly, triumphing over them in Him" (Col. 2:15)

5. It began receiving its citizens on the Day of Pentecost, but it shall not reach its culmination until the Second Coming of Christ and the end of time "Then comes the end when he delivers the kingdom to God the Father after destroying every rule and every authority and power." (I Cor. 15:20ff)

6. Certain "dispensational" teachers today would teach that this passage "the fourth empire" represents a revived Roman empire of the future which will come to an end by a sudden catastrophic judgment, a literal war with literal weapons, led by a literal Christ upon a literal earth, reigning in a literal Jerusalem, after which the kingdom of God will be set up. The destruction of the Gentile world power, according to this view, occurs not at the first coming of Christ, but the the second.

7. One such teacher says a revived Babylonian king-kingdom, with Babylon as the capital of Antichrist, is the fourth empire, and the Stone is the 1000 yr. kingdom of God.

8. One writer who calls himself a "premillennialist" writes, "The discerning reader will readily observe that . . . these systems (i.e. the interpreta-

tions of Allis, Leupold and Young) rest upon a theory of church-kingdom identity—that the kingdom of God and the church are precisely identical. This is a position which cannot be sustained by Scripture, despite valiant attempts to make the Bible support it."

9. It is inconveivable to me how any "Discerning reader" of the N.T. cannot observe that both Christ and the apostles clearly equated the kingdom of God and the church as one and the same. It seems clear that the dispensational views of the kingdom of God miss completely the fact that the true significance of the kingdom of God is its spiritual nature (cf. Eph. 6:10-13, etc.).

D. Felicitious King 2:46-49
1. The king seemed greatly relieved to know the interpretation of his dream
2. Perhaps he was relieved to know that there was nothing really foreboding toward him personally in this dream.
3. Perhaps he was simply relieved to have his mind's troubling anxiety to know set at rest.
4. I do not believe he had been converted from his polytheism to an acceptable loyalty to Jehovah-God as yet.
5. He did promote Daniel and his three companions and gave glory to Daniel's God. Daniel was making some progress in his personal evangelism.

CONCLUSION

I. IS THERE A LESSON IN NEBUCHADNEZZAR'S DREAM FOR US?
A. I believe that there is
B. I believe there are great lessons of faith, God's nature, and God's moral government of the universe to be learned from all the O.T.
C. I believe that we can see in the O.T. and the fulfillment of its prophecies, purpose, destiny, truth, holiness, and hope in man's future if man puts his future in the will of God

II. WHAT IS THE LESSON OF THIS DREAM AND ITS INTERPRETATION?

A. Leupold sums up the meaning of the dream: "Heretofore all that history seemed to amount to was: kingdom conquering and replacing kingdom. That however, is not an inevitable, unalterable cycle. For a new power, not conditioned by man's control, shall come into operation and shall break the old order of things and establish a lasting and definite victory. . . . On this victorious note the interpretation ends."

B. THUS THE DREAM SKETCHED THE COURSE OF THE HISTORY OF THE WORLD IN BOLD STROKES. IT PREDICTED HOW GOD WAS GOING TO SOLVE MAN'S DILEMMA, MAN'S NEED WHICH HUMAN GOVERNMENT COULD NOT SOLVE.

C. Even after the kingdom of God has been established and its power to change men into the image of God has been demonstrated, men have still blundered along trying to establish a lasting world power. But each product of human effort shall go the way of all flesh including republics, dictatorships, democracies, United Nations, etc., NONE OF THEM CAN CONQUER MAN'S ENEMY, SATAN AND SIN!

D. There is no need to think of a literal, violent, catastrophic war of the kingdom of God against world power in some millenial kingdom as the interpretation of this Stone

E. The gospel has the power to destroy strongholds and imaginations and every thought that exalts itself against God and to bring every thought into captivity unto Christ (II Cor. 10:3-5).

F. There is no force that can conquer sin except the force created within the will, mind and heart of man by the faithfulness, love, mery and righteousness of God!

III. THE FIFTH KINGDOM

A. It is of superhuman origin, does not owe its source to human plans/power

B. It begins small

C. It supplants all other kingdoms; provide man's real need

D. It will be eternal; neither arms nor persecution, philosophy, science nor ridicule will ever conquer it.

E. It grows great and prevails universally and will someday be the only government on a new earth wherein dwelleth righteousness

THE LESSON OF DANIEL

A proud king reigned in Babylon the great;
A pure youth dreamed, to goodness consecrate.
The youth turned eyes to Heaven, with a prayer;
The king appraised his wealth and kingdom fair.
But God disdained the kingdom—it was gone;
The humble youth prayed earnestly at dawn.
No lions' den nor furnace breathing fire
Can frighten him whom Godly thoughts inspire.
The tyrant's taunts are as the winter grim
Whose insults pass as God's bright spring comes in.
The hosts of error, clad in stern array,
Inflame the world, then glumly fade away.
Proud kings and mighty kingdoms suffer loss;
Love lives!—through Godly visions and a Cross.

—Thomas Curtis Clark

EXAMINATION TWO

REFUTATIONS

(Answer the following by giving the argument which will correct the statement)

1. The magicians, enchanters, sorcerers and Chaldeans of Nebuchadnezzar's court were superstitious ignoramuses. Refute!

2. Daniel arrived at his interpretation of the king's dream from his education in Babylonian culture. Refute!

3. The ten toes of the great image represent 10 Roman emperors beginning with Pompey. Refute!

110

ASSOCIATIONS

(Associate the persons or events of column one with the correct person or event of column two)

1	2
Belteshazzar	angel
gold	Arioch
Chaldean	Daniel
Nebuchadnezzar	Abed-nego
silver	empire of Babylon
king's captain	Hananiah
Syrian language	Persia
bronze	wise-man
Shadrach	Ahaz
iron-clay	king of Babylon
stone	Greece
	magician
	Rome
	beast
	kingdom of God
	Aramaic

MEMORIZATIONS

(Fill in the blanks:)

And in the days of _____ _____ shall the God of heaven set up a _____ that shall never be _____, nor shall the _____ thereof be left to another people; but it shall _____ in pieces and consume all these kingdoms, and it shall stand _____

EXPLANATIONS

1. Explain why Nebuchadnezzar was troubled in his spirit by the dream of the great image.
2. Explain the significance of Daniel's statement that God "changeth the times and the seasons . . . removeth kings, and setteth up kings . . ."
3. Explain the reason for depicting four great world empires as *one* image.

4. Explain the significance of the "stone" dashing the image to pieces.
5. Explain the relevance of this dream and its interpretation for 20th centry Christians.

CHAPTER THREE

I. DIVINE DELIVERANCE—3:1-30

a. PAGAN DEITY

TEXT: 3:1-7

1 Nebuchadnezzar the king made an image of gold, whose height was threescore cubits, and the breadth thereof six cubits: he set it up in the plain of Dura, in the province of Babylon.

2 Then Nebuchadnezzar the king sent to gather together the satraps, the deputies, and the governors, the judges, the treasurers, the counsellors, the sheriffs, and all the rulers of the provinces, to come to the dedication of the image which Nebuchadnezzar the king had set up.

3 Then the satraps, the deputies, and the governors, the judges, the treasurers, the counsellors, the sheriffs, and all the rulers of the provices, were gathered together unto the dedication of the image that Nebuchadnezzar the king had set up; and they stood before the image that Nebuchadnezzar had set up.

4 Then the herald cried aloud, To you it is commanded, O peoples, nations, and languages,

5 that at what time ye hear the sound of the cornet, flute, harp, sackbut, psalter, dulcimer, and all kinds of music, ye fall down and worship the golden image that Nebuchadnezzar the king hath set up;

6 and whoso falleth not down and worshippeth shall the same hour be cast into the midst of a burning fiery furnace.

7 Therefore at that time, when all the peoples heard the sound of the cornet, flute, harp, sackbut, psaltery, and all kinds of music, all the people, the nations, and the

languages, fell down and worshipped the golden image that Nebuchadnezzar the king had set up.

QUERIES

a. Why did Nebuchadnezzar make an image of gold?
b. Why did he command that it be worshipped?
c. Why all the different musical instruments at once?

PARAPHRASE

King Nebuchadnezzar ordered that a great image, ninety feet high and nine feet wide, overlaid with gold, be fashioned and erected on the Plain of Dura, in the province of Babylon. Then he sent messages to all the princes, governors, captains, judges, treasurers, counsellors, and other minor judiciary and all the rulers of the different provinces that they should come to the dedication of this great statue. When all these different officials had arrived and were standing before the statue, a herald shouted out, Oh people of all nations and languages, this is the king's command: when you hear the sound of these instruments all together, the horn, flute, harp, trigon, psaltery, bagpipe and all kinds of music, you are to fall on your face and worship king Nebuchadnezzar's statue. Anyone who refuses to obey will immediately be thrown into a flaming furnace. So when these instruments were all played at once, everyone—whatever his nation, language or religion—fell to the ground and worshipped king Nebuchadnezzar's statue.

COMMENT

v. 1 . . . THE KING MADE AN IMAGE OF GOLD . . . Nebuchadnezzar's motive for such a grand undertaking is not stated. It is quite possible that, overcome with pride because of his conquests and influenced by Daniel's identification of him as the head of gold of the great dream-image, the king erected this image to do honor to his gods for victory as well as to do honor to himself.

The image was 60 v 6 cubits (dimensions expressed in terms of Babylonian sexagesimal system), which would measure today 90 x 9 feet. Imposing but not impossible.

It may have been in the form of an obelisk, nine feet in breadth at the base. Grotesque, to be true, but this is characteristic of much of Babylonian sculpture. Diodorus records a statue of a god which was forty feet in height and weighed 1000 Babylonian talents. The Colossus of Rhodes was 70 feet tall. Some of the Buddhist images of Buddha are equally as imposing and grotesque.

The plain of Dura according to one archaeologist was about 12 miles southeast of the city of Babylon where there is excavated a rectangular brick structure forty-five feet square and twenty five high which may have formed the pedestal of a colossal image. The Babylonian empire was divided into provinces over which "satraps" ruled. This great image was located somewhere in the *province* of Babylon, probably very near the capital city of Babylon.

v. 2-3 THEN NEBUCHADNEZZAR THE KING SENT TO GATHER TOGETHER THE SATRAPS . . . For the formal, dedication of this great golden image Nebuchadnezzar sent RSVP invitations to all of the officials of the kingdom. If all the under-rulers of the realm were there, there would also be a great throng of thousands of people. Such a dedication would have a great psychological effect upon officials and people of the power of the empire and the king. It would bind the empire together in patriotic and religious bonds. In those days practically all nations believed that success in military conquests was attributable to the power of the victor's gods over the gods of the vanquished. If a nation had prevailed over another nation, the thing that happened behind the scenes was that the victorious nation's gods had prevailed over the defeated. The king was merely expecting men to do what men naturally expected to do—pay homage to Babylon's god for many victories. There was no primary intention, on Nebuchadnezzar's part, to practice any religious persecution, or to interfere with anyone's worship of his own gods, or to compel men to accept a new god as their own. In those days all men were expected to practice syncretism in religion. That is, it was taken for granted that they would do homage to the god or gods of any particular nation or culture in which they found themselves. At the same time, they might worship their own particular deity

without fear of interference if they did homage to the local
deity also. In fact, the worship of as many gods as one
might know about was the vogue of the day.

In the list of Babylonian officials we have three, perhaps four, of the official terms of office in the Persian
language. So many Persian titles some fifty years before
the Persians ruled the world proves rather disconcerting at
first glance. Consider, however, the fact that Daniel lived
well into the Persian empire and was a man of great stature
in that government. Now Daniel would surely have taken
pains as nearly as possible to bring his book up to date and
to have kept it so in case certain portions had been written
earlier during the days of Babylon. Daniel would not want
to leave his book for a new generation of Jewish exiles in
the Persian era cumbered with a lot of antiquated terms
which would need interpretation for the generation which
knew only Persian terms. The use of Persian words by
Daniel certainly lends no credence to the liberal theory that
an unknown author of the Maccabean era wrote the book
and used the pseudonym, Daniel.

Satrap literally means "kingdom-guardian" and according to Gesenius means, ". . . the governors or viceroys of
the large provinces among the ancient Persians . . . being
in the provinces the representatives of the sovereign, whose
state and splendor they also rivalled." Daniel is using a
Persian term in Nebuchadnezzar's day to describe some
official who would be immediately next to the king in rank
—a "prince" or an immediate lieutenant of the king. Daniel
probably was a *satrap*. The other official titles probably
descend in rank down from the satrap to the sheriff.

v. 4-7 . . . AT WHAT TIME YE HEAR . . . WHOSO FALLETH
NOT DOWN AND WORSHIPPETH SHALL . . . BE CAST INTO THE
MIDST OF A BURNING FIERY FURNACE . . . The individual
musical instruments are enumerated: *cornet* (horn of a
beast made into a musical horn) ; *flute* (to whistle, suggests
an instrument with a shrill sound) ; *harp* (or zither, a
stringed instrument) ; *sackbut* (a triangular board with
short strings which gave off high-pitched notes) ; *lyre* (a
stringed instrument with twenty strings) ; *psaltery* (another
stringed instrument of triangular shape); *dulcimer* (trans-

lated by some "bagpipe" whether like the Scotch or not is
unknown); *and all kinds of music* (may have been percus-
sion instruments of all kinds), from the Greek *sumphonia*
(symphony).

Critics claim that here we find Greek words in the text
of Daniel in the names of at least three of these musical
instruments and therefore, the book of Daniel must have
been written at least as late as Alexander's Greece (approx.
330 B.C.). Leupold offers the most complete argument
against this claim. To assume that Greek words would begin
to appear in Hebrew or Aramaic only after Alexander's
Greek empire had been established is to ignore historical
evidence which points to contacts with the Greeks before
Nebuchadnezzar's time. (a) Relations between Assyria
(which empire preceded even the Babylonian) and Greece
were established already before the bginning of the Assyrian
Empire had its peak; (b) Ionian Greeks established merchan-
tile connections very early as the Assyrian population began
crowding the Semitic peoples toward Asia Minor; (c) From
very early times Sinope (on the Black Sea) was an outpost
of trade between Assyria and Greece; (d) in the Assyrian
army of Esarhaddon (682 B.C.) as well as later in the
Babylonian army of Nebuchadnezzar, Greek mercenary
troops were found; (e) in the very early musical and
philosophical culture of Greece we find influences of Semitic,
Assyrian and Babylonian culture; (f) finally, if Daniel had
been written in the days of Antiochus Epiphanes, it would
be very difficult to explain *why so few words of Greek*
origin occur in the Aramaic of Daniel.

Young writes, ". . . as we know from recent archaeological discoveries, there was not a century of the Iron Age
during which objects of Greek origin, mostly ceramic in
character, were not being brought into Syria and Palestine.
Greek traders and mercenaries were familiar in Egypt and
throughout Western Asia from the early seventh century on,
if not earlier. As early as the sixth century B.C. the coasts
of Syria and Palestine were dotted with Greek ports and
trading emporia, several of which have been discovered during the past five years."

One can imagine the unharmonious din that would be caused at the shrieking, blowing and thrumming of such a diverse collection of instruments. But the "sound" was not intended to furnish a soothing symphony for cultured critics. It was to serve as a very impressive *signal* that the time had come to worship the king's image.

The *furnace* was probably a furnace used commercially as a lime-kiln, or brick-kiln. Eastern potentates of that day were accustomed to practice methods of cruel punishment for the slightest disobedience to their commands. Refusal to do homage to the image, since it was erected by the king and for his glory, would be regarded as equivalent to treason to the state. No heathen of any race or language would have scruples against doing homage to another god or image since it simply involved the acknowledgement that the gods of Babylon were at that time more powerful than their own gods. But for devout Jews to worship this statue would have been a violation of the first principle of their religion that there is a Living God and He is One God and The Only True God.

A traveller of some three centuries ago (1671-77) by the name of Chardin went to the territory of Persia and noted that two furnaces of fire were kept burning for a month for consuming those who overcharged for food.

The religious implications of this event are rather incidental compared with the political significance. Yet the Jews who were firm in their faith had no alternative but to desist.

The question always arises, where was Daniel? The following text indicates that only the three Hebrew companions of Daniel were arrested and thrown into the furnace of flaming fire. As a matter of fact, we do not know why there is no mention of Daniel in this chapter, and it is pure conjecture to state otherwise. We would conjecture, however, that Daniel might have been on some official mission away from the immediate vicinity of the Plain of Dura and his mission was of such importance that his presence at the great image was excused by the king.

The love of the Babylonians for music is recorded in Isaiah 14:11; Psalms 137:3; Herodotus 1:191.

QUIZ

1. What was the size of the image made by Nebuchad-nezzar?
2. Where is the Plain of Dura?
3. What is a satrap?
4. What is a dulcimer?
5. What kind of furnace was probably to be used for traitors?
6. Why would doing homage to a new god not bother any heathen of that day?

b. PERNICIOUS DENOUNCEMENT

TEXT: 3:8-12

8 Wherefore at that time certain Chaldeans came near, and brought accusation against the Jews.
9 They answered and said to Nebuchadnezzar the king, O king, live for ever.
10 Thou, O king, hast made a decree, that every man that shall hear the sound of the cornet, flute, harp, sackbut, psaltery, and dulcimer, and all kinds of music, shall fall down and worship the golden image;
11 and whoso falleth not down and worshippeth, shall be cast into the midst of a burning fiery furnace.
12 There are certain Jews whom thou hast appointed over the affairs of the province of Babylon; Shadrach, Meshach, and Abed-nego; these men, O king, have not regarded thee: they serve not thy gods, nor worship the golden image which thou hast set up.

QUERIES

a. Who were the Chaldeans who brought accusation?
b. Why their accusation?

PARAPHRASE

During this very time some of the Chaldeans, the leading class of court wisemen, came before the king and maliciously accused the Jews of disobedience to the king's edict.

They said, O king, Hail, live forever! You made a royal decree that everyone must fall down and worship the golden image at the signal of all the musical instruments playing together. Your edict was that anyone who refuses will be thrown into a flaming furnace. But there are some Jews—Shadrach, Meshach, and Abednego—whom you have put in places of high position of government in the province of Babylon, who have defied you and they refuse to serve your gods and to worship the golden image you set up.

COMMENT

v. 8 . . . CERTAIN CHALDEANS . . . BROUGHT ACCUSA-TION . . . The "Chaldeans" as we learned before were a prominent class of court astrologers or wisemen (cf. 2:2ff). They held high positions of influence in government and, as in almost every human organization—especially civil structures, there is a great amount of jealousy and status seeking. There is a common Semitic expression in the Aramaic text here which translated literally reads, ". . . they devoured the pieces of the Jews . . ." and would be better translated, ". . . they accused the Jews with malice aforethought . . ." Jealousy and envy over the quick promotion and success of the Hebrew youths motivated the Chaldeans throughout. Their wounded vanity and unreasoning jealousy is made to look like a patriotic disclosure as the words of accusation fall from their lips.

v. 9-12 . . . CERTAIN JEWS . . . SERVE NOT THY GODS . . . The accusation is also made to sound like a charge of ingratitude. Here the king has honored these men by appointment to high office and they will not even so much as return the honor by doing homage to the golden image the king has made.

QUIZ

1. Why do we think the accusation against the Jews was motivated by envy?
2. How did the Chaldeans make their accusation sound patriotic?
3. Why do we think they made the charge sound like the Jews were ungrateful?

119

c. PROFESSION OF DEDICATION

TEXT: 3:13-18

13 Then Nebuchadnezzar in his rage and fury commanded to bring Shadrach, Meshach, and Abed-nego. Then they brought these men before the king.

14 Nebuchadnezzar answered and said unto them, Is it of purpose, O Shadrach, Meshach, and Abed-nego, that ye serve not my god, nor worship the golden image which I have set up?

15 Now if ye be ready that at what time ye hear the sound of the cornet, flute, harp, sackbut, psaltery, and dulcimer, and all kinds of music, ye fall down and worship the image which I have made, well: but if ye worship not, ye shall be cast the same hour into the midst of a burning fiery furnace; and who is that god that shall deliver you out of my hands?

16 Shadrach, Meshach, and Abed-nego answered and said to the king, O Nebuchadnezzar, we have no need to answer thee in this matter.

17 If it be so, our God whom we serve is able to deliver us from the burning fiery furnace; and he will deliver us out of thy hand, O king.

18 But if not, be it known unto thee, O king, that we will not serve thy gods, nor worship the golden image which thou hast set up.

QUERIES

a. What did Nebuchadnezzar mean by his question to the three youths?

b. Why did they "have no need to answer" the king in this matter?

c. Does their answer exhibit a lack of faith in God?

PARAPHRASE

Then Nebuchadnezzar, in a furious rage, ordered Shadrach, Meshach, and Abednego to be brought in before him. As incredible as it is, is it still true, he asked, O Shadrach, Meshach, and Adebnego, that you are refusing to serve my gods or to worship the golden image I set up? There must be some misunderstanding on your part so I will give you one more chance. When the musical instruments are played, giving the signal, if you fall down and worhip the statue, all will be well. But if you refuse, you will be thrown into a flaming furnace within the hour. And what god can deliver you out of my hands then? The three Hebrew youths replied, O Nebuchadnezzar, if we went into lengthy explanations you would not understand, therefore, there is no need for us to make such an answer. Either our God will deliver us and the issues will then be cleared up—for our God is well able to deliver us from any circumstances—or else, for reasons best known to Him, He will not deliver us. But in either case, please understand, O King, we will not alter our position nor serve your gods nor worship the golden image which you set up.

COMMENT

v. 13-14 . . . NEBUCHADNEZZAR IN HIS RAGE AND FURY COMMANDED TO BRING SHADRACH, MESHACH, AND ABED-NEGO . . . The king is incredulous! He cannot believe that anyone would defy his royal edict—least of all three foreigners placed in such high positions by his special favor. Their apparent ingratitde shocked him at first and then spurred him into a furious rage. The pharse "Is it of purpose . . ." would be better translated "Is it true . . ." At least the king is fair enough to give the three men an opportunity to answer for themselves. Nebuchadnezar must have recognized the envy and jealousy behind the accusations made by the Chaldeans.

v. 15 NOW IF YE BE READY . . . BUT IF YE WORSHIP NOT . . . The king is also ready to give them a second chance to obey the royal edict. But that is all. If they do not worship the next time they hear all the musical instruments giving the signal to do so, they shall be speedily (that very hour) cast into the flaming furnace. Then, boastingly, what god can protect you from my power? It would seem that Nebuchadnezzar had already seen sufficient evidence of the power of the Hebrew God that he would have spoken with some restraint. But it is easy to forget if one does not believe with all the heart in the first place.

v. 16-18 . . . WE HAVE NO NEED TO ANSWER THEE IN THIS MATTER . . . This is not an answer of insolence. It is an answer of reality. The Hebrew lads know that due to the king's spiritual ignorance and blindness extensive explanations of their reasons for obedience to Jehovah-God and disobedience to paganism would be useless. There is no need of lengthy explanations because either God will deliver them from the fire and the whole issue of who is the most powerful, Nebuchadnezzar or Jehovah, will be cleared up, or else, for reasons best know to God, he will not deliver them from the fire. In either case, they are not going to worship the image of Nebuchadnezzar. They were wholly committed to the will of God as they knew it. Whatever the consequence of obeying His will, they were persuaded it would serve His purposes. They have no revelation that God will certainly work a miracle on their behalf and protect them from the furnace. All they know is that His word prohibits worshipping idols and His word promises divine approval and salvation ultimately to those who commit themselves to doing His will. These Hebrew lads did not lack faith in God. They exemplify the most complete, unreserved faith of the Old Testament saints.

QUIZ

1. Why did Nebuchadnezzar give the Hebrew lads a second chance?
2. What is Nebuchadnezzar's boast?
3. Is the answer of the Hebrew lads one of fatalism or faith?
4. Did the Hebrew lads know God was going to deliver them miraculously?

d.   PERFECT DELIVERANCE

TEXT: 3:19-25

19   Then was Nebuchadnezzar full of fury, and the form of his visage was changed against Shadrach, Meshach,

and Abed-nego: therefore he spake, and commanded that they should heat the furnace seven times more than it was wont to be heated.

20 And he commanded certain mighty men that were in his army to bind Shadrach, Meshach, and Abed-nego, and cast them into the burning fiery furnace.

21 Then these men were bound in their hosen, their tunics, and their mantles, and their outer garments, and were cast into the midst of the burning fiery furnace.

22 Therefore because the king's commandment was urgent, and the furnace exceeding hot, the flame of the fire slew those men that took up Shadrach, Meshach, and Abed-nego.

23 And these three men, Shadrach, Meshach, and Abednego, fell down bound into the midst of the burning fiery furnace.

24 Then Nebuchadnezzar the king was astonished, and rose up in haste: he spake and said unto his counsellors, Did not we cast three men bound into the midst of the fire? They answered and said unto the king, True, O king.

25 He answered and said, Lo, I see four men loose, walking in the midst of the fire, and they have no hurt; and the aspect of the fourth is like a son of the gods.

QUERIES

a. Why heat the furnace seven times hotter than before?
b. What caused the soldiers of the king to fall into the flames?
c. Who was the fourth person in the furnace?

PARAPHRASE

Then Nebuchadnezzar was filled with fury and his face was distorted with rage. At once he commanded that Shadrach, Meshach, and Abednego be bound by certain of his most powerful soldiers and thrown into a flaming furnace which he had ordered to be fired up seven times hotter than it was before. The three Hebrew youths were then bound up securly hand and foot with all their fine regalia of boots, leggings, caps and robes on, and cast into the very center

123

of the flaming furnace. Driven by the fury of the king's anger, the soldiers were in such haste they did not take precautions concerning the intensity of the leaping flames and as they shoved the Hebrew lads into the furnace they themselves were burned to death by the flames. After the three Hebrew lads had fallen into the furnace, king Nebuchadnezzar bent over to look into the aperture but he rose to his feet quickly with astonishment on his face. He said to his counsellors, Did we not cast three men bound hand and foot into that flaming furnace? They answered, Indeed we did, O King. Then Nebuchadnezzar said, Look! I see four men loose, walking around in the middle of that inferno, and none of them are burned. The fourth man in there is like a son of the gods.

COMMENT

v. 19-21 . . . COMMANDED THAT THEY SHOULD HEAT THE FURNACE SEVEN TIMES MORE THAN IT WAS WONT TO BE HEATED . . . Their vow of resolution after being offered a second chance angered the king to the extreme. He was hot with anger. His face was distorted with rage. His command to heat it "seven times more . . ." is a figure of speech much like our "ten times as much" or "hundred times more." It would be impossible to measure precisely when the heat was exactly seven times greater.

The furnaces resembled our present day lime kilns. They were stone or brick, open at the top and approachable by an elevated path or inclined plane because the kiln was built against a hillside from which the approach was made. At the bottom there must have been an opening that was large enough to enable men to peer into the flames if they stooped or got down on their knees.

The three Hebrew lads had appeared, evidently, at this occasion of state dressed in their finest apparel. Ordinarly, their finery would be stripped off before committing them to the furnace. In this case, however, due to the urgency of the king's command, the victims were taken just as they were, bound hand and foot, and cast into the roaring inferno.

The description of their apparel begins with boots, trousers, caps and ends with robes. They were cast into the flames fully clothed. Clothing would serve as extremely combustible fuel to feed the flames and serve to make the burning-up of the persons faster.

v. 22-23 . . . BECAUSE THE KING'S COMMANDMENT WAS URGENT, AND THE FURNACE EXCEEDING HOT, THE FLAME OF THE FIRE SLEW THOSE MEN . . . The king's order given with furious rage written all over his countenance and pouring forth from his mouth spurred his powerful soldiers to careless and fatal haste. They rushed headlong toward the opening of the furnace on the top close enough to hurl their victims in but they went too close and the leaping, licking flames, roared out from that inferno many times hotter than ever before and burned the soldiers to death. They succeeded, however, in casting the Hebrew men into the very center of that furnace. The fact that the soldiers were burned to death instantly when they merely came close to the flames and the fact that the Hebrew men did not even have the smell of smoke upon them makes this miracle most outstanding.

v. 24-25 . . . DID WE NOT CAST THREE MEN . . . INTO THE . . . FIRE? . . . LO, I SEE FOUR MEN . . . WALKING IN THE . . . FIRE . . . AND THE . . . FOURTH IS LIKE A SON OF THE GODS. The king took up a position at a safe distance from the furnace, yet at a vantage point where he could stoop down and peer inside through the opening at the bottom of the furnace. His furious rage at being disobeyed by, in his estimation, these ingrateful Hebrews caused him to want to witness their execution. But instead of seeing them writhing in agony as they are roasted alive, he sees a scene which utterly astounds him! It is so astonishing he is incredulous. He asks his counselors for confirmation of the number of men cast into that inferno for he has counted an extra one. He sees, in fact, six amazing things. (1) he sees not three but four; (2) they are not bound but free; (3) they are not lying down or standing still but walking about; (4) they are not being consumed by the fire but are unhurt; (5) the appearance of the fourth was like unto a son of the gods; (6) they were not frantically searching for a way of escape, but were evidently calmly resigned to let their God handle the situation.

The statment of Nebuchadnezzar, ". . . like a son of the gods. . ." concerning the fourth person he saw in the furnace is to be expected from a pagan king. The KJV translates the king's statement, ". . . like the Son of God," but that is not gramatically defensible. The literal meaning is ". . . son of deity," and the Aramaic, in reproducing the sense of Nebuchadnezzar's statement does so by the language of paganism. What the king saw was a being with supernatural qualities and appearance. The king was impressed with this being's divine appearance and its superhuman abilities but speaks as a typical heathen when he likens the fourth person to a "son of the gods." We believe the fourth person was an angel of the Lord, whether one of the angels of high rank or not is uncertain (cf. Dan. 10:13, 21, regarding Michael, the arch-angel). To hold that the fourth person was the pre-incarnate Son of God robs the incarnation, in our estimation, of its uniqueness and seems to contradict plain teaching of scripture that the appearance of the Son of God took place uniquely at His birth by the virgin Mary and His subsequent life (cf. John 1:1-18; Heb. 1:1-14). In the passage in Hebrews 1:1-14 we are told of God's previous ministry to the fathers through the agency of angels and this is to emphasize the uniqueness of the ministry of the Son "in these last days." God did many things through the agency of angels. We will discuss angels in a Special Study in connection with chapter ten.

QUIZ

1. Why was Nebuchadnezzar full of fury? How angry was he?
2. How hot was "seven times more than it was wont to be heated?"
3. Why were the soldiers burned to death?
4. Why mention the apparel of the three Hebrew men?
5. Name six things which caused the king to be astonished?
6. Who was the fourth person "like a son of the gods?"

e. PHILANTHROPIC DECREE

TEXT: 3:26-30

26 Then Nebuchadnezzar came near to the mouth of the burning fiery furnace: he spake and said, Shadrach, Meshach, and Abed-nego, ye servants of the Most High God, come forth, and come hither. Then Shadrach, Meshach and Abed-nego came forth out of the midst of the fire.

27 And the satraps, the deputies, and the governors, and the king's counsellors, being gathered together, saw these men, that the fire had no power upon their bodies, nor was the hair of their head singed, neither were their hosen changed, nor had the smell of fire passed on them.

28 Nebuchadnezzar spake and said, Blessed be the God of Shadrach, Meshach, and Abed-nego, who hath sent his angel, and delivered his servants that trusted in him, and have changed the king's word, and have yielded their bodies, that they might not serve nor worship any god, except their own God.

29 Therefore I make a decree, that every people, nation, and language, which speak any thing amiss against the God of Shadrach, Meshach, and Abed-nego, shall be cut in pieces, and their houses shall be made a dunghill; because there is no other god that is able to deliver after this sort.

30 Then the king promoted Shadrach, Meshach, and Abed-nego in the province of Babylon.

QUERIES

a. Why did Nebuchadnezzar call the Hebrew men out of the furnace?

b. How did the Hebrew men "change the king's word?"

c. Does the King's decree mean he now believes in Jehovah?

PARAPHRASE

Then Nebuchadnezzar came as close as he could to the opening in the flaming furnace and shouted, Shadrach, Me-

shach and Adebnego, you servants of the Most High God,
Come out of there and Come here! So they came out of
the furnace and approached the king.   Then a great company of the king's princes, governors, captains, and counsellors crowded around them and saw that the fire had not
even touched the Hebrew men—not a hair of their heads
was singed; their shoes were not even scorched; there was
not even the slightest smell of smoke on their persons!
Then the king said, Blessed be the God of Shadrach, Meshach, and Abednego, for he sent his angel to deliver these
servants who trusted him completely.   By their trust and
miraculous deliverance they have caused the king to cancel
his decree concerning their execution.   Their determination
to be true to their God and not serve other gods was manifested when they willingly submitted their bodies to be
burned alive.   Therefore, I make this new decree, that any
person of any nation, language, or culture who speaks a
word against the God of Shadrach, Meshach, and Abednego
shall be hacked limb from limb and his house publicly desecrated.   No other God can do what this God does! So the
king, from that time forward, favored these Hebrew young
men and they were successful and prosperous because of
the king's favor.

COMMENT

v. 26-27 . . . CAME FORTH OUT OF THE MIDST OF THE
FIRE . . . THE FIRE HAD NO POWER UPON THEIR BODIES . . .
Nebuchadnezzar saw that in spite of his royal authority and
in spite of his having physically committed the Hebrew
men to the furnace and in spite of the intensity of the
flames these men were not going to be consumed.   There
was nothing left for the king to do but admit defeat and
call them forth from the furnace.   Stationing himself at
a safe distance from the furnace he yelled over the roar of
the flames that they should come out and stand before him.

As they stood before the king a great company of the
king's officials gathered around them and were utterly
amazed that not a hair on their head was singed and there
was not even the slightest smell of smoke upon them.   The
shoes with which they walked upon the white-hot coals were

not scorced at all. Daniel wants to be understood by his future readers that a large body of reliable witnesses satisfied themselves as to the perfect deliverance from certain death experience by these three Hebrew men. Deliverance was so complete and supernatural that their clothing did not even smell of fire or smoke. Under natural circumstances one who has been anywhere near a fire will bear the odor of smoke on his person or clothing.

v. 28 NEBUCHADNEZZAR . . . SAID, BLESSED BE THE GOD OF SHADRACH, MESHACH, AND ABED-NEGO . . . Nebuchadnezzar has not only witnessed with his own eyes a stupendous physical miracle of deliverance but he has also been touched by the whole-hearted faith of these Hebrews. The king's immediate reaction is a word spoken in praise of the God of these Hebrews.

Yet, his manner of designating God as the God of Shadrach, Meshach, and Abednego, is the manner of a heathen polytheist. The king is merely admitting that their God, compared to other gods, has distinguished Himself by manifesting a power that is greater than any other god. So far it has not even occurred to the king to confess the Hebrew God as the Only True God and to denounce pagan gods as false.

That fourth person seen in the furnace by the king and formerly called by him "a son of the gods" is now called "His angel" by the king. This is to be expected since Babylonian religion was replete with doctrines of angels, demons, helping spirits and the like. As to the whereabouts of this fourth person we assume it returned to its heavenly abode.

Note the various impressions made on Nebuchadnezzar by these Hebrew men: (1) the complete "trust" or faith they had in their God—such faith has impressed more than one heathen potentate; (2) their deliverance had overruled the decree of the powerful Nebuchadnezzar—he was forced to admit defeat; (3) they were willing to surrender their physical bodies to apparent excruciating death by being burned alive rather than worship pagan deities.

Note further in his decree the king does not deny his own national gods but simply makes a decree in a negative way that no one should speak any thing remiss (error or falsehood that would tend to lead the minds of men astray in regard to the things they have seen the God of the Hebrews demonstrate). Nebuchadnezzar does not decree, in a positive sense, that Jehovah is to be worshipped as the one and Only God.

The king's promised punishment for violation of this decree is exactly like that pronounced upon his own magicians should they fail to tell him his dream (cf. ch. 2).

v. 30 THEN THE KING PROMOTED . . . Leupold says the word "promoted" does not mean they were advanced to a new office in the structure of government but the word means the king "supported and favored them so that their position was made easier and their work more successful in spite of the opposition of those that begruged them their success."

Keil notes that the incidents recorded in this chapter teach us "how the true worshipers of the Lord under the dominion of the world power could and would come into difficulties, imperiling life, between the demands of the lords of this world and the duties we owe to God. But we also learn that, if in these circumstances they remain faithful to their God, they will in a wonderful manner be protected by Him; while He will reveal His omnipotence so graciously that even the heathen world rulers will be constrained to recognize their God and give Him glory." (See our sermon at the end of this chapter for similar remarks).

QUIZ

1. Where was the king when he called for the Hebrew men to come out?
2. What happened to the fourth person in the furnace?
3. Why did Daniel note the many people who surrounded the Hebrew men upon their exit from the furnace?
4. What is the significance of mentioning that they did not even smell of fire?
5. Name at least three things about the Hebrew men's faith that amazed Nebuchadnezzar.
6. Why do we think the king is not a true believer in Jehovah?
7. What does this chapter teach us for today?

SERMON NUMBER THREE
"FOUR IN A FIERY FURNACE"

Text: Daniel 3

INTRODUCTION

I. CHAPTERS TWO AND THREE ARE CONNECTED

    A. Second chapter showed final outcome of growth and success of WORLD-POWER—the world-power must eventually crumble

    B. Yet, while its power lasts, must it not be feared by God's own because of the harm it can and will do to God's saints?

    C. Chapter Three answers, NO! He that is with us is greater than he that is with them!

II. CHAPTER THREE A STUMBLING BLOCK TO UN-BELIEVERS

    A. Farrar calls the chapter "historic fiction"

        1. Then he says its purpose is "to inculcate the noblest truths . . ."

        2. and he says "always regarded it as one of the most precious among the narrative chapters of Scripture."

        3. also . . . "it is not only superb in its imaginative grandeur, but still more in the manner in which it sets for the piety of ultimate faithfulness."

    B. But a purely fictional or mythological deliverance is small comfort to a man who is confronted by a factual peril of death.

    C. If we have no guaranty of the truth of the account, we have no guaranty of the validity of any comfort we may draw from the account.

    D. I believe this is a valid, historically accurate account of a miraculous deliverance from death by fire . . . these were real men and the miracle really happened. It is referred to in Hebrews 11:34 ". . . quenched the power of fire . . ."

III. THERE ARE GREAT LESSONS HERE . . . THERE
HAVE BEEN MANY PARALLELS TO SUCH PERSE-
CUTION AND FAITH

A. There are lessons on religion and the state; faith;
God's power

B. There is one recent parallel in John Noble who
endured 12 years of persecution, lived by faith, and
was miraculously delivered time and again in Russian prison camps.

C. We have outlined the chapter for sermon purpose
thus:

1. Religion and The State 3:1-15
2. Resistance and The Sanctified 3:16-23
3. Rescue and the Sovereign 3:24-30

DISCUSSION

I. RELIGION AND THE STATE 3:1-15

A. Nebuchadnezzar's image

1. Probably after he had completed his major conquests and was feeling the magnitude and
strength of his empire

2. The image maybe copied from his dream to represent world-power established by himself

3. Maybe represented one of his gods since heathen
philosophy was that when they won victory their
gods had triumphed over gods of those they had
defeated

4. It was 90 ft. high and 9 ft. wide, gold-plated
(cf. Isa. 49:19)

5. The sound of such a conglomeration of musical instruments did not exactly sound like a symphony
but they were intended only to give an arresting
signal designed to impress the hearers by their
variety and their volume . . . this they did quite
well

6. Whatever its appearance and regardless of what
is symbolized, all the officials of the kingdom
were commanded to worship it.

B. There are various attitudes world-power has taken toward religion, depending upon the attitudes of the state's governors

  1. All the gods worshipped by others were to be recognized

  2. New ones might be introduced by authority of the state

  3. The gods which the state approved and acknowledged were to be honored by all

  4. If any persons denied their existence, and their claims to homage, they were to be treated as enemies of the state.

  5. These principles are followed even today by world-powers which are heathen, pagan and atheistic (for atheism is a religion and in Russia all who do not worship it are enemies of the state)

  6. Russia has been committed for over 50 years to the proposition that the Living God is a myth; religion an opiate for oppressed working classes; after 1917 revolution 2/3 of all clergymen in Russia were executed; 4/5 of all church buildings closed or turned into museums for instruction in "scientific atheism." A prisoner related to John Noble his trial. After sentencing to 25 yrs. hard labor in Siberia his judges laughed and asked him if he believed in God; the prisoner replied he certainly did; the Russian judge then pointed to a picture of Stalin hanging on the wall and said, "That is our God, and the only God we have." BUT THREE YEARS LATER THEIR GOD WAS DEAD—DISHONORED IN DEATH AS SOON AS HIS BODY WAS COLD! China is even worse in its deification of Mao Tse Tung!

  7. The three Hebrew children were experiencing the results of world-government perverting its God-ordained purpose . . . it was dictating what man should worship rather than protecting man's liberty to worship as he pleased.

C. The only proper attitude of world-power toward religion:

133

1. There is to be, on the subject of religion, perfect liberty to worship God in the manner that shall be most in accordance with the views of the individual himself, PROVIDED IN DOING IT HE DOES NOT INTERFERE WITH THE RIGHTS OR DISTURB THE WORSHIP OF OTHERS. State is not merely to tolerate exercise of religion, for toleration implies that state has right of control which it does not —the word is liberty.

2. The state is to protect all in the enjoyment of these equal rights. Its authority does not go beyond this. Its duty demands this.

3. For this reason Christians need to beware of their zeal to insist that the government take action to restore religion to the public school system. Forcing the government to such action might force the government to make laws regarding the establishment of a state-controlled religion.

4. A nation cannot be Christianized by force; and a Bible verse a day will not keep immorality away.

5. We should never expect the public school to do the job that parents and churches must do. We've been passing the buck for too long.

6. In Connellsville, Pa., citizens have taken the law into their own hands and defied the Supreme Court and the Constitution. Prayer is *compulsory* there now, no matter what the Supreme Court said. In fact, the Lord's Prayer and ten verses of Scripture are required each day, the same rite which was declared unconstitutional by the U.S. Supreme Court in 1963.

7. HOW CAN CHRISTIAN PEOPLE, WHO ARE CONSTANTLY BEWAILING THE BREAKDOWN OF LAW AND ORDER IN SOCIETY, DISREGARD THE HIGHEST COURT IN THE U.S.? EVEN IF WE DISAGREE, DOES THAT GIVE US THE PREROGATIVE TO DISOBEY? DO WE "RENDER UNTO CAESAR" ONLY WHEN WE AGREE WITH CAESAR?

8. What the Supreme Court outlawed was state-controlled religious worship and requiring young people to worship in a way that was contrary to their consciences . . . IN FACT, CHILDREN CAN STILL READ THEIR BIBLES . . . TEACHERS CAN READ BIBLES TO THE CLASS FOR EDUCATIONAL PURPOSES . . . BUT LET US NOT INSIST UPON STATE-CONTROLLED RELIGION!!!

II. RESISTANCE AND THE SANCTIFIED 3:16-23

A. Upon what basis did the three young men refuse to worship Nebuchadnezzar's idol?
  1. Whole-hearted belief in the Living God
     a. Whole-hearted belief is an intelligent belief. Not one of emotion alone.
     b. It is not obstinancy. Obstinancy is where a man has made up his mind, and resolves to act, without any good reason or investigation of the evidences
  2. Unhesitating determination to DO what is right. Not what is expedient or popular, or lucrative, BUT WHAT IS RIGHT
  3. With such convictions we will always do our God-given duty regardless of the consequences and put our trust in God believing that if He pleases He can protect us from danger.
  4. There is no need for saying more than they said to the king. They believe that God will either deliver them and the issues will then be cleared up, or, for reasons best known to Him, He will not be able to deliver them—even at that they will not alter their position for even in their death they believe God's purposes will be served.
  5. They were thrown into a fiery furnace whose heat was so hot it consumed the men who got close enough to throw them in.
B. When the pride of world-power is wounded or its authority threatened and it is not founded on the principles of the God-ordained liberties of its constituents, it persecutes.

1. The three Hebrew youths were thrown into a fiery furnace whose heat was so hot it consumed the soldiers who were throwing them in
2. John Noble writes: "I have seen Christianity under the most terrible persecution it has suffered since the days of Nero . . . and I am convinced it was God's will that I be a member of that persecuted Church for several years in order to testify that God is with it and is sustaining it."
3. Brutal whippings; starvation for 15 days; solitary confinement for days in dungeons; working long hours in 50-70° below zero weather; 9000 people died of disease and starvation in 3 years in one camp alone; women raped and abused by guards; men sadistically tortured. One man, to keep from being sent to the mines, put his hand on a stool palm down, took a hatchet and chopped off all four fingers—the guards came and took the delirious man to the camp infirmary where the stumps were trimmed and sewed up without anasthetic and threw him in the dungeon for 60 days for sabotage.

C. The viciousness and beastiality of the persecutions some of the sanctified have been called upon by the Lord to endure are almost beyond human comprehension

1. The early saints under Nero and successors: lighted as human torches to illuminate his chariot races; women and babies and old men unarmed thrown to face lions starved to death; forced to fight gladiators; made slaves and treated in most despicable manner
2. The true believers who were persecuted by a Roman church which had become united with the state: hacked to pieces, hanged, torn limb from limb on a rack, flogged to death with a whip.
3. Modern saints persecuted by Nazis, Communists in Russia, China and Cuba, and even here in the U.S.

4. "Indeed all who desire to live a godly life in Christ Jesus will be persecuted. . ." 2 Tim. 3:12

5. ". . . a servant is not greater than his master . . . if they persecuted me, they will persecute you . . ." John 15:20

6. "persecution arises on account of the word . . ." Mt. 13:21

7. "You have need of endurance, so that you may do the will of God and receive what is promised . . ." Heb. 10:36

III. RESCUE AND THE SOVEREIGN 3:24-30

A. ". . . the Lord knows how to rescue the godly from trial, and to keep the unrighteous under punishment until the day of judgment . . ." II Pet. 2:9

1. The 3 Hebrew youths were rescued by an angel (not the Son of God) but some supernatural being sent by God. Nebuchadnezzar got the shock of his life. Not only were the 3 not harmed nor was there even upon them the smell of smoke but there was a FOURTH MAN IN THE FURNACE!

2. Peter writes, ". . . the eyes of the Lord are upon the righteous, and his ears are open to their prayer . . . Now who is there to harm you if you are zealous for what is right?" He continues, ". . . it is better to suffer for doing right, if that should be God's will, than for doing wrong."

3. We are not to be surprised at any fiery ordeal for it has come to prove us . . . we are to rejoice to be able to share in Christ's sufferings because we know the spirit of glory and of God rests upon us. I Pet. 4:12ff Therefore let those who suffer according to God's will do right and entrust their souls to a faithful Creator.

4. God has not promised to deliver every suffering saint by a miracle from physical harm. But it is better that we should not fear him who is able to destroy the body, but Him who is able to destroy both body and soul in hell.

5. We should not expect exact and perfect judgment to be enacted upon earth while we live here.

6. If the righteous were never persecuted, poor, hungered, many would believe not in God but in the "loaves which fill their bellies."

7. While it is proper for God to miraculously save some saints in order to demonstrate His faithfulness—it would not be proper for Him to save all and thus have many coming to Him simply for the reward and not for the sake of who He is

B. Examples of deliverance

1. John Noble tells of a cell-mate of his father's in prison camp. This cell-mate was terrified he might be placed in a cell with non-christian. He miraculously stayed with Noble's father. He was starving to death and dying of disease—got down to 80 lbs. and could not even eat what little food they had. He constantly called for wife and daughter. Noble and has father prayed earnestly that the dying man might receive some word about his family. Very next day, a man from his home town, a neighbor was assigned to the very next cell. Upon receiving news that his family was safe, this man prayed, thanking God, and saying he was now ready to die if it was God's will. BUT HE BEGAN TO IMPROVE, REGAINED HIS HEALTH, AND TWO YEARS LATER WAS RELEASED AND REJOINED HIS WIFE AND DAUGHTER.

2. J. Russell Morse's accounts of prison and deliverance are accounts of modern day acts of the providence of God in rescuing his saints.

3. You have heard of others, I am sure. THERE IS NO DOUBT ABOUT IT—GOD KNOWS HOW TO RESCUE THE GODLY FROM TRIAL!

4. But, it is not always God's purpose to rescue from physical harm. Sometimes His purpose is better served by suffering and death. WHAT WE MUST BELIEVE AND TRUST IS THAT WHEN GOD'S PURPOSES ARE SERVED IN OUR LIVES, WE WILL ALWAYS BE VICTORIOUS. "Rejoice and be exceedingly glad when men shall persecute you and say all manner of evil against you for my names sake, for so persecuted they the prophets before you."

CONCLUSION

NEBUCHADNEZZAR'S REACTION REMINDS ME OF ONE OF JOHN NOBLE'S MOST TOUCHING STORIES Date: November, 1950. Place: Vorkuta slave labor camp. Three nuns, of which church and order Mr. Noble was uninformed, assigned to work at making bricks for construction work throughout the whole Arctic area of Russia.

The nuns told their guards they regarded doing any work for the communist regime as working for the Devil and they were servants of God and they were not going to work despite any threats they might make.

They were put on punishment rations—black bread and rancid soup, day after day. Each morning they were ordered to go out to the clay pits in the brick factory and each morning they refused. They were placed in strait jackets—hands tied in back of them, then the rope with which their wrists were bound was passed down around their ankles and drawn up tight—their feet were pulled up behind them and their shoulders wrenched backward and downward into a position of excruciating pain. NOT A SOUND OF PROTEST ESCAPED THEIR LIPS.

Then the commandant ordered water poured over them so that the cotton material in the strait jackets would shrink . . . they moaned softly and lapsed into unconsciousness. This was done more than once. Kept in this state for 2 hours.

The commandant decided they were either going to work or he was going to have to kill them in the attempt to make them do so. They would not so he ordered that they be taken out in the bitter wind of the Arctic winter and left to stand there immobile all day long to watch the other women work. The guard went over expecting to see them frozen to death but found them kneeling, praying, relaxed and warm.

At this the commandant ordered their gloves and caps be removed so they would be exposed to the full fury of the wind. All through the 8 hour day they knelt on that windy hilltop in prayer. Three days in a row they were thus exposed—and while those working with boots and caps and

139

gloves were complaining of frostbite and frozen feet—not one indication of frostbite could be found in the nuns.

News of what was happening spread throughout the camp. Everyone was murmuring that indeed God had brought a miracle to pass. Even hardened MVD men found excuses to come by the brick factory and take a furtive look at the three figures on the hill. Women working down in the pits crossed themselves and nervously mumbled prayers. Even the commandant was sorely disturbed. IF NOT A RELIGIOUS MAN, HE WAS AT LEAST A SOMEWHAT SUPERSTITIOUS ONE AND HE KNEW WELL ENOUGH WHEN HE WAS WITNESSING THE HAND OF A POWER THAT WAS NOT OF THIS EARTH!

By the fourth day, the guards themselves were afraid of the unearthly power they were witnessing and they flatly refused to touch them or have anything more to do with them. The commandant was afraid to go and order them out into the hill any more. So they were not disturbed in their prayers, and were taken off punishment rations.

When I left Vorkuta 4 years later, those nuns were still at the brick factory and none of them had done a day's work for the communist regime. They were regarded with awe and respect. The guards were under instructions not to touch them or disturb them. They were preparing their own food and even making their own clothes. Their devotions were carried on in their own way and they seemed at peace and contented. Though prisoners, they were spiritually free. NO ONE IN THE SOVIET UNION HAD SUCH FREEDOM OF WORSHIP AS THEY!

Later on, when I had the opportunity as a locker-room attendant for the MVD men to talk with some of the more hardened Russian Communists about religion, not one failed to mention the Miracle of the Nuns.

YES, GOD KNOWS HOW TO DELIVER THE GODLY.

EXAMINATION THREE

REFUTATIONS

(Answer the following by giving the argument which will correct the statement)

1. This image of Nebuchadnezzar was erected because of God's command to do so. Refute!
2. The three Hebrew friends of Daniel did not worship the image, but Daniel did. Refute!
3. The fourth person Nebuchadnezzar saw in the fiery furnace was Jesus Christ. Refute!

ASSOCIATIONS

(Associate the person or thing of column 1 with the correct parallel of column 2)

1	2
dulcimer	location of the image
image	Cyrus
Meshach	Abed-nego
hosen	Daniel
angel	Mishael
satrap	tree
sheriff	bagpipe
Dura	triangular board instrument
cubit	kingdom guardian
furnace	Nebuchadnezzar
sackbut	kiln
	lesser official
	boots
	a son of the gods
	city of Babylon
	measurement

MEMORIZATIONS

(Fill in the blanks:)

Nebuchadnezzar spake and said, Blessed be the _____ of Shadrach, _____, and Abed-nego, who hath sent his _____, and delivered his servants that _____ their bodies, that they might not _____ nor _____ any god, except their own God.

141

EXPLANATIONS

1. Explain the probable reason Nebuchadnezzar commanded that all people worship his image.
2. Explain why they had the Hebrew men thrown into the fiery furnace.
3. Explain how the guards were consumed by the fire.
4. Explain the deliverance of the three Hebrew youths.
5. Explain the reaction of Nebuchadnezzar to this miracle.

CHAPTER FOUR

I. DESPOT'S DISGRACE—4:1-37

a. EMPEROR'S EPHEMERAL EXCURSION AND EDICT

TEXT: 4:1-6

1 Nebuchadnezzar the king, unto all the peoples, nations, and languages, that dwell in all the earth: Peace be multiplied unto you.
2 It hath seemed good unto me to show the signs and wonders that the Most High God hath wrought toward me.
3 How great are his signs! and how mighty are his wonders! his kingdom is an everlasting kingdom, and his domain is from generation to generation.
4 I, Nebuchadnezzar, was at rest in my house, and flourishing in my palace.
5 I saw a dream which made me afraid; and the thoughts upon my bed and the visions of my head troubled me.
6 Therefore made I a decree to bring in all the wise men of Babylon before me, that they might make known unto me the interpretation of the dream.

QUERIES

a. Is it possible that Nebuchadnezzar would make such a humiliating confession?

b. Was Nebuchadnezzar now converted to the God of Israel?
c. Why did the king's dream make him afraid?

PARAPHRASE

This is the proclamation of Nebuchadnezzar the king which he sent to the whole world—to people of every nation and language that dwelt in all the earth—May your peace be multiplied. I consider it necessary and proper at this time to publicly announce to you the great and marvelous signs and wonders which the Most High God has done toward me. They were incredible—the miraculous dreams and experiences—surely demonstrating that his kingdom is everlasting and his dominion is over all of mankind forever. I, the great emperor, Nebuchadnezzar, was dwelling in luxury, contentment, safely and secure in my great palace, when one night I had a dream that terrified me and caused me great agitation of soul. So I called in all the wise men of Babylon and ordered that they tell me the meaning of my dream.

COMMENT

v. 1-2 NEBUCHADNEZZAR THE KING, UNTO ALL THE PEOPLES . . . There are many who would deny the historicity of this chapter. Their arguments revolve around two points (a) alleged lack of historical confirmation in records outside the Bible; (b) alleged intrinsic improbability. The critics say (1) other O. T. historical books do not mention the insanity of Nebuchadnezzar (2) there is no record of this event among heathen writers of antiquity (3) Josephus had no information except the O.T. when he wrote of this event (4) Origen and Jerome could find no historical grounds for this event (5) If these things had happened, Nebuchadnezzar would have made sure they were recorded permanently so how come they are absent from Babylonian records? (6) If the record of the event was lost how was the event ever known, recovered and recorded by Daniel?

Let us consider these alleged discrepancies in order: (1) There are thousands of events of, not only Nebuchadnezzar's life, but hundreds of other important persons concerned with Israel which are not recorded in the historical books of the O.T. None of the books of the O.T. pretend to be complete in every detail even of the history of Israel. An argument from the silence of other O.T. books is no argument at all against the record of Daniel; (2) for that matter, the argument from the silence of profane historians is no argument against the record of Daniel—*only if there were profane records stating that such an event never happened would there be an argument against Daniel.* But, as a matter of fact, there are two historians of antiquity who mention certain events in the life of Nebuchadnezzar which support the historicity of Daniel's record: Berosus and Abydenus. Berosus was a Chaldean, and a priest in the temple of Belus, during the days of Alexander the Great. Abydenus (268 B.C.) was a pupil of Berosus. Berosus wrote three books relative to the history of the Chaldeans, of which only some fragments are preserved in Josephus and Eusebius. Both these writers derived their knowledge from the traditions of the Chaldeans, and both should be regarded as good authorities. Berosus mentions "Nabolassar, king of Babylon and of the Chaldeans." He then mentions the expedition of his son, "Nabuchodonosor" (Nebuchadnezzar), against the Egyptians; the capture of Jerusalem; the burning of the temple; and the captivity of the Jews. After these and other statements about the conquests of Nebuchadnezzar and the magnificence of his capital, Berosus gives the following narrative:

> "Nabuchodonosor, after he had begun to build the forementioned wall, fell sick and departed this life when he had reigned forty-three years, whereupon his son, Evil-Merodach, obtained the kingdom."

This quotation may be found in Josephus vs. Apion. It confirms the account of Daniel: (1) in referring to some sickness in the case of Nebuchadnezzar that was unusual which probably preceded, for a considerable time, his death, and, (2) this statement of Berosus accords, in respect to *time,* remarkably with that in Daniel inasmuch as both accounts agree that the sickness occurred after he had built Babylon, and towards the close of his reign.

144

The other quotation, that of Abydenus, is found in the works of Eusebius:

"After these things (Nebuchadnezzar's conquests) as it is said by the Chaldeans, having ascended his palace, he was seized by some god, and speaking aloud, he said: 'I Nebuchadnezzar, O Babylonians, foretell your future calamity, which neither Belus, my ancestor, nor queen Beltis, can persuade the destinies to avert. A Persian mule will come, employing your own divinites as his auxiliaries; and he will impose servitude upon you. His coadjutor will be the Mede, who is the boast of the Assyrians. Would that, before he places my citizens in such a condition, some Charybdis or gulf might swallow him up with utter destruction! Or that, turned in a different direction, he might roam in the desert (where are neither cities, nor footsteps of man, but wild beasts find pasturage, and the birds wander), being there hemmed in by rocks and ravines! May it be my lot to attain to a better end, before such things come into his mind!' Having uttered this prediction, he forthwith disappeared."

The points of agreement between Abydenus and Daniel in the matter of the Babylonian's insanity or sickness are amazing: (1) The sickness or seizure occurred after Nebuchadnezzar's conquests and sometime before his death; (2) In both Daniel and Abydenus, the king is on the top of his palace; (3) The king was seized by some divinity, (and it is worthy of note that Abydenus does not ascribe the seizure to either an idol or to any god worshipped by the Chaldeans, but to God simply, as to a God that was not known); (4) in the language which Neb. is reported by Abydenus to have used respecting the return of the Persian king after his conquest, there is a remarkable resemblance to what is said in Daniel. How did such a prediction concerning Cyrus come to be attributed to Nebuchadnezzar?—the only reasonable conclusion is that this tradition has its origin from certain factual events involving Nebuchadnezzar's insanity—thus Daniel's account and that of Abydenus both have their origin in a factual event. There are things in both the statements of Berosus and Abydenus which cannot be accounted for except on the assumption of the truth of such an occurrence as that which is stated in the historical record of Daniel.

v. 3 HOW GREAT ARE HIS SIGNS! . . . The destructive critics claim this edict is "historically absurd" because it makes Nebuchadnezzar appear to be too familiar with Biblical phraseology, (cf. Psa. 145:13). However, with the impact of Daniel's extensive influence as third in the kingdom it is neither "absurd" or incredible that the Babylonian king's vocabulary in addressing Daniel's God would have such familiar phrases in it. Furthermore, it is altogether possible that Nebuchadnezzar requested the direct assistance of Daniel in phrasing this edict. Still further, excerpts from the Babylonian psalms and other literature often remind one of Biblical psalms.

This edict sheds interesting light, as Young puts it, "upon the open, magnanimous character of the great king." One thing is evident as the character of Nebuchadnezzar unfolds itself in Daniel's narrative, this pagan king is not nearly so biased and prejudiced and close-minded as many unbelievers today who have less reason to be so. Nebuchadnezzar was shaken by his experience! He was impressed as he had never been before! If he, the mightiest monarch who had ever ruled to that time, could be rendered so totally impotent and incompetent then the only noble or honest thing to do was to admit it. Perhaps the element of fear was also a strong motivation for Nebuchadnezzar's doxology.

One thing the king had to admit, no human king thus far was so mighty that he could prolong his own reign if Daniel's God willed it otherwise. And it was very apparent that the rule of Daniel's God was everlasting and omnipotent. The history of the world since the days of Nebuchadnezzar confirms this great fact! All earthly rulers die; all authority lodged in the hands of earthly monarchs is soon withdrawn; and not one of them can insure that his authority will extend even to the next generation.

v. 4-6 . . . I SAW A DREAM WHICH MADE ME AFRAID
. . . The mighty king was "at rest" which indicates more
precisely that he was feeling secure and completely free
from apprehension. His wars were over; his kingdom was
tranquil and prosperous beyond his fondest dreams. He
had built a magnificent city; gathered about him the wealth
and the luxuries of the world and now he was preparing to
while away the remainder of his life enjoying it all.

The word translated "afraid" is even stronger than
"terrified." He was literally petrified with fear. Although
he did not at first understand the dream, he was well enough
versed in signs and portents to understand that the falling
of so mighty a tree signified some mighty overthrow. And
even afterward he reflected upon the dream as he lay in
his bed, his consternation increased. The wierd and exaggerated visions of the dream kept flashing before his
mind's-eye as he thought about its meaning.

The very first thing that morning when he arose the
king sent with all haste an official decree that all the wise-
men and seers of the nation's capital should be summoned
to the palace to interpret his dream for him.

QUIZ

1. What is the answer to the attack upon the historicity
of chapter 4 by critics who point to the silence of the
other O.T. books and profane history about Nebuchadnezzar's insanity?
2. What is a probable explanation to the biblical phraseology of Nebuchadnezzar's edict concerning the greatness and everlastingness of God?
3. What does "at rest" indicate concerning the king's
circumstances before his dream?
4. Why would this mighty monarch be "afraid?"
5. Why did the king call for his wise-men?

b. RULER'S REVERIE RELATED, PART I

TEXT: 4:7-12

7 Then came in the magicians, the enchanters, the Chaldeans, and the soothsayers; and I told the dream before

147

them; but they did not make known unto me the interpretation thereof.

8 But at the last Daniel came in before me, whose name was Belteshazzer, according to the name of my god, and in whom is the spirit of the holy gods: and I told the dream before him, saying,

9 O Belteshazzar, master of the magicians, because I know that the spirit of the holy gods is in thee, and no secret troubleth thee, tell me the visions of my dream that I have seen, and the interpretation thereof.

10 Thus were the visions of my head upon my bed: I saw, and, behold, a tree in the midst of the earth; and the height thereof was great.

11 The tree grew, and was strong, and the height thereof reached unto heaven, and the sight thereof to the end of all the earth.

12 The leaves thereof were fair, and the fruit thereof much, and in it was food for all: the beasts of the field had shadow under it, and the birds of the heavens dwelt in the branches thereof, and all flesh was fed from it.

QUERIES

a. What does Nebuchadnezzar understand about "the spirit of the holy gods?"

b. Was Daniel a "magician"? Doesn't the Law of Moses forbid this?

c. Why did God choose to use a "tree" in Nebuchadnezzar's dream?

PARAPHRASE

But when they came in—all the scholars, astrologers, wise-men, and diviners—and I told them the dream, they could not interpret it. At that moment Daniel came in—the man I named Belteshazzar after my god—the man in whom is the spirit of the holy deity, and I told him the dream. O Belteshazzar, chief of the wise-men, I said, know that the spirit of the holy deity is in you and no secret is too difficult for you—behold! my dream that I have seen. Tell me what my dream means: I was dreaming and suddenly I saw a tree right in the center of the world all by itself and its height was very great. The tree was growing and becoming strong, and its height was reaching higher and higher into the sky until it could be seen by everyone in the world. Its leaves were fresh and green, and its branches were weighted down with fruit, enough for everyone to eat; wild animals rested beneath its shade and birds from all over the sky rested in its branches and all the people of the world were nourished from it.

COMMENT

v. 7 THEN CAME IN THE MAGICIANS . . . ETC. All these titles refer to the same general class of persons—those considered to be endued with superhuman wisdom; who were supposed to be qualified to explain remarkable occurrences, to foretell the future, and to declare the will of the gods from dreams, signs and wonders. It is not strange to find the occult in that age when there was yet a limited revelation; when so much of the world's population dwelt in darkness and self-induced moral perverseness (cf. Rom. 1:18ff); and when the boundaries of science were not as extended as they are today. But in the age of enlightenment —with the Christian revelation and explosion in scientific knowledge—it is almost incredible that so many people today are becoming enmeshed in the superstitious and credulous web of the occult. Popular songs ("Aquarius") and books by the thousands are hawking the wares of the "mystic revolution" all over the 20th century world. One weekly U.S. news magazine estimates that 10 million Americans are "hard-core adherents" to astrological forecasting. Another 40 million, it reported, dabble in the subject: "It appears clear that what was once regarded as an offshoot of the occult is a rapidly evolving popular creed," it said. One American magazine publisher puts out some 30 separate horoscope magazines. During 1968 it sold 8 million copies of one edition. The executive editor of Doubleday & Co., said in the N.Y. Times of August 11, 1968, "American publishers have discovered of late that there is a great deal of money to be made in convincing readers that the fault is not in themselves but in their stars . . . The public in-

terest has been way ahead of the publisher's response . . .
People in general want to read about these things. After
all, there is the possibility of discovering the meaning of life.
We can't get enough good books on the subject."

"In astrology," says the president of a well-known
astrological organization, "the earth is at the center of the
universe and the individual is the center of attention.
Everybody's favorite topic is himself." A 22-year-old Boston
girl put her finger on this point when she said, "Astrology
. . . is a very personal tying of the individual to the universe.
Science led us away from God and now science (meaning
astrology?!) will bring us back." The astrologer holds out
the vision of a world ruled by forces operating with clock-
work regularity. These forces supposedly guide the individual to greater heights of achievement—they help him
succeed, attain, understand. When things go wrong,
one can blame the stars. When good things happen, you
thank your lucky star. Astrologers tell people what they
WANT to hear. The thing that is so incredible is that 20th-
century-man would have laughed at the way the soothsayers
and diviners exploited the superstitions of Nebuchadnezzar,
not realizing that they are being exploited in the same way
today. Nebuchadnezzar learned that in the God of Daniel,
Jehovah-God—the God who has revealed Himself in history
by miraculous deeds and direct propositional revelations in
human language to selected prophets, is the only source of
immutable truth. AND THAT IS STILL TRUE FOR 20TH-
CENTURY-MAN! Daniel's God is omnipotent and immutable
—He changeth not!

v. 8 . . . AT THE LAST DANIEL CAME IN . . . IN WHOM
IS THE SPIRIT OB THE HOLY GODS . . . Why Daniel was not
with the other wise-men when they came into the presence
of the king we do not know. Leupold suggests two possi-
bilities: (a) he may have been busy assemblying the wise
men and could not come earlier; (b) he may have chosen
to defer his coming, timing it carefully to coincide with the
moment when the failure of the Chaldeans was most evident.

Most commentators insist that Nebuchadnezzar's statement, "in whom is the spirit of the holy gods," is an explicit expression of his polytheism. However, Young believes

that the phrase is only rightly interpreted when the word "god" is made singular, "god" or "deity," as in our paraphrase. The king was very much aware that the God of Daniel was different from his own gods, so, he reasons, "The power or wisdom which is from the highest deity is to be found in Daniel." Young says there is "a wealth of philological evidence (linguistic material) to support" the position of a singular "god," (cf. Gen. 41:38).

v. 9   O BELTESHAZZAR . . . TELL ME . . . THE INTERPRETATION . . . It is evident from the following context that the emperor does not this time insist that Daniel relate to him the content of the dream, for the emperor tells Daniel the details of the dream. He wants Daniel to tell him the meaning of the symbolism he dreamed.

For comments on Daniel's Babylonian name, Belteshazzar, see our notes on 1:7. Leupold claims that the translation "chief of the magicians" does not accurately represent to the modern mind the position of Daniel. In our day "magicians" are thought of as purveyors of "slight of hand" magic. This meaning was never connected with the Greek word *magoi* from which we get the word "magician" or, as the *magi* (wise-men) in the account of the birth of Christ. Leupold thinks a better translation would be "chief of the scholars."

We are informed of the absolute confidence Nebuchadnezzar had in Daniel's possession of divine wisdom! This does not seem to be for the purpose of proving to the king that Daniel has such abilities (as in Daniel 2). It almost seems as if the king had deliberately refused to hear Daniel until he was forced by necessity to turn to him as a last resort. Young believes that this is actually the case—"If others can interpret the dream, he will go to them rather than to Daniel. With this God, Nebuchadnezzar, as yet wanted no dealings." Calvin also believes that it was "extreme necessity" which compelled the ruler to turn to Daniel for interpretation of his dream. "And hence we gather that no one comes to the true God, unless impelled by necessity." (Calvin) It is most certainly true that no one comes to God by accident! We are convinced more and more that most unbelief is due to moral resistance, not to intellectual ignorance. Every man has sinned and sinned because he deliberately chose to resist the moral light he possesses! (Romans, chapters 1, 2, and 3 and Jn. 3:19-21)

v. 10-11 . . . I SAW, AND, BEHOLD, A TREE IN THE MIDST OF THE EARTH . . . The phrase is progressive. The king was contemplating or studying the dream as he was dreaming. Not only so, but the tree was in the process of growing as he was dreaming. This tree was occupying a central position on the earth. Its centrality was to indicate its preeminence and importance for the entire earth. It grew until it reached into the sky, towering to the heavens, sending out its branches afar. It was a "sight" to behold to everyone in the earth.

Trees were figurative, especially in Oriental dreams, of monarchs. Ezekiel 31:3ff compares the Assyrian monarch with a cedar of Lebanon (cf. also Ezek 17:1ff; Isa. 2:13; 10:18-19; Jer. 22:7, 23). Barnes notes, "Nothing is more obvious than the comparison of a hero with a lofty tree of the forest, and hence it was natural for Nebuchadnezzar to suppose that this vision had a reference to himself." Herodotus relates a dream of Xerxes, who, ready to set out against Greece, beholds himself crowned with an olive shoot, the branches of which stretch out over all the earth; of Croesus that he will destroy the men of Lampascus "like a fir" since this tree when cut down, sends forth no fresh shoots, but dies outright; of Astyages the Mede who dreamed of a vine growing from the womb of Mandane, his daughter, and spreading over the entirely of Asia, the vine being Cyrus. This should in no way imply that the dream of Nebuchadnezzar was not unique. The record of Daniel is plain to indicate that the Babylonian monarch's dream was a divinely imposed dream, a revelation from God. It was supernaturally imposed—it was unique.

v. 12 . . . AND IT WAS FOOD FOR ALL . . . All who lodged in the tree found fruit upon it. All living things on the earth are represented as finding sustenance and security in this great, towering, affluent tree. A really imposing sight! But this is not all of the dream. And what perplexed the king most was the remainder of the reverie!

QUIZ

1. What is so surprising about finding a popularity of the occult today?
2. What is meant by "the spirit of the holy gods?"
3. What confidence did Nebuchadnezzar have in Daniel's abilities?
4. Why did the king wait until the last resort to seek Daniel's interpretation?
5. How great was the "tree" in the king's dream?
6. Why would this portion of the dream not be so perplexing to the king?

c. RULER'S REVERIE RELATED, PART II
TEXT: 4:13-18

13 I saw in the visions of my head upon by bed, and, behold, a watcher and a holy one came down from heaven.

14 He cried aloud, and said thus, Hew down the tree, and cut off its branches, shake off its leaves, and scatter its fruit: let the beasts get away from under it, and the fowls from its branches.

15 Nevertheless leave the stump of its roots in the earth, even with a band of iron and brass, in the tender grass of the field; and let it be wet with the dew of heaven: and let his portion be with the beasts in the grass of the earth:

16 let his heart be changed from man's, and let a beast's heart be given unto him; and let seven times pass over him.

17 The sentence is by the decree of the watchers, and the demand by the word of the holy ones; to the intent that the living may know that the Most High ruleth in the kingdom of men, and giveth it to whomsoever he will, and setteth up over it the lowest of men.

18 This dream I, king Nebuchadnezzar, have seen; and thou, O Belteshazzar, declare the interpretation, forasmuch as all the wise men of my kingdom are not able to make known unto me the interpretation; but thou art able; for the spirit of the holy gods is in thee.

153

QUERIES

a. Who are the "watchers" and "holy ones?"
b. Why leaven "the stump of its roots" in the earth?
c. What are the "seven times" which are to pass over him?

PARAPHRASE

Then as I lay there dreaming, I saw a divine guardian descending from the heavens. He was shouting, Cut down this great tree; trim off its branches; shake off its leaves, and scatter its fruit. Get the animals out from under it and drive the birds from its branches, but leave its stump and roots in the ground, banded with a chain of iron and brass, surrounded by the tender grass. Let the dews of heaven drench him and let him eat grass with the wild animals! For a certain period of time let him have the mind of an animal instead of a man. This sentence upon the tree is decreed by the divine guardians and is no idle fancy but a divine revelation of an impending fact. The purpose of that which is decreed is to show men everywhere that there is one Ruler who is higher than the highest among men, the Most High, and that He rules over all the kingdoms of men. The Most High gives rule of the nations to whomsoever He will. He prefers to use those who are humble to rule over nations and men, and deposes the proud and arrogant. And now, O Belteshazzar, this is what I, king Nebuchadnezzar have dreamed. Declare to me speedily what all this means. No one else can help me; all the wisest men of my kingdom have failed me. You alone can tell me because the spirit of deity is in you.

COMMENT

v. 13   I SAW . . . A WATCHER . . . A HOLY ONE . . . Some divine vigilante or divine guardian (an angel) manifested himself (perhaps more than one, cf. v. 17) to the king. Angels are called watchers in the religion of Zoroaster so it may be that a pagan king is using the term familiar to him concerning divine apparitions although it is more likely a simple, straigthforward description of what he saw. Angels are vigilant ones—they keep guard unceasingly (cf. Heb. 1:14; Matt. 18:10; see also our special study on *Angels* in connection with chapter 10 of this commentary). This is the only portion of scripture in the whole Bible where angels are called by the name "watcher" but even this title is descriptive of part of their ministry even as is the word "angel". The king earlier described the manifested divine being he saw in the fiery furnace as "one like a son of the gods" (cf. 3:25). Some way or another the angel exhibited its supernatural nature to the king and he was impressed.

v. 14   HE CRIED ALOUD, . . . HEW DOWN THE TREE . . . The divine vigilante suddenly shouted loudly and confidently, to someone (probably other divine beings), Cut down this towering, proud tree.   Drastic, complete demolition of the tree is commanded—even to stripping it of its leaves and fruit and the scattering of all life depending upon it.   As great and impressive as this tree is, so also, great was the fall thereof (cf. Matt. 7:24-27).   One commentator has remarked on the scattering of animals and birds . . . "a lively image of subjects alarmed by the fall of their sovereign . . ."

v. 15-16 . . . LEAVE THE STUMP . . . LET IT BE WET WITH . . . DEW . . . LET HIS PORTION BE WITH THE BEASTS IN THE GRASS . . . LET HIS HEART BE CHANGED FROM MAN'S . . . Just as unexpected as the complete demolition of the tree earlier, now comes the command to leave "the stump" indicating the possibility of reviving the tree. Furthermore the "stock of its roots" is to be left indicating there shall be something left of this particular tree which may again grow.   The "band of iron" probably refers, as Keil says, "to the withdrawal of free self-determination through the fetter of madness," (cf. Ps. 107:10; Job 36:8).   This is the insanity referred to in our comments on 4:1.

From now on it seems as if the angel has stopped speaking in symbolic figures and is, for all practical purposes, interpreting some of the particulars of the fulfillment of this dream. "Let him be wet," changes the subject from the tree to the man.   This man shall find himself in such an insane state, like a dumb animal, that he shall not

155

know enough to keep under cover at night.   It will even
be his lot to share with cattle the grass they eat.   Robert
Wilson, in *Studies in The Book of Daniel*, quotes from a
work entitled *Dictionary of Psychological Medicine*, "the
complete loss of personal identity, and the conviction of
being changed into one of the lower animals, accompanied
frequently by a corresponding belief on the part of the
beholders, is one of the most remarkable facts which the
psychological history of the race reveals."   In the same
book a well-accredited case is cited of a man who imagined
himself to be a wolf, and attempted to act like one.   This
phenomenon of man imitating animal in a state of mental
illness is called lycanthropy.   To all intents and purposes
he behaves as a beast would behave, thus it is expressed
as being changed in heart from a man to a beast.   It is
obvious that the physical heart is not meant.

This state is to continue until "seven times shall pass
away over him."   This could mean seven years.   But in a
book like this, where the symbolical use of numbers stands
out so prominently, the emphasis obviously rests on the
seven as depicting some complete, fully-determined period
of time, known to God and purposely begun and terminated
by God—not necessarily seven years.   Dispensationalists see
in this a period of humiliation of seven years for Nebuchadnezzar which in turn symbolizes the end of the Gentile age
(that is, the period between Christ's coming *for* ["the
rapture"] and His coming *with* ["the judgment"] His
saints).   This period is supposed to be for seven years, and
is that which most dispensationalists identify as Daniel's
70th week (see 9:24ff).   Allis, in *Prophecy and The Church*,
comments that the dispensational interpretation of Daniel 4
shows the extremes they are prepared to carry their interpretations to in order to establish their doctrines.   Daniel
plainly indicated that this dream applied directly and exclusively to Nebuchadnezzar and was completely fulfilled
in the strange and tragic experience through which the king
personally and individually passed.   The dispensationalists
see in the "tree" the type of Gentile domination, and in the
cutting down of the tree the judgment of the apostate
professing-church at the end of this age, after the rapture
of the true Church.   The "seven times" become the seven

year interval between the rapture and the appearing; and Nebuchadnezzar's changed attitude is regarded as foreshadowing the millennium.

v. 17-18 THE SENTENCE IS BY THE DECREE OF THE WATCHERS . . . By this statment the king is informed positively that the dream he had had is no idle and meaningless fancy on his part, but it is a divine revelation of an impending fact to be accomplished in his own person. But the most significant part of this entire event is the purpose for which it is designed—"to the intent that the living may know that the Most High ruleth in the kingdom of men, and giveth it to whomsoever he will . . . etc." And it is a lesson for all men of all ages, inscribed in the archives of history, that there is one Ruler which is higher than the highest among men—the Most High (cf. Isa. 10:5ff; Jer. 27:5-7). Babylon, and especially as it was in the days of the proud and arrogant Nebuchadnezzar, came to symbolize the pride and the spirit of arrogance and rebellion of world power against God. So this dream and its fulfillment portrays that the pride of the world power will receive its just recompense of reward. We shall have more to say on this in following chapters.

After stating the content of the dream, the king, somewhat appealingly, commands Daniel to interpret it. The king appeals again to his confidence in Daniel's superior abilities over the other wise men of Babylon for it is evident to the king that Daniel is in possession of "the spirit of deity."

QUIZ

1. What does the term "watcher . . . a holy one" signify about the person who announced to Nebuchadnezzar his dream?
2. What does the "hewing" down of the tree signify?
3. What does the leaving of the stump signify?
4. What does leaving it to be wet with dew signify?
5. What does "let his portion be with the beasts in the grass" signify?
6. Is it possible for people to be insane enough to act like animals?

7. What is the purpose of this dream and its fulfillment to the person of Nebuchadnezzar? to all men of all ages?

d.   RULER'S REVERIE REVEALED, PART I

TEXT: 4:19-23

19   Then Daniel, whose name was Belteshazzar, was stricken dumb for a while, and his thoughts troubled him. The king answered and said, Belteshazzar, let not the dream, or the interpretation trouble thee. Belteshazzar answered and said, My lord the dream be to them that hate thee, and the interpretation thereof to thine adversaries.

20   The tree that thou sawest, which grew, and was strong, whose height reached unto heaven, and the sight thereof to all the earth;

21   Whose leaves were fair, and the fruit thereof much, and in it was food for all; under which the beasts of the field dwelt, and upon whose branches the birds of the heavens had their habitation:

22   it is thou, O king, that are grown and become strong; for thy greatness is grown, and reacheth unto heaven, and thy dominion to the end of the earth.

23   And whereas the king saw a watcher and a holy one coming down from heaven, and saying, Hew down the tree, and destroy it; nevertheless leave the stump of the roots thereof in the earth, even with a band of iron and brass, in the tender grass of the field, and let it be wet with the dew of heaven; and let his portion be with the beasts of the field, till seven times pass over him;

QUERIES

a. Was Daniel's "dumbness" natural or miraculous?
b. Why did Daniel want the dream to be applied to the king's enemies?
c. Why was Daniel unafraid to tell the king the true interpretation?

PARAPHRASE

Then Daniel, whose Babylonian name was Belteshazzar, stood there stunned and silent for a time, aghast at the meaning of the dream. Finally the king said to him: Belteshazzar, do not fear to tell me plainly the interpretation of this dream. Daniel replied: O king, this is a dream that would please your enemies, for what it portends they would surely like to see fulfilled upon you. For this tree you saw growing and becoming strong and its height was reaching into the heavens and which was seen by everyone in the world—whose leaves were fresh and green and branches weighted down with fruit—under which wild animals rested and upon whose branches birds from all over the sky rested—this tree, Your Majesty, is you. For you have grown mighty and great; your greatness and sovereignty extends over all the earth and sea and sky. Then you saw a holy guardian coming down from heaven, saying, Cut down the tree and destroy it; but leave the stump and the roots in the earth surrounded by tender grass, bound with a chain of iron and brass. Let it be wet with the dew of heaven and for a certain period of time let him eat grass with the animals of the field.

COMMENT

v. 19 THEN DANIEL . . . WAS STRICKEN DUMB FOR A WHILE AND HIS THOUGHTS TROUBLED HIM . . . The Holy Spirit gave Daniel the meaning of the dream almost at once and he was overwhelmed immediately by the awesomeness and terrifying nature of the judgment about to come upon the king. In interpreting the dream he had to pronounce a judgment upon this man who had treated him justly and had even promoted him to a position of great influence. There can be little doubt that Daniel was attached to Nebuchadnezzar, and that this attachment was the cause of his agitation of mind. Daniel's hesitancy is, therefore, highly honorable. Daniel was a man who would not violate his conscience at the king's command; but neither would he be unloyal to the king when it was not a matter of conscience. Men who are loyal to God will always be found to be most loyal to kings. Men like Daniel, though they may refuse to comply with the sinful commands of rulers, will be the first to weep for them and pray for them! This was no miraculously induced dumbness nor does it seem to be motivated by paralyzing fear for his own safety—not if Daniel's previous actions are any indication of his courage and faith.

We are not to suppose either that Daniel had any specific, malevolent hatred for the enemies of Nebuchadnezzar. A more correct translation of this phrase would render it, "this is a dream that would please your enemies, for what it portends they would surely like to see fulfilled upon you." Literally it is translated, "The dream is for thy enemies . . ."

The king, aware that something serious and perhaps evil was portended by the dream, yet not possibly aware that it would be so drastic, was gripped with anxiety to know and therefore urged Daniel to speak plainly and freely, without fear, what he knew about this dream. So Daniel begins to relate to the king what God has revealed to His prophet concerning this dream.

v. 20-23 . . . IT IS THOU, O KING . . . For explanation of verses 20, 21, and 23 see notes on 4:9-15. Daniel's recapitulation of the description of the tree and what is to happen to it is almost word for word in the very terms used by the king. Having repeated the description of the dream for the sake of emphasis and impression, Daniel comes to the point with his, "It is you, O king!" Like the prophet Nathan before him ("Thou are the man!") Daniel dares to confront the world's mightiest potentate with the judgment of God.

QUIZ

1. Why was Daniel "stricken dumb?"
2. Was Daniel attached to the king in a sympathetic way? Why?
3. What did Daniel mean by, ". . . the dream be to them that hate thee . . . ?"

e. RULER'S REVERIE REVEALED, PART II

TEXT: 4:24-27

24 this is the interpretation, O king, and it is the decree of the Most High, which is come upon my lord the king:

25 that thou shalt be driven from men, and thy dwelling shall be with the beasts of the field, and thou shalt be made to eat grass as oxen, and shalt be wet with the dew of heaven, and seven times shall pass over thee; till thou know that the Most High ruleth in the kingdom of men, and giveth it to whomsoever he will.

26 And whereas they commanded to leave the stump of the roots of the tree; thy kingdom shall be sure unto thee, after that thou shalt have known that the heavens do rule.

27 Wherefore, O king, let my counsel be acceptable unto thee, and break off thy sins by righteousness, and thine iniquities by showing mercy to the poor; if there may be a lengthening of thy tranquillity.

QUERIES

a. Did the king actually "dwell with the beasts of the field?"
b. How do "the heavens rule?"
c. What is the meaning of "a lengthening of thy tranquillity?"

PARAPHRASE

Your Majesty, the Most High God has decreed—and it will surely happen—that you will be driven from association with sane and normal people and you will live in the fields like an animal, eating grass like an ox, your body wet with dew from staying out in the fields over night. For a definite period of time this will be your condition until you learn that the Most High God rules in the kingdom of men and gives power to rule to anyone He chooses. But inasmuch as the stump and the roots of the tree in your dream were to be left in the ground, it is decreed that you will be restored to sanity and your rule over Babylon will be given back to you; this will be done when you have learned that Heaven is sovereign over all men on the earth. This is true, O king, and if you will take heed to what I am saying to you and repent by ceasing to do evil and do what you know is right, showing mercy to the poor and weak, perhaps God will prolong your present state of peace and security and withdraw this impending judgment.

COMMENT

v. 24-25 . . . TILL THOU KNOW THAT THE MOST HIGH RULETH IN THE KINGDOM OF MEN . . . Daniel specifies in no uncertain terms that the object of his revelation is the king himself. The world's most powerful and magnificent potentate will be driven from normal associations with other men and will be bereft of human rationality. He will literally live like a wild animal—even to eating grass like an ox and living oft-times out in the open. That this is not unheard of among the insane may be thoroughly documented. We ourselves have observed it in some of our modern-day mental institutions. It is plain from the text that Daniel was revealing this malady would be supernaturally induced—it was not from natural causes.

As we observed before, the term "seven times" probably means simply a specific and, in the purpose of God, an adequate time for the accomplishing of God's providential goal—it does not necessarily mean seven years.

The most important part of Daniel's revelation is the focus or purpose of the king's insanity. The intent of the matter is to give mankind, specifically this heathen king and his subjects, and the captive covenant people, a proof that the fortunes of kings and empires are in the hand of Jehovah—that His providence perpetually interposes in the affairs of men, distributing thrones and empires, always for the good of the faithful, but according to His will. This revelation would be especially relevant for the Jews in pagan bondage and slavery. Their spiritual immaturity would cause them to doubt the faithfulness of God to His promised covenant made with their forefathers (Abraham, Isaac, Jacob, Moses, David, etc.). Definite, prophetic, electrifying, empirical evidence was needed that God was able and would, in His own good time, overrule the power of paganism and carry on the fulfillment of His covenant in His faithful people.

"Our God is in the heavens; He hath done whatsoever He pleased" (Psa. 115:3). "The Lord hath prepared His throne in the heavens; and His kingdom ruleth over all" (Psa. 103:9). God governs in the affairs of kingdoms and nations, and the Scriptures declare that the care of Providence extends to the most minute and inconsiderable parts of the creation; and, therefore, much more does it extend to the affairs of men and the fates of kingdoms (cf. Matt. 6:26; Jer. 27:5ff). The Bible expressly asserts the setting up and pulling down of rulers and empires are from God (cf. Psa. 75:2-7). There are many instances in the Bible of God's overruling the conduct of men, even of the wicked, to accomplish His own great designs, when the persons themselves had nothing in view but their own interests. Who could have thought that anything good would come from the murderous, selfish and perverted actions of the brothers of Joseph when they threw him into a pit and sold him into slavery in Egypt? Their only purpose was to get rid of one they envied and hated. But God had a very important purpose—the deliverance of the covenant family and thousands of others. Therefore, Joseph tells his brothers, "It was not you that sent me hither, but God" (Gen. 45:8). See our Special Study Nine, pgs. 93-113, entitled Theo-Ramic Philosophy of History, in *Minor Prophets*, pub. College Press.

v. 26-27 . . . BREAK OFF THY SINS BY RIGHTEOUSNESS . . . The part of the dream depicting the stump of the roots of the tree left in the ground predicted the possibility of Nebuchadnezzar's rule being restored to him conditioned upon his acknowledgment that Daniel's God rules omnipotently. This, as we learn later, is exactly what transpired, (cf. 4:34ff).

Evidently Nebuchadnezzar was guilty of the common fault of monarchs—inequity, tyrannism, violence in dealings with the ruled. He was "missing the mark" (sinning) according to God's moral standards of government. So the prophet of God demands that the king "break with his sins" and practice justice, equity and kindness in the administration of government. There can be no mistaking it that God holds all rulers, pagan and godly, responsible for meeting His moral standards in governing (cf. Amos, chap. 1-2). "Blessed are the merciful, for they shall receive mercy!" If the king shows mercy to the poor and weak, he shall receive mercy from God. There will be, perhaps, an extension of his present time of peaceful and prosperous rule. The promise does not include the withdrawal of judgment of insanity, because the fundamental and overriding sin of Nebuchadnezzar is pride and it appears that he did not pay much heed to this warning by Daniel. In fact, he may have been offended and slightly angered with Daniel— there is no mention of having rewarded Daniel as he had done on similar occasions earlier.

QUIZ

1. Is such insanity as predicted of Nebuchadnezzar impossible?
2. To what extent does God rule in the affairs of kings and empires?
3. Why would God be concerned about the sins of a pagan ruler?
4. Why did Daniel not promise the withdrawal of God's judment of insanity if the king would break with his sins?

f. DESPOT'S DERANGEMENT

TEXT: 4:28-33

28 All this came upon the king Nebuchadnezzar.
29 At the end of twelve months he was walking in the royal palace of Babylon.
30 The king spake and said, Is not this great Babylon, which I have built for the royal dwelling-place, by the might of my power and for the glory of my majesty?

31 While the word was in the king's mouth, there fell a
    voice from heaven, saying, O king Nebuchadnezzar, to
    thee it is spoken: The kingdom is departed from thee:
32 and thou shalt be driven from men; and thy dwelling
    shall be with the beasts of the field; thou shalt be made
    to eat grass as oxen; and seven times shall pass over
    thee; until thou know that the Most High ruleth in the
    kingdom of men, and giveth it to whomsoever he will.
33 The same hour was the thing fulfilled upon Nebuchad-
    nezzar: and he was driven from men, and did eat grass
    as oxen, and his body was wet with the dew of heaven,
    till his hair was grown like eagles' feathers, and his
    nails like birds' claws.

QUERIES

a. Why the mention of the "end of twelve months?"
b. Why was Nebuchadnezzar so proud of Babylon?
c. How was his hair "like eagles' feathers?"

PARAPHRASE

And all that Daniel predicted in his interpretation of
the dream happened to Nebuchadnezzar. One year after
the king had the dream, he was strolling on the roof of the
royal palace in Babylon, and remarking proudly, Behold my
great city of Babylon—the city I have built by my own
skill, power and ingenuity. I built it as my royal residence
and a monument to my own greatness. It is still standing
and I still rule over it! Does this not prove how omnipotent
I am? But as he was in the very act of speaking a voice
from heaven said to him, O king Nebuchadnezzar, this
message is for you: The rule of this kingdom is now going
to be taken from you. You are about to be driven out of
your glorious palace to live with the animals of the fields,
and to eat grass like the oxen for a certain period of time,
until, that is, you finally realize that God rules in the affairs
of men and that it is by His sovereign power and decision
that men are providentially allowed to rule the kingdoms
of the earth. That very hour this prophecy was fulfilled.
Nebuchadnezzar became insane and was hidden somewhere
in his palace and he lived like the animals of the field, ate

grass like an ox, slept out in the open; and his hair grew, became unkempt and as long as eagles feathers; his finger-nails and toenails grew long like birds' claws.

COMMENT

v. 28-30 . . . IS NOT THIS GREAT BABYLON . . . The fulfillment of the predicted judgment verifies with finality the prophetic commission of Daniel. There can be no question in the mind of Nebuchadnezzar after this. Neither should there be any doubt in the minds of the Jewish nation in captivity that Daniel was God's spokesman and that God was active, providentially overruling all the seemingly omnipotent machinations of pagan world power to preserve His covenant people.

The accuracy of Nebuchadnezzar's boast has been re-markably confirmed. Ancient historians, Josephus (quoting Berosus) and Eusebius (quoting Abydenus), wax eloquent about the grandeur of old Babylon. The East India House inscription, now in London, has six columns of Babylonian writing telling of the stupendous building operations which the king carried on in enlarging and beautifying Babylon. He rebuilt more than twenty temples and directed construction work on the docks and defenses of the city. Most of the bricks taken out of Babylon in the archaeological excavations bear the name and inscription of Nebuchadnezzar stamped thereon. One of the records of Nebuchadnezzar sounds almost like the boast which Daniel recorded in verse 30; it reads, "The fortifications of Esagila and Babylon I strengthened and established the name of my reign forever."

Many critical scholars hold that the book of Daniel was not written in the time of Daniel (600 B.C.ff) but that it was composed some four hundred years later, about 168-165 B.C. However, on the basis of the critical view, it is difficult to explain how the supposed late writer of the book of Daniel knew that the glories of Babylon were due to Nebuchadnezzar's building activities. One higher critic, Pfeiffer, sweeps the problem under the rug by simply making the arbitrary statement, "we shall presumably never know" how the writer of Daniel knew that Babylon was the result of Nebuchadnezzar's building projects, as the excavations have proved. This is a very handy, but un-scientific, method of dispensing with facts!

The king's last statement shows that his ulitmate ob-jective was the glorification of his own name—"for the glory of my majesty."

v. 31-32   WHILE THE WORD WAS IN THE KING'S MOUTH . . . The king had not even finished boasting about himself and he was interrupted by a voice from heaven pronouncing execution of the judgment upon him. The administration of the kingdom which he considered to be his exclusive pre-rogative, was taken from him and he was driven to live and act like the beasts of the field. See our comments earlier on the dream, (4:15-16).

v. 33   . . . HIS HAIR . . . LIKE EAGLE'S FEATHERS . . . HIS NAILS LIKE BIRD'S CLAWS . . . This is an additional de-scription of the king's physical state during his insanity. His hair was left to grow naturally, untrimmed, and is aptly described as growing long like eagles' feathers. His fingernails and toenails, uncared for, would also grow to great lengths. This is only natural if he actually lived as the beasts of the field.

Although he was insane and physically grotesque, he was not exposed to the curious gaze of the multitudes, or to harsh treatment, or derision. He did not, evidently, be-come the gazing stock of all that passed by but was, no doubt, confined in the precincts of the royal palace. There he acted like an animal, eating grass, sleeping out on the ground, etc. The affairs of state were, no doubt, carefully taken in hand by his wisemen, princes, and probably by the establishment of a kind of council of ministers—expecting him to return to sanity and resume control of the govern-ment. One commentator cites a number of historical paral-lels to such temporary measures.

QUIZ

1. What would the fulfillment of the dream mean to the Jews?
2. How great and glorious was the city of Babylon?
3. Is there any way to confirm the greatness of Babylon?

4. How are the opinions of the destructive critics proved false by archaeology?
5. What do you suppose Nebuchadnezzar looked like in his state of insanity?
6. Where do you suppose he was confined in his insanity?

g. SOVEREIGN'S SURRENDER

TEXT: 4:34-37

34 And at the end of the days I, Nebuchadnezzar, lifted up mine eyes unto heaven, and mine understanding returned unto me, and I blessed the Most High, and I praised and honored him that liveth for ever; for his dominion is an everlasting dominion, and his kingdom from generation to generation;

35 and all the inhabitants of the earth are reputed as nothing; and he doeth according to his will in the army of heaven, and among the inhabitants of the earth; and none can stay his hand, or say unto him, What doest thou?

36 At the same time mine understanding returned unto me; and for the glory of my kingdom, and my majesty and brightness returned unto me; and my counsellors and my lords sought unto me; and I was established in my kingdom, and excellent greatness was added unto me.

37 Now I, Nebuchadnezzar, praise and extol and honor the King of heaven; for all his works are truth, and his ways justice; and those that walk in pride he is able to abase.

QUERIES

a. To what extent did Nebuchadnezzar's worship of God go?
b. How did the king's understanding return to him?

PARAPHRASE

At the end of the days appointed by the Most High God I, Nebuchadnezzar, surrendered to the sovereignty of the God of Heaven, and my sanity returned to me. Then I praised and worshiped the Most High God and honored The Eternal One. His dominion is everlasting and His rule is sovereign in every age of man to the end of time. All the power of mankind is as nothing when compared to Him. He does whatever He desires and executes His will among heavenly beings and earthly beings alike and no one can stop Him or challenge Him, saying, What do You mean by doing these things? As soon as my reason had returned to me, then my honor and reknown also returned to me as also the glory of my kingdom. My counsellors and court officers sought my leadership again and I was reestablished as head of my kingdom, with even greater honor than before. Now I, Nebuchadnezzar, praise and glorify and honor the King of Heaven, the Judge of all, Whose every act is right and just; for He is able to take those who walk proudly and punish them into the dust!

COMMENT

v. 34-35 . . . I BLESSED THE MOST HIGH . . . The mighty potentate seems to have learned well the lesson God wanted him to learn. There is no reason at all to question the statement of facts made here. The sincerity of his motive will have to await the final judgment when all the secrets of men will be revealed. One thing seems almost certain, Nebuchadnezzar is convinced of the omnipotence of Daniel's God! He admits to God's sovereignty in both the unseen and seen world—and that universally so! There is no potentate among mortals or immortals to be compared with Him, as far as the king is concerned.

It also seems certain that the king is thanking Daniel's God for the restoration of his sanity and his kingdom. This, in itself, is a great condescension on Nebuchadnezzar's part.

v. 36-37 . . . NOW I . . . PRAISE AND EXTOL AND HONOR THE KING OF HEAVEN . . . Nebuchadnezzar was not only restored to full control of the government and so acknowledged by his men of state, but "excellent greatness was added unto me." One is reminded of Job—"And the Lord blessed the latter days of Job more than his beginning . . ." (Job 42:12). Does this act of God indicate some acceptable manifestation of faith by this pagan king? Could we say the pagan king had been converted? We do not know! It would seem proper to believe that God was pleased with the faith of Nebuchadnezzar, however immature and limited it may be. Edward J. Young lists the following in favor of Nebuchadnezzar:

"(a) There is discernable a progress in his knowledge of God (cf. 2:47 with 3:28 and finally with 4:34, 35).
 (b) The king acknowledges the utter sovereignty of God with respect to his own experience (4:37b).
 (c) The king utters true statements concerning the omnipotence of the true God (4:34-35).
 (d) The king would worship this God, whom he identifies as King of heaven (3:37a). These reasons lead me to believe that, although the faith of Neb. may indeed have been weak and his knowledge meagre, yet his faith was saving faith, and his knowledge true."

Compared with the advantages Pharaoh enjoyed and the utter rejection he made of God's will, Nebuchadnezzar had a conversion experience. Certainly Nebuchadnezzar was equally receptive and responsive to the will of God as the King of Nineveh at the preaching of Jonah. To what extent God will accuse or excuse Nebuchadnezzar at the judgment is solely God's prerogative. It is now our blessed privilege to preach the Good News of salvation by faith in Christ. Let us bless God that we do not live in the pagan darkness of the days of Nebuchadnezzar. Perhaps the major purpose served in this incident was to bolster the hope of that faithful remnant of Jews down in Babylon that their God could, and would, overcome and carry out His redemptive, messianic purpose in them soon.

QUIZ

1. Did Nebuchadnezzar really praise the name of Jehovah?
2. Out of what kind of motive did he do so?
3. Was Nebuchadnezzar converted to faith in Daniel's God?
4. What other person would it be interesting to use as a comparison with Nebuchadnezzar?
5. What might be the major purpose of God's acting thus with Nebuchadnezzar?

SERMON NUMBER FOUR

DESPOT'S DISGRACE

Text: Daniel 4:1-37

INTRODUCTION

I. DIFFERENCE IN ATTITUDE IN NEBUCHADNEZ-ZAR NOW THAN IN THIRD CHAPTER
   A. In chapter three the mighty king of Babylon made an image (perhaps resembling himself somewhat)
   1. Everyone was to bow down and worship it
   2. But the Hebrew children wounded his pride by refusing to do so
   3. He arrogantly condemned them to the fiery furnace
   4. But God delivered them
   B. Now, nothing but thoughts of peace are in his heart
   1. Now he extols and praises the God of Heaven......
   2. And Neb. is an old man—not easily changed

II. THIS CHAPTER IS REMARKABLE ALSO IN THAT IT IS A BABYLONIAN STATE DOCUMENT
   A. This is a Statutory Declaration by the king
   1. Obviously quite different in its terms from anything Neb. has declared before
   2. He spoke about Jehovah-God before in chapters 2 and 3 in a sort of respectful salute, as he would any other god
   3. This, however, is a universal, official document with the king publicly bowing his proud neck in submission to Daniel's God
   4. So, here in this 4th chapter, we have this State Document from the archives of Babylon . . . the personal testimony of one of the great monarchs of all history, his own account of how he, a proud self-willed, ruthless tyrant, was brought to repentance before God, and then was restored by the God of all grace.

171

B. This incident is also remarkable in that it shows the amazing patience of God with even a stubborn pagan ruler
   1. God spoke twice before to Neb. in chapter 2 in the dream of the image
   2. God spoke again in the deliverance of the Heb. children from the furnace

III. THIS IS THE KIND OF THING GOD DOES FROM TIME TO TIME IN HISTORY
   A. From time to time God, in history, has reminded the whole human race forcibly of Himself
      The flood, Tower of Babel, Sodom and Gomorrah, Pharaoh Ex. 9:16
   B. The preamble to this declaration (verse 1) is interesting
      1. It is beneficent, "Peace be multiplied unto you."
      2. It is voluntary, "It seemed good to me . . ." it is his own idea
      3. It is experimental. The moment Neb. has had this transforming experience he wants to tell everybody else about it. If you have a full heart your mouth will speak, and if your mouth doesn't speak then your heart is empty.
      4. It is enthusiastic, "How great are his signs"

DISCUSSION

I. THE DREAM DECLARED, 4:4-18
   A. Its effect on Nebuchadnezzar at the first
      1. He was at ease in his house when it happened
         a. This is going back 8 years to the old Neb. in circumstances of security and luxury
         b. Beware of ease and plenty. It is difficult to be prosperous without being proud (later he represents himself boasting about Babylon which he built)
         c. Prosperous and proud, at rest and flourishing, but a stranger to God
         d. THERE IS A DECEITFUL PEACE. GOD ALONE CAN GIVE PEACE, BUT THE DEVIL CAN GIVE A COUN-

TERFEIT OF GOD'S PEACE AND THERE IS A DE-
CEITFUL PEACE THAT LULLS THE SOUL INTO A
FALSE SECURITY:

   e. TO BE UNTROUBLED IS NOT EVIDENCE OF SAFETY:
TO BE PROSPEROUS DOES NOT MEAN THAT ALL IS
WELL.

2. The dream disturbed him (lit. "petrified with fear")

   a. How easily our peace and ease can be disturbed!

   b. Guilty men, of course, are easily frightened.

   c. Shakespeare rightly says, "Conscience doth make cowards of us all"

   d. And, though Neb. did not know what his dream meant, it destroyed his false peace—IT WAS GOD IN MERCY HELPING HIM OUT OF A FOOL'S PARADISE

3. What is he going to do?

   a. He turns to the wrong people—how human this story is!

   b. Men get troubled: their hearts fail them for fear; but they don't go to the messengers of God—THEY RUN TO THE POLITICIANS AND THE PSYCHOLOGISTS, OR THEY TURN TO ANY QUACK WHO HAS ANYTHING TO SAY ON A SOAPBOX

   c. Popular songs "Aquarius" and books by the 1000 are hawking the wares of the "mystic revolution" all over the 20th century world. One weekly U.S. news magazine estimates that 10 million Americans are "hard-core adherents" to astrological forecasting. Another 400 million dabble in the subject. "In astrology," says the president of a well-known astrological organization, "the earth is at the center of the universe and the individual is the center of attention. Everybody's favorite topic is himself." THIS IS WHY PEOPLE WILL GO TO EVERY SOURCE BUT THE BIBLE . . . BECAUSE THE BIBLE DOES NOT FOCUS ON MAN, EXCEPT TO TELL HIM HE IS A SINNER, IT FOCUSES ON GOD AND HIS SON! (cf. Jn. 3:19-20)

B. Content of the dream
  1. The tree
     a. Trees were used to symbolize greatness in world rulers (cf. Ezek. 31)
     b. This is a tremendous tree, a miracle tree, a skyscraper of a tree, so big that all the earth can see it
     c. One cannot help remembering the image Neb. set up in the plain, gold, gleaming, everybody able to see it. All life is dependent upon this tree
     d. Herodotus relates a dream of Xerxes, who, ready to set out against Greece, beholds himself crowned with an olive shoot, the branches of which stretch out over all the earth . . . Coroesus also dreamed that he would destroy the men of Lampascus "like a fir" since this tree when cut down, sends forth no fresh shoots, but dies outright, etc.
  2. The watcher (a divine vigilante) (watching over the affairs of men)
     a. Hew down the tree and watch the hangers on scatter
     b. Leave a stump, possibility of the tree being revived
     c. Bound with band of iron probably refers to withdrawal of free-self-determination through the fetter of madness
     d. In a book entitled *Dictionary Of Psychological Medicine* are these words, "the complete loss of personal identity, and the conviction of being changed into one of the lower animals, accompanied frequently by a corresponding belief on the part of the beholders, is one of the most remarkable facts which the psychological history of the race of man reveals." In the same book a well-accredited case is cited of a man who imagined himself to be a wolf, and attempted to act like one. This phenomenon of man imitating animal is a state of mental illness is called lycanthropy. To all intents and

purposes he behaves as a beast would, thus it is expressed as being changed in heart from a man to a beast.

3. The purpose
   a. It is decreed by the watchers, it is no idle and meaningless fancy or an upset stomach
   b. "to the intent that the living may know that the Most High ruleth in the kingdom of men, and giveth it to whomsoever he will . . . etc." (cf. Isa. 10:5ff; Jer. 27:5-7)
   c. IT IS A LESSON FOR ALL MEN OF ALL AGES, INSCRIBED IN THE ARCHIVES OF HISTORY, THAT THERE IS ONE RULER WHICH IS HIGHER THAN THE HIGHEST AMONG MEN—THE MOST HIGH GOD. THIS WOULD BE MORE APPROPRIATE TO INSCRIBE IN THE MEETING ROOM OF THE UNITED NATIONS THAN WHAT THEY HAVE THERE! ONE WOULD LIKE TO DECLARE THIS IN THE MIDST OF THE KREMLIN!

II. THE DREAM DIVINED, 4:19-27

A. Thou art the man!
   1. Daniel was not too anxious to have to tell the king what it meant
   2. Neb. had treated him justly and had even promoted him, so Dan. might even have been attached to him
   3. Daniel was a man who would not violate his conscience at the king's command; but neither would he be unloyal to the king when it was not a matter of conscience
   4. Men like Daniel, though they may refuse to comply with the sinful commands of rulers, will be the first to weep for them and pray for them!
   5. Daniel dares to confront the world's mightiest potentate with the judgment of God—like Nathan confronted David

B. You shall be driven from among men
   1. Neb. was to dwell with the beasts of the field, and made to eat grass like an ox, and this for a determined time by God

2. The most important part of Daniel's revelation is the focus or purpose of the king's insanity. The intent of the matter is to give mankind, specifically this heathen king and his subjects, and the captive covenant people of God, a proof that the fortunes of kings and empires are in the hand of Jehovah —that His providence perpetually interposes in the affairs of men, distributing thrones and empires, always for the good of the faithful, but according to His will. "Our God is in the heavens; He hath done whatsoever He pleased" Psa. 115:3; "The Lord hath prepared His throne in the heavens; and His kingdom ruleth over all" Psa. 103:9

C. Break off your sins
1. It is possible that Neb. rule might be restored to him
2. Conditioned upon his repentance
3. Cease to do evil—begin to do good ("break off your sins by practicing righteousness), cf. I Jn. 3:7-8
4. IT IS BECAUSE OF SIN THAT GOD'S CHASTENING MUST COME . . . WHAT A PITY WE TALK SO LIGHTLY OF SIN VERY OFTEN, WHEN THE BIBLE MAKES SO MUCH OF IT!
5. Here, with Daniel and Neb., is an example of how God would have preachers preach to sinners
   a. Preach to men out of a heart full of concern
   b. Interpret the ways of God to them—point out their sin if need be
   c. Extend the mercy of God upon His conditions and terms

III. THE DREAM DEMONSTRATED, 4:28-33

A. Nebuchadnezzar was not impressed
1. The accuracy of Neb. boast has been remarkably confirmed. Ancient historians wax eloquent about the grandeur of old Babylon. The East India House inscription, now in London, has six columns of Babylonian writing telling of the stupendous building operations which the king carried on in enlarging and beautifying Babylon.

    a. He rebuilt more than 20 temples

    b. Directed construction work on the docks and defenses of the city

    c. Most of the bricks taken out of Babylon in archaeological excavations bear the name and inscription of Neb. stamped thereon

  2. He had no sooner bragged than the judgment of God fell

B. He was driven from among men

  1. He lost his right mind to such an extent that he did not even know to come in out of the damp nights

  2. He ate grass in his deranged state

  3. He was evidently unattended until his hair grew long (always thought long hair in men and insanity were to be associated) and his nails were long like birds claws

  4. Although he was insane and physically grotesque, he was evidently not exposed to the curious gaze of the multitudes, harsh treatment, or derision. He was, no doubt, confined in the precincts of the royal palace. There he acted like an animal, eating grass, sleeping out on the palace ground. The affairs of state were, no doubt, carefully taken in hand by his wisemen, princes, and perhaps even his son. A number of historical parallels could be cited to such temporary measures.

C. Critics attack this miracle as unhistorical

  1. They say other O.T. historical books do not mention the insanity of Neb. and, there is no record of this event among heathen writers of antiquity

  2. First, there are 1000s of events, of not only Neb. life, but 100s of other important persons concerned with Israel which are not recorded in the historical books of the O.T. None of these books pretend to be complete in every detail even of the history of Israel. An argument from the silence of other O.T. books is no argument at all against the record of Daniel

3. Second, the argument from the silence of profane historians is no argument against the record of Daniel—ONLY IF THERE WERE PROFANE WRITERS STATING THAT SUCH AN EVENT NEVER HAPPENED WOULD THERE BE AN ARGUMENT AGAINST DANIEL

4. As a matter of fact, there are two historians of antiquity who mention certain events in the life of Neb. which support the historicity of Daniel's record: Berosus and Abydenus. Berosus, a Chaldean priest in the time of Alexander the Great. Abydenus (268 B.C.) was a pupil of Berosus. Berosus wrote: "Nabuchodonosor, after he had begun to build the forementioned wall, fell sick and departed this life whe he had reigned 43 years, whereupon his son, Evil-Merodach, obtained the kingdom." Abydenus tells of a prediction of Neb. about insanity for one of his enemies after which his enemies after which Neb. disappeared for a time.

CONCLUSION—4:34-37

I. THE MIGHTY POTENTATE FINALLY SURRENDERS TO HIS SOVEREIGN
   A. There is no reason at all to question the statement of facts made here
      1. The sincerity of his motive will have to await the final judgment when all the secrets of men will be revealed
      2. One thing seems almost certain, Neb. is convinced of the omnipotence of Daniel's God!
      3. He admits God's sovereignty in both the unseen and seen world—and that universally so!
      4. It also seems certain that the king is thanking Daniel's God for the restoration of his sanity and his kingdom.
   B. Does God's restoration of Neb. indicate some acceptable manifestation of conversion by this pagan king?
      1. It would seem proper to believe that God was

pleased with the faith of Neb., however immature and limited it may be

2. Ed. J. Young lists the following in favor of Neb. acceptance of God

    a. There is discernable a progress in his knowledge of God (cf. 2:47 with 3:28 and with 4:34-35)

    b. The king acknowledges the utter sovereignty of God with respect to his own experience

    c. The king utters true statements concerning the omnipotence of the true God (4:34-35)

    d. The king would worship this God, whom he identifes as King of heaven.

3. To what extent God will accuse or excuse Neb. at the judgment is solely God's business. Neb. was as responsive it would seem as the king of Nineveh at the preaching of Jonah.

II. Graham Scrobbie writes:

"Here we take leave of Nebuchadnezzar. How does he bid us farewell? Not only as a sane man but as a converted man. The last thing related of him is the humble public confession which he made, and the noble testimony to the true God, which, for the benefit of all men, he delivered in the edict contained in this chapter. With the restoration of his reason and his kingdom came the regeneration of his soul. There is nothing in this Book more sublime than this testimony of Nebuchadnezzar's. To him light came at eventide, and he turned his throne into a pulpit, and his State papers into sermons, that his erring subjects might learn the wonders of Omnipotence, be led to honor the Most High, and have peace multiplied unto them through His Name. Nebuchadnezzar's testimony is the political message for all earth's kings and rulers until Christ shall come— "GOD RULES." This is the king's final message to the world. "Those that walk in pride He is able to abase." LET US REMEMBER THAT WHEN IT SEEMS TO US THAT THE WICKED PROSPER AND THE RIGHTEOUS SUFFER. THE LORD REIGNETH . . . REJOICE!" AMEN!

EXAMINATION FOUR

REFUTATIONS

(Answer the following by giving the argument which will correct the statement)

1. Nebuchadnezzar believed his dream about the tree to be a sign from the Babylonian wise-men. Refute!
2. Daniel viciously prayed that the king's dream should come true upon his enemies. Refute!
3. This account of such a dream is only another example of pagan mythology which has found its way into the biblical text. Refute!

ASSOCIATIONS

(Associate the person or thing of column 1 with the most nearly correct parallel of column 2; some of column 2 are not correct)

1	2
watcher	king of Babylon
beast's heart	flute
seven times	complete period
tree	Nebuchadnezzar
King of heaven	Daniel
eat grass	Belshazzar
	lycanthropy
	insanity
	angel
	God

MEMORIZATIONS

(Fill in the blanks:)

It had seemed good unto me to show the _____ and _____ that the _____ God hath wrought toward _____. How _____ are his signs! and how _____ are his wonders! his kingdom is an _____ kingdom, and his _____ is from generation to generation.

Now I, Nebuchadnezzar, _____ and _____ and honor the King of _____ : for all his works are _____, and his ways _____ ; and those that walk in _____ he is able to _____ .

EXPLANATIONS

1. Explain the meaning of Nebuchadnezzar's dream as Daniel interpreted it.
2. Explain how the prophecy concerning the king's insanity might have actually happened.
3. Explain what you think the scriptures indicate to be the result in Nebuchadnezzar's relationship of Jehovah-God.

BELSHAZZAR

Midnight came slowly sweeping on;
   In silent rest lay Babylon.
But in the royal castle high
   Red torches gleamed and courtiers cry.
Belshazzar there in kingly hall
   Is holding kingly festival.
The vassals sat in glittering line,
   And emptied the goblets with glowing wine.
The goblets rattle, the choruses swell,
   And it pleased the stiff-necked monarch well.
In the monarch's cheeks a wild fire glowed,
   And the wine awoke his daring mood.
And, onward still by his madness spurred,
   He blasphemes the Lord with a sinful word;
And he brazenly boasts, blaspheming wild,
   While the service courtiers cheered and smiled.
Quick the king spoke, while his proud glance burned,
   Quickly the servant went and returned.
He bore on his head the vessels of gold,
   Of Jehovah's temple the plunder bold.
With daring hand, in his frenzy grim,
   The king seized a beaker and filled to the brim,

181

And drained to the dregs the sacred cup,
    And foaming he cried, as he drank it up,
"Jehovah, eternal scorn I own
    To thee. I am monarch of Babylon."
Scarce had the terrible blasphemy rolled
    From his lips, ere the monarch at heart was cold.
The yelling laughter was hushed, and all
    Was still as death in the royal hall.
And see! and see! on the white wall high
    The form of a hand went slowly by,
And write—and wrote, on the broad wall white,
    Letters of fire, and vanished in night.
Pale as death, with a steady stars,
    And with trembling knees, the king sat there;
The horde of slaves sat huddering chill;
    No word they spoke, but were deathlike still.
The Magicians came, but of them all,
    None could read the flame-script on the wall.
But that same night, in all his pride,
    By the hands of his servants Belshazzar died.

—Heinrich Heine (1820)

CHAPTER FIVE

I. DEGENERATE DESPOT'S DEMISE—5:1-31

a. TERROR

TEXT: 5:1-7

1 Belshazzar the king made a great feast to a thousand of his lords, and drank wine before the thousand.

2 Belshazzar, while he tasted the wine, commanded to bring the golden and silver vessels which Nebuchadnezzar his father had taken out of the temple which was in Jerusalem; that the king and his lords, his wives and his concubines, might drink therefrom.

3 Then they brought the golden vessels that were taken out of the temple of the house of God which was at

182

Jerusalem; and the king and his lords, his wives and his concubines, drank from them.

4 They drank wine, and praised the gods of gold, and of silver, of brass, of iron, of wood, and of stone.

5 In the same hour came forth the fingers of a man's hand, and wrote over against the candlestick upon the plaster of the wall of the king's palace; and the king saw the part of the hand that wrote.

6 Then the king's countenance was changed in him, and his thoughts troubled him; and the joints of his loins were loosed, and his knees smote one against another.

7 The king cried aloud to bring in the enchanters, the Chaldeans, and the soothsayers. The king spake and said to the wise men of Babylon, Whosoever shall read this writing, and show me the interpretation thereof, shall be clothed with purple, and have a chain of gold about his neck, and shall be the third ruler in the kingdom.

QUERIES

a. Who is "Belshazzar" and what happened between his reign and that of Nebuchadnezzar?

b. Why insist upon drinking wine from the "vessels of the temple which was in Jerusalem?"

c. Where did the "fingers of a man's hand" come from?

PARAPHRASE

Belshazzar the king of the district of Babylon put on a great feast for a thousand of his army officers and they all got drunk. As Belshazzar was getting drunk, he ordered his servants to bring the gold and silver vessels which his predecessor, Nebuchadnezzar, had carried off from the temple of the Jews in Jerusalem. When the servants arrived with these vessels he and his army officers, his wives and his concubines in insolent defiance of the god of the Jews drank toasts to their pagan gods of metal and wood. Suddenly, in the midst of their drunken revelry, they saw the fingers of a man's hand writing on the plaster of the wall opposite the lampstand. The king himself saw the fingers as they wrote. His face grew pale with terror, and such fear gripped him his hips began to tremble violently and his knees knocked together. He began screaming that the diviners, wise-men and astrologers be brought with haste. As they began coming into the banquet hall the king shouted loudly, Whoever reads that writing on the wall, and tells me what it means, I will dress in purple robes of royal honor and put a golden chain of regal authority around his neck, and I will place him in very high authority in my kingdom.

COMMENT

v. 1 BELSHAZZAR THE KING . . . Hostile critics of the Bible have seen their "beautiful theories murdered by the brutal facts" of history as it is now available in the case of Belshazzar. For a hundred years these critics attempted to use the absence of historical reference to Belshazzar as a weapon to destroy the historical trustworthiness of the record of Daniel. Recently, however, archeological and historical data has been discovered which thoroughly substantiates the historicity of Daniel's account concerning belshazzar.

Berosus lists the succession of kings of Babylon, beginning with Nabopolassar who came to the throne upon the overthrow of the Assyrian power, as follows:

625 B.C.—Nabopolassar (died)
604 B.C.—Nebuchadnezzar (died)
562 B.C.—Amel-Marduk (Evil-merodach) (assassinated by Neriglissar)
560 B.C.—Nergal-shar-usur (Neriglissar) (died— throne to infant Labashi-Marduk)
556 B.C.—Labashi-Marduk (deposed by priestly party —replaced by Nabonidus)
555 B.C.—Nabunadi (Nabonidus) (exiled and pensioned by Persian conquerors)
538 B.C.—Capture of Babylon by Cyrus (Belshazzar was killed)

Berosus has also been validated as a reliable historian by the archaeological data published for all the monuments and inscriptions amply confirm his sequence of the Babylonian kings. The critics, prior to the discovery of these amazing documents, argued from silence. At the same time the defenders of the Bible were forced to argue from silence. Now, however, every bit of evidence is on the side of those who accept the historical accuracy of the Bible and the critics, still arguing from silence, do so squarely in the face of empirical, scientific testimony!

We quote in full from *Archaeology And Bible History*, by Joseph P. Free, pages 231-235, pub. Scripture Press:

EVENTS IN BABYLON, c. 562-560 B.C.; ARCHAEOLOGICAL LIGHT ON JEHOIACHIN AND EVIL-MERODACH (II KINGS 25:27-30)

Nebuchadnezzar died about 562 B.C. He was succeeded by his son, Evil-merodach, who allowed Jehoiachin to come out of prison (II Kings 25:27-30), and gave him an allowance of provisions (25:30). We have already noted the discovery of clay tablets at Babylon listing the payment of rations of oil, barley and other food to workmen and political prisoners. Among those listed as recipients of these provisions was Jehoiachin of Judah (See last part of Ch. 19, section on "Archaeological Confirmation of Jehoiachin's Exile . . .").

Archaeological evidence of Evil-merodach (Amil-Marduk in Babylonian) was found on a vase at Susa in Persia, reported by the French archaeological expedition there. This vase bore an inscription which read, "Palace of Amil-Marduk, King of Babylon, son of Nebuchadnezzar, King of Babylon." The people of Persia (called Elam in ancient times) had apparently carried this vase from Babylonia to Persia at the time of one of their military invasions of the Mesopotamian area.

LAST EVENTS IN THE NEO-BABYLONIAN EMPIRE, c. 560-539 B.C.; NABONIDUS AND BELSHAZZAR (DANIEL 5).

Evil-merodach ruled for only two or three years (c. 562-560 B.C.) and was then assassinated by his brother-in-law, Neriglissar (Nergalsharezer), who is identical with the Nergalshaerezer of Jeremiah 39:3. After a rather successful administration of four years (c. 560-556 B.C.), Neriglissar died, leaving the throne to his infant son, Labashi-Marduk, who was deposed by the priestly party in nine months, and replaced by Nabonidus (Nabuna'id), a Babylonian of the priestly group.

Nabonidus (556-539 B.C.) tells us in his inscriptions that he had been a trusted general in the army of his predecessors. As king, Nabonidus maintained the stability of the empire, and spent much time in directing the building and strengthening of the fortifications on the Euphrates River. One of his great joys came in the rebuilding of temples which lay in ruins. His record telling of the rebuilding of the temple of Shamash at Sippar, and the finding of the foundation record of Naram-Sin has already been cited (See this book, Ch. 19, section on "The Finding of the book of the Law...").

Whereas the secular sources indicated Nabonidus as the last king of the Neo-Babylonian Empire, the Bible indicates Belshazzar as the last ruler (Dan. 5). This apparent contradiction and difficulty has been resolved by the archaeological discoveries of recent years. It will be dealt with in the following section.

ARCHAEOLOGICAL CONFIRMATION CONCERNING NABONIDUS AND BELSHAZZAR (DANIEL 5)

The author of this book received the following letter from a college sudent:

"I am a history major at the university. This semester I am taking a course in Ancient History.

"As my religious beliefs are orthodox and some Dr.—'s are not, there are naturally quite a few points where we do not agree. The particular point which she and I are discussing at the present time concerns the book of Daniel. Dr.— believes that Daniel errs in his book when he speaks of Belshazzar as king of the Chaldeans in Daniel 5:1. She says that Nabonidus was king of Babylon at the time of its fall and not Belshazzar. She takes the position that Belshazzar was never king, and, from the way she has spoken, I believe she even doubts his actual existence. She also has taught that Daniel errs when he says that Babylon was taken by siege. According to other accounts there was not a siege of Babylon. It was just handed over to Cyrus.

"I feel as though I should have proof for my beliefs whenever it is possible to obtain it. I am writing to you to ask you if you would be willing to give me your point of view on the matter or refer me to some source which, in your opinion, states the facts correctly."

The author of this book replied to the above letter as follows:

The Biblical statements concerning Belshazzar have been used for a long time by liberals to demonstrate that the Bible is not accurate. It is quite true that up to one hundred years ago our historical sources (outside of the Bible) showed that Nabonidus was the last king of Babylon and was not killed when the city was taken by the Persians, but was given a pension by his conquerors. Ancient historians such as Berossus (c. 250 B.C.) and Alexander Polyhistor give us this information that Nabonidus was the last king of Babylon. On the other hand, the Bible indicates that Belshazzar was the last ruler of Babylon and that he was killed when the city was taken (Dan. 5:30). Modern liberal commentators, such as Hitzig, have taken the view that the name Belshazzar was a pure invention on the part of the writer of Daniel.

Archaeological discoveries, however, show that the Bible is accurate in regard to its indications concerning Belshazzar. About the middle of the nineteenth century a great number of clay tablets were excavated in the region which was ancient Babylonia, and were sent to the British Museum. During the last half of the nineteenth century many of these tablets were examined by Dr. Theophilus G. Pinches, prominent Assyriologist of London. One of these clay tablets contained the name Belshazzar, which showed that such a man actually existed. Another tablet was found to bear the names of Belshazzar and Nabonidus, showing that there was some connection between these two people, and another tablet referred to Belshazzar as the king's son. Another tablet was examined which proved to be a contract, containing an oath taken in the name of Nabonidus and Belshazzar. In ancient Babylonia oaths were taken in the name of the reigning king. This tablet, then, gave indication that Belshazzar was actually co-ruler with his father, Nabonidus.

In subsequent years, the work of Raymond P. Dougherty, late professor of Assyriology at Yale University, furnished further illumination on the situation concerning Belshazzar. Dougherty showed that during the later part of his reign Nabonidus spent a great deal of his time in Arabia, probably for the purpose of consolidating that part of his empire, although some scholars have suggested that he was doing what we would call archaeological work, and others have suggested that he stayed in Arabia because he liked the climate. In any event the clay tablets show us the reason for the raising of Belshazzar to the position of ruling monarch—namely, because of the absence of his father from Babylon. The English scholar, Sidney Smith, has published an inscription which evidently refers to Nabonidus and which says, "He entrusted the kingship to him," indicating the bestowal of royal authority upon Belshazzar.[20]

There is no first-rate liberal today, as far as the writer knows, who urges this old objection concerning Belshazzar. An example of the way in which liberals recognize the facts in the case may

---

19. R. P. Dougherty, *Nabonidus and Belshazzar*, (New Haven: Yale University Press, 1929) (DNB)
20. *Ibid.*, p. 108.

be taken from the book, *What Mean These Stones,* by Millar Burrows, where he points out that "the solution of this apparent discrepancy was apparent when evidence was found that during the last part of his reign Nabunaid (Nabonidus) lived in Arabia and left the administration of the government to his son Belshazzar."

The detailed facts are that Nabonidus, in one sense the last king of Babylon, was not killed by the invading Persians, but was given a pension by his conquerors. On the other hand, Belshazzar, elevated to the position of ruler of Babylon by his father, was killed when the city of Babylon was taken, as indicated in Daniel 5:30. The matter concerning Belshazzar, far from being an error in the Scriptures, is one of the many striking confirmations of the Word of God which have been demonstrated by archaeology.

For more detail on this data see Boutflower (IABD, pgs. 114-141). There is no doubt now that Belshazzar was a historical personage. That Daniel calls him "king" in no way implies that Daniel understood him to be emperor of all the Babylonian empire. The Hebrew and Aramaic languages do not have a word for "emperor" who is over kings. One word, "king," covers all such and similar relationships. Belshazzar was the "king" of the city of Babylon and its district—and perhaps a few adjoining districts.

Since the question of the relationship of Nabonidus and Belshazzar to Nebuchadnezzar comes here first it may be well to bring in the subject of the "queen" in v. 10. Some have supposed her to be the queen-mother of Belshazzar. Nabonidus was not related to Nebuchadnezzar and came to the throne by means other than royal family succession. However, since only seven years had elapsed between Nebuchadnezzar's death and the accession of Nabonidus to the throne, it could have easily been possible that a young widowed wife of Nebuchadnezzar was available for Nabonidus to marry. Such a marriage would give the "usurper" Nabonidus social or royal standing (Herod the Great had this in mind, no doubt, when he married the Hasmonean princess, Mariamne). Thus the queen would be the queen-mother to Belshazzar. There is also the possibility that Belshazzar, might have been a real "son" of Nebuchadnezzar and not Nabonidus, living at the same time Nabonidus was living. When Nabonidus married the widowed queen he may have adopted the son, Belshazzar, and thus secured an heir for himself, a scion of the illustrious family of Nebuchadnezzar.

Robert Dick Wilson in (SBD, pg. 117ff) has shown among the Arabs and the Babylonians the word "son" lent itself to no less than twelve separate uses, including "grandson" and "adopted son"; and the word for "father" has seven separate and istinct uses.

v. 2-4 BELSHAZZAR, WHILE HE TASTED THE WINE, COMMANDED TO BRING THE GOLDEN AND SILVER VESSELS . . . THEY DRANK WINE AND PRAISED THE GODS OF GOLD . . . Leupold remarks that "the Oriental . . . king and his most renowned men of state sat on an elevated dias in the banquet hall. The drinking of wine followed after the meal had been eaten; it signifies the procedure that might be termed a 'drinking bout.' "

When the wine was beginning to have its inebriating effect, supplying that pseudo-boldness and courage which is characteristic of its intoxicating ingredients, this debauched monarch commanded the holy vessels of the Jewish Temple be brought that they might be used in their revelry. This was plainly an act of open defiance, calculated to insult the God whose Temple stood in Jerusalem. Using the vessels of the Jewish Temple, Belshazzar and his drunken court drank toasts to their idols. Leupold points out that this is "a deed unparalleled in the records of antiquity." The heathen were noted for destroying and ransacking the temples of their victims but they always erected new temples for the deities of the conquered nations or placed their sacred things in their own pantheons. The gods of all peoples were venerated; a man respected his own gods as well as the gods of others.

As is plainly shown in verses 22ff., Belshazzar sad ample opportunity to know better than this. His action then was plainly one of insolence brought on by drunken

The Handwriting On the Wall

191

debauchery. His predecessor, Nebuchadnezzar, was guilty of *pride*. Belshazzar was guilty of *insolence*. There has been a marked degeneracy in the moral and rational fibre of the Babylonian leadership.

Belshazzar is the typical profligate and frivolous monarch of paganism. The presence of the king's "wives" and "concubines" was usually not tolerated at banquets. It was, however, permitted when debauchery began to run rampant. added insult to the holy God of heaven.

How many people were at this banquet? Royal feasts in antiquity were often huge. Athenaeus relates that the Persian king daily fed 15,000 men from his table. One marriage festival given by Alexander the Great was attended by 10,000 guests.

All the data we have thus far gathered on Belshazzar indicates that he occupied a position of co-regency with Nabonidus; yet while Belshazzar occupied a position, technically, subordinate to that of Nabonidus, actually, he seems to have had nearly all the prerogatives of a monarch. He was actually entrusted with the kingship over Babylon, and he managed it like a king. Now it is important to remember the book of Daniel is not an official document of the Neo-Babylonian Empire. It was written for the Jews, the people of God, who had to deal with the man who ruled in Babylon. This man was Belshazzar—not Nabonidus. The man whose royal word could affect the Jews was Belshazzar. Very properly, therefore, he is called "king" and "king of Babylon."

v. 5-7 . . . CAME FORTH THE FINGERS OF A MAN'S HAND, AND WROTE . . . UPON THE PLASTER . . . Just as the feast "began to swing," a human hand appeared and with the fingers began to inscribe some words upon the white plaster of the king's banquet hall. The royal table sat on the dais and close to a back wall. That portion of the great hall (about 50' x 160') was lit with a great candelabrum, the light of which reflected on the plastered wall behind the royal seat. Another interesting testimony of archaeology is that the walls of the palace at Babylon were covered with white plaster. This mention of white plaster is interesting because the Aramaic word translated plaster literally means chalk.

The sight of this hand was clearly seen by the king. It had a rapid, sobering effect on the king! Seeing only a hand, the king's imagination would have free reign to think of all manner of terrible beings who might be the owner of that hand. The color drained from his face leaving it ghostly white and he began to shake violently so that his hips seemed to go clear out of their sockets and his knees knocked together so the knocking could be heard by those standing near him! The arrogant, insolent king of a few moments ago, defying the Almighty, now stands transfixed with terror!

Unable to sit down because of his shaking, hardly able to stand because of his overpowering fear, the king screams (literally, with excessive loudness), to hide his trembling voice, Summon my wise-men immediately! "His thoughts troubled him . . ." may indicate that his conscience began to bother him. We have commented earlier on the categories of seers in the Babylonian court.

Belshazzar hastily promises anyone of them elevation to a place of preeminence in the kingdom if one of them can decipher the writing on the wall for him. Just what the position "third in the kingdom" means is debated by the commentators. Young thinks it means "a thirdling or triumvir, 'one of three'." The Triumvirate would then include, in order of authority, Nabonidus, Belshazzer, and whoever deciphered the writing (as the sequence of events shows would be Daniel). Leupold maintains it reads literally *talti* which is not the ordinal numeral "third," which would have to be *telithi*. It therefore probably means "adjutant or officer." It no doubt involves a very high dignity, but no man is able to determine exactly what dignity.

QUIZ

1. Prove that Belshazzar was a real, historic personage.
2. How may Nebuchadnezzar be designated the "father" of Belshazzar?
3. Who was the "queen"?

4. How many people might be in attendance at this banquet?

5. What was Belshazzar's purpose in drinking wine from the temple vessels?

6. Describe Belshazzar's condition upon seeing the hand writing on the wall.

7. Should Belshazzar have known better than to act this way with the Jews sacred vessels? Why?

b. TURMOIL

TEXT: 5:8-16

8 Then came in all the king's wise men; but they could not read the writing, nor make known to the king the interpretation.

9 Then was king Belshazzar greatly troubled, and his countenance was changed in him, and his lords were perplexed.

10 Now the queen by reason of the words of the king and his lords came into the banquet house: the queen spake and said, O king, live for ever; let not thy thoughts trouble thee, nor let thy countenance be changed:

11 there is a man in thy kingdom, in whom is the spirit of the holy gods; and in the days of thy father light and understanding and wisdom, like the wisdom of the gods, were found in him; and the king Nebuchadnezzar thy father, the king, I say, thy father, made him master of the magicians, enchanters, Chaldeans, and soothsayers;

12 forasmuch as an excellent spirit, and knowledge, and understanding, interpreting of dreams, and showing of dark sentences, and disolving of doubts, were found in the same Daniel, whom the king named Belteshazzar. Now let Daniel be called, and he will show the interpretation.

13 Then was Daniel brought in before the king. The king spake and said unto Daniel, Art thou that Daniel, who art of the children of the captivity of Judah, whom the king my father brought out of Judah?

14 I have heard of thee, that the spirit of the gods is in thee, and that light and understanding and excellent wisdom are found in thee.

15 And now the wise men, the enchanters, have been brought in before me, that they should read this writing, and make known unto me the interpretation thereof; but they could not show the interpretation of the thing.

16 But I have heard of thee, that thou canst give interpretations, and dissolve doubts: now if thou canst read the writing, and make known to me the interpretation thereof, thou shalt be clothed with purple, and have a chain of gold about thy neck, and shalt be the third ruler in the kingdom.

QUERIES

a. Is this "change" in the king's countenance a second change?

b. Who is the "queen" and why was she not in the banquet at the start?

c. What was "third ruler in the kingdom?"

PARAPHRASE

And as the wise men kept coming in and were finally all assembled, it was found that none of them could interpret the writing inscribed on the wall or tell the king what it meant. The king grew more and more hysterical; his face reflected the terror he felt, and his officers, too, were shaken. But when the queen-mother heard what was happening, she rushed to the banquet hall and said to Belshazzar, Pull yourself together and try to be calm, your Majesty; don't be so pale and frightened over this. There is a man in your kingdom who has the spirit of the holy gods within him. In the days of your forefather, king Nebuchadnezzar, this man was found to be as full of wisdom, insight and understanding as if he had the very spirit of the gods in him. And in the reign of your forefather Nebuchadnezzar he was made chief of all the magicians, astrologers, wisemen and soothsayers of Babylon. Call for this man, Daniel —or Belteshazzar, as the king called him—for his mind is filled with superhuman knowledge and understanding. He can interpret dreams, solve riddles and solve knotty problems. He will tell you what the writing means. So Daniel was rushed in to see the king. The king said, So you are Daniel! You are the Daniel that my forefather, king Nebuchadnezzar, brought from Judah as a captive of war! Well, I have been reminded that you manifest the spirit of the holy gods within you by the insight, enlightenment and extraordinary wisdom you displayed during Nebuchadnezzar's reign. These wisemen, soothsayers and enchanters of mine were assembled to interpret for me this handwriting on the wall, but they are not able to do so. I have been informed that you are able to give interpretations and solve knotty problems. If you are able to make the interpretation of this handwriting known to me, I will clothe you in a robe of purple and put a golden chain of authority about your neck and elevate you to the position of talti in the kingdom.

COMMENT

  v. 8-9 THEN CAME IN ALL THE KING'S WISE MEN . . . The original language indicates that the wise men did not all come in at once in one body but kept coming in until finally, when they were all assembled, it was found that not one could offer the least bit of help. Why the wisemen could not interpret these characters on the wall we shall deal with in verses 24-28. Suffice it now to say the king was filled with consternation at not knowing their meaning.

  It became evident to Belshazzar that the terrifying frustration of not being able to know what was written would not be solved by the mighty "brain-trust" of Babylon (all its wise men together). He grew very nearly hysterical and his countenance reflected his terror. Staring into the face of this august body of wise men he recognized that they, too, were as much at a loss as he was to calm his fears for they were seized with perplexity also.

  v. 10-12 NOW THE QUEEN . . . CAME . . .AND SAID . . . THERE IS A MAN . . . Undoubtedly the queen mother was the widow of Nebuchadnezzar, because she was so familiar with past events concerning the relationship of Daniel to Nebuchadnezzar. Queen mothers held a very significant position in ancient oriental courts—even more authoritative than that of the reigning queen. She entered the banquet hall of her own accord and without pausing to obtain permission of the monarch. Leupold suggests she had absented herself from this banquet in moral protest against the profligacy and indifference to duties of defense by Belshazzar. Whatever her reason for being absent it is evident that the reason for her coming to the banquet hall is to bring some calm reason and valuable information to this "play-boy" despot who was "coming unglued." The queen mother had probably received a report from someone at court that the situation was critical, and, in view of the fact that the Medes and Persians were camped outside the great city, someone was going to have to take the hysterical king in hand and bring the head of the government to his senses.

Boutflower says of the queen, "She was not the mother of Nabonidus. That lady, as we learn from the Annalistic Tablet, died in the camp at Sippara in the ninth year of Nabonidus. But since she appears in Daniel 5, in the character of queen-mother, and speaks with remarkable dignity and self-possession, it is reasonable to suppose that she was the widow of Nebuchadnezzar, whom Nabonidus had married, and who—now that her husband was a prisoner in the hands of the enemy—had assumed the post of queen-mother."

The queen speaks to Belshazzar of Daniel as if Belshazzar should have remembered this prophet. She informs the emperor that Daniel had had a very close and significant relationship to Nebuchadnezzar. She informs the king of the belief that the "spirit of the gods" resided in Daniel, and that the king's grandfather, Nebuchadnezzar, had promoted Daniel to "chief of the magicians." In other words, the queen is informing Belshazzar that Nebuchadnezzar had put this wise man Daniel thoroughly to the test and he had demonstrated supernatural knowledge, discernment and ability to solve "knotty matters," which is the literal meaning of "dissolving of doubts." The queen's advice is that Daniel be called to "solve this knotty problem."

v. 13-16 . . . ART THOU THAT DANIEL . . . I HAVE HEARD OF THEE . . . THAT THOU CANST GIVE INTERPRETA- TIONS . . . There is no indication in the original language that the statement of the king is interrogative. Even if it is a question, it is only rhetorical, for the king apparently did not expect an answer, since he proceeds with his request immediately. The king may have made a simple declara- tion with a tone of surprise, "So you are that Daniel about whom I have heard." Belshazzar may even have heard of Daniel long before this but indulging himself in profligacy and frivolity, had never taken the trouble to consult him. It is noteworthy that Belshazzar, in spite of all his in- difference to administration of the city and his indulgence in riotous living, did not forget all the details of his grand- father's military history.

The remainder of Belshazzar's speech is verbatim quota- tion of the queen's speech, except the promise of reward. Since all his own wisemen had failed, the king was now willing to reward this Hebrew if he could tell him the interpretation of the words on the wall.

Thanks to the excavations of Koldewey, not only has the throne-room of the Neo-Babylonian kings been dis- covered, but the doubly-recessed niche opposite the central entrance, which marks the spot where the throne must have stood, and precisely where the conscience-stricken Belshaz- zar must have sat!

QUIZ

1. Describe the confusion and consternation of Belshazzar and his wise men.
2. Who was the queen, and why was she not at the banquet?
3. Why did the queen come to the feast at this particular time?
4. What was her advice to Belshazzar and why?
5. What sort of archaeological evidence do we have con- cerning this event?

c. TRANSGRESSION

TEXT: 5:17-23

17 Then Daniel answered and said before the king, Let thy gifts be to thyself, and give thy rewards to another; nevertheless I will read the writing unto the king, and make known to him the interpretation.

18 O thou king, the Most High God gave Nebuchadnezzar thy father the kingdom, and greatness, and glory, and majesty:

19 and because of the greatness that he gave him, all the peoples, nations, and languages trembled and feared before him: whom he would he slew, and whom he would he kept alive; and whom he would he raised up, and whom he would he put down.

20 But when his heart was lifted up, and his spirit was hardened so that he dealt proudly, he was deposed from his kingly throne, and they took his glory from him:

21 and he was driven from the sons of men, and his heart was made like the beasts, and his dwelling was with the wild asses; he was fed with grass like oxen, and his body was wet with the dew of heaven; until he knew that the Most High God ruleth in the kingdom of men, and that he setteth up over it whomsoever he will.

22 And thou his son, O Belshazzar, hast not humbled thy heart, though thou knewest all this,

23 but hast lifted up thyself against the Lord of heaven; and they have brought the vessels of his house before thee, and thou and thy lords, thy wives and thy concubines, have drunk wine from them; and thou hast praised the gods of silver and gold, of brass, iron, wood, and stone, which see not, nor hear, nor know; and the God in whose hand thy breath is, and whose are all thy ways, hast thou not glorified:

QUERIES

a. Why did Daniel refuse the gifts promised by the king?

b. How much of God's part in Nebuchadnezzar's insanity did Daniel believe Belshazzar knew?

c. To what extent did Daniel expect Belshazzar to "glorify" God?

PARAPHRASE

Daniel answered, Keep your gifts yourself, or give them to someone else. Your generosity is appreciated. However, I will tell you the true writing upon the wall and its interpretation regardless of remuneration. Your Majesty—the Most High God gave Nebuchadnezzar, your ancestral predecessor, the kingdom of Babylon and elevated him to greatness, glory and majesty. This God gave Nebuchadnezzar such greatness that all the nations of the world surrendered in fear to his sovereignty. He killed any who offended or opposed him and offered mercy to everyone who did not offend him. At the decree of Nebuchadnezzar lesser kings rose or fell. But when he allowed pride to make his heart callous so that he dealt with people haughtily, God removed him from his royal throne and his majesty was stripped from him. God caused him to be shut off from association with men and his nature became like that of a wild animal and he actually lived among the wild donkeys; he ate grass like the oxen; he stayed out in the open often enough at night to sometimes have his body covered with the dew of heaven. Eventually he recognized that the Most High God rules in the political affairs of men, nations and kingdoms, and that the Most High God elevates and deposes whomsoever He will over kingdoms and nations. And you, his ancestral successor, O Belshazzar—you knew all this, yet you have reigned in a proud and haughty manner as if you did not know it. You have exalted yourself and defied the God of Heaven, and brought to this profane feast the vessels from God's temple; and you and your officers and wives and concubines have been drinking wine from them while worshipping gods of silver, gold, brass, iron, wood, and stone—gods that neither see nor hear, nor know anything at all. You have defied the God who gives you the breath of life and controls your destiny!

COMMENT

v. 17-19 , . . LET THY GIFTS BE TO THYSELF . . .THE MOST HIGH GOD GAVE NEBUCHADNEZZAR THY FATHER THE KINGDOM . . . Some have assumed that Daniel was being insolent in this address to the king. Daniel, in v. 17, is merely stating that he will gladly read the writing for the king but he desires no remuneration. Reading the handwriting on the wall is a service rendered both for his God, for God's people, and for the king. Daniel does not think of reward first in such service. He is not at all like the mercenary wise men of Babylon. They will say what the king wants to hear for the right price. Daniel will tell the truth without reward.

Daniel's next step is preparation of the ground-work to reach the haughty heart of Belshazzar. The purpose of the prophet is to convict the proud potentate of his moral failure, in the hope that Belshazzar will repent. Daniel prepares the king's heart by reminding him that his predecessor (Nebuchadnezzar) came to the throne and its subsequent greatness by the sovereign power of the Most High God. It is Daniel's God who raises up and puts down (cf. Psa. 115:15-16; Acts 17:26; Ezek. 29:18-20; Jer. 25:9; Isa. 10:5ff). God gave Nebuchadnezzar such greatness that he exercised unhampered, unrestrained power. No one told him what to do. The whole world was under his power.

v. 20-21 BUT . . . HIS HEART WAS LIFTED UP . . . With such power and glory as Nebuchadnezzar had one would think he was justified in being proud. But when he lifted up his heart and did not give glory to the Most High God, divine correction was needed and instigated, (see chapter 4 for comments on Nebuchadnezzar's chastening). Now the point is this—how much more does the proud and haughty Belshazzar deserve the chastening of the Most High God for he has hardly turned his hand in order to be in the position he holds. He has not even the slightest reason to boast—he has come to the throne by circumstances of birth and not by effort.

v. 22-23 . . . THOU KNEWEST ALL THIS . . . BUT HAST LIFTED UP THYSELF AGAINST THE LORD OF HEAVEN . . . There is no questioning the theology of these verses. Even pagan kings are held morally responsible by God. All men are accountable to learn moral and religious lessons from history. By means of events in nature and history God reveals His existence and His character (in a limited way, of course) (cf. Acts 14:15-18; 17:22-31; Rom. 1:18-23; Psa. 19:1ff., etc.) and all men everywhere are expected to learn what God approves and what He disapproves. If there is one lesson the prophets teach it is the sovereignty of God in politics, private and public morals, over all men, saint and sinner, pagan and patriarch alike. And if there is one thing history teaches it is that, generally speaking, kings and potentates (and mankind at large) have followed the course of Belshazzar—arrogance, materialism, pride and indifference to the lessons of history! History teaches that civilization commits spiritual, moral, and intellectual suicide when it makes for itself and worships impotent, false gods. Yet men of every generation insist on remaining blind to this lesson from history. Every generation makes and worships its own gods and each generation destroys itself spiritually, morally and intellectually all over again. Barnes says: "Nothing is more absolute than the power which God holds over the breath of men, yet there is nothing which is less recognized than that power, and nothing which men are less disposed to acknowledge than their dependence on him for it."

QUIZ

1. Was Daniel insolent in his answer to the king in v. 17?
2. How does Daniel prepare the king's mind for the moral lesson he wants to teach?
3. What is the point of relating Nebuchadnezzar's downfall?
4. Was Belshazzar not responsible since he was not a Jew?
5. How many people usually learn moral lessons from history?

d. TRAGEDY

TEXT: 5:24-31

24 then was the part of the hand sent from before him, and this writing was inscribed.
25 And this is the writing that was inscribed: MENE, MENE, TEKEL, UPHARSIN.
26 This is the interpretation of the thing: MENE; God hath numbered thy kingdom, and brought it to an end.
27 TEKEL; thou art weighed in the balances, and art found wanting.
28 PERES; thy kingdom is divided, and given to the Medes and Persians.
29 Then commanded Belshazzar, and they clothed Daniel with purple, and put a chain of gold about his neck, and made proclamation concerning him, that he should be the third ruler in the kingdom.
30 In that night Belshazzar the Chaldean king was slain.
31 And Darius the Mede received the kingdom, being about threescore and two years old.

QUERIES

a. In what language were the words written?
b. Why would the king reward Daniel for such a terrible message?
c. What is the significance of mentioning the age of Darius?

PARAPHRASE

And then God sent the fingers to write the message upon the wall: *Mene, Mene, Tekel, Upharsin*! This is what it means: *Mene* means "numbered"; thus God has fixed the limit the days of your reign, and they are ended. *Tekel* means "weighed"; thus you have been weighed in the balances of God and have failed the test. *Peres* means "divided, and thus your kingdom will be divided up between the Medes and the PePrsians. Somewhat grateful that the spspense was ended, and determined to keep his promise, Belshazzar made royal decree that Daniel was to be robed in purple, and that a golden chain of authority was to be placed around his neck. The king then announced that Daniel was elevated to third ruler in the kingdom. But, lo, that very same tragic night Belshazzar, the Chaldean monarch, was slain; and Gubaru (Darius the Mede) entered the city and began reigning at the age of sixty-two.

COMMENT

v. 24-28 . . . THIS IS THE WRITING THAT WAS IN-SCRIBED: MENE, MENE, TEKEL, UPHARSIN. The phrase "sent from before him," indicates the supernatural nature of the apparition—that is, the portion of the hand (fingers) which appeared and did the inscribing upon the wall were very plainly from some supernatural origin.

The language of the supernatural message was probably Aramaic and in the ancient alphabetic characters which we find in the oldest Hebrew and Aramaic inscriptions such as the Moabite Stone, the Siloam Inscription, and the Aramaic inscriptions from Zenjerli.

1. *Mene* is the passive participle of *menah*, "to number" and means not only "to count," but also "to fix the limit of" speaking of end or finish or expiration. According to the divine principle that when men sow to the flesh they shall reap corruption, this king and his kingdom's number is up!

2. *Tekel* is a passive participle, the Aramaic equivalent of the Hebrew root *shaqal*, and means "to weigh." The idea is that Belshazzar has been put in the balances of God and weighed or tested to see if he balances to God's standards. (cf. I Sam. 2:3; Job 31:6; Psa. 62:9; Prov. 16:2). He does not!

3. *Peres: Pharsin* is the plural form of *peres*; *u* is the customary form of the conjunction "and." It means to "break or divide." There may be in the word *peres* an allusion to the word *paras* which means "Persian." So it is revealed to Daniel that this kingdom is to be divided up and given to the Medes and the Persians.

Leupold notes, "This sequence: "Medes' first, then
'Persians,' indicates a point of historical accuracy that fits
in beautifully with the idea of Daniel's authorship of the
book. The supremacy in this dual kingdom remained but
a short time with the Medes and that while Daniel was still
on the scene, and then passed permanently to the Persians,
a fine point that a writer who lived in the Maccabean age
would hardly have thought of recording. Yet the form
upharsin, 'Persians,' gives the emphasis to the much longer
Persian supremacy."

v. 29-30 . . . IN THAT NIGHT BELSHAZZAR THE CHAL-
DEAN KING WAS SLAIN . . . Daniel refused the rewards of
the king before he made his revelation of the words upon
the wall because he wanted to make it abundantly clear
that, come what may, he was determined to declare the
truth. It now being clear that he had no mercenary motives,
there is no reason why the gifts should at this time be
refused.

How did Belshazzar die? He was slain! But by whom?
Daniel does not say. Verses 30 and 31 may or may not be
separated by an extended time, so far as we know. Actually,
verse 31 should be verse 1 of the sixth chapter, and Edward
J. Young so treats it. However, Boutflower believes that
Jeremiah (in Jer. chapters 50-51) foretells Babylon's demise by "strategem" (Jer. 50:24); that this strategem is
"connected with her water-defences" (51-36); that the city
will be taken with such surprise "the reeds will be burned
with fire" (51:32); that this stratagem will be executed
"when a great feast is going on, at which all the principal
men of the land are gathered together . . . and they will
be drunken" (51:39, 57). Now it is evident that Daniel
does not give any details about the seizure of the city of
Babylon by the Medes and the Persians. But Daniel's
silence does not necessarily contradict the trustworthy accounts of other ancient historians!

When we investigate the ancient historians (Herodotus
who is believed to have visited Babylon only some 80 years
after its downfall; Xenophon who wrote his history about
100 years after Herodotus visited Babylon; Berossus, a
Chaldean priest who wrote a history about 300 B.C.; The

Nabonidus Chronicle; and the Cyrus Cylinder) here is what we find:

a. According to Herodotus, Cyrus (the Persian king) was a long time in preparing for the siege of Babylon, and the Babylonians advanced to meet him. Being defeated, they retreated and barricaded themselves inside their city walls. Eventually, Cyrus diverted the waters of the Euphrates so that his troops could march into the city by the bed of the stream when the water was shallow. The city fell when a festival was being celebrated.

b. Xenophon mentions the diverting of a stream which flowed through Babylon. Then, one night when the Babylonians were observing a festival with drinking and revelry, Cyrus turned aside the course of the river and entered the city. The entrance was actually made by Gobryas (or Ugbaru), one of Cyrus' generals. Bobryas entered the royal palace and slew the wicked king Belshazzar. Xenophon represents the Babylonians as being extremely hostile to Cyrus.

c. Berossus writes that Nabonidus (father of Belshazzar and co-regent) met the approaching Cyrus and being defeated, fled to Borsippa. Cyrus then captured Babylon and tore down is walls. Nabonidus surrendered and was sent to Carmania where he lived in exile, supported by a small pension from the Persians, until he died.

d. The Nabonidus Chronicle mentions that in the month Tishri (October) Cyrus fought and destroyed the people of Akkad at Ophis on the Tigris river; on the 14th day he captured Sippar without fighting. Nabonidus fled; on the 16th day Gobryas (Ugbaru), the governor of Gutium, and the troops of Cyrus without fighting entered Babylon. This chronicle is one of the multitudinous clay tablets found in Asshurbanipal's library by Rassam and Layard and is sometimes called the Annalistic Tablet. The tablet measures 4 inches by 3½, in four columns, two on the obverse and two on the reverse. The tablet is of sun-dried clay and it is no wonder that considerable portions of it are illegible. The record breaks off at a point of deep interest—the burial of Belshazzar and the installation of Gabaru as his successor (whom Whitcomb suggests was the mysterious Darius the Mede of Daniel 5:31ff.). A translation of a portion of this chronicle may be read in Boutflower, pages 126-127.

e. The Cyrus Cylinder, written evidently by a priest of Merodach, who must have come into contact with some of the Hebrew captives at Babylon, since his style and tone of thought are Hebraistic (one of the most Hebraistic which have come from Babylonia to Assyria), also states that Cyrus entered Babylon without encounter or battle. The great theme of the Cylinder is that Cyrus is the chosen of Merodach, and that Merodach has given him the empire of Babylon.

Note now the points of agreement: (1) A preliminary battle between the Medo-Persian coalition and the Babylonians fought, according to the Chronicle at Opis; according to Herodotus fought at a short distance from the city; (2) The statement as to the death of the king's son (Belshazzar) on the night of the capture of Babylon in the Nabonidus Chronicle would seem to agree with Daniel 5:30; (3) The statement that the attack on the palace was led by Ugbaru (Gobryas), who, according to Xenophon, was one of the two leaders of the attacking party. Xenophon speaks of Gobryas as the Babylonian governor of a wide district (Gutim), who had been very badly treated by the Babylonian king and had gone over to the side of Cyrus; (4) According to the Cylinder, Cyrus held a great reception after the capture of Babylon—this agrees with the statement of Xenophon that very soon after the taking of the city Cyrus admitted to his presence the Babylonians, who flocked around him in overwhelming numbers.

Here then is a summary of the fall of perhaps the richest, most magnificent empire of antiquity. As far as we know from the Greek historians, the siege was not a bloody one. After the preliminary battle fought near Opis, the Babylonians retreated within their walls, and continued their busy commercial life, scoffing at the efforts of their beseigers, who, under pretense of raising up an earthen wall of siege encircling the city, were steadily and thoroughly preparing the strategem of diverting the river which enabled them to gain an entrance into the part of the city still unconquered. There was thus no fighting till the last fatal night, when all was sudden, sharp, and soon over. As the sequel shows, whether told by Xenophon or recorded on the Cylinder, Cyrus did his best to conciliate the inhabitants, and they for their part responded heartily to his efforts. Hence it was possible for the official documents to emphasize these facts and to represent the entry of Cyrus into Babylon as a peaceful one. And indeed it was, except for that single night of carnage, when the impious Belshazzar was slain. Cyrus then evidently crowned Cambyses, his son as co-ruler of all the Persian domain and gave him the honor of burying the slain Belshazzar while he appointed Gubaru (Darius the Mede) (see notes on 5:31) as governor of Babylon. Having set this part of his vast empire in order, Cyrus took his generals and his army off to other worlds to conquer.

v. 31   AND DARIUS THE MEDE RECEIVED THE KINGDOM . . . Who is "Darius the Mede?" John C. Whitcomb, Jr., in his very important book entitled *Darius, The Mede*, published by Eerdmans, contends that mistakes were made in translation of the Nabonidus Chronicle when two different names in this Chronicle were both translated Gobryas. One name (on line 15) was *Ugbaru*, the governor of Gutium, who entered Babylon with the army of Cyrus and conquered the city. On lines 19-20 of the same Chronicle is the name *Gubaru*, who appointed satraps. In line 22 Ngbaru is said to have died. It is Mr. Whitcomb's suggestion that Ugbaru was indeed Gobryas who conquered the city in the name of Cyrus, but it was Gubaru who had been appointed governor of Babylon and beyond the River, and who is one and the same person as Daniel's Darius of 5:31. Gubaru (Darius) was governor of Babylon and the River beyond on the very day that Cyrus first set foot in the conquered city, which was on October 29 (seventeen days after its conquest by Ugbaru or Gobryas), and he continued in that position throughout the reign of Cyrus and through more than half the subsequent reign of Cambyses the son of Cyrus. The great prominence given to Darius the Mede (Gubaru) in the book of Daniel is more readily explained if we assume his identification with a person by the name of Gubaru whose reign extended not only over a period of three weeks (the time within which Ugbaru was dead after capturing Babylon) or even a year, but of fourteen years (539-525 B.C.) !

The cuneiform signs for "Ug" and "Gu" are quite different, and could not possibly have been confused by the Persian scribe whose text (the Nabonidus Chronicle) we now possess.

Thus it is Mr. Whitcomb's conclusion "that there is one person in history, and only one, who fits all the Biblical data concerning Darius the Mede. He is never mentioned by the Greek historians, but appears in various sixth century B.C. cuneiform texts under the name of Gubaru."

Listed below are the various cuneiform references to Gubaru, the Governor of Babylon and the Region beyond the River, in chronological order:

539 B.C., October 29 (3rd day of Marcheswan, Accession Year of Cyrus)—Nabonidus Chronicle, Col. III, Line 20.

535/534 B.C. (4th Year of Cyrus)—Pohl 43, 45, 46.

533/532 B.C. (6th Year of Cyrus)—Tremayne 56:5, 92.4.

532/531 B.C. (7th Year of Cyrus)—Contenau 142.

531/530 B.C. (8th Year of Cyrus)—Tremayne 70:5, Phol 61.

530/529 B.C. (Accession Year of Cambyses)—Dougherty 103:11; Keiser 169:22; Niles & Keiser 114:15.

529/528 B.C. (1st Year of Cambyses)—Strassmaier 96:3, 4, 8; Clay 20:13, 14, 15.

528/527 B.C. (2nd Year of Cambyses)—Contenau 150, 152; Dougherty 120:3, 14; Tremayne 127:12, 128:19.

527/526 B.C. (3rd Year of Cambyses)—Tremayne 137:22, 160:12.

526/525 B.C. (4th Year of Cambyses—Tremayne 168:8, 172:13; Pinches Text.

525/524 B.C. (5th Year of Cambyses)—Tremayne 177:9, 178:16; Contenau 168.

QUIZ

1. In what language were the words probably written upon the wall of the king's banquet hall?
2. What is the meaning of *Mene, Mene, Tekel, Upharsin?*
3. Describe the final conquest of the city of Babylon.
4. Who is Darius the Mede?

SERMON NUMBER FIVE

BELSHAZZAR, THE PLAYBOY OF BABYLON

Text: Daniel 5

INTRODUCTION

I. BELSHAZZAR REALLY LIVED?

   A. For many years unbelieving critics of the Bible insisted that since there were no historical records (discounting the Bible as historically accurate, of course) that such a person as Belshazzar ever lived, the Bible is filled with myths

   B. But archaeological discoveries made about 1850 uncovered clay tablets in the region that was formerly Babylon and on these clay tablets was the name Belshazzar; both the names of Nabonidus and Belshazzar on another; one in which oaths were taken in the name of Belshazzar and Nabonidus indicating that they were co-rulers; subsequent work in this information showed that Nabonidus spent a great deal of his time in Arabia, which shows the reason for the raising of Belshazzar to the position of ruling monarch

II. BELSHAZZAR HAD EVERYTHING THE WORLD COUNTS VALUABLE

A. He had riches; Babylon was probably the richest of the four great world empires

B. He had power; he had at his command the power and wealth of the capital city

C. He had opportunity to indulge himself in every sensual pleasure

III. BUT WHAT DID BELSHAZZAR CONTRIBUTE TO THE BETTERMENT OF MAN?

A. He would not even be remembered if it were not for this account in the Bible

B. None of the playboys of this world have ever contributed. They are too busy getting, thinking of self

DISCUSSION

I. THE PLAYBOY AT WORK

A. Feasting, and Fornicating

   1. The text does not describe his sexual escapades, however, it speaks of his wives and concubines engaged in drunken revelry.

   2. Anyone who knows about drinking parties that involve people knows what goes on as a consequence of drinking.

   3. Alcohol lowers the moral resistance of anyone

B. Blaspheming

   1. When the wine was beginning to have its inebriating effect and supplying that pseudo-boldness and courage which is characteristic of its intoxicating ingredients, this debauched monarch commanded that the holy vessels of the Jewish Temple be brought so they might be used in their drunken feast to toast their idols.

   2. Leupold points out that this was a "deed unparalleled in the records of antiquity."

   3. This was plainly an act of open defiance, calculated to insult the God whose Temple stood in Jerusalem.

C. There is another playboy like Belshazzar (perhaps many millions)
   1. Hugh Hefner: started Playboy in 1953 with $600 of his own money, $60,000 in borrowed funds, and a photo of Marilyn Monroe in the nude.
   2. Parlayed his editorial mixture of sex and the "good life" into a $70,000,000 empire whose magazine is second in reading only to Reader's Digest in Western Europe
   3. Playboy is far more than a girlie book . . . it is a point of view.
   4. That point of view is hedonism, which teaches that pleasure is the sole good in life and that moral duty is fulfilled in the gratification of pleasure-seeking instincts.
   5. This is not new; it is as old as the Greeks at least, and even goes back to Belshazzar.
   6. But pleasure-seeking is a treadmill never-ending. Someone has aid pleasure sought is pleasure lost. Hedonists are left with only themselves—their frustrations, their weaknesses, their greed, their desires.
   7. Playboy magazine makes it clear through its photographs of nude women, its articles and its cartoons and party jokes that females are to be exploited, used whenever and wherever possible, as long as it's all in "good clean fun" and the girl goes along with the gag. That it is a gag, and that the joke is usually on the girl and ultimately on all mankind, is certain! Whether you want to be the one who uses a woman as a thing, or whether you want to be the woman who is willing to be used as a thing, it is all the same. This might be adequate for animals, but it falls a bit short for human beings.

THE BASIC PHILOSOPHY IS, "I'M FOR ME, AND EVERYONE ELSE IS A POTENTIAL ITEM ON MY MENU . . . THE BASIC LAW IN THIS KIND OF JUNGLE IS SELF-FULFILLMENT. AND WHO WOULD ARGUE THAT THERE IS ANYTHING MORE SELF-FUL-FILLED THAN A TIGER, CROCODILE, OR PYTHON THAT HAS JUST FEASTED ON ITS PREY?"

II. THE PLAYBOY AWAKE

A. It is all very well to live it up, scoff at God, indulge self, exploit other people, as long as there is no God.

   1. This is what Belshazzar thought.

   2. All this talk about a Jewish God who has powers supernatural, fooey!

   3. Belshazzar was god! He would do as he pleased!

   4. But, lo, God thought it expedient to openly and dramatically reveal His supernatural character to this arrogant hedonist.

   5. Belshazzar began to tremble until his hips went out of socket and his knees knocked together and those at the feast could see his face grow ashen gray with the pallor of death.

B. Such an awakening has come to many a playboy or playgirl:

   1. Very often it is not connected with any miraculous manifestation of God such as Belshazzar had.

   2. Usually it is just the simple conscience of man telling him he stands guilty before his creator of exploiting other people for selfish ends.

   3. Though still many more will never awake to their peril until they meet the holy God at the judgment and they are banished to the realm of darkness, impurity and evil, lies and abominations.

   4. Some of Hefner's girls have awakened to the fact that he is merely using them to serve his own selfish purposes . . . that they are nothing more than things he uses to satisfy himself and he does not care one bit for them, they have exposed him in magazines.

   5. IT IS THE DUTY OF EVERY CHRISTIAN, YOUNG AND OLD, TO USE THE POWERFUL WORD OF GOD TO GUIDE THE HELL-BENT, SELFISH, SENSUAL-MINDED WORLD BACK TO TRUE HAPPINESS IN GOD'S WILL.

III. THE PLAYBOY WEIGHED

A. What brings on this playboy attitude?

   1. "And you his son, Belshazzar, have not humbled your heart, though you knew all this, but you

have lifted up yourself against the Lord of heaven. . . "

2. ". . . you have praised the gods of silver and gold, of bronze, iron and stone, which do not see or hear or know, but the God in whose hand is your breath, and whose are all your ways, you have not honored."

3. Wm. Banowsky says in *It's A Playboy World,* "When men lose their sense of established standards, they tend to fall victim to an urge for pleasure or a lust for power. And when the loss of standards occurs during a period of peril, men seem to prefer pleasure to power. It is one of the sad facts of war that the specter of danger and death causes many soldiers to want to spend the evening before the terrible battle with the prostitute rather than the priest. It has been said that there are more brothels in Saigon, today, than in any other city of comparable size in the world."

4. We have lived in years of war for decades now and the easiest anesthesia to deaden the constant ache of emptiness is proving to be the simple pursuit of pleasure.

5. Frank Sinatra has been quoted as saying, "I'm for anything that gets you through the night, be it prayer, pills, or a bottle of Jack Daniels."

6. D. H. Lawrence, author of *Lady Chatterly's Lover,* says, "My great religion is a belief in the blood, the flesh, as being wiser than the intellect. We can go wrong with our minds, but what our blood feels and believes and says is always true. The real way of living is to answer one's wants."

7. Affluence, unbelief, uncertainty all bring on the popular idea that the answer is to be found in pleasure with its two indivisible components, sensuality and immediacy.

B. Playboyism has been weighed and found wanting.

1. Many pleasure-seekers in our modern world have been driven to the desperate conclusion that it is

impossible to achieve and, therefore, the pathway to pleasure is in the grave.

2. Ernest Hemingway write in *Death In The Afternoon*, "There is no remedy for anything in life. Death is the sovereign remedy for all our misfortunes."

3. The very rich, beautiful, and famous often learned that pleasure is a hard master, an appetite that grows on what it feeds. It is a physiological fact that a stimulated muscle reflexively demands greater stimulation, and people become enslaved by their passions in much the same way. With each overindulgence, the level of physical and emotional expectation gradually rises so that an increasingly greater thrill is required to satisfy the urge. Eventually, the thrill begins to diminish but the hunger for stimulation is ever present, now stronger than ever. Without finding full satisfaction, the hunger need settles into the monotony of filling and emptying. One beings by seeking pleasures to fill his boredom and ends by being bored with his pleasures. As Shakespeare said, "If all the years were playing holidays, to sport would be as tedious as to work."

CONCLUSION

I. PLAYBOYISM BRINGS TRAGEDY

A. It destroys the image of God in man.
   1. Belshazzar allowed himself to become as an animal.
   2. He served no human or spiritual purpose except to glut himself on sensual pleasures;
   3. So, God took away his existence.

B. Enslaving oneself to the passions of the flesh takes away freedom.
   1. The philosophy of playboyism is aggrandizement of the self, with all its accompanying disorders of arrogance, exaggerated self-importance, and unrealistic self-expectation.
   2. Ayn Rand, praised by Hefner, author of *Atlas Shrugged*, and *The Virtue of Selfishness*, writes,

"Man exists for his own sake, the pursuit of his own happiness is his highest moral purpose, that he must not sacrifice himself to others nor sacrifice others to himself."

3. What is necessary for the sake of survival itself, as well as for the sake of the moral life, is a more realistic understanding of the terms of genuine freedom. Freedom is something to be earned, and individual responsibility—discipline at the personal level—is always the price of freedom at the corporate level.

4. We take an important step forward when we realize that, like it or not, we are going to be governed by something.

5. Only when individual men are free, because they are disciplined, can the society of men be free. Edmund Burke said, "Men are qualified for civil liberties in exact proportion to their disposition to put moral chains upon their own appetites. Society cannot exist unless a controlling power upon will and appetite be placed somewhere, and the less of it there is within, the more there must be without. It is ordained in the eternal constitution of things that men of intemperate minds cannot be free. Their passions forge their fetters."

6. "NO MAN IS FREE WHEN HE IS A SLAVE TO HIS FLESH." Seneca

II. THERE IS NOTHING BUT FRUSTRATION AND DEATH IN THE PURSUIT OF PLEASURE AND THINGS

A. John W. Gardner, former Sec. of HEW, in his book, *Self-Renewal,* said, "It is not unduly harsh to say that the contemporary idea of happiness cannot possibly be taken seriously by anyone whose intellectual or moral development has progressed beyond that of a three-week-old puppy . . . Despite almost universal belief to the contrary, gratification, ease, comfort, diversion in the state of having achieved all one's goals do not constitute happiness for man.

The reason Americans have not trapped the bluebird of happiness, despite the most frantic efforts the world has ever seen, is that happiness as total gratification is not a state to which man can aspire. The irony is that we should have brought such unprecedented dynamism to the search for such a static condition. Comforts and the pleasure of good living will never be enough. If they were, the large number of Americans who have been able to indulge their whims on a scale unprecedented in history would be deliriously happy. They would be telling one another of their unparalleled serenity and bliss instead of trading tranquilizer prescriptions."

B. What is the solution? Malcom Muggeridge wrote, "how infinitely sad it is that the present moral upheaval should amount to nothing more than a demand for Pot and Pills, for the most tenth-rate sort of escapism and self-indulgence ever known. How pathetic that when the world is waiting for a marvelous release of creativity, all we actually get is the resort of any old slobbering debauchee anywhere in the world at anytime—DOPE AND THE BED."

C. Mr Muggeridge puts in the plainest possible words the conviction that is also deepest in the life of any committed Christian, "So I come back to where I began, to that other King, one Jesus; to the Christian notion that man's efforts to make himself personally and collectively happy in earthly terms are doomed to failure. HE MUST INDEED, AS CHRIST SAID, BE BORN AGAIN, BE A NEW MAN, OR HE'S NOTHING. SO AT LEAST I HAVE CONCLUDED, HAVING FAILED TO FIND IN PAST EXPERIENCE, PRESENT DILEMMAS AND FUTURE EXPECTATIONS, ANY ALTERNATIVE PROPOSITION. AS FAR AS I AM CONCERNED, IT IS CHRIST OR NOTHING."

III. JESUS TOLD A PARABLE ABOUT A PLAYBOY

A young man who wanted to be free to do his own thing. Terribly bored with the family farm, he demanded his inheritance immediately so that he could go to the glittering city and lead his own life. But the selfish satisfactions were short-lived. Though the son surrendered himself to every pleasure, he did not find freedom; he did not find joy. Having refused to serve his father, he ended up serving pigs. When the terrible bondage of self-indulgence was complete "he came to himself." He realized that even the slaves in his father's house were much better off than he. When he found the courage to go back home, to ask for a job, his father met him saying, "It is not another slave I seek, but a son." What Jesus was saying is that every man must choose to be either a son or a slave; and that the greater freedom of sonship always involves the greater responsibility—personal discipline.

EXAMINATION FIVE

REFUTATIONS

(Answer the following by giving the argument which will correct the statement)

1. Belshazzar was not a true historical personage. Refute!
2. Daniel was being sarcastic when he told Belshazzar, ". . . thy gifts be to thyself . . ." Refute!
3. Belshazzar was not responsible for his actions since he knew nothing about the God of Israel's actions towards his ancestors. Refute!

ASSOCIATIONS

(Associate the persons or events of column one with the correct person or event of column two)

1	2
Belshazzar	Daniel
concubine	Nebuchadnezzar
queen	purse
Belteshazzar	Vashti
talti	authority
vessels	mistress

Mene
Judah
Tekel
chain
Upharsin

mother
king of Babylon
third
numbered
Meshach
weighed
threescore
divided

MEMORIZATIONS

(Fill in the blanks:)

And thou his son, O Belshazzar, hast not _____.
thy heart, though thou _____ all this, but hast _____
up thyself against the Lord of heaven; and they have
brought the _____ of his house before thee, and thou
and thy lords, thy wives and thy _____ have drunk wine
from them; and thou hast praised the _____ of silver
and gold, of brass, iron, wood, and stone, which _____
not, nor _____, nor _____; and the God in whose
hand thy _____ is, and whose are all thy ways hast
thou not glorified.

EXPLANATIONS

1. Explain why Belshazzar was called "king" of Babylon,
   when history says it was Nabonidus who was king of
   Babylon at that time.
2. Explain the relationship of the "queen" to Belshazzar.
3. Explain why Belshazzar was so serrified at the handwriting on the wall.
4. Explain why the wise-men of Babylon could not read
   the writing on the wall.
5. Explain how Belshazzar was slain that night.

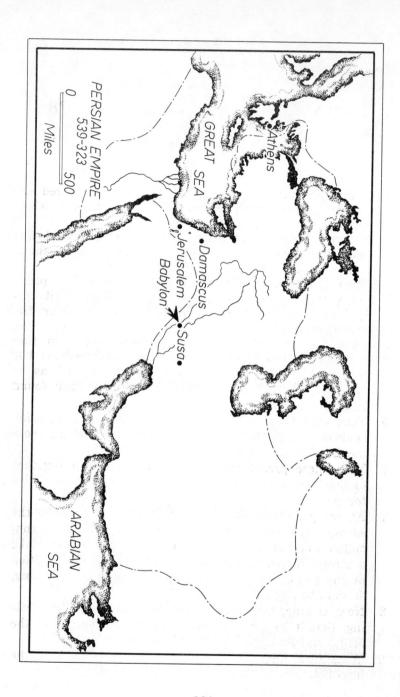

PERSIAN EMPIRE
539-323

0   500
Miles

GREAT
SEA

Athens

Damascus
Jerusalem
Babylon
Susa

ARABIAN
SEA

CHAPTER SIX

I. LAWYERS AND LIONS—6:1-28

a. PERFIDY

TEXT: 6:1-9

1 It pleased Darius to set over the kingdom a hundred and twenty satraps, who should be throughout the whole kingdom;

2 and over them three presidents, of whom Daniel was one; that these satraps might give account unto them, and that the king should have no damage.

3 Then this Daniel was distinguished above the presidents and the satraps, because an excellent spirit was in him; and the king thought to set him over the whole realm.

4 Then the presidents and the satraps sought to find occasion against Daniel as touching the kingdom; but they could find no occasion nor fault, forasmuch as he was faithful, neither was there any error or fault found in him.

5 Then said these men, We shall not find any occasion against this Daniel, except we find it against him concerning the law of his God.

6 Then these presidents and satraps assembled together to the king, and said thus unto him, King Darius, live for ever.

7 All the presidents of the kingdom, the deputies and the satraps, the counsellors and the governors, have consulted together to establish a royal statute, and to make a strong interdict, that whosoever shall ask a petition of any god or man for thirty days, save of thee, O king, he shall be cast into the den of lions.

8 Now, O king, establish the interdict, and sign the writing, that it be not changed, according to the law of the Medes and Persians, which altereth not.

9 Wherefore king Darius signed the writing and the interdict.

QUERIES

a. Why should Daniel be appointed a "president" over the satraps?

b. Why could they find no fault with Daniel's relationship to the kingdom?

c. Why was the law of the Medes and Persians unalterable?

PARAPHRASE

Gubaru (Darius) divided the administration of the kingdom over which Cyrus had placed him among 120 governors. Over these lesser governors he appointed three presidents (Daniel was one of them) to whom they should be accountable in order that the finances of the kingdom might be managed profitably and efficiently. Daniel quickly proved more capable than all the other presidents and governors. He had great ability and the king began to think of placing him over the entire empire as his administrative officer. This made the other presidents and governors very jealous, and they began searching for some fault in the way Daniel was administering the affairs of his office for the king so that they could accuse him to the king. But they could not find one mistake or fault. Daniel was faithful, honest, and absolutely accurate and efficient. After deliberating, their conclusion was that their only opportunity to bring him into disfavor with the king would be through his religion. They decided to go to the king and use him to trap Daniel. After all due ceremony of saluting the king with, "O King Darius, may you live forever," the governors approached the king so eagerly they very nearly bordered on disrespectful behavior in his court. They said, "We presidents, governors, counsellors, and deputies unanimously suggest that you should make a law, irrevocable under any circumstances, that for the next thirty days anyone who should pray to any god except yourself, Your Majesty, shall be thrown to the lions. Your Majesty, we suggest your signature on this law; sign it so that it cannot be cancelled or changed; it will be a law of the Medes and Persians that cannot be revoked." So King Darius signed the law.

COMMENT

v. 1-2 . . . DARIUS . . . SET OVER THE KINGDOM A
HUNDRED AND TWENTY SATRAPS . . . We have discussed the
problem of identifying this "Darius" in the preceeding chapter. The Nabonidus Chronicle substantiates the fact that
Gubaru (Darius) appointed governors in Babylon. These
men were an expedient of the king to make the administering of the Persian system of taxes profitable. The king's
treasury must suffer no losses. This was a definite characteristic of the Persian era—the hoarding of money (see our
comments on chap. 2:39). Over these 120 administrators
(satraps) the king appointed three top-echelon cabinet
members (presidents) and Daniel was one of the three.

Through the courtesy of Dr. John C. Whitcomb and
Eerdmans Publishing Co., we now insert a study of the
Medes and Persians from Mr. Whitcomb's book, *Darius
The Mede*, pages 68-74:

HISTORICAL SKETCH OF THE
MEDES AND PERSIANS
DOWN TO 520 B.C.

Around 1500 B.C. Aryan peoples first moved
into that high plateau region to the east of the
Tigris River and to the south of the Caucasus
Mountains and Caspian Sea which constitutes the
northwestern part of a large country known since
1935 as Iran (from "Airyana" or "land of the
Aryans"). The two principal Aryan tribes were the
Medes and the Persians. The Medes lived to the east
and south of Lake Urmia, and the Persians lived in
Parsua, a region to the west of that large lake.

It is in 836 B.C. that we find the first mention
of the Medes and Persians in Assyrian records. In
that year, Shalmaneser III received tribute from the
kings of "Parsua" and reached eastward to the lands
of the "Mada." Just one hundred years after this,
Tiglathpileser III invaded Parsua and received tribute from Medina chiefs. *Deioces* was the first to
unite the nomadic Median tribes into one nation;
but he was taken captive by the Assyrians in 715
B.C. and was deported to Syria. His successor,

Cyaxares I paid tribute to Sargon, king of Assyria, and attacked the Assyrian province of Harhar in 702 B.C.

About the year 700 B.C., Cimmerian and Scythian tribes began to move south into the Iranian plateau, pushing the Medes before them. Also, the Persians moved south from Parsua to a region south of the Elamite land of Anzan (or Anshan) and named it Parsumash in memory of their original home. At this time their leader was *Achaemenes* (700-675 B.C.), founder of the Achaemenian dynasty, who is noted for having led troops from Parsumash and Anzan against Sennacherib at Halulina in 681 B.C.

Phraortes, king of the Medes, began his twenty-two-year reign in 675 B.C. by forming an anti-Assyrian coalition of Medes and Cimmerians, and causing the Persians to become his vassal. But the Persians, under the leadership of *Teispes* (675-640 B.C.), son of Achaemenes, regained their independence from the Medes following the death of Phraortes in 653 B.C. The Persians were also able to conquer some territory to the east of Parsumash, which they named Parsa; and after the destruction of Elam by the Assyrians in 646 B.C., Teispes assumed the title, "Great King, King of the City Anshan."

Cyaxares II (635-585 B.C.), the new Median king, remained under the power of the Scythians during the first twenty-eight years of his reign; but he finally threw off their yoke and succeeded again in dominating the Persians. In 615 B.C. he led the Medes in a mighty invasion of Assyria, and with the aid of Nabopolassar, King of Babylon, conquered Nineveh in 612 B.C. Two year later he delivered the final blow to the Assyrian army by defeating Ashuruballit at Harran. Absorbing all of northern Mesopotamia, he moved into Asia Minor, met the powerful Lydians, and was forced to establish a common frontier with them at the river Halys (May 28, 585 B.C.).

In the meantime, Teispes had divided his territory between his two sons, *Ariyaramnes* (640-615)
and *Cyrus I* (640-600), the former taking the eastern region of Parsa and the latter ruling over Parsumash and the city of Anshan. However, both of
these Persian Kings remained vassals of the Medes.
The son and grandson of Ariyaramne, *Arsames* and
Hystaspes, remained petty rulers; but the son of
Cyrus I, *Cambyses I* (600-559), married Mandane
the daughter of *Astyages* (585-550), successor to
the throne of Media. Their son was *Cyrus II, the
Great.* Amytis, another daughter of Astyages, became a wife of Nebuchadnezzar; and it was for her
sake that he ordered the famous Hanging Gardens
of Babylon to be constructed. The Achaemenian dynasty down to the time of Cyrus II, the Great, may
be represented by the following genealogical table
(the earlier dates are approximate) :

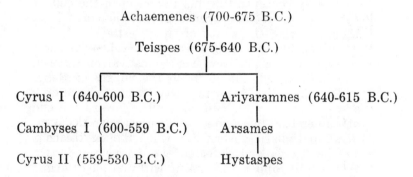

Achaemenes (700-675 B.C.)
│
Teispes (675-640 B.C.)
│
┌──────────────────┴──────────────────┐
Cyrus I (640-600 B.C.)   Ariyaramnes (640-615 B.C.)
│   │
Cambyses I (600-559 B.C.)   Arsames
│   │
Cyrus II (559-530 B.C.)   Hystaspes

Cyrus II became king of Anshan about 559 B.C.,
and soon began an insurrection against the weak
and corrupt Astyages, king of the Medes, with the
help of Nabonidus, the new king of Babylonia. Astyages attempted to crush the revolt, but his general
Harpagus, whom he had previously wronged, deserted the cause of Astyages, and brought his soldiers
over to the side of young Cyrus. The Median king
was soon seized by his men, and the Persians took
the capital city of Ecbatana in 550 B.C. without

a battle. From this time forward, the Medes and Persians fought and served together as one unit under the brilliant leadership of Cyrus.

After the conquest of Media, Cyrus moved swiftly to the west, absorbing all of the Median territories as far as the river Halys in Asia Minor. When Croesus, the fabulously wealthy king of Lydia, refused to recognize the sovereignty of Persia, Cyrus defeated him in battle and took over his empire (546 B.C.). Seven years later he was ready to launch the great assault against Babylon itself.

The Neo-Babylonian empire was in no condition to resist a Medo-Persian invasion in the year 539 B.C. During the preceding fourteen years Nabonidus, the Neo-Babylonian king, had not so much as visited Babylon, leaving the administration of that great city in the hands of his profligate son Belshazzar, whose name appears on the cuneiform tablets as "the son of the king." Nabonidus weakened the empire by concentrating his favors upon the cult of the god Sin at the expense of Babylonian deities, thus incurring the wrath of the priesthood.

Realizing that danger was near, Nabonidus came to Babylon for the New Year's festival of April 4, 539 B.C., and began to bring the images of Babylonian divinities into the city from surrounding areas. But it was all to no avail. Toward the end of September, the armies of Cyrus under the command of Ugbaru, governor of Gutium, attacked Opis on the Tigris and defeated the Babylonians. On October 10 Sippar was taken without a battle and Nabonidus fled. Two days later Ugbaru's troops were able to get into Babylon while Belshazzar, completely oblivious of the doom that awaited him, was engaged in a riotous banquet within the "impregnable' 'walls of the city. The fateful day was October 12; in that same night Belshazzar was slain. Not ling afterwards Nabonidus was taken captive.

Cyrus entered Babylon on October 29 and presented himself to the people as a gracious liberator and benefactor. He permitted the gods whom Na-

bonidus had brought into Babylon to be carried
back to their respective cities, and pursued a benevolent policy toward various captive peoples who had
suffered under the rule of Nebuchadnezzar and his
successors. The Jews were favored with a special
decree permitting them to return to Palestine and
rebuild their ruined temple (Ezra I).

The same day that Cyrus came to Babylon, Gubaru, the new governor or satrap of Babylon and
the Region beyond the River, began to appoint sub-
governors to rule with him over the vast territories
and populations of the Fertile Crescent. On November 6, Ugbaru, the conqueror of Babylon, died;
and in March the mother of Belshazzar (Nitocris,
wife of Nabonidus and daughter of Nebuchadnezzar)
died in Babylon and was publically mourned for
five days. Turning the administration of the huge
satrapy of Babylonia over to Gubaru, Cyrus left for
Ecbatana toward the end of his accession year.

In the meantime, *Cambyses*, son of Cyrus, lived
in Sippar and represented his father at the New
Year's festivals in Babylon as "the King's son." He
was also given the task of preparing for an expedition against Egypt. In 530 B.C., Cyrus appointed
his son to be his successor and co-regent just before
setting out upon a campaign to the far northeast
in the Oxus and Jaxartes region; and at the New
Year's festival of March 26, 530 B.C., Cambyses
assumed the title "King of Babylon" for the first
time, while Cyrus retained the broader title "King
of Lands." In the autumn of the same year news
reached Babylonia that Cyrus had died on the field
of battle. Cambyses was now the sole ruler of the
great Persian Empire.

After securing his position on the throne, Cambyses began his conquest of Egypt. He defeated
Psammetichus III at Pelusium in 525 B.C. and occupied the entire country. But news of troubles in the
homeland disturbed him; and when, on his way
home in Palestine, he heard that a pretender had
taken the throne, he committed suicide. Fearing

disloyalty, Cambyses had previously ordered his brother Smerdis (or Bardiya) to be killed; but now a man named Gaumata set himself up as the king of Persia, claiming to be Smerdis. The Pseudo-Smerdis, as he was later called, gained a huge following by remitting taxes for three years throughout the Empire.

This would have been the end of the Achaemenian dynasty had not *Darius,* son of Hystaspes and great-grandson of Ariyaramnes (brother of Cyrus I), retained the loyalty of the Persian army. Within the brief space of two months he succeeded in capturing and killing the Pseudo-Smerdis (522 B.C.), and during the next two years defeated nine kings in nineteen battles. His own account of these victories is recorded in the famous Behistun Inscription, carved on the face of a rock cliff three hundred feet above the level of the plain near the old road from Ecbatana to Babylon. Thus the second major phase of Achaemenian rule was launched, to end only with the conquests of Alexander the Great in 331 B.C.

DATED EVENTS IN THE
YEAR OF BABYLON'S FALL

New Year's festival observed by the
  Babylonians (4th of Nisan)   April 7, 539 B.C.
Opis attacked by Cyrus (Tishri), Sept.-Oct., 539 B.C.
Sippar captured by Cyrus
  (14th of Tishri)   Oct. 10, 539 B.C.
Babylon taken by Ugbaru
  (16th of Tishri)   Oct. 12, 539 B.C.
First tablet dated in the reign of
  Cyrus (Tishri)   Sept.-Oct., 539 B.C.
Babylon entered by Cyrus; and Gubaru,
  his governor, appoints governors in
  Babylon (3rd of Marchesvan)   Oct. 29, 539 B.C.
Next to last Nabonidus tablet
  (10th Marchesvan)   Nov. 5, 539 B.C.
Death of Ugbaru
  (11th of Marchesvan)   Nov. 6, 539 B.C.

Second Cyrus tablet
  (24th of Marchesvan)   Nov. 19, 539 B.C.
Last Nabonidus tablet (Kislev), Nov.-Dec., 539 B.C.
Beginning of period of mourning for some
  prominent person, possibly Belshazzar's
  mother (28th of Adar)   Mar. 21, 538 B.C.
End of period of mourning
  (3rd of Nisan)   Mar. 26, 538 B.C.
Cambyses, son of Cyrus, enters the Temple,
  apparently for some religious ceremony
  (4th of Nisan)   Mar. 27, 538 B.C.

NEO-BABYLONIAN AND PERSIAN KINGS

1. *Nabopolassar* (Nabu-apal-usur) - founder of the Neo-Babylonian Empire. (626-605 B.C.)
2. *Nebuchadnezzar* (Nabu-kudurri-user)—his son and the greatest of the Neo-Babylonian kings. (605-562 B.C.)
3. *Evil-Merodach* (Amel-Marduk) — his son. (562-560 B.C.)
4. *Neriglissar* (Nergal-shar-usur) — a son-in-law of Nebuchadnezzar. (560-556 B.C.)
5. *Laborosoarchad* (Labashi-marduk) — his son (a few months in 556 B.C.)
6. *Nabonidus* (Nabu-na'id) — probably the husband of Nitocris, a daughter of Nebuchadnezzar, and the father of *Belshazzar*, who shared the throne during the last years of his reign. (556-539 B.C.)
1. *Cyrus the Great* (539-530 B.C.)
2. *Cambyses* (530-522 B.C.)
3. *Gautama*, or Smerdis, or Bardiya (a few months in 552 B.C.)
4. *Darius I - Hystaspes* (521-486 B.C.)
5. *Xerxes* (586-465 B.C.)
6. *Artaxerxes I - Longimanus* (464-423 B.C.)
7. *Darius II - Ochus* (423-404 B.C.)
8. *Artaxerxes II - Memnon* (404-359 B.C.)
9. *Artaxerxes III - Ochus* (359-338 B.C.)
10. *Arses* (338-335 B.C.)
11. *Darius III* (335-331 B.C.)

v. 3-4 . . . DANIEL WAS DISTINGUISHED ABOVE THE
PRESIDENTS . . . THE PRESIDENTS . . . SOUGHT TO FIND OCCA-
SION AGAINST DANIEL . . . Many commentators insist that the
"excellent spirit . . . in him" was a direct, supernatural, extraordinary gift of God to Daniel such as the special gifts of the
Holy Spirit in the N.T. We cannot agree. We believe it involved much more than technical excellence. It was not
mere talent that raised Daniel to such exceeding favor with
the king. No doubt he had talent, but talent without moral
strength counts for little in such a position as Daniel was
placed. Moral strength is not an irresistible gift of the
Holy Spirit. It is the moral character even more than the
brain that determines the man.

This "excellent spirit" means literally that in Daniel the
spirit was predominent, was uppermost, was enthroned. Excellent is something that excels, goes beyond, predominates.
We might translate literally, "A spirit that excelled was in
him . . . a spirit that jutted out was in him." The spiritual
was the chief thing—not the flesh. This excellent spirit
was (a) A spirit of self-control; (b) A spirit of genuine
piety—to him God was a reality, a living and reliable friend,
to whom he could take every difficulty, and on whom he
could trust in every danger; (c) A spirit of unshaken faith
in God. The man of excellent spirit, in whom spirit excels
is (1) a man of purpose; (2) a man of prayer; (3) a man of
perception; (4) a man of power. Daniel was all of this. By
unswerving faith in God Daniel made use of every circumstance and did not allow circumstances to rule him.

It does not take jealous enemies to find some flaws in
all of us — but not even these envious schemers could find
fault with Daniel's responsibilities to his pagan ruler! This
does not mean, of course, that Daniel was no sinner, but
there was no open departure from righteousness and justice
which could be brought against him. Daniel was above reproach in honesty, fairness, fidelity, and integrity toward
his king.

Daniel's irreproachable integrity is little short of incredible in view of his circumstances! He had come to this
land against his will as a prisoner of war; he was requested
by a pagan despot to study pagan literature and science

and be trained to serve in a pagan court surrounded by luxury, sensuality, lust, self-seeking, idolatry, and ruthless cruelty. In the middle of all this there grew up this fair flower of a character, pure, true, holy, and stainless, by the acknowledgement of enemies, and in which not even accusers could find a mault! There are no circumstances in which a man must have his garments spotted by the world! In fact, unfavorable circumstances are the most favorable for the development of the godly character. Development of godly character comes, not by what we draw from the things around, but by what we draw from the things from above (Col. 3:1-4).

v. 5-9 . . . WE SHALL NOT FIND ANY OCCASION AGAINST THIS DANIEL, EXCEPT WE FIND IT AGAINST HIM CONCERNING THE LAW OF HIS GOD . . . MAKE A STRONG INTERDICT . . . This is a typical trick of corrupt politicians. If no flaw in a man's social or vocational relationships can be found, the unjust enemy will try to pit the godly man's relationship to God against his relationship to necessary secular loyalties. The enemies of God attempted the same trick against the Son of God but He defeated it in much the same way as Daniel—"render unto Caesar the things that are Caesar's and unto God the things that are God's."

It should not seem unusual even to twentieth century minds that pagan societies would deify their rulers. Adolph Hitler was practically defied in the office of "Fuehrer." Lenin has been practically deified by the Russian communists. The kings of Egypt were worshipped as gods as far back as recorded history can determine. The envious presidents, satraps, and other officials were not suggesting anything unusual to king Darius. Even Herod (Acts 12) revealed in the foolishness of the Jews calling him a god!

They had heard of Daniel's religious practices and observed how faithful he was to them. They were convinced that Daniel would not compromise his religious convictions even at the threat of his life. Thus their scheme is presented to the king—its purpose hidden from him.

It was common for the Babylonians to administer capital punishment by burning (the fiery furnace). To the Persians, who were worshippers of fire, this was regarded

Nevertheless Daniel Prayed

as something of an abomination, and so they destroyed their condemned criminals by casting them to savage beasts.

Darius yielded to the subtle flattery of thinking of himself as being prayed to as a god. Prayer had a very significant place in Persian religion. It was the chief factor in their worship. A great part of the holy writings (the Zend-Avesta, etc.) contains only formulas of prayer and a certain type of litanies. Prayer is regarded as irresistible, as operating with a certain magic power. To omit prayer would mean the collapse of the world. One can readily see why Daniel's enemies centered their attention on prayer.

It is a logical deduction that if the Persian king is a god or an earthly representative of a god, then his decrees ought to be irrevocable (cf. Esther 1:19; 8:8). Diodorus Siculus, ancient historian, reports a case where Darius III (335 B.C.) passed sentence of death upon a certain Charidemos, but "immediately he repented and blamed himself, as having greatly erred; but it was not possible to undo what was done by royal authority." These jealous politicians had taken this custom into account and were banking on it to help them achieve their purpose when the king should later discover their trick!

QUIZ

1. Where did the Medes and the Persians originate?
2. When were the Babylonians and Persians allied and for what purpose?
3. What did Cyrus II, the Great, do for the Jews in captivity?
4. Why is Daniel's irreproachable integrity so unique?
5. What trick did the enemies of Daniel use after no flaw in his job can be found?
6. How important was prayer in the pagan Persian religion?

b.   PERSISTENCE

TEXT: 6:10-18

10   And when Daniel knew that the writing was signed, he went into his house; (now his windows were open in his chamber toward Jerusalem); and he kneeled upon his

knees three times a day, and prayed, and gave thanks before his God, as he did aforetime.

11 Then these men assembled together, and found Daniel making petition and supplication before his God.

12 Then they came near, and spake before the king concerning the king's interdict: Hast thou not signed an interdict, that every man that shall make petition unto any god or man within thirty days, save unto thee, O king, shall be cast into the den of lions? The king answered and said, The thing is true, according to the law of the Medes and Persians, which altereth not.

13 Then answered they and said before the king, That Daniel, who is of the children of the captivity of Judah, regardeth not thee, O king, nor the interdict that thou hast signed, but maketh his petition three times a day.

14 Then the king, when he heard these words, was sore displeased, and set his heart on Daniel to deliver him; and he labored till the going down of the sun to rescue him.

15 Then these men assembled together unto the king, and said unto the king, Know, O king, that it is a law of the Medes and Persians, that no interdict nor statute which the king establisheth may be changed.

16 Then the king commanded, and they brought Daniel, and cast him into the den of lions. Now the king spake and said unto Daniel, Thy God whom thou servest continually, he will deliver thee.

17 And a stone was brought, and laid upon the mouth of the den; and the king sealed it with his own signet, and with the signet of his lords; that nothing might be changed concerning Daniel.

18 Then the king went to his palace, and passed the night fasting; neither were instruments of music brought before him: and his sleep fled from him.

QUERIES

a. Did Daniel deliberately provoke their wrath by praying, v. 10?

b. How did the king labor all day to rescue Daniel?

c. Why seal the stone?

PARAPHRASE

But though Daniel knew about the decree of king Darius, he went home and knelt down as usual in his upstairs room, with its windows open toward Jerusalem, and prayed three times a day, just as he was accustomed to do every day, giving thanks to his God.   Then Daniel's enemies all gathered secretly at his house and found him praying there, as they knew he would, to his Jehovah God.   They rushed back to the king and subtly reminded him, You have signed a decree, have you not, O king, that demands that any man who shall pray to any god except yourself, within the next thirty days, shall be thrown to the wild lions?   The king answered, Yes, that is absolutely correct.   And, according to the law of the Medes and Persians, my decree cannot be altered or abrogated!   The satraps, presidents and others who had been spying on Daniel then said to the king, This fellow, Daniel, one of the Jewish captives, is paying no attention to you or your law.   He is praying to his God three times each day.   Hearing this, the king was very angry with himself for signing the law, and made up his mind he would try to save Daniel.   He spent the rest of the day trying to figure out some way to rescind the law or stop the execution of it. In the evening the men came again to the king and said, O king, there is nothing that can be done.   You signed the law and it cannot be changed.   Fearfully the king gave the order for Daniel's arrest, and so Daniel was brought to the den of lions.   The king said to him, May your God, whom you worship continually and who has delivered you in the past, deliver you now.   And they threw Daniel into the den of lions.   A stone was brought and placed over the access into the den through which the animals were driven.   The king sealed it with his own official signet ring, and that of his government, so that no one would dare rescue Daniel from the lions.   Then the king returned to his palace and was awake the whole night in a state of deep depression and agitation of soul.   He could not eat, he could not sleep and he had no desire to have his usual entertainment.

COMMENT

v. 10-11 . . . DANIEL . . . WENT INTO HIS HOUSE . . . AND KNEELED . . . AND PRAYED Daniel did the only thing he could do. He was not deliberately courting martyrdom or persecution, but if he had evaded the issue he would have given the appearance of trusting his God only when it was physically profitable. Very plainly there were only two alternatives: (a) Continue to worship God as he had been doing all along and face the probability of death and trust in God; (b) Submit to the decree of the king, save his neck, and declare his unbelief and cowardice. Daniel believed God!

The original text indicates his chamber was an "upper chamber." One of those rooms built upon some corner of the roof or a special tower-like chamber on top of the house, with latticed windows no doubt for coolness, where one could be alone for rest and meditation. Daniel, being one of the presidents, would have no mean place of abode. But he had some mean enemies! Praying toward Jerusalem seems to have its origin in I Kings 8:33ff. His jealous contemporaries appear to have set up a watch at his window (all of them gathered so as to have plenty of witnesses). When they had seen enough they made haste for the king's palace.

v. 12-13 . . . HAST THOU NOT SIGNED AN INTERDICT . . . DANIEL . . . REGARDETH NOT . . . These envious politicians are crafty psychologists. They are also liars. First they "psych" the king into an even more emphatic declaration of his decree and the absolute impossibility of its being revoked. Then they applied nationalistic prejudice to "psych" the king against Daniel by referring to him as "that fellow (Daniel) . . . one of the Jewish prisoners of war . . ." To top it all off they exaggerated the truth in their own scheming imaginations into a lie and said that Daniel had no regard for the king. Now it is true that Daniel would not give precedence to any king or any king's law over God and His laws. However, it was not true that Daniel had no proper regard for the king's authority in other realms. In fact, it had already been recognized by the king that Daniel did have high regard for him and his country. But the king is under great pressure.

v. 14-15 . . . THE KING . . . WAS SORE DISPLEASED . . .
SET HIS HEART . . . TO RESCUE HIM . . . Darius was no
moron. He knew he had been tricked. He also knew he was
about to lose his most efficient, truthworthy, and loyal president which did not make him happy. No doubt the schemers
were not prepared for this reaction. Just how Darius went
about his attempt to rescue Daniel from this predicament
we are not told. It is easy to infer, from verse 15, that he
argued, reasone, and attempted to coerce his advisors to
relent on this decree—that he not be held to the irrevocable
nature of a royal decree this time. But they would not relent! They "belabored" the king over and over again with
the inviolability of Medo-Persian law. They probably even
dropped a threatening inneundo here and there that they
would take the matter to Cyrus if he should desist from
his duty. This, of course, is the kind of political pressure
that broke down what little moral fibre Pontius Pilate had
when he would have released Jesus as a man who had done
no evil. The phrase "Thou art not a friend of Caesar,"
modified with the times, has rung in the ears of many a
man faced with such a moral decision between right and
wrong — and they have surrendered to the wrong for fear
of Caesar. What should ring in their ears are the words of
the Lord, "Do not fear him who is able only to destroy the
body, rather fear Him who is able to destroy both body and
soul in hell!"

v. 16-18 . . . THEY BROUGHT DANIEL, AND CAST HIM
INTO THE DEN OF LIONS . . . The king seems to have some
hope that Daniel's God, whom he worshipped so faithfully,
would by some mighty wonder deliver him. Perhaps Darius
had even heard stories of Daniel's past deliverance under
the Babylonians. It would be too far-fetched to think that
Darius had come to any personal faith in Jehovah God such
as Daniel himself had. Darius was at least truly interested
in seeing Daniel saved because he had high regard for the
seer.

Some think the lion's den must have had a gate or a
normal door-type entrance at the side where ferocious animals were driven in, plus an opening on top through which
condemned criminals were dropped into the midst of the

ravenous beasts. The top opening would not need to be closed since it would be completely inaccessible from within while the side gate was doubly secured by rolling a large stone in front of it. Darius then placed some type of seal upon the stone door and the imprint of his signet ring and that of the government therein. Guards were probably placed there at the insistence of Daniel's enemies so no one would tamper with the door or attempt to rescue Daniel.

The king, wrestling with his conscience and depressed at the thought of losing so trustworthy a friend as Daniel, was nearly beside himself all night. He could not eat, he was in no mood for any kind of entertainment, and he could not sleep. Many times he probably paused from pacing the floor of his palace room and looked and listened toward the lions den to catch some indication of hope, against hope, that Daniel might survive the night. He no doubt remonstrated with himself over and over at being tricked by his own pride and by evil and envious men, all of whom put together were not worth this trustworthy administrator, Daniel. Little did he know what great power the God of Daniel had.

QUIZ

1. What were Daniel's alternatives when he learned of the king's decree?
2. Describe the crafty way in which the enemies of Daniel pressured the king?
3. Why was the king upset when he finally realized what must be done?
4. How did the king probably trp to rescue Daniel?
5. Did Darius have Daniel's faith that his God would rescue him?
6. How upset was the king?

c. PRESERVATION

TEXT: 6:19-28

19 Then the king arose very early in the morning, and went in haste unto the den of lions.
20 And when he came near unto the den to Daniel, he cried with a lamentable voice; the king spake and said

to Daniel, O Daniel, servant of the living God, is thy
God, whom thou servest continually, able to deliver
thee from the lions?

21 Then said Daniel unto the king, O King, live for ever.

22 My God hath sent his angel, and hath shut the lions'
mouths, and they have not hurt me; forasmuch as before him innocency was found in me; and also before
thee, O king, have I done no hurt.

23 Then was the king glad, and commanded that they should
take Daniel up out of the den. So Daniel was taken
up out of the den, and no manner of hurt was found
upon him, because he had trusted in his God.

24 And the king commanded, and they brought those men
that had accused Daniel, and they cast them into the den
of lions, them, their children, and their wives; and the
lions had the mastery of them, and brake all their bones
in pieces, before they came to the bottom of the den.

25 Then king Darius wrote unto all the peoples, nations,
and languages, that dwell in all the earth: Peace be
multiplied unto you.

26 I make a decree, that in all the dominion of my kingdom
men tremble and fear before the God of Daniel; for he
is the living God, and stedfast for ever, and his kingdom that which shall not be destroyed: and his dominion shall be even unto the end:

27 he delivereth and rescueth, and he worketh signs and
wonders in heaven and in earth, who hath delivered
Daniel from the power of the lions.

28 So this Daniel prospered in the reign of Darius, and in
the reign of Cyrus the Persian.

QUERIES

a. Why did the king cry "with a lamentable" voice?
b. Just how innocent was Daniel before the living God?
c. Why did the king have the wives and children of Daniel's
   enemies thrown into the lion's den?

PARAPHRASE

Very early the next morning the king hurried to the
lions' den. As he ran toward the den he began crying out,
O Daniel, servant of the living God, was your God, whom

God Rewards Faith

you worship faithfully, able to deliver you from death by
the lions? Then the king was almost overcome with relief
to hear Daniel's voice as he answered, O king, may thy
days be many. My God has sent His angel to shut the lions'
mouths so that they cannot harm me. My God has protected me because I am innocent of the wrong of which I
have been accused, and you know that I have done no wrong
to you, O king. The king was so glad that he was nearly
beside himself and he ordered that Daniel be hoisted up out
of the lions' den. When Daniel had been brought up not a
scratch was found on him. Daniel's deliverance was due to
his complete trust in God. Immediately the king ordered
that the men who had accused Daniel, along with their wives
and children, be brought and thrown into the lions' den. As
they were being cast into the den, the lions leaped upon them
and tore their bodies apart before they even hit the bottom
of the pit. Afterwards king Darius issued this decree ad-
dressed to everyone under his administration: May all my
subjects dwell in peace! I hereby decree that in all the areas
where Cyrus has appointed me to rule men shall pay due
respect to the God of Daniel. His God is the living, un-
changing God whose kingdom shall never be destroyed and
whose power is omnipotent. Daniel's God delivers His people, preserving them from harm and He does it by performing great miracles in heaven and earth. This is the
omnipotent God who delivered Daniel from the power of the
lions. So Daniel prospered in the days Darius ruled for
Cyrus in Babylon and during all the rest of the reign of
Cyrus who ruled all the empire.

COMMENT

v. 19-22 . . . THE KING AROSE VERY EARLY IN THE
MORNING . . . The king coul dhardly contain himself until
the very beginning of sunrise. At the first sign of dawn
he gathered a few servants and went with much haste to
the lions' den. Hoping against hope he came near the pit
yelling the name of Daniel. Drawing up to the hole opened
at the top of the pit he yelled with a voice of pain and
pleading, down into it, "Daniel! You who serve Jehovah
God as your God, are you still alive?" When he heard the
voice of Daniel replying, he was very evidently overjoyed

(v. 23). Daniel answers, respectful as ever, informing the king that the angel of Jehovah was sent to shut the mouths of the lions. Scriptures abound in revelation concerning the activity of angels of God" "as ministering spirits sent forth to minister for them who shall be heirs of salvation" (Heb. 1:14). We have outlined a special study on angels in Daniel chapter 10.

Daniel does not mean to infer that he was sinless but simply that he was "innocent" of the charges for which he had been thrown to the lions and, therefore, because of his complete trust in God and not in himself, God delivered him. He also politely, but frankly, reminded the king that the king was well aware of his innocence.

v. 23-24 . . . THEN WAS THE KING GLAD . . . The original indicates the king was "exceedingly glad." Daniel was hoisted out of the pit through the opening at the top. Not one scratch was found on his body. The lions had been completely restrained from harming him in any way.

Then Oriental justice was meted out. The men who had lied about Daniel were ordered brought, along with their wives and children, and they were cast into the jaws of death they had been so ready to give Daniel. Their fate is mentioned by Daniel, not out of malice, but objectively, in order to show that Daniel's deliverance was miraculous. The lions did no harm to Daniel, not because they were not hungry or because they were docile, but because some supernatural power prevented them from putting even the slightest scratch upon him.

v. 25-28 THEN KING DARIUS WROTE UNTO ALL THE PEOPLES . . . Darius ruled in the region of Babylon and beyond the River (see comments at beginning of this chapter), so he wrote to all under his sub-rule (Cyrus the Great was ruler over all the empire). It would be too much conjecture to think Darius was doing anything more than commanding that Daniel's God be worshipped along with all the other gods of the Persian pantheon. He does not confess Daniel's God to be the only True God. He knows now that Daniel's God is able to do miraculous wonders, but he believes his gods are able to do such wonders also.

so ends the historical portion of the book. Daniel's purpose has been to record the mighty demonstration of God's miraculous power to deliver and the sovereignty of God over the greatest of pagan powers. These historical demonstrations are to provide the basis for the prophecies of deliverance for the captive Jews that follow in Daniel's book. The visions of deliverance and the visions of 600 years of history God unfolds through the pen of Daniel are to be believed! The people of God will be victorious over all bondage and persecution! They will have their Messiah and messianic kingdom! Their "prince" will usher in a time of spiritual renewal (chap. 9)! If God can deliver from the fiery furnace, from the lions' den, and can bring down a Nebuchadnezzar and a Belshazzar—then He can deliver these captives!

QUIZ

1. What was the attitude of the king as he went to the lions' den?
2. What was his attitude when he heard Daniel's voice?
3. Why mention that the lions tore the Persians asunder?
4. What is the purpose of the historical section of Daniel?

SERMON NUMBER SIX

LAWYERS AND LIONS

Text: Daniel 6

INTRODUCTION

I. WHO IS DARIUS THE MEDE?

    A. John C. Whitcomb, Jr., in his book, *Darius, The Mede,* contends that an error was made in transcription of the Nabonidus Chronicle when two different names were both translated "Gobryas."

        1. One name was Ugbaru, the governor of Gutium, who entered Babylon with the army of Cyrus and conquered the city.

        2. The other name is Gabaru, who appointed satraps.

3. In line 22 of this Chronicle, Ugbaru is said to have died.

4. Mr. Whitcomb suggests that Ugbaru was indeed Gobryas who conquered the city in the name of Cyrus, but Gubaru is the one who was appointed governor of Babylon and is the same person as Darius, the Mede.

B. He is mentioned in Daniel 9:1 as the son of Ahasuerus.

1. The fact that no cuneiform text known to us mentions the name of Gubaru's father (Darius) is no evidence tsat his father could not have been Ahasuerus.

C. Gubaru was appointed governor of Babylon and the River beyond on the very day Cyrus first set foot in the conquered city, October 29, 539 B.C.

1. He continued in that position throughout the reign of Cyrus and through more than half of the subsequent reign of Cambyses, the son of Cyrus.

2. The great prominence given to Darius the Mede (Bubaru) in the book of Daniel is readily explained if we assume his identification with a person by the name of Gubaru whose reign extended over 14 years (539-525 B.C.)!

II. DANIEL'S HIGH POSITION IN PERSIAN GOVERNMENT

A. It is interesting that Daniel maintains high position in government with the drastic change of administration from Babylonian to Persian.

1. Usually a "clean sweep" of former government officials is made when an Oriental king conquers an enemy's government.

2. We would like to know some of the details of Daniel's circumstances during the csange of government, but we have none.

B. Daniel was appointed as one of the top-echelon cabinet members, "a president."

1. There were three such "presidents."

2. They sad subordinated under them 120 satraps.

3. The Persians were great administrators, they had an excellent revenue system, public works system, postal system, etc.
4. The satraps and the presidents were charged with seeing that the king's treasury should suffer no loss of revenue.

C. Daniel's position was doubtless granted because of his character.
   1. Technically, he was probably well schooled in government affairs, especially of the province of Babylon, so the Persians would want to use his knowledge of Babylon people and history.
   2. Morally, he was above reproach. The Persian king had doubtless been informed or tested Daniel for himself and was assured that Daniel was trustworthy and would serve his ruler well.

DISCUSSION

I. PERFIDY, 6:1-9

A. Moved by jealousy and prejudice the other officials of Darius' kingdom sought to have Daniel dishonored and deposed from office, probably in order to have a relative or friend appointed in his place.
   1. It may be simply that the excellence of Daniel's technical performance and moral integrity made him favored in the king's counsels and his contemporaries grew envious.
   2. It does not take jealous enemies to find some flaw in all of us—but not even these envious schemers could find faults with Daniel's responsibilities to his pagan ruler!
   3. This does not mean that Daniel was no sinner—but there was no open departure from faithfulness and justice and honesty that could be brought against him.
   4. Daniel's irreproachable integrity is little short of incredible in view of his circumstances. He had come to this land against his will as a prisoner of war; he was requested by a pagan despot to study pagan literature and science and be trained

to serve in a pagan court surrounded by luxury, sensuality, lust, self-seeking, idolatry, and ruthless cruelty; to serve a ruler who held his people in slavery.

5. In the middle of all this there grew up this fair flower of a character, pure, true, holy, and stainless, by the acknowledgement of enemies, and in which not even accusers could find a fault!

6. There are no circumstances in which a man must have his garments spotted by the world! NOT EVEN IN PRISON, AS WE SHALL LEARN LATER! In fact, unfavorable circumstances are the most favorable for the development of the godly character. Development of godly character comes not by what we draw from the things around, but by what we draw from the things from above (Col. 3:1-4).

B. The next move was to try to pit the godly man's relationshi pto God against his relationship to necessary secular loyalties.

1. The enemies of God attempted the same trick against the Son of God but He defeated it in much the same way as Daniel—"render unto Saesar the things that are Caesar's and unto God the things that are God's."

2. Villanous men have used the same tactics for centuries against godly people of whom they are envious. God-fearing men seeking political office even in America have been subtly villified with innuendo and inferences that they will be less than loyal or less than humane because they are religiously conservative and fundamental. The American press has assassinated the characters of some political figures of this decade because these men were god-fearing and not afraid to say so (Lester Maddox, George Wallace, and others too numerous to mention).

C. Communists have imprisoned, tortured, and killed millions of Christians on "trumped up" charges.

1. Richard Wurmbrand tells in his book *Tortured For Christ*, of being kidnapped right off a public

street and imprisoned because they said, ". . . you are telling your people to just be patient and the Americans will come and deliver them . . . you are also telling them the communists will not continue to rule! These are counter-revolutionary lies!" He had said none of this!

2. Haralan Popoff in his book, *I Was A Communist Prisoner,* tells how he and many other Christian ministers were arrested and tried as spies against the state when they had done nothing but preach the Gospel.

3. Once Wurmbrand was released by having been "ransomed" with payment of $6,000. The Communists told him, "Go to the West and preach Christ as much as you like, but don't touch us! Don't speak a word against us! We tell you frankly what we plan for you if you do tell what happened. First of all, for $1,200 we can find a gangster to liquidate you, or we can kidnap you . . . We can also destroy you morally by spreading a story about you with a girl, theft, or some sin of your youth. The Westerners—especially Americans—are very easily deceived and duped."

D. Why such perfidy against God-fearing people?

1. Because darkness cannot stand the light (cf. John 3:19-20).

2. Atheism, materialism, polytheism cannot tolerate the idea of God, The Only True and Holy God

3. Wurmbrand writes, "The cruelty of atheism is hard to believe. When a man has no faith in the reward of good or the punishment of evil, there is no reason to be human . . . I heard one torturer say, 'I thank God, in whom I don't believe, that I have lived to this hour when I can express all the evil in my heart.' "

4. Lenin wrote, "Every religious idea, every idea of God, even flirting with the idea of God, is unutterable vileness of the most dangerous kind, contagion of the most abominable kind. Millions of sins, filthy deeds, acts of violence and physical con-

tagion are far less dangerous than the subtle, spiritual idea of a God."

5. Men cannot be kept in bondage to be exploited by selfish, wicked, ungodly tyrants if the truth of God is preached and lived, therefore those who love and serve God will be persecuted. (cf. Jn. 15:18ff.)

II. PERSISTENCE, 6:10-18

A. Daniel did the only thing he could do. He was not deliberately courting martyrdom or persecution, but if he evaded the issue he would have given the appearance of trusting his God only when it was physically profitable.

1. He had only one alternative: submit to the decree of the king, save his neck, and declare his unbelief and cowardice. DANIEL BELIEVED GOD!

2. These words ring down the corridors of time, "Whether it is right in the sight of God to listen to you rather than to God, you must judge; for we cannot but speak of what we have seen and heard." "We must obey God rather than men. . . (Acts 5:19-20; 5:29)."

3. Wurmbrand writes, "It was strictly forbidden to preach to other prisoners . . . A number of us decided to pay the price for the privilege of preaching, so we accepted their terms. It was a deal; we preached and they beat us. We were happy preaching. They were happy beating us, so everyone was happy."

4. Wurmbrand tells of a preacher who was tortured by being made to stand for two weeks day and night, but he resisted. They finally brought in his 14-year-old son and began to whip the boy in front of the father saying that they would continue to beat him until the preacher said what they wished him to say. The poor man was half mad. He bore it as long as he could. When he could not stand it any more, he cried to his son, "Alexander, I must say what they want! I can't bear your beating any more!" The son answered,

"Father, don't do me the injustice to have a traitor as a parent. Withstand! If they kill me, I will die with the words 'Jesus and my fatherland.'" The communists, enraged, fell upon the child and beat tim to death, with blood spattered over the walls of the cell. He died praising God!

B. Daniel's sentence was to be thrown to the lions. This was no tame pack of lions, for we learn later that when the men who had conspired against Daniel were thrown in, the lions tore them asunder before they even hit the bottom of the pit.

1. Some of the tortures Wurmbrand had to endure because of his faith:

   a. Tortured with red-hot irons and pokers and knives.

   b. Starving rats driven into his cell against which he had to defend himself.

   c. Some Christians tied to crosses for 4 days and nights; the crosses put on the floor and hundreds of prisoners had to fulfill their bodily necessities over the faces and bodies of the crucified ones.

   d. A priest, after being driven nearly insane with tortures, was forced to consecrate human excrement and urine and give Holy Communion to Christians in this form.

2. Some of the tortures Haralan Popoff had to endure because of his faith:

   a. Locked in a filthy cell literally plastered with bed-bugs (he killed 539 his first night in the cell).

   b. Stand with face eight inches from a wall for ten days and nights without food or drink or sleep while questioned and while tormented with food and drink nearby. His blood drained from his head to his legs; his face became yellow; his legs swelled to twice their normal size.

   c. He was beaten, spat upon, thrown in an underground dungeon, made to work under the whip of prison guards, starved on one piece of bread

and six-tablespoons of watery soup per day
when he did get anything to eat.

C. Others have endured as much or more

1. The question we all ought to ask is, "Would my
faith in God and Christ stand such a test?"

2. It could happen to American Christians right here
in America without a Russian or Chinese communist ever setting foot on our shores.

3. Our own government could be toppled and taken
over by godless Americans and the government
made into a people's god.

4. If your chldren were beaten to death before your
eyes, could you still trust in Jesus and take Him
at His word?

5. If you had to go without eating for ten days,
could you still believe God loved you?

6. If you were threatened not to tell others about
Christ, would you?

III. PRESERVATION, 6:19-28

A. God sent his angels to shut the mouths of the lions.
Daniel's God was not impotent!

1. This was a glorious manifestation of the power of
Jehovah God against the ultimate that a pagan
monarch could do.

2. Men cannot even take the lives of other men unless
God permits it.

3. The Bible abounds in illustrations of this.

B. Wurmbrand writes of his deliverance: ". . . they
broke four vertebrae in my back, and many other
bones. They carved me in a dozen places. They
burned and cut eighteen holes in my body. Doctors
in Oslo, seeing all this and the scars of the lung
tuberculosis which I also had, declared that my being
alive today is a pure miracle! According to their
medical books, I should have been dead for years.
I know myself it is a miracle. God is a God of
miracles."

C. Daniel was preserved for a purpose. Evidently God
had many years for Daniel to serve Him yet in being
an agent of God's revelation to the covenant people

of their future. Daniel also served as a contact between pagan government and captive people.

1. All whom God saves out of danger and death are saved for His purposes, not simply for ther fleshly ease.

2. Many never survive the persecutions and executions of physical life . . . THOSE WHO DO SHOULD BE THANKFUL FOR THE OPPORTUNITY TO CONTINUE TO SERVE HIM ON EARTH! FOR CHRISTIANS WHO DO NOT SURVIVE, WE SHOULD BE THANKFUL THEY HAVE GONE TO BE WITH HIM, AND THEY DO REST FROM THEIR LABORS, AND THEIR WORKS DO FOLLOW AFTER THEM!

3. Wurmbrand writes, "I believe God performed this wonder (his release) so that you could hear my voice crying out on behalf of the Underground Church behind the Iron Curtain."

4. Even those who die bear fruit: "A Christian was sentenced to death. Before being executed, he was allowed to see his wife. His last words to his wife were, 'You must know that I die loving those who kill me. They don't know what they do and my last request of you is to love them, too. Don't have bitterness in your heart because they kill your beloved one. We will meet in heaven.' These words impressed the officer of the secret police who attended the discussion between the two. Afterward he told me the story in prison, where he had been put for becoming a Christian."

5. Those of us who live in affluent America have no idea what it is to suffer for our faith in Christ. But why have we been spared? What purpose does God have in being so merciful and beneficient toward us? IS IT NOT IN ORDER THAT WE SHALL HAVE ABUNDANCE TO SHARE WITH THOSE ALL OVER THE WORLD WHO DO NOT HAVE . . . AND MATERIAL GOODS ARE NOT PRIMARILY THE THINGS WE SHOULD BE SO READY TO SHARE . . . WE SHOULD PUT OUR MATERIAL GOODS TO WORK IN ORDER TO SHARE WITH OTHERS THE GOOD NEWS OF CHRIST! The goods are merely means to the end of the good news!

CONCLUSION

I. LESSONS TO BE LEARNED

A. Popoff writes, "Tritchkov's prediction that I would rot there and never get to see my family again was not fulfilled. Our lives and destinies do not depend on human ambitions and predictions but on a higher will and power—God opened the door to the dungeon."

B. Wurmbrand writes, "There is only one method of resistance to brainwashing. This is "heartwashing." If the heart is cleansed by the love of Jesus Christ, and if the heart loves Him, you can resist all tortures."

C. Wurmbrand, "One great lesson arose from all the beatings, torturings and butchery of the communists: that the spirit is master of the body."

D. "Preachers in the West usually assume that those whom they have in church are really convinced about the main truths of Christianity, which they are not. You rarely hear a sermon proving the truth of our faith. But behind the Iron Curtain, men who have never learned to do it give their converts a very serious foundation."

II. LEADERS TO BE CONVERTED

A. Darius may not have been converted, but he was forced by the facts to admit the existence of Daniel's God and he acted in accordance with that.

B. Wurmbrand writes, "But can a communist leader be converted? Surely, because he is unhappy and insecure just like his victim . . . The communists, who very often are as sincere in their beliefs as Christians are in theirs, are passing through a great crisis . . . They had believed that communism would create a brotherhood among nations. Now they see that communist countries quarrel with each other like dogs . . . They had really believed that communism would create an earthly paradise, opposed to what they call the illusory paradise in heaven. And now their peoples are hungry . . . The communists had believed in their leaders. Now they have read in their own newspapers that Stalin was a mass murderer and Khrushchev an idiot . . . There is a void in the hearts of communists. This void can be filled by Christ alone . . . There is something positive in the enormous amount of drunkenness in communist countries. There is the longing for a wider life, which communism cannot give. The average Russian is a deep, great-hearted, generous person. Communism is shallow and superficial. He seeks the deep life and, finding it nowhere else, he seeks it in alcohol. He expresses in alcoholism his horror about the brutal and deceiving life he has to live."

"We must win rulers: political, economic, scientific, artistic personalities. They are the engineers of souls. They mold the souls of men. Winning them, you win the people they lead and influence."

C. There is only one force which can overthrow communism or any other pagan power over men. . . This force is the truth of God in the Gospel of Christ.

The underground church has already won communist rulers for Christ. Gheorghiu Dej, Rumania's prime minister, died a converted man after confessing his sin and changing his sinful life.

In communist countries there are communist members of the government who are hidden Christians. This can spread.

D. IT HAPPENED IN DANIEL'S TIME . . . IT HAPPENED IN THE APOSTLE PAUL'S TIME . . . IT HAPPENED IN ALEXANDER CAMPBELL'S TIME. IT CAN HAPPEN IN OUR TIME!

IF WE FEAR GOD AND ARE NOT AFRAID OF
LAWYERS AND LIONS!

EXAMINATION SIX

REFUTATIONS

(Answer the following by giving the argument which will correct the statement)

1. Darius was the conquerer of Babylon. Refute!

2. Daniel did not serve Darius well because he felt he was not obligated to serve a pagan king faithfully. Refute!

3. Darius took pleasure in committing Daniel to the lion's den for disobeying the king's edict. Refute!

ASSOCIATIONS

(Associate the persons or events of column one with the correct person or event of column two)

1	2
Darius	Medo-Persian origin
president	concubine
Cyrus	Ugbaru
Cambyses	Belshazzar
Gobryas	Gubaru
Aryans	lake
Elam	mountain
law	son of Cyrus
lion	king of Persia
angel	administrator
	Medo-Persian territory
	city of Jews
	unalterable
	execution
	deliverance

MEMORIZATIONS

(Fill in the blanks:)

. . . That in all the _____ of my kingdom men tremble and fear before the _____ of Daniel; for he is the _____ God, and steadfast for ever, and his kingdom that which shall not be _____: and his dominion shall be even unto the end: he delivereth and _____, and he worketh _____ and _____ in heaven and in earth, who hath delivered Daniel from the power of the _____.

EXPLANATIONS

1. Explain who Darius the Mede was.
2. Explain why the enemies of Daniel persuaded the king to make an edict about praying to any other God except the king.
3. Explain why the king was so concerned about the safety of Daniel after he had ordered Daniel thrown to the lions.
4. Explain why the king commanded the accusers of Daniel and their families to be thrown to the lions after Daniel had been delivered by the angel of the Lord.
5. Explain why the law of the Medes and Persians could not be revoked.

The Four Symbolic Beasts

256

CHAPTER SEVEN

I. BEASTS AND THE BEAUTY—7:1-28

a. MALEVOLENT BEAST

TEXT: 7:1-8

1 In the first year of Belshazzar king of Babylon Daniel had a dream and visions of his head upon his bed: then he wrote the dream and told the sum of the matters.

2 Daniel spake and said, I saw in my vision by night, and, behold, the four winds of heaven brake forth upon the great sea.

3 And four great beasts came up from the sea, diverse one from another.

4 The first was like a lion, and had eagle's wings: I beheld till the wings thereof were plucked, and it was lifted up from the earth, and made to stand upon two feet as a man; and a man's heart was given to it.

5 And, behold, another beast, a second, like to a bear; and it was raised up on one side, and three ribs were in its mouth between its teeth: and they said thus unto it, Arise, devour much flesh.

6 After this I beheld, and, lo, another, like a leopard, which had upon its back four wings of a bird; the beast had also four heads; and dominion was given to it.

7 After this I saw in the night-visions, and, behold, a fourth beast, terrible and powerful, and strong exceedingly; and it had great iron teeth; it devoured and brake in pieces, and stamped the residue with its feet: and it was diverse from all the beasts that were before it; and it had ten horns.

8 I considerd the horns, and, behold, there came up among them another horn, a little one, before which three of the first horns were plucked up by the roots: and, behold, in this horn were eyes like the eyes of a man, and a mouth speaking great things.

QUERIES

a. What symbolic meaning do the "four winds" and the "great sea" have?
b. What do the four beasts symbolize?
c. Who is the "little horn" of the fourth beast?

PARAPHRASE

One night back during the first year of Belshazzar's reign over Babylon, Daniel had a dream and he wrote it down. This, in essence, is his vision: I was having a very graphic vision in my dreamin, at night, and behold the four winds of heaven burst forth upon the great sea. Then four huge, terrifying beasts came up out of the sea, each different from the other. The first was like a lion, but it had wings like an eagle. And as I watched, its wings were pulled off so that it could no longer fly. But it was stood on its hind legs like a man would stand, and a man's mind was given to it. The second beast was like a bear with its feet on one side lifted as if it were going to stride ahead. It held three ribs in its mouth between its teeth. I heard a voice saying to it, Get up, Devour many people! The third of these strange beasts was like a leopard, but it had in its back wings like those of birds; and it had four heads. And extensive power was given to it over all mankind. Then, as my dream continued, I saw a fourth beast coming up out of the sea too fearful and dreadful to describe, and it was incredibly strong. It devoured some of its victims by tearing them apart with its huge iron teeth; others it crushed beneath its powerful feet. It was far more brutal and vicious than any of the other beasts, and it had ten horns. And as I was observing the horns, suddenly another small horn appeared among them, and three of the first ones were pulled out by the roots to give the little horn room; this little horn had a man's eyes and a boastful, bragging mouth.

COMMENT

v. 1-3 . . . THE FOUR WINDS OF HEAVEN BRAKE FORTH UPON THE GREAT SEA . . . Young believes the four winds symbolize some power of God to stir up the nations (sea).

Keil suggests, "heavenly powers and force by which God sets the nations of the world in motion." Leupold disagrees, saying, "that would yield the result that disturbances in the world are attributable to heavenly forces whereas they are more correctly termed the result of purely earthly causes." He believes that the unrest of nations which brings one king and kingdom to power after another is caused directly by the deliberate unregenerate actions of these nations. He prefers "to regard the winds as a second earthly factor in the picture and a rather appropriate one at that." There is some indication in scripture that God does "stir up the spirit" of certain rulers and nations and is providentially active in the affairs of history (cf. Isa. 10:5-16; 45:1-7; Jer. 27:5-7; II Chron. 36:22-23; Ezra 1:1-4, etc.). It should be apparent, however, from the context of the whole body of scripture that God does not overrule the will of man and force a man to think something he does not want to think. God does use natural means at various times to overrule the actions of men but not their wills. So a position somewhere between that of Young and Leupold would seem scriptural to us.

Now with the symbolic figure water the matter is much clearer in scripture. It seems to be widely accepted that the "great sea" symbolizes mankind, and especially Gentile world powers hostile to God and Israel (cf. Isa. 8:7ff.; Jer. 46:7-9; 47:2; Isa. 17-2ff. and Rev. 17:1-15). Thus when the four "beasts" appear as rising from the sea, that clearly indicates that tse disturbed state of the world (whether the disturbing force be God or man or both) gives origin to the successive world powers that appear on the scene of history.

This chapter is somewhat of a "flashback" to the days before Darius and the Medo-Persian takeover. It was during the first year of Belshazzar's rule of Babylon that Daniel himself was given a dream-vision. While the dream was still fresh in his mind, he wrote it down in its essentials. He was undoubtedly restrained by the Spirit of God from including all the unnecesary so as not to present a bewildering array of details not necessary to the reader's understanding.

The most adequate figurative representation of these powers is four "beasts." Leupold dwells at length upon this:

"There may be something of human greatness about empires as chapter two allows.   There is just as much justification for the point of view that in their relation to one another and in their mode of acquiring power the world powers are rapacious *beasts* of great strength and are no longer human.   As long as a nation makes no bid for imperial control it may preserve a more humanized attitude and character.   As soon as it enters the lists to become a leader among the nations, all resemblance to the finer human traits is laid aside, and the beast comes to the forefront.   This flatters human vanity but litt,e but is one of the truest facts ever revealed by the Scriptures. All subtle self-flattery of the nations to the contrary, this is still the most telling and accurate description of the outstanding trait of the nations that aim to exercise control over other nations."

We believe "beast" represents in an even more general way all world power. Eventually all worldly rulers and governments will be banished and the only kingdom remaining in a new heaven and new earth will be the kingdom of God.   This forms a key or basis for interpreting all apocalyptic literature of the Bible, including the book of Revelation. *Beast* does not mean one specific world empire, unless a certain beast is named and some point of interpretative reference is specifically named by the inspired writers.

v. 4-6 . . . FIRST . . . A LION . . . A MAN'S HEART . . . GIVEN TO IT . . . ANOTHER . . . LIKE UNTO A BEAR . . . AND LO, ANOTHER, LIKE A LEOPARD . . . It should be evident to the thorough student that these four beasts are parallel to the four parts of the great mental statue in chapter two. The lion represents Babylon for Babylon was the first power to achieve world dominion.   Egypt is Babylon's only predecessor who came near to such world dominion but Egypt never came near to dominating the world like Babylon did.   Babylon was the sead of the statue in chapter two and here she is represented by the "heads" of two animal kingdoms—the lion and the eagle. Furthermore, the peoples of that day were familiar with such figures as the winged lions that guarded the gates of royal palaces among the Babylonians.   They were practically emblems of the Babylonian power. The prophets use the lion to symbolize Babylon as well as using the eagle for the same purpose (cf. Jer. 49:19; 50:17, 44; Jer. 48:40; 49:22; Ezek. 17:3, 12). The plucking out of the wings from the lion and the standing like a human plus the giving of a human heart symbolizes a time when the Babylonian power was de-beasted and humanized. This undoubtedly refers to the humiliation of Nebuchadnezzar as related in chapter four when his proud nature and lust for conquest were taken from him by God. The nation, of course, shared the king's experience since he was its moving spirit.

The second beast in Daniel's dream-vision was like a bear. After the lion in regality comes the bear and symbolizes the Medo-Persian empire. The bear is more slow and heavy-going than the lion and well represents the distinction between Babylon and Persia. Young thinks the bear was standing with two feet on one side raised for the purpose of going forward and this symbolizes the two-sided (Medo-Persian) nature of the empire with one side (Persian) going on ahead of the other. The three ribs it is devouring in its mouth merely represents the beast as not content with one body but devouring many. Any delineation of the "three ribs" as specific empires devoured by the Medo-Persian conquest would have to be totally arbitrary since the Medo-Persian coalition conquered more than three (some arbitrarily say the three ribs represent Babylon, Lydia and Egypt). The bear is commanded by God after it has substantial conquests in its jaws to arise and attempt to devour more. The Persian Empire was voracious; it devoured quite a bit more than did Babylon and attempted to devour as far as Macedonia and Greece. All in all, the vision emphasizes a greedy voraciousness over against the royal dignity that marked the first beast.

The third beast, like a leopard with four wings and four heads, symbolizes Alexander the Great and the Grecian empire. About 150 years after Persian hordes had invaded Greece and burned Athens (although the Persians had been driven back to Asia Minor) Greek militants still preached vengeance. War demanded unity and Greece remained fragmented in rival city-states, exhausted by the Peloponnesian War. Into the vacuum rode Philip II (of Macedon), intent upon uniting Greece and invading Persia. A master in the art of war, he developed the celebrated Macedonian Phalanx —rank upon rank of infantrymen with shields closely joined and spears more than twice as long as those of their foes. Shock troops—skilled horsemen of Thessaly and Macedonia— flanked the solid phalanxes. As Philip rode south, the Greeks resisted. In Athens, orators denounced the north-erner; Demosthenes' eloquent thunder still echoes in our word "philippic." The decisive clash came in 338 B.C. at Chaeronea, northwest of Athens. Philip commanded on the right wing while his 18-year-old son Alexander led a cav-alry charge from the left. They wheeled and chewed up the Greek center. All Greece save Sparta now submitted, and Philip was free to lead a united force against Persia. When an assassin's knife cut him down, young Alexander made his father's dream his own. Alexander left Pella on a bright spring day in 334 B.C. leading 30,000 foot soldiers and 5000 cavalry—and the next 11 years were spent in a whirlwind of warfare, hardships, and revelry. Entering Babylon in the spring of 323 B.C., worn out by wounds, hardship, and overdrinking, he fell ill of a fever. Soon he could neither move nor speak. He was propped up and each officer and soldier filed past. He acknowledged each man with his eyes or a slight movement of his head. Within two days Alexander died. He was not yet 33 years old. His empire stretched half-way around the world—from Europe to Asia—from Macedonia to the Himalayas in India and China.

This ferocious, agile, swift beast is a very appropriate symbol of Alexander's empire. The four heads on the beast symbolize the four-way division of this great empire at Alexander's death, (although Young disagrees and insists they merely represent "the four corners of the earth, sym-bolizing the ecumenicity of his kingdom). At his untimely death his empire disintegrated into four major kingdoms which were ruled over by his chief generals (Ptolemy— Egypt; Antigonus—Asia; Cassander—Macedonia; and Lysi-machus—Thrace) Antigonus was later killed in a battle, his Asiatic empire came to an end, and Seleucus (Ptolemy's leading general) was given Palestine and Syria over which to rule (see extended historical account in chapter 11).

These four kingdoms continued as prominent factors in world politics until the next empire appeared on the scene and amalgamated the parts into a whole.

The interesting note at the end of verse 6, ". . . and dominion was given to it," reveals very clearly that all of Alexander's accomplishments were providentially given to him by the Most High God. Alexander did not actually achieve by ordinary conquests the victories that were his lot, but that he had been singled out by divine providence to have the world dominion come into his hands. He was, in a very particular way, a man of destiny!

v. 7-8 . . . BEHOLD A FOURTH BEAST, TERRIBLE AND POWERFUL . . . IT HAD TEN HORNS . . . CAME UP AMONG THEM ANOTHER HORN, A LITTLE ONE . . . There is no beast in all the fauna sufficiently fierce and terrible to symbolize so abnormal a type of empire. Everything points to the Roman world power as being the empire typified by this beast. Using its great iron teeth it broke things in pieces and devoured them, and what it could not devour it stamped with its feet, grinding it into dust. Rome was singularly voracious, cruel and destructive—even vindictive as a world power. She could never get enough of conquest. Often she conquered just out of sheer spiteful vengeance. Rome had no interest in raising the conquered nations to any high level of development. All her designs were exploitation and imperialism. If they could not "devour" a victim by plunder and taxation, they would "stamp" it under their feet, sacked and burned, left in desolate ruins.

The ten horns symbolize a complete, multiplicity of powerful rulers. As with the "three ribs" in the bear's mouth, should one attempt to designate specifically ten different emperors of Rome he would have to make a very arbitrary selection. The number ten symbolizes completeness.

The seer's attention is directed to a "little horn" which supplants three that were rooted up. Leupold suggests that the whole idea between ten, three that are rooted up, and one which supplants the three, is comparative. If *one* replaces *three*, it becomes comparatively quite a bit larger than any one of the others. Yet the "little" *one* does not grow as strong as the whole empire—the *ten*.

This "little horn" has eyes like a man and a mouth speaking great things, which, as we shall show later in verses 15-28, are characteristic of the ruler of the Roman atholic papacy. The fact that Daniel observed the little orn having human eyes indicates his attention was inentionally drawn away from the beastly character of the :ourth kingdom to what seems to be a human personality growing out of the fourth beast. This human personality has power (symbolized by "horn") and utters great, boastful, things (characterized in verses 25 as "words against the Most High"). A more extensive interpretation of the "little horn" will be made in subsequent verses.

QUIZ

1. Does God ever "stir up" men or events upon the earth to fulfill His purposes?
2. What is symbolized by the "four beasts" coming up from "the sea?"
3. Which world-empire does the lion represent, and why?
4. Which, the bear?
5. Which, the leopard? What about its four heads?
6. Why was the fourth empire not represented by an animal?
7. What do the ten horns hymbolize? What about the "little horn?"

b. MAGNIFICENT BEAUTY

TEXT: 7:9-18

9 I beheld till thrones were placed, and one that was ancient of days did sit: his raiment was white as snow, and the hair of his head like pure wool; his throne was fiery flames, and the wheels thereof burning fire.

10 A fiery stream issued and came forth from before him: thousands of thousands ministered unto him, and ten thousand times ten thousand stood before him: the judgment was set, and the books were opened.

11 I beheld at that time because of the voice of the great words which the horn spake; I beheld even till the

beast was slain, and its body destroyed, and it was given to be burned with fire.

12 And as for the rest of the beasts, their dominion was taken away: yet their lives were prolonged for a season and a time.

13 I saw in the night-visions, and, behold, there came with the clouds of heaven one like unto a son of man, and he came even to the ancient of days, and they brought him near before him.

14 And there was given to him dominion, and glory, and a kingdom, that all the peoples, nations, and languages should serve him: his dominion is an everlasting dominion, which shall not pass away, and his kingdom that which shall not be destroyed.

15 As for me, Daniel, my spirit was grieved in the midst of my body, and the visions of my head troubled me.

16 I came near unto one of them that stood by, and asked him the truth concerning all this. So he told me, and made me know the interpretation of the things.

17 These great beasts, which are four, are four kings, that shall arise out of the earth.

18 But the saints of the Most High shall receive the kingdom, and possess the kingdom for ever, even for ever and ever.

QUERIES

a. Who is the "one that was ancient of days?"

b. How could the fourth beast be slain and the other beasts have their lives prolonged?

c. When shall the saints of the Most High receive the kingdom?

PARAPHRASE

I watched as thrones were set in place and the Eternal, Omniscient One, sat down to judge. His clothing was snow-white, and the hair of his head pure as wool. He sat upon a fiery throne which had flaming wheels, and a river of fire flowed from before him. Myriads upon myriads of angels ministered to Him; so many myriads stood before Him, they could not be numbered. Then the court began its session and The Books were opened. Then I carefully ob-

served what the great horn was doing: it was arrogantly
speaking blasphemous and boastful things against the Eternal One, and as I was observing, the brutal fourth beast
was killed and its body submitted to the burning of fire. As
for the other three beasts, they also had their dominion
taken away one after another, each at its appointed time;
for to each God gave its duration of life, depending on the
circumstances involved and the time appointed in the providence of God. And as I was seeing these visions in the
night, lo, there arrived on the scene a Man—or so He seemed
to be—brought there on clouds from heaven; He approached
the Eternal One and was presented to Him. He was given
dominion and honor and sovereignty in order that all peoples, nations, and tongues should serve and obey Him. His
dominion is an everlasting dominion that never passes away,
and His kingdom is an eternal kingdom that is never destroyed. As for me, Daniel, I was confused and disturbed
by all I had seen because I did not know the meaning of it.
So I approached one of the angels standing by the throne
and asked him for an authoritative interpretation of all
these things, and he explained their meaning to me. As to
these great beasts which, to be explicit, are four in number,
the meaning is that four kings with their earthly, tem-
poral kingdoms shall arise and succeed one another in dominion for a while. But they shall each one fall and dis-
appear, while it will be the sanctified ones of God who shall
receive and possess that kingdom which is everlasting—
even forever and ever.

COMMENT

v. 9-10 . . . THRONES WERE PLACED . . . ANCIENT OF
DAYS DID SIT . . . BOOKS WERE OPENED . . . Who sits upon
the other thrones (pl.) Daniel does not tell us, and any statement on our part would be conjectural. The plurality of
thrones is to emphasize majesty and power, but Young
thinks the angels that serve God in judgment are the other
throne (cf. Psa. 89:8; Isa. 6:2; Rev. 1:4; 4:4; 8:2; Mt. 13:
36-50).

Ancient of Days signifies one who has liver ever since
anyone can remember. The emphasis is upon the omniscience and eternality of God. The Eternal One is well aware

of all the deeds and acts of men and kingdoms and is, therefore, well able to pronounce judgment in all justice. He is clothed in holiness and purity, symbolized by his white garments, and His nature is wisdom symbolized by His white hair.

His throne is fire, and fire issues forth from it representing the judicial power and also splendor and majesty (cf. Psa. 50:3; 97:3; Rev. 4:4-5; Ex. 3:2; Deut. 4:24; I Tim. 6:16; Heb. 12:29). Fire may also symbolize a purifying, purging, sanctifying agent issuing forth from the throne of God. Wheels symbolize the omnipresent nature of God's judicial action. His throne is not bound to one place but rules universally (cf. Ezek. chap. 1).

Thousands of thousands and ten thousand times ten thousands are simply expressions relating to the same multitude of myriads and myriads of heavenly creatures gathered to minister to the Ancient of Days and do His bidding in the judgment.

The Books are symbolical of the fact that God records and remembers the actions of men (cf. Isa. 65:6; Jer. 17:1; Mal. 3:16; Lk. 10:20 and Rev. 20:12), and here the reference is particularly to the deeds of the four beasts and the little horn. The rest of the O.T. (other than Daniel) knows only one Book (cf. Ex. 32:32-33; Psa. 69:28; 139:16) but in the N.T. it is books (pl.). God has not only a record of the deeds of men but a record of all who are His. To be blotted out of His book is to be lost and condemned to an eternal separation from Him unto punishment. Unless one is a member of the eternal kingdom of the Ancient of Days this is his destiny. To be associated with any other than the Eternal One is to be associated with one of the beasts whose doom is sealed.

v. 11-12 . . . THE HORN SPAKE . . . THE BEAST WAS SLAIN . . . YET THEIR LIVES WERE PROLONGED . . . Daniel is abruptly and dramatically shown that the little horn which grew into greatness has not passed out of the vision. This horn is still doing what it was before (v. 8)—speaking ungodly and blasphemous words against the Most High. This blasphemy provokes the Ancient of Days to action against the fourth beast and the horn to destroy them.

The beast, as a whole, was slain and its body given "to the burning of fire," indicating, in the present tense, continuing action of burning. The Aramic original, as is given in the marginal reference of the A.S.V., must be rendered in the present, continuing, tense; that is perpetual punishment, not annihilation, although the beast is banished and conquered.

The rest of the beasts (the first three) had previously had their dominion taken away, one after the other, each at its appointed time. This is the meaning of the phrase, "yet their lives were prolonged for a season and a time." The meaning is, "even though the first three beasts were allowed a prolonged life for a predetermined time by God, still, in His own good time, God took away their dominion also." It may also mean that the essence of the first three beasts (worldliness) was prolonged in the culminating worldliness of the fourth beast; still, when the fourth was slain, they, too, had their dominion taken away.

v. 13-14 . . . THERE CAME . . . ONE LIKE UNTO A SON OF MAN . . . AND THERE WAS GIVEN TO HIM DOMINION . . . If the fourth beast and the little horn constitute all that opposes God from the Roman empire up to the man of lawlessness, then the fact that it is depicted as being destroyed and given over to burning indicates this text is referring to the Second Advent of the Lord Jesus Christ. The second chapter of Daniel states that during the time of the "fourth" kingdom, the kingdom of God would be established and this would be the fatal blow to worldly dominion. This seventh chapter merely indicates the consummation of the kingdom of God and the final destruction of the fourth kingdom, which began when the kingdom of God was first established and Christ despoiled the principalities and powers (cf. Col. 2:15). The revelation here given to Daniel omits all the history between the beginning of the fourth beast and the little horn and its final overthrow which is the Christian dispensation (that is from the founding of the kingdom of God on the day of Pentecost and the Second Coming of Christ—indicated as three and one-half times in 7:25—during which time the horn made war with the saints and prevailed over them . . . 7:21). (See the chart at the end of this chapter).

It would have been irrelevant to Daniel's readers to have been told in detail what was to transpire during an unknowable time between the fourth world empire and the final coming of the Lord (the Christian age). What would be relevant and edifying to his readers would be to know that worldly dominion would ultimately be overthrown by the blessed kingdom of God which was to be completely victorious.

Furthermore this kingdom was to be presided over by the Divine-Human Messiah (one like unto a son of man). Their Saviour-king would be like them, son of man, yet he would come on the clouds and be Divine at the same time. This very prophecy is undoubtedly the reason Jesus used the phrase "son of man" in reference to Himself so often— He was attempting to convince the Jews that He was the One who had come to establish the kingdom of God which would be ultimately victorious over the beast and the horn. But His human nature was a stumbling block to so many who had their own interpretation of His Messianic nature.

His dominion will be universal. Only those people from every nation and tongue who have surrendered to His will shall abide. They shall willingly serve Him in an everlasting condition because they were willing to serve Him in their temporary, fleshly condition. Any who have given allegiance to the beast will be punished with everlasting punishment along with the beast, (cf. Rev. 14:9-12).

v. 15-18 . . . BEASTS . . . ARE FOUR KINGS . . . BUT THE SAINTS . . . SHALL RECEIVE THE KINGDOM . . . FOR EVER . . . EVER . . . AND EVER . . . Daniel is startled with the vividness and dramatic nature of this apocalyptic vision and his mind is exceedingly agitated to know what it is all about. He approached one of the angels and asked for "an authoritative interpretation" of the vision. So in "a nutshell" he is given the interpretation. It will be enlightening here to quote from Leupold: "Why does the sequence of historical kingdoms in this vision extend no farther than the Roman (the fourth beast) whereas we know that many developments came after the Roman Empire and have con-

tinued to come before the judgment? . . . One suggestion
. . . is the fact that prophets generall, barring the conclusion of chapter 9 in Daniel, never see the interval of time
lying between the first and the second coming of Christ. In
the matter of history, therefore, Daniel does not see beyond Christ's days in the flesh and perhaps the persecution
that came upon the early church."

"In the second place, it may be correctly argued that
the pattern of empire development adopted by the Romans
has been followed by practically all the succeeding world
powers. Roman law is said still to be the pattern of juris-
prudence. Roman classic literature dominates the literature produced since that time. In fact, the powers that
can be said to have anything like world dominion are segments of the old Roman Empire, and so the fourth beast
is still in a sense alive though Rome was overthrown."

In connection with Leupold's first suggestion see our
comment in *Minor Prophets*, by this writer, published by
College Press, on Joel 2:27-28, pages 184-188; see also page
32 in the same work on "Shortened Perspective."

The one point of emphasis not to be lost sight of in
this vision is: THE SAINTS SHALL HAVE AN EVERLASTING
KINGDOM, while those who give allegiance to the beast
make every attempt to achieve dominion and glory and
eternality; but they shall be destroyed, for in so doing they
must set themselves in opposition to the program of God.

QUIZ

1. Who sat upon the thrones other than the "Ancient of
   Days?"
2. What do the flames and wheels symbolize concerning the
   throne?"
3. Was the fourth beast completely annihilated by the fire,
   vs. 11?
4. Whaat is the significance of the term, "one like . . . a
   son of man?"
5. What is the main point of this vision?
6. Why is nothing said of what transpires between the
   fourth kingdom and the judgment?

c. MEANING BESTOWED

TEXT: 7:19-28

19 Then I desired to know the truth concerning the fourth beast, which was diverse from all of them, exceeding terrible, whose teeth were of iron, and its nails of brass; which devoured, brake in pieces, and stamped the residue with its feet;

20 and concerning the ten horns that were on its head, and the other horn which came up, and before which three fell, even that horn that had eyes, and a mouth that spake great things, whose look was more stout than its fellows.

21 I beheld, and the same horn made war with the saints, and prevailed against them;

22 until the Ancient of Days came, and judgment was given to the saints of the Most High, and the time came that the saints possessed the kingdom.

23 Thus he said, The fourth beast shall be a fourth kingdom upon earth, which shall be diverse from all kingdoms, and shall devour the whole earth, and shall tread it down, and break it in pieces.

24 And as for the ten horns, out of this kingdom shall ten kings arise: and another shall arise after them; and he shall be diverse from the former, and he shall put down three kings.

25 And he shall speak words against the Most High, and shall wear out the saints of the Most High; and he shall think to change the times and the law: and they shall be given into his hand until a time and times and half a time.

26 But the judgment shall be set, and they shall take away his dominion, to consume and to destroy it unto the end.

27 And the kingdom and the dominion and the greatness of the kingdoms under the whole heaven, shall be given to the people of the saints of the Most High: his kingdom is an everlasting kingdom, and all dominions shall serve and obey him.

28 Here is the end of the matter. As for me, Daniel, my thoughts much troubled me, and my countenance was changed in me: but I kept the matter in my heart.

QUERIES

a. Why was the look of the one horn more "stout" than its fellows?
b. How is the one to be diverse from the ten v. 24?
c. How would he change times and the law?

PARAPHRASE

Then I wanted to know with certainty about the fourth beast which was so different from all the preceeding three, so exceedingly brutal, with teeth of iron and claws of bronze that tore things into pieces, devoured much, and stamped with its feet all that was not devoured. I also wanted to have an authoritative interpretation concerning the ten horns on the head of this terrible beast and of the other horn which came up from among the ten and which destroyed three of its predecessors. That was the one horn that had eyes and a mouth that spoke blasphemous and boastful things against God and it was stouter than all the other horns. As I was watching, and waiting for the interpretation, this same strong horn made war upon the saints and was allowed to gain an apparent advantage over them. But this was only apparent, for when the Ancient of Days came, judgment was executed (and the saints assisted in its execution) upon this horn, and the saints then possessed the kingdom. The angel said to me, This fourth beast is the fourth world empire that will rule the earth. It will be different from all the others in that it will be much more universal in its dominion conquering and consuming every thing in its path. The ten horns upon this beast signify the totality of diversity in the composition of his universal empire when it is fully extended. This one horn shall be, comparatively, as powerful as a part of this great empire but not as great and powerful as the whole empire. This one powerful ruler shall speak words against the Most High God and shall attempt to subjugate the saints by persecution. He will be so presumptuous against God as to inovate changes in moral and religious commandments and ordinances instituted by God. God's people will be persecuted by him for a definite length of time known only to God. But God has the judgment of this blasphemer set at a determined time, and at that time God and His people ssall have the final victory, and this one's dominion will be taken away from him and he will be punished eternally. At this judgment all the kingdoms of the earth shall become the kingdoms of God and His people, and His kingdom shall abide forever and ever, and men who serve and obey Him shall dwell in it securely. That was the end of the dream and nothing more was revealed to me at that time. As for me, I was deeply affected by this revelation and my wondering about it all—I even grew pale in the face over my perplexity—but I did not forget it all; I kept thinking about it often.

COMMENT

v. 19-20 THEN I DESIRED TO KNOW THE TRUTH CONCERNING THE FOURTH BEAST . . . The phrase "the truth" is in opposition to incomprehension, not accuracy. What had been shown in symbolic form concerning the fourth beast was absolutely accurate but its meaning was not understood. There is one additional symbolism attached to the one horn arising out of the ten in that its "look was more stout than its fellows." It was more formidable than any one of the other of the ten. In the following interpretation it will be seen why this one is comparatively stronger than any one of the others (see also our interpretation of 7:8).

v. 21-22 . . . THE SAME HORN MADE WAR WITH THE SAINTS . . . UNTIL THE ANCIENT OF DAYS CAME . . . Again, something new is said of the one horn that was not said of it in verses 1-8. It is to make war upon the saints and even seem to prevail over them. This is to continue until the final judgment, which God has already determined against it, shall be executed. This refers, without doubt, to the final consummation of all things; the Second Coming of Christ, the great judgment; the destruction of the heavens and earth; the creation of a new heaven and earth wherein dwelleth righteousness; all this is to be inferred

273

from the following verses (23-28). The judgment of the one
horn is coincidental with the ultimate victory of God and
possession of His kingdom by the saints. Thus Daniel is
shown the eventual rise of the Roman Empire (the fourth
beast); its great, universal, complete power for a long
period of time (the ten horns); a ruler of arrogance, pride,
hate for God's true people; power shall arise and be as
powerful as a part of this Roman empire—more powerful
than any one part—but not as powerful as the entire empire at its apex.

v. 23-25 . . . A FOURTH KINGDOM . . . AND ANOTHER
SHALL ARISE . . . SPEAK . . . AGAINST THE MOST HIGH . . .
WEAR OUT THE SAINTS . . . CHANGE . . . TIMES AND THE
LAW . . . This is the crucial section of chapter 7. We think
a scriptural case may be made for the following interpretation: The fourth beast is the Roman empire in its beginning conquest of the world, tearing to pieces, devouring
and stamping the residue with its feet; the ten horns is
the Roman empire in its long and complete rule of the
known world under successive emperors until its downfall;
the little horn which grows great is the Roman Catholic
papacy which succeeded the Roman empire in controlling
nations and rulers and is parallel to the man of lawlessness
of II Thessalonians 2:1-12; and the Roman state, succeeded
by the Roman papacy, is parallel to Revelation chapter 13
and the two beasts.

The little horn grown great speaks words against the
Most High; wears out the saints; thinks to change the
times and the law; has power to do so for a specific time;
then is destroyed when the saints possess the kingdom.

The "man of lawlessness" of II Thessalonians is connected with *"the* falling away" (not just *a* falling away)
which undoubtedly means the great Roman apostasy. A
"man of lawlessness" would be a man who was not subject to any law. He would be the one who would think
to *change* any commandment of God which would suit his
purpose of deceiving men and maintaining his rule over
them. When we speak of the "man of lawlessness," our
minds frequently connect him with "antichrist" mentioned
in I John 2:18, 22; 4:3; II John 7, as Wilbur Fields states

in *Thinking Through Thessalonians,* published by College
Press, and we quote, "However, the Bible does not specifically connect them, and any connection that we might make
between the two woul dhave to be regarded as only speculations.   We hear lots of preaching about THE antichrist.
But John makes it rather clear that antichrist is not one
supremely evil person, but that anyone who denies that
Jesus is the Christ or that He came in the flesh is antichrist.   There were antichrists even in John's time . . . But
we stand on very shaky support when we teach that there
will be some one particularly terrible ANTICHRIST in the
future."

The little horn grown great is NOT the Antichrist.
He may be one antichrist.   But we believe he is the man
of lawlessness which represents the office of the Roman
papacy.   Mr. Fields summarizes what we believe is the correct interpretation of the "man of lawlessness" (which we
identify with the little horn of Dan. 7):

1. The falling away (of II Thess. 2) refers to . . .
   corruption . . . of apostolic teaching by heathenism
   . . . and resulted in development of the Roman
   Catholic religion . . . this apostasy is still in
   progress.
2. The man of sin . . . refers to the papacy . . . visible,
   personal head of the "falling away."
3. That which hinders the appearance of the man of
   sin (II Thess. 2:6-7) . . . was the Roman government . . . for several centuries . . . held in check
   the attempts of power-hungry Roman bishops to
   take control of both the spiritual affairs of man
   and the political authority as well.

Arguments for this view:

1. The "mystery of lawlessness" which resulted in the
   falling away and the appearance of the man of sin,
   was already at work in Paul's time . . . Paul could
   not have been referring to things that would not
   happen until the 19th and 20th centuries when he
   spoke of the "falling away." There are numerous
   references in the N.T. which show that false doc-

     trines, unauthorized power grabs where already developing (cf. Jude 4, III Jn. 9; Acts 20:29-30; II 2:1, Col. 2:8).

2. In I Tim. 4:1-3 Paul told how some would depart from faith; forbid to marry; command abstinence from meats, etc. . . . a clear prophecy of the Roman Catholic apostasy.

3. If some Antichrist is going to rule the world, then Daniel's prophecy, in Daniel 2, would have to be wrong in indicating that there would be only four empires before God's kingdom should prevail and fill the earth.

4. The use of the term *mystery* suggests that there may be a connection with Rev. 17:5, where the great harlot is given the name MYSTERY. This mystery woman in Revelation is ROME. For she is identified as that city that sits on seven mountains (or hills) and rules over the kings of the earth (Rev. 17:9, 18). Rome is the only city on earth that fulfills those descriptions. (The harlot is also united as one with the two beasts of Revelation 13, the second of which we believe also represents Roman Catholicism).

A thorough study of II Thessalonians 2:1-12 is demanded on the part of the student who wishes to understand the "little horn" of Daniel 7. We would suggest there is no finer or more scholarly discussion of this difficult N.T. passage than that of Wilbur Fields, *Thinking Through Thessalonians,* published by College Press.

We call the readers attention now to Revelation, chapter 13. There the *first* beast is symbolized as a composite of leopard, bear and lion, with ten horns and seven heads. This first beast represents the concentration and personification of world-power, through the whole period of history, continuing as one entity, but manifesting itself under various forms in various ages; with many and diverse modifications. This first beast was dealt a death-blow and a *second* beast arose which exercises all the authority of the first beast . . . and makes the earth and its inhabitants worship the first beast. The second beast works great signs, etc. This second beast looked like a lamb. The second beast is represented as bringing to life again *or healing* the first beast. It should be seen by the careful student that this symbolism of Revelation 13 parallels in many ways exactly the symbolism of Daniel 7: Lion, Bear, Leopard and Non-descript Beast symbolized in both; out of beastliness grows another form of world-power and persecution diverse from its predecessor; the time it has to hold sway over man is the same 3½ times (years) and 24 months; its judgment and overthrow comes at the consummation of all things when the saints shall possess the kingdom.

Daniel is informed that the "saints" shall be given into the hand of the little horn grown great until 3½ times: 3½ is half of 7—half of a complete or perfect number—and therefore symbolizes a definite period of time which God knows and has not revealed to man but not perfect or eternal in duration; 3½ years is the same as 42 months or 1260 days (both used as units of time in Revelation and denote the time between the beginning of the Church of Christ on Pentecost (Acts 2) and the consummation at the Second Coming of Christ, which is also represented by 1000 years—a round number not to be taken literally.

v. 26-28 BUT THE JUDGMENT SHALL BE SET . . . The little horn grown great (also the man of sin and the beast like a lamb) shall not endure. His overthrow is appointed in God's own good time and is certain. God has already made up His mind about this—all that remains is the execution of it; when it is to occur no one knows—not even the angels of heaven (cf. Mt. 24:36. 44, etc.). But when it does occur the seventh angel will blow his trumpet and there will be loud voices in heaven, saying, The kingdom of the world has become the kingdom of our Lord and of his Christ, and he shall reign for ever and ever (cf. Rev. 11:15; I Cor. 15:20-28). All of this was enough to agitate the soul of Daniel and he could not forget it but kept it in his heart.

This chapter should stir us up too! A definite and glorious note of victory pervades the whole chapter. With such a revelation as this offers to God's people to know how history must run its course, and how the kingdom of God alone will stand in the glorious consummation,

277

the christian can trust and love his Lord. Only the member of the kingdom of God had the tope of enduring the certain and sure judgment of the world—and what a hope it is—possession of the kingdom of God. God is permitting His saints to be given over to the persecution of the beast in order to purify their lives and strengthen their faith in Him. God knows that a man's moral fiber is never perfected until it is put to the test. He knows that He shall never have a believer's full allegiance until that allegiance is tried. Praise Him for His love! He desires only that we be better than we are!

QUIZ

1. What two new things are added to the description of the "little horn" that were not given in 7:8?
2. What two N.T. apocalyptic passages are parallel to Daniel 7?
3. What is the "little horn"?
4. Where does it come from?
5. How does changing times and the law characterize it?
6. What is "a time and times and half a time?"

SERMON NUMBER SEVEN

BEASTS, AND THE BEAUTY

Text: Daniel 7:1-28

INTRODUCTION

I. DANIEL'S VISION
   A. It was a dream vision.
      1. God often used dreams to give vivid, memorable, communications of His will to mankind.
      2. Even in N.T. times God still uses this method (Paul and the Macedonian).
      3. It is evident to me that these dream-revelations were far different from modern day experiences with ESP (extra-sensory perception). There was never any doubt that these came directly from

God. They were more specific and detailed and if greater length than ESP.

B. Located as it is in Daniel's book, it is a sort of flashback.
1. He is telling us the dream God sent him back in the first year ob Belshazzar's reign.
2. He recorded the dream for all posterity.
3. It, therefore, has a message for us.

II. FOUR WINDS OF HEAVEN AND THE GREAT SEA

A. Four winds represent the powers that stir up or set in motion the persons, events and circumstances which bring forth the earthly conflicts between good and evil—between Bod's enemies and His people.
1. There is some indication in scripture that God does "stir up the spirit" of certain rulers and nations and is providentially active in the affairs of history (cf. Isa. 10:5-16; 45:1-7; Jer. 27:5-7; II Chron. 36:22-23; Ezra 1:1-4, ect.).
2. It is also apparent from scripture that God does not overrule the will of man and force man to think something he does not want to think. God does overrule the actions and circumstances of man at various times by providential use of nature . . . BUT NEVER DOES HE IRRESISTIBLY OVERRULE MAN'S WILL. . . .
3. So the four winds represent all the forces, both Divine and finite, which stir up or set in motion these conflicts.

B. The great sea symbolizes mankind, and especially Gentile world powers hostile to God and Israel (cf. Isa. 8:7ff.; Jer. 56:7-9; 47:2; Isa. 17:2ff. and Rev. 17:1-15).
1. When the four beasts appear as rising from the sea, that clearly indicates that the disturbed state of the world gives origin to the successive world powers that appear on the scene of history.
2. The devil, getting the cooperation of man, can fill man's heart with evil, degeneration, tyranny and corruption and man's circumstances are very

nearly unbearable—his lack of peace of mind and soul do become more than he can stand. Then God stirs someone's soul with the Truth, the linging to be free, to be holy and pure, and the battle is on.

3. Revelations, reformations, restorations, crusades, wars, renaissances have all brought forth such struggles and have all given birth to successive forms of world-power.

DISCUSSION

I. THE MALEVOLENT BEAST, 7:1-8

A. Beast—general
1. The most adequate figure to represent world-power is *beast.*
2. The beast
   a. Concentrates entirely, even instinctively, on the flesh. Has there ever been any government not unlike this?
   b. Is amoral; that is, it is guided in its actions by instinct to preserve the flesh; is not this the way world powers react?
   c. Is a predator; it survives only by preying upon weaknesses. World power, since it is carnally oriented, survives only in the same manner— Government must gobble up territories and rights of the individual for its survival.
   d. Since it has no abiding life in it, sooner or later it dies; so with all world powers.

B. The Lion, and Eagle
1. Represent Babylon
2. In the great statue of Dan. 2, Babylon is represented as the head of Gold.
3. Here she is represented by the heads of two animal kingdoms the lion and the eagle.
4. People of that day were familiar with such figures as the winged lions that guarded the gates of royal palaces among Babylonians. They were practically symbols of Babylonian power. This is familiar symbolism throughout the O.T. prophets.

5. Plucking out the wings from the lion and the standing like a human plus the giving of a human heart symbolizes a time when the Babylonian power was de-beasted and humanized to some extent. This undoubtedly refers to the humiliation of Nebuchadnezzar (ch. 4) when his proud nature and lust for conquest were taken away from him by God. The nation, of course, shared the king's experiences since he was its moving spirit.

C. The Bear
   1. Represents Medo-Persia.
   2. The bear is more slow and plodding than the lion and well represents a major difference between Babylon and Persia.
   3. Two feet raised on one side for the purpose of going forward symbolizes the two-sided (Medo-Persian) nature of the empire with one side (Persian) going on ahead of the other.
   4. Three ribs in its mouth merely represents the beast not content with one nation but devouring man. Any delineation of the three ribs as specific empires devoured by Medo-Persian conquest would have to be totally aribtrary since they definitely conquered more than three.
   5. Persian empire was voracious—commanded by God after it has substantial conquests in its jaws to arise and attempt to devour more.
   6. It devoured more than Babylon and attempted to devour as far as Macedonia and Greece.

D. The Leopard with four wings and four heads
   1. Represents Greece.
   2. 150 years after Persian hordes invaded Greece and burned Athens, Greek militants still preached vengeance. War demanded unity; Greece remained fragmented in city states rivaling one another.
   3. Into this vacuum rode Philip of Macedon intent upon uniting Greece and invading Persia. As Philip rode south, the Greeks resisted him. In

Athens, orators denounced the northerner; Demosthenes' eloquent thunder still echoes in our word "philippic." Just northwest of Athens the decisive clash came. Philip commanded on the right wing while his 18-year-old son, Alexander, led a cavalry charge from the left. All Greece except Sparta submitted. An assassin's knife cut Philip down before he could cross the Aegean and invade the Persian domain, but Alexander made his father's dream his own. Alexander left Pella on a bright spring day in 334 B.C. leading 30,000 foot soldiers and 5,000 cavalry—and the next 11 years were spent in a whirlwind of warfare, hardships, and revelry. Entering Babylon in the spring of 323 B.C., on his way back to Greece, worn out by wounds, hardship and overdrinking, he fell ill of a fever. Soon he could neither move nor speak. He was propped up and each officer and soldier filed past. He acknowledged each man with his eyes or a slight movement of his head. Within two days Alexander died. He was not yet 33 years old. His empire stretched half way around the world—from Europe to Asia—from Macedonia to the Himalayas in India and China.

4. This ferocious, agile, swift beast is a very appropriate symbol of Alexander's empire.
5. The four heads on the beast symbolize the four-way division of this empire at his death (Ptolemy-Egypt; Antigonus - Asia; Cassender - Macedonia; Lysimachus-Thrace; Antigonus was later killed in a battle, his Asiatic empire came to an end, and Seleucus (Ptolemy's leading general) was given Palestine and Syria over which to rule. These four kingdoms continued as prominent factors in world politics until the next empire appeared on the scene and amalgamated the parts into a whole.
6. "Dominion was given" to this beast (Alexander), indicating very clearly that all of Alexander's accomplishments were providentially given to him by the Most High God (Rom. 9:14-24).

E. The Fourth Beast, With Ten Horns

1. No beast in all the fauna sufficiently fierce and terrible to symbolize so abnormal a type of empire.

2. Everything points to the Roman empire as being represented by this beast. It has iron teeth and jaws—Iron was the fourth kingdom of the great statue (ch. 2).

3. What it could not devour it stamped with its feet grinding it into dust. Rome was singularly voracious, cruel and destructive—even vindictive (Carthage) as a world power.

4. Rome had no interest in raising the conquered nations to any high level of development. Often she conquered just out of sheer spiteful vengeance. All her designs were exploitation and imperialism. If they could not devour a victim by plunder and taxation, they would stamp it under their feet, sacked and burned, left in desolate ruins.

5. Ten horns symbolize a complete, multiplicity of powerful rulers. Like three ribs, one should not attempt to designate specifically ten different emperors of Rome—again it would be speculative arbitrariness to do so. The number 10 symbolizes completeness.

F. Now the LITTLE HORN

1. Supplants three that were rooted up.

2. The whole idea between ten, three that are rooted up, and one which supplants the three, is comparative. If one replaces three it becomes comparatively quite a bit larger than any one of the others.

3. YET, THE LITTLE ONE DOES NOT GROW AS STRONG AS THE WHOLE EMPIRE—THE TEN!

4. Has eyes like a man and a mouth speaking great things.

5. We shall show later these are characteristics of the Roman papacy.

6. The fact that Daniel observed the little horn having human eyes indicates his attention was intentionally drawn away from the beastly

character of the fourth kingdom to what seems to be a human character growing out of the fourth beast.

7. This human personality has power (horn) and utters great, boastful things (against the Most High, vs. 25).

II. THE MAGNIFICENT BEAUTY, 7:9-18

A. 1. Surrounded by thrones, symbolizing omnipotence
2. Ancient of Days, symbolizing Eternality
3. Raiment white as snow, symbolizing Purity and Holiness
4. Hair like pure wool, symbolizing omniscience
5. Fire represents judicial power and splendor.
6. Tens of Thousands serving Him, symbolize sovereignty
7. Books, symbolize God's remembrance of all that transpires on earth and His authority to call men to account.
8. THE BLASPHEMY OF THE LITTLE HORN PROVOKES THE ANCIENT OF DAYS TO ACTION AGAINST THE FOURTH BEAST AND THE HORN TO DESTROY THEM.
9. So the beast, as a whole, is slain and its body given to the burning of fire. Present tense indicating continual burning, eternal burning.
10. The rest of the beasts, even though the first three were allowed to prolong their life for a predetermined time by God; still, in His own good time, God took away their dominion also. It may mean that the essence of the first 3 beasts (worldliness) was prolonged in the culminating worldliness of the fourth beast (and the little horn), still when the fourth was slain they too had their dominion taken away.

B. 1. If the 4th beast and the little horn constitute all that opposes God from the Roman empire up to the man of lawlessness (Pope), then the fact that it is depicted as being destroyed and given over to burning indicates this text is referring to the 2nd Advent of Christ.

2. Daniel 2 states that during the time of the 4th kingdom, the kingdom of God would be established and this would be the fatal blow to worldly dominion. THIS SEVENTH CHAPTER MERELY INDICATES THE CONSUMMATION OF THE KINGDOM OF GOD AND THE FINAL DESTRUCTION OF THE FOURTH KINGDOM (WHICH DESTRUCTION BEGAN WHEN THE KINGDOM OF GOD WAS FIRST ESTABLISHED AND CHRIST DESPOILED THE PRINCIPALITIES AND POWERS (cf. Col. 2:15).

3. The revelation here given to Daniel omits all the history between the beginning of the fourth beast and the little horn, and its final overthrow which is the consummation of the Christian dispensation, (Christ's 2nd coming). This span of silence is indicated at 3½ times in 7:25—during which time the horn made war with the saints and prevailed over them.

C. Details of this silent period would have been irrelevant to Daniel's contemporaries.

1. What would be relevant and edifying to his contemporaries would be to know that worldly dominion would ultimately be overthrown by the blessed kingdom of God, which was to be completely victorious.

2. Furthermore this kingdom was to be presided over by the Divine-Human Messiah (one like unto a son of man). He would be like them, son of man, yet he would come on the clouds and be Divine. This very prophecy is undoubtedly the one Jesus referred to when he so often used the phrase "son of man" referring to Himself. He was attempting to convince the Jews that He was the One who had come to establish the kingdom of God which would ultimately be victorious over the beast and the horn.

D. Why no reference to other worldly powers after the Roman empire

1. The prophets usually never have revealed to them the interval of time lying between the first and second coming of Christ.

2. The pattern of empire development adopted by the Romans has been followed by practically all the succeeding world powers so the 4th beast is still in a sense alive though Rome was overthrown.

3 The little horn grown great carries on in the great conflict.

E. The one point of emphasis not to be lost sight of in this vision: THE SAINTS SHALL HAVE AN EVERLASTING KINGDOM. While those who give allegiance to the beast make every attempt to achieve dominion and glory and eternality, they shall be destroyed, for in so doing they must set themselves in opposition and rebellion against the will of God.

III. THE MEANING BESTOWED, 7:19-28

A. The horn which came up appeared to be stouter than its fellows.

1. It made war with the saints, and even seems to prevail over them.

2. This is to continue until the final judgment which God has already determined shall be executed.

3. This judgment of the horn is coincidental with the ultimate victory of God and possession of His kingdom by the saints and is, therefore, the great judgment day at the consummation of the ages.

B. The little horn grown great is the Roman Catholic Papacy which succeeded the Roman empire in controlling nations and rulers, and is parallel to the man of lawlessness of II Thess. 2:1-12; and the Roman state, succeeded by the Roman papacy, is parallel to Revelation 13 (the two beasts).

1. This little horn grown great

a. Speaks words against the Most High.

b. Wears out the saints.

c. Thinks to changes the times and the law.

d. Has power to do so for a specific time.

e. Then is destroyed when the saints possess the kingdom.

2. The "man of lawlessness" of II Thess. 2

a. Connected with *the* falling away (undoubtedly the great Roman apostasy)

    b. Such a man would not consider himself subject to any law.

    c. Such a man would think to change any commandment of God which would suit his purpose of deceiving men and maintaining his rule over man.

    d. THIS IS NOT THE ANTI-CHRIST! THE BIBLE NOWHERE CONNECTS THE TWO! THERE ARE MANY ANTI-CHRISTS.

    e. That which HINDERED the appearance of the man of sin was the Roman government which for several centuries held in check the attempts of power-hungry Roman bishops to take control of both the spiritual affairs of men and the political authority as well.

    f. The mystery of lawlessness which brought on the great apostasy was already at work in Paul's time, so Paul could not have been referring only to things that would not happen until the 19th or 20th centuries

    g. If some Anti-Christ is going to rule the world, then Daniel's prophecy in Dan. 2 would have to be wrong in indicating that there would be only four empires before God's kingdom should prevail and fill the earth.

    h. The use of the term mystery suggests that there may be a connection with Rev. 17:5, where the great harlot is given the name MYSTERY. This mystery woman in Rev. is ROME (she sits on seven mountains, and rules over the kings of the earth. Rome is the only city on earth that fulfills those descriptions. The Harlot is also united as one with the two beasts of Rev. 13, the second of which we believe also represents Roman catholicism).

C. Revelation 13

    1. First beast is symbolized as a composite of leopard, bear and lion with ten horns and seven heads. This first beast represents the concentration and

personification of world power, through the whole period of history, continuing as one entity, but manifesting itself under various forms in various ages, with many and diverse modifications. This FIRST BEAST WAS DEALT A DEATH BLOW, AND A SECOND BEAST ARISES.

2. The Second beast exercises all the authority of the first beast. It makes the earth and its inhabitants worship the first beast. It works great signs, etc. It looks like a lamb. It is represented as bringing to life again, or healing, the first beast.

3. It is evident that Revelation 13 and its symbolism parallels in many ways exactly the symbolism of Daniel 7.

   a. Lion, Bear, Leopard and Non-descript Beast symbolized in both

   b. Out of beastliness grows another form of world power and persecution diverse from its predecessor; in both

   c. The time it has to hold sway over man is the same 3½ times and 42 months.

   d. Its judgment and overthrow comes at the consummation of all things when the saints shall possesses the kingdom.

D. Period of Time

   1. Dan. 7 is informed that the saints shall be given into the hand of the little horn grown great until 3½ times. 3½ is half of 7—half of a complete or perfect number—and therefore symbolizes a definite period of time which God knows and has not revealed to man but not perfect or eternal in duration.

   2. 3½ years is the same as 42 months or 1260 days (both of the latter figures used as units of time in Rev. and denote the time between the beginning of the church of Christ on Pentecost (Acts 2) and the consummation at the 2nd coming of Christ, also represented by 1,000 years—a round number not to be taken literally).

CONCLUSION

I. NO MATTER HOW POWERFUL OR HOW SUBTLE, GOD'S ENEMIES SHALL NOT ENDURE

A. The beasts, the Fourth Beast, the Little Horn grown Great (also the man of lawlessness and the beast like a lamb) shall not endure.

B. His overthrow is appointed in God's own good time and is CERTAIN! He has pledged it with the despoiling of the principalities and powers by making a public example of them, triumphing over them in Christ.

C. God has already made up His mind about this—all that remains is the execution of the decision; WHEN IT IS TO OCCUR, NO ONE KNOWS, NOT EVEN THE ANGELS OF HEAVEN (Mt. 24:36; 24:44, etc.) IT IS NOT FOR US TO KNOW! (Acts 1:7).

D. When it does occur
1. The 7th angel will blow his trumpet and there will be loud voices in heaven, saying, "The kingdom of the world has become kingdom of our Lord and of His Christ, and He shall reign for ever and ever (cf. Rev. 11:15; I Cor. 15:20-28).
2. All of this was enough to agitate the soul of Daniel and he could not forget it, but kept it in his heart.

II. THIS CHAPTER SHOULD STIR US UP TOO!

A. A definite and glorious note of victory pervades the whole chapter

B. With such a revelation as this offers to God's people; to know how history must run its course, and how the kingdom of God alone will stand in the glorious consummation, the Christian can trust and love His Lord.

C. Only the member of the kingdom of God has the hope of enduring the certain and sure judgment of the world—and what a hope it is—possession of the kingdom of God.

D. God is permitting His saints to be given over to the persecution of the Beast in order to purify their lives and strengthen their faith in Him—so they may see the transitory nature and the way of destruction chosen by the Beast (IF ONLY HIS SAINTS WILL BELIEVE IN HIM). God *knows that a man's moral fibre* is never perfected until it is put to the test. He knows that He shall never have a believer's full allegiance until that allegiance is tried. PRAISE HIM FOR HIS LOVE! HE DESIRES ONLY THAT WE BE BETTER THAN WE ARE!

EXAMINATION SEVEN

REFUTATIONS

(Answer the following by giving the argument which will correct the statement)

1. The "son of man" in 7:13 was Jesus Christ appearing to Daniel. Refute!
2. The four beasts of chapter seven have no parallel in the book of Daniel. Refute!
3. The fourth beast is communist Russia. Refute!

ASSOCIATIONS

(Associate the persons or events of column one with the correct person or event of column two)

1	2
Rome	eagle
Greece	mankind
God	communism
angel	the pope
Persia	fourth beast
Babylon	Ancient of days
ten horns	leopard
man of lawlessness	Japan
great sea	son of man
four winds	bear
	heavenly forces
	lion
	completeness

CHART OF
DANIEL CHAPTER SEVEN
(and parallels)

Victory of God's Kingdom
over
The Beast

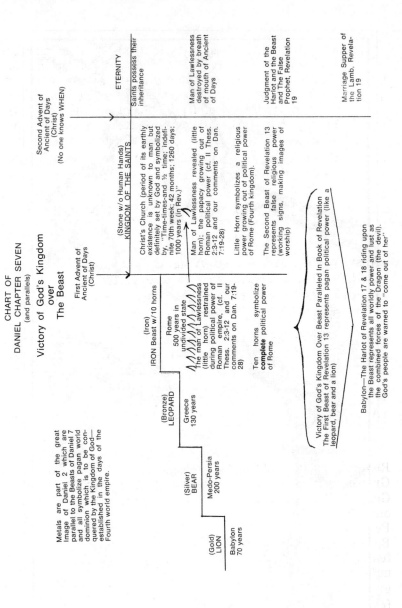

Metals are part of the great Image of Daniel 2 which are parallel to the Beasts of Daniel 7 and all symbolize pagan world dominion which is to be conquered by the Kingdom of God—established in the days of the Fourth world empire.

(Gold) LION
Babylon 70 years

(Silver) BEAR
Medo-Persia 200 years

(Bronze) LEOPARD
Greece 130 years

(Iron) IRON Beast w/ 10 horns
Rome 500 years in undivided state

The man of Lawlessness (little horn) restrained during political power of Roman empire, (cf. II Thess. 2:3-12 and our comments on Dan. 7:19-28)

Ten horns symbolize **complete** political power of Rome

First Advent of Ancient of Days (Christ)

(Stone w/o Human Hands) KINGDOM OF THE SAINTS

Christ's Church (period of its earthly existence is unknown to man but definitely set by God and symbolized by, "Time-times-and ½ time; indefinite 70th week; 42 months; 1260 days; 1000 years (in Rev.)"

Man of Lawlessness revealed (little horn); the papacy growing out of Roman political power (cf. II Thess. 2:3-12 and our comments on Dan. 7:19-28)

Little Horn symbolizes a religious power growing out of political power of Rome (Fourth kingdom).

The Second Beast of Revelation 13 represents false religious power (working signs, making images of worship)

Second Advent of Ancient of Days (Christ)
(No one knows WHEN)

ETERNITY

Saints possess their inheritance

Man of Lawlessness destroyed by breath of mouth of Ancient of Days

Judgment of the Harlot and the Beast and The False Prophet, Revelation 19

Marriage Supper of the Lamb, Revelation 19

Victory of God's Kingdom Over Beast Paralleled In Book of Revelation
The First Beast of Revelation 13 represents pagan political power (like a leopard, bear and a lion)

Babylon—The Harlot of Revelation 17 & 18 riding upon the Beast represents all worldly power and lust as the combined forces of the Dragon (the devil). God's people are warned to "come out of her"

291

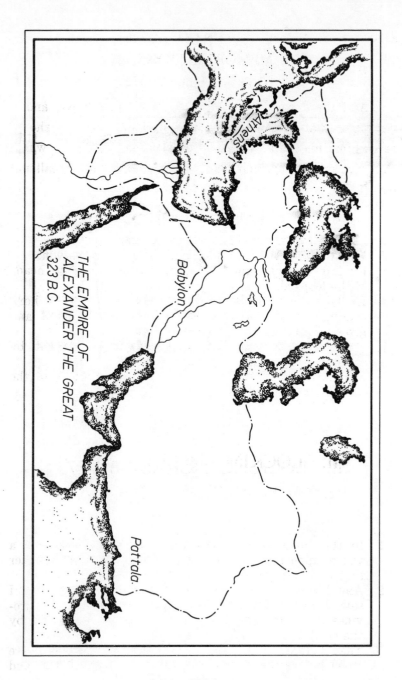

THE EMPIRE OF
ALEXANDER THE GREAT
323 B.C.

Athens

Babylon

Pattala

291A

MEMORIZATIONS

(Fill in the blanks:)

And there was given him _____ and glory, and a _____ that all the peoples, nations and _____ should serve him: his _____ is an everlasting _____, which shall not pass away, and his _____ that which shall not be _____.

EXPLANATIONS

1. Explain why the lion had eagles' wings.
2. Explain why the bear had three ribs in his mouth.
3. Explain the meaning of the four wings and four heads of the leopard.
4. Explain the probable interpretation of the small horn coming out of the ten horns of the fourth beast and growing strong and blaspheming God.
5. Explain the overall philosophy of history taught by chapter 7.
6. Explain how chapter 7 is parallel to chapter 2 of the book of Daniel.

CHAPTER EIGHT

II. LOCKING HORNS—8:1-27

a. THE GOAT AND THE RAM

TEXT: 8:1-8

1 In the third year of the reign of king Belshazzar a vision appeared unto me, even unto me, Daniel, after that which appeared unto me at the first.

2 And I saw in the vision; now it was so, that when I saw, I was in Shushan the palace, which is in the province of Elam; and I saw in the vision, and I was by the river Ulai.

3 Then I lifted up mine eyes, and saw, and, behold, there stood before the river a ram which had two horns: and

the two horns were high; but one was higher than the other, and the higher came up last.

4 I saw the ram pushing westward, and northward, and southward; and no beasts could stand before him, neither was there any that could deliver out of his hand; but he did according to his will, and magnified himself.

5 And as I was considering, behold, a he-goat came from the west over the face of the whole earth, and touched not the ground: and the goat had a notable horn between his eyes.

6 And he came to the ram that had the two horns, which I saw standing before the river, and ran upon him in the fury of his power.

7 And I saw him come close unto the ram, and he was moved with anger against him, and smote the ram, and brake his two horns; and there was no power in the ram to stand before him; but he cast him down to the ground, and trampled upon him; and there was none that could deliver the ram out of his hand.

8 And the he-goat magnified himself exceedingly; and when he was strong, the great horn was broken; and instead of it there came up four notable horns toward the four winds of heaven.

QUERIES

a. Where is Shushan in the province of Elam?

b. What is the significance of the last horn of the ram coming up higher than its first horn?

c. Why was the he-goat moved with anger against the ram?

PARAPHRASE

In the third year of the reign of king Belshazzar, I, Daniel, had a second vision from the Lord, somewhat like the first. In this vision I found myself at Susa, the capital of the province of Elam, standing beside the Ulai River. As I was loooking around, I saw a ram with two horns standing on the river bank; these two horns were large, but one was larger than the other and this larger of the two grew up last! The ram butted everything out of its way as it butted toward the west, the north and the south, and there was no one who could stand against it or render aid to its victims. This ram did as he pleased and became very great. And as I contemplated what all this might mean, lo, a he-goat came from the west, traversing his course of progress over all the earth so swiftly that he hardly even touched the ground. This he-goat had one very great horn between his eyes. He butted furiously at the two-horned ram, and the farther he came, the angrier he became toward the ram. He charged into the ram and broke off both his horns and when the ram was helpless the he-goat knocked it down and stamped it with his feet and none could deliver the ram from being destroyed by the he-goat. The he-goat then became proud and powerful, but suddenly, at the apex of his greatness, his horn was broken. In its place grew four strong horns pointing toward the four corners of the world.

COMMENT

v. 1-2 . . . A VISION APPEARED TO ME . . . IN SHUSHAN . . . BY THE RIVER ULAI . . . Elam was a country situated on the east side of the Tigris river opposite Babylonia in a mountainous region. Its population was made up of a variety of tribes. Their language, different from the Sumerian, Semitic, and Indo-European tongues, was written in cuneiform script. It has not yet been deciphered to any great extent. Elam was one of the earliest civilizations. In Sumerian inscriptions it was called Numma (high mountain people), which term became Elamtu in Akkadian texts; in classical literature it was known as Susiana, the Greek name for Susa, the capital city of Elam. The river Ulai runs through the province of Elam, flowing on through the city of Susa, into the Tigris-Euphrates.

Why did Daniel deem it necessary to mention these places? Because Shushan was later to become the summer capital of the Persian Empire. When the vision appeared to Daniel, nothing concerning the future importance of this site was known. But since the fortunes of Persia were involved, the future center of Persian life and activity was the best background. The yet unknown Sushan no doubt needed to be located for many of Daniel's readers—which certainly bears witness to the predictive nature of the Scriptures.

Archaeological effort in the last part of the 1880's uncovered in Shushan the great palace of King Xerxes (486-465 B.C.) in which Queen Esther lived. Many Jews lived here in the captivities and became prominent in the affairs of the city as the books of Esther and Nehemiah show.

v. 3-4 . . . BEHOLD, THERE STOOD BEFORE THE RIVER A RAM WHICH HAD TWO HORNS . . . ONE WAS HIGHER THAN THE OTHER . . . HE DID ACCORDING TO HIS WILL . . . MAGNIFIED HIMSELF . . . The ram is Medo-Persia (cf. 8:20). The two horns are the two component parts of the empire, Media and Persia. The taller one came up last, which coincides with the history of this empire when Persia eventually became supreme and assimilated the Medes. How does the ram typify Persia? The ram is an emblem of princely power (cf. Ezek. 34:17; 30:18; and vs. 20). The contrast between a ram and a he-goat is remarkably close to the relationship between Persia and Greece. The ram likes to butt things and yet there is something of a staid and sober character to it and not quite as flambouyant as the he-goat.

The history of Persia's rapid conquest of the world is symbolized by the butting of the ram toward the west, north and south. It did not butt toward the east because she herself was the eastern most part of her empire. The "three" points of the compass agree with the "three" ribs in the mouth of the bear (chapter 7). The statement that "no beasts could stand before him" refers to the imagery of chapter 7 also ,and the command there, "Arise and devour much flesh." There was little resistance to the Persian conquest of the world until Philip of Macedon (Alexander the Great's father) of whom we have spoken earlier. The phrase "he did as he pleased" was in a special sense true of the Persian Empire. Whatever rulers and people wanted in the course of their conquests, that they did, no matter how irregular or strange it might seem to others.

That the Persian conquerors "magnified" themselves may be exemplified by this historical sketch from *Archae-*

ology and Our O.T. Contemporaries, by James Kelso, pub. by Zondervan; pgs. 167-172.

In Isaiah God speaks of Cyrus as His shepherd and His anointed i.e., Messiah. These two terms designate Cyrus as a king chosen by God to be His agent in world history. And Cyrus was, indeed, one of history's most significant monarchs. Look at this abridged summary of the Persian empire which Cyrus created. For the first time in history the Persians give us a world empire dominated by Aryans. The previous Hamitic and Semitic world empires had made a tragedy of international government. But Persia brought in a veritable millennium for subject peoples. These Persians were virtually an unknown people until Cyrus in one generation made them masters of the world. Cyrus was at least as great a military genius as Alexander.

To create his empire Cyrus had to capture about twenty strong enemies including Lydia where Croesus, the richest man in the world, ruled Asia Minor; and Babylonia, the greatest of the ancient powers before Cyrus. He ruled from the Aegean Sea on the west to the Jaxartes River and the Himalayas on the east. All of these he consolidated into an empire that lasted two centuries. This is the final test of military power and it is here where Alexander was a total failure as his empire fell to pieces immediately upon his death.

Under Darius the Persian empire increased somewhat and was then twice the size of any previous world empire. Darius governed from the Balkans and Egypt on the west well into India on the east. The Persian empire ran for two centuries and gave the world the longest peace in history until the Pax Romana. About the middle of the Persian empire, Nehemiah, the last great political figure in the Old Testament, appeared. The Persian and the Roman empires were far more similar than formerly realized.

296

The Persian peace brought in one of the great-est periods of commercial expansion. They intro-duced an international language (Aramaic), rapid communications and good roads. They also put coinage on an international basis. In the sphere of politics Persia was the first world government to attempt to bring different races and nationalities under a central government which assured to all the *rights* and *privileges* of government as well as its burdens. They allowed the various subject races and existing civilizations to go on side by side with their own. They even permitted the Jews to coin their own money! Furthermore Persia inter-ferred as little as possible in local government matters. Alexander himself found the Persian system of government so excellent that he took over almost bodily the Persian policy of world empire and simply grafted on to it his own Hellen-istic policies.

The Persians' respect for truth and honor and their humane and chivalrous character was the secret of their nation's success. Their kings might lack these qualities, but the subject states of the empire seldom suffered seriously as most of the Persian subordinates were true to Persian ideals. The Persian's diplomatic and commercial language was Aramaic, not Persian! Thus Aramaic became one of the world's influential languages. Its in-scriptions are found as far east as India. In Roman times the Levant had a renaissance of this language, which was then called Syriac, and it replaced Greek. The Persians were the founders of religous freedom on a world basis. Note that the Jews speak well only of the Persian empire. Rome returned to many of the Persian practices.

Many of the features of good government which these Persians introduced are those which we have often thought of as America's unique con-tribution to world history. We should be doing far more than we are in the light of over two thousand years of international history and especial-

The Ram and the He-Goat
298

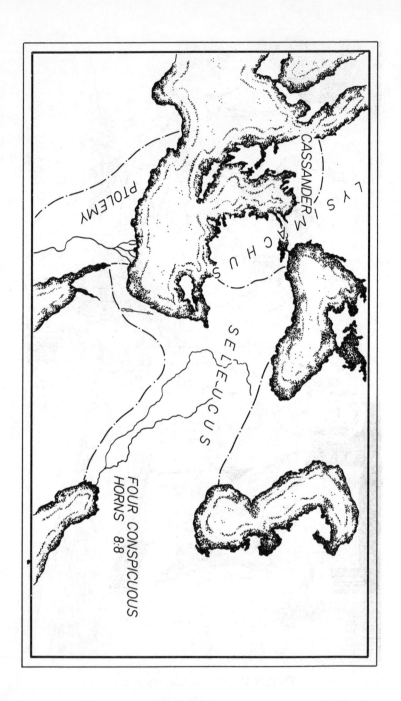

CASSANDER

PTOLEMY

LYSIMACHUS

SELEUCUS

FOUR CONSPICUOUS
HORNS 8:8

The Death of Alexander the Great

ly in 1900 years of the teachings of Jesus Christ.
The Persians deserve far more credit in world history than they have received. Unfortunately, too
often the Greeks have been their historians, and
your bitter enemy seldom speaks well of you.

Now let us return to the days of Cyrus. In antiquity the nations who were successful in war
brought home to their capital city the chief idols
of the conquered peoples as the major prize of victory. Thus mighty Babylon held the world's largest collection of gods in antiquity. When Cyrus
conquered that empire he completely reversed this
policy. He told all the conquered peoples to come
to Babylon and take home their national gods.
With Israel there was no idol, but the temple vessels taken away by Nebuchadnezzar were returned
to Jerusalem in the care of Shesh-bazzar, fourth
son of Jehoiachin. Under Darius, the Persian
government even helped bear the expense of erecting Israel's new temple.

v. 5-8 . . . BEHOLD, A HE-GOAT . . . SMOTE THE RAM
. . . THE GREAT HORN WAS BROKEN . . . THERE CAME UP
FOUR NOTABLE HORNS . . . The buck-goat is a fitting symbol
for the empire of Greece (cf. v. 21) for it represents ruggedness and power (cf. Zech. 10:3). It represents surefootedness and quickness. In I Macc. 1:3 Alexander's conquests are thus discribed: "He went through to the ends
of the earth and took spoils of a multitude of nations; and
the earth was quite before him," His conquests were
so rapid the he-goat is represented as "not touching the
ground," or literally, skimming over the earth. He came
from *ma-arabh* (where the sun sets—the west). This he-goat had a "horn of conspicuousness'" (a prominent horn)
between its eyes. This prominent horn represents Alexander *the Great*.

The "river" is significant for it symbolizes the historic
clash of the Greeks and the Persians at the Granicus river
where they met in their first Asiatic war. The "great
anger" points to the cry for vengeance from the Greek city
states after years of assaults across the Aegean sea by the
Persian hordes in 490-480 B.C. and battle at Marathon, Sa-

lamis, Plataea and Athens. When Darius landed near the plain of Marathon in 490 B.C. the city of Athens dispatched a runner, Pheidippides, to Sparta to summon long-pledged aid. He covered 140 miles in two days, but he raced in vain. For the famed fighters of Sparta, celebrating a festival of Apollo, could not go to war during that holy time. Athens hastily mobilized militia, and her general Miltiades gave the order: "Take food and march." Miltiades, by shrewdly outwitting and outflanking his foe (the Persian army) and by courageously charging into the ranks of the Persians (Merodotus wrote, "They were the first Greeks . . . who charged their enemies at a run . . .") defeated Darius at Marathon. Most Greeks hailed Marathon as glorious proof of their invincibility. But Themistocles, an Athenian statesman, warned that the Persians would return. Like Churchill in Britain between world wars, Themistocles went unheeded by the masses and was mocked by political opponents. The rich fought his plan for a tax-financed navy, perferring the self-supported citizen army. Across the Aegean, meanwhile, the Persian empire was conscripting men, ships, and arms for a land-and-sea invasion of Greece. In 481, Xerxes, successor to his father's throne, massed three forces on the Asian shore of the Hellespont. Athens Sparta, Corinth, and Aegina responded by forming a defensive league that would eventually include 31 city-states. But most Greeks, awed by Persian might, favored neutrality or even alliance with the invaders.

Xerxes bridged the channel with boats. His Egyptian subjects, renowned as the world's best ropemakers, produced the great bridge cables (a sample of their craft has been excavated in an Egyptian quarry: rope 18 inches in diameter attached to a 70-ton block of stone). Sod covered the mile-long plank roadway and high screens lined it so that animals crossing on it would not shy at the seething current. Across the Hellespont in 480 tramped an army that ancients numbered in the millions. Some 1000 ships paralleled the army's march, landing men and supplies as the invaders headed westward through Thrace, Macedonia, and Thessaly. The fleet traversed a canal Xerxes had ordered cut through the Mount Athos peninsula. He must have paid for the work in gold darics (named for Darius). A 300-coin cache has been found there. The Persians lived off the land. But unlike the Greeks, they were great meat eaters, so their fleet maintained food dumps holding beasts for slaughter and stores of salt meat of every kind. The depots also had piles of papyri for paper-work—a military feature alien to Greeks.

This massive army consisted of Persian warriors in leather jerkins and fish-scale armor, high-booted Phrygians, Mysians bearing sharpened stakes, wooden-helmeted men of the Caucasus, Scythians in pointed caps, Iranians behind tall wicker shields, an Arabian camel corps, ass-drawn chariots from India — and Ethopians in lionskins who brandished stone-headed clubs and spears tipped with gazelle horn. The exotic horde marched on toward Athens, drinking rivers dry, ravaging the land. But this slave army, said Herodotus, marched under the lash. And ahead lay a pass called Thermopylae, defended by a band of freemen.

Xerxes, enthroned near the pass to watch his men pour through, laughed at a scout's report of vain Greek warriers bathing and preening on the eve of battle. But a Greek, serving Xerxes, heard the report and understood: the troops were Spartans, ritualistically preparing to die. "O king!" he exclaimed, "now you are face to face with the most valiant men in Hellas." Aeschylus, veteran of the battle in the Salamis Strait, re-created it in his play *The Persians*. He told how the Greeks' bronze-sheathed rams smashed into the Persians "till hulls rolled over, and the sea itself was hidden, strewn with their wreckage, dyed with blood of men. The dead lay thick on all the reefs and beaches, and flight broke out . . ."

Bearing news of the Salamis disaster, messengers sped across the Aegean, rode the Royal Road from Sardis to Susa, and galloped along the highways that linked the satrapies of the Persian empire. "Neither snow, nor rain, nor heat, nor gloom of night stays these couriers from the swift completion of their appointed rounds," wrote Herodotus, which centuries later became the official motto of the U.S. Post Office. The following summer the Persian messengers had more bad news to spread: An army of some 100,000 Greeks had wiped out the last of the invaders in a battle at Plataea in the hills of Thebes.

And the rest belongs to the history of Alexander the Great, the *he-goat* whose armies went about their task of conquest as though it were being done to avenge a great wrong: His anger grew to the point where it was nothing less than rage—Alexander was bent upon obliterating every vestige of Persian control in the earth.

Alexander and his men spent the winter of 331 B.C. luxuriating in the splendor of Persepolis. One evening, encouraged by his drunken colleagues, Alexander burned the palaces of Xerxes in revenge against that king, who had put Athens to the torch 150 years before. "Avenge Greece," cried Alexander, hurling the first firebrand. "As soon as sleep had restored his senses," wrote Curtius, "Alexander regretted what he had done."

Half the peoples were already subjugated. But to win all Persia, Alexander would have to conquer the rest. His greatest efforts were still to come. In the spring of 330 B.C. Alexander marched north to Ecbatana, Persia's summer capital, now Hamadan. His object: the capture of Darius himself. But the Persian fled through the Caspian Gates, a pass over the Elburz Mountains. The Macedonian pursued him, averaging an extraordinary 36 miles a day. When he caught the straggling baggage train, he found Darius dead, murdered by his own disillusioned generals. King of Persia at last, Alexander marched to Zadracarta, modern Gorgan, to assume not only the title but the pomp of an oriental monarch.

At the Beas River, just inside present India, Alexander faced a real mutiny for the first time. His homesick men, unnerved by the fierce fight against Porus, concerned by reports of even greater armies ahead, refused to go on. Alexander summoned his officers and tried to rally them. Silence greeted him. Then Coenus, a faithful general, rose, removed his helmet, and addresssd Alexander: "O king, I speak not for those officers present, but for the men . . . Those that survive yearn to return to their families, to enjoy while they yet live the riches you have won for them . . . A noble thing, O king, is to know when to stop." Angered and disappointed by the speech, Alexander sulked in his tent for three days. When as last he bowed to the will of his men, they rejoiced.   "Alexander," they said, "has allowed us, but no other, to defeat him."   He led his men back to the Jhelum to begin the journey home.

As Arrian wrote, "Alexander had no small or mean conceptions, nor would ever have remained contented with any of his possessions . . . but would always have searched far beyond . . . being always the rival, if of no other, yet of himself."   As he turned from further conquests in India it is reported that he "wept because there were no more worlds to conquer."   He died in Persepolis at the age of 32.

Idolized by his men, hailed as divine in lands he won, Alexander passed into the legends of three continents.   Central Asia worshippd him as Iskander, founder of cities (one, Bucephala, honored his horse).   Chiefs in Turkistan claim descent from him; Afghan mothers frighten naughty children with tales of Iskander.   Persians called him son of Darius; Egyptians, son of the last Pharaoh, Nectanebo.   Ethiopia made him a saint, and Islam enrolled him as a prophet.   Mogul art shows him in a diving bell seeking the sea's secrets.   Medieval Europe depicted him as a knight of chivalry.   Romans, first to call Alexander "the Great," held themselves heirs to his empire and ambitions.   Augustus wore Alexander's head on a signet ring, emulated his deeds and divinity.   Even Buddha owes his image to Alexander's march into the Orient.   Inspired by statues Greeks brought to Bandhara, sculptors created Buddha in the image of Apollo, but added to his forehead the Oriental third eye, which emits spiritual light.

He won an empire covering more than one and one half million square miles.   He had mapped unknown territory, built cities, opened trade routes, stimulated the exchange of ideas.   From the Mediterranean to the Hindu Kush, Greek became the lingua franca of court and commerce.

His vast realm survived for only a few years as the Diadochi—his "successors"—fought each other for power. Verse 8 and its "four notable horns" coming up in the place of the great horn (Alexander) are parallel to the four heads of the "leopard" of chapter 7 and represent the four-way division of Alexander's empire between Ptolemy, Antigonus, Cassander and Lysimachus (see our comments on Dan. 7:4-6).

QUIZ

1. Why did Daniel mention all the geographical locations in verse 2?
2. Whom does the ram symbolize and how extensive was his empire?
3. What is the significance of the ram "doing as he pleased?"
4. Who is represented by the "he-goat?"
5. Why is the "he-goat" represented as moving with anger against the ram?
6. How extensive was the empire of the "he-goat?"
7. What is represented by the "four notable horns?"

b. THE GREAT HORN AND
THE RIGHTEOUS PRINCE

TEXT: 8:9-17

9   And out of one of them came forth a little horn, which waxed exceeding great, toward the south, and toward the east, and toward the glorious land.

10 And it waxed great, even to the host of heaven; and some of the host and of the stars it cast down to the ground, and trampled upon them.

11 Yea, it magnified itself, even to the prince of the host; and it took away from him the continual burnt-offering, and the place of his sanctuary was cast down.

12 And the host was given over to it together with the continual burnt-offering through transgression; and it cast down truth to the ground, and it did its pleasure and prospered.

13 Then I heard a holy one speaking; and another holy one said unto that certain one who spake, How long shall be the vision concerning the continual burnt-offering, and the transgression that maketh desolate, to give both the sanctuary and the host to be trodden under foot?

14 And he said unto me, unto two thousand and three hundred evenings and mornings; then shall the sanctuary be cleansed.

15 And it came to pass, when I, even I Daniel, had seen the vision, that I sought to understand it; and, behold, there stood before me as the appearance of a man.

16 And I heard a man's voice between the banks of the Ulai, which called, and said, Gabriel, make this man to understand the vision.

17 So he came near where I stood; and when he came, I was affrighted, and fell upon my face: but he said unto me, Understand, O son of man; for the vision belongeth to the time of the end.

QUERIES

a. Why does the "little horn" come forth from the four?
b. Who is the "host" and the "prince of the host?"
c. What is the "time of the end?"

PARAPHRASE

And from one of the four notable horns, came one little horn growing slowly at first, soon becoming very strong, and it extended itself toward the south and the east and toward the glorious, holy land of God's people, Canaan. This arrogant horn extended its evil power against the hosts of God's people and some of them were slain, that is, many of God's heavenly saints were killed. Yes, this presumptuous and boastful horn even exalted itself over God himself taking it upon himself to prohibit the daily sacrifices in the temple of the Jews which God had commanded to be offered, and the horn desecrated the temple until it was defiled beyond use. And God allowed some of the Jews and His temple to come under the power of this horn because of the apostasy of some who agreed to the defilement of the temple by the horn. This despicable horn carried on such an immoral paganization of the holy land that justice, truth, and righteousness seemed to vanish and evil seemed to be triumphing. Just then I heard two angels talking one another. One said to the other, How long will it be until the daily sacrifices are restored again? How long until the desecration of the temple is avenged and God's people triumph? The other replied, a time just short of seven years, that is 2300 days, will transpire and then the

307

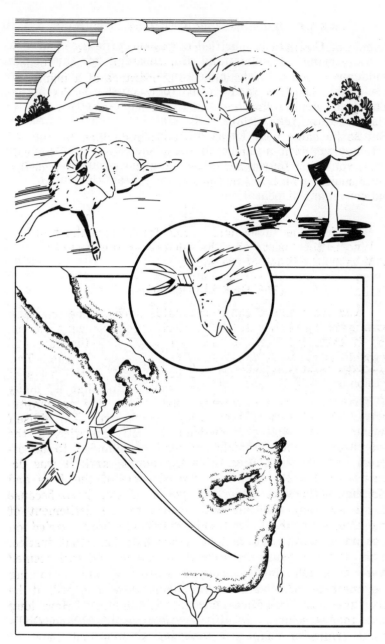

The Little Horn Developed

temple of God will be purified of pagan defilement. And as I was trying to understand the meaning of this vision, suddenly a being in the appearance of a man stood before me and I heard a man's voice from across the river Ulai. The voice said, Gabriel, make this prophet understand the vision he has just received. So Gabriel started toward me. But as he came near I was too frightened to stand up and I fell down with my face to the ground. He said, son of man, you must understand that the events you have seen in your vision will not take place until near the end of the old convenant dispensation.

COMMENT

v. 9-10 . . . CAME FORTH A LITTLE HORN . . . WAXED GREAT, EVEN TO THE HOST OF HEAVEN . . . The description given here and in subsequent verses of this chapter is so definite and specific that the "little horn" here can be no other than Antiochus IV (Epiphanes) and his immediate predecessors (The Seleucids). Ptolemy I, one of the four who succeeded Alexander to his empire, appointed Seleucus Nicator (312-280 B.C.) to administer Syria for him. There followed almost a century and a half of war between the Ptolomies and the Seleucids for sovereignty in Syria and Palestine. This is discussed at length in chapter eleven of this work. In this text all the Seleucid rulers between Seleucus Nicator and Antiochus the IV are passed over with the phrase, "came forth a little horn, which waxed exceeding great, toward the south . . . and east . . . and the glorious land." Verse 10 brings the reader abruptly to Antiochus Epiphanes (about 175-165 B.C.).

It is important to note that the "little horn" here *grows out of* one of the four which definitely belong to the Grecian Empire. It cannot, therefore, be the same little horn of chapter 7 which overthrew three of the ten which were definitely connected to the fourth beast. The Scofield Reference Bible declares this passage (8:10-14) to be the "most difficult in prophecy." While it refers the passage to Antiochus IV, still it connects the horn of chapter 8 to the horn of chapter 7 inferring they are one and the same. Such seems clearly contradictory in view of the

fact that the Scofield Reference Bible declares the fourth
beast of chapter 7 to be the Roman Empire.

The "glorious land" can be none other than the Holy
Land, Palestine. This horn "waxed great" or extended its
power south and east from Syria, even into Palestine, to the
very borders of Egypt. The "host of heaven" and the
"stars" are simply God's covenant people (and not any special group of Jewish priests or rulers). One may find a
number of references or figurative parallels where God's
saints of the O.T. are likened unto the stars of heaven
(Jer. 33:22; Dan. 12:3, etc.) ; they are also referred to as
the "hosts" (cf. Ex. 7:4; 12:41).

The terrible, presumptuous deeds of Antiochus IV
against the saints of God were in reality arrogant wickednesses against Heaven itself.

v. 11-12 . . . IT MAGNIFIED ITSELF, EVEN TO THE PRINCE
OF THE HOST . . . AND THE HOST WAS GIVEN OVER TO IT . . .
This little horn (Antiochus Epiphanes) arrogated to himself the prerogatives of Almighty God. He actually considered himself equal to God and commanded that likenesses
of himself be placed in the temple of the Jews and worshipped as god. That this Syrian ruler actually forbade the
Jews to offer their regular sacrifices is confirmed by I Macc.
1:44-47: "And the king sent letters by the hand of messengers unto Jerusalem and the cities of Judah, that they
should follow laws strange to the land, and should forbid
whole burnt offerings and sacrifice and drink offerings in
the sanctuary; and should profane the sabbaths and feasts,
and pollute the sanctuary and them that were holy." Antiochus did not actually tear down the temple, but he desecrated it to such a point, even commanding that a swine be
slain on the temple altar, that it was not fit for use. He
also substituted an altar to Jupiter for the altar of burnt
offering. This was the crowning abomination.

Great numbers of the people of Israel consorted with
Antiochus and welcomed his Hellenization of their culture.
Many of them were given over to transgression. God permitted it—He did not cause it! The same principle is
evident here as is annuonced in II Thess. 2:11-12. If men
wish to be deluded it is in the economy of God's creating
them as free, moral agents, that they shall be permitted to

310

be so deluded. If, however, they wish to know the truth and love the truth, God will always make it possible that they shall have the opportunity to know it and practice it.

This pagan ruler "cast down truth to the ground," and all descriptions of evil flourished and prospered for a time. Every copy of Jewish scriptures that could be found was burned and many faithful Jews were slain. One need only read I Maccabees to know of the terrible paganization and attendant persecution of this time. (For more detailed information concerning the reign of Antiochus IV see our comments on 11:20ff)

v. 13-14 . . . HOW LONG . . . THE TRANSGRESSION THAT MAKETH DESOLATE . . . UNTO TWO THOUSAND AND THREE HUNDRED EVENINGS AND MORNINGS . . . God sent His angels into the presence of Daniel to discuss the matter under consideration so that Daniel might through their words arrive at an authoritative interpretation. These are things angels desire to look into (cf. I Pet. 1:10-12). One angel seems to be more knowledgeable than the other concerning the times and seasons of God's counsels, (see our Special Study on Angels at the end of chapter 10).

There are two principal interpretations of verse 14: (a) it means 1150 days; those who adopt this view insist that the prophecy is related to the daily morning and evening sacrifices and 2300 such sacrifices would therefore be offered on 1150 days. They also connect this to the horn of chapter 7, especially with 7:25, which they contend is 3½ years (a time, times and half a time) and 1150 days is nearly equivalent to 3½ years. It should be obvious, however, that 1150 days do not equal 3½ years, even when these years are regarded as comprising only 360 days each or a total of 1260 days. It should also be obvious that the "horn" of chapter 7 and the "horn" of chapter 8 are different "horns." (b) it means 2300 days and is probably a derivative of Genesis 1, where an "evening and a morning" are reckoned as a full day. In the O.T. an expression such as 40 days and 40 nights does not mean 20 days, nor does 3 days and 3 nights mean either 6 days or 1½ days; it means 3 days. Keil says: "A Hebrew reader could not possibly understand the period of time 2300 evening-mornings of 2300 half days or 1150 whole days, because evening and morning at the creation constituted not the half but the whole day." So we must understand the phrase as meaning 2300 whole days.

But how are the 2300 days to be applied to the history of Antiochus? The number 2300 shows that the period must be defined in round numbers (the number 10 and any multiple of it is an incomplete number or a "round" number and should not be taken literally), measuring only nearly the actual time. This conforms to all genuine prophecy because genuine prophecy never makes mantic prediction of exact days and hours its primary focus. The period (2300 days) are undoubtedly referring to the period of Antiochus' abominable treatment of the Jews. This began in the year 171 B.C., one year before his return from his second expedition to Egypt. In this year began the laying waste of the sanctuary. The termination would then be the death of Antiochus (164 B.C.). The 2300 days cover a period of six years and about 4 months. Keil believes that the number (being a little short of 7 years) possesses a symbolic meaning, namely, not quite the full duration of a period of divine judgment. It does seem to be used to cover approximately the period of the persecution under Antiochus. Leupold says: "The fact that it is expressed in days reminds the troubled Israelites that the Lord will not let this period extend a day beyond what they can bear." Thus when these days (the period that is not even a full period of divine judgment) shall have come to an end, "then shall the sanctuary be cleansed." This makes it very plain that what is really marked by the 2300 days is the period of the desecration of the sanctuary.

v. 15-17 . . . I SOUGHT TO UNDERSTAND . . . GABRIEL, MAKE THIS MAN TO UNDERSTAND . . . THE VISION BELONGETH TO THE TIME OF THE END . . . Daniel knows only, so far, that the overthrow of the sanctuary and the sufferings of the saints were not to last even through an entire divine judgment period. But he seeks to understand more. And at the mere desire (not even an audible prayer was made by Daniel) lo, an angel of God stands before him. Here and in 9:21 Gabriel is named; in 10:13ff. Michael is named. The only O.T. book in which angels receive names is Daniel, and Gabriel and Michael are the only two who are named. This is so in the N.T., Luke 1:19, 26; Jude 9.

The presence of perfect holiness before Daniel causes him, sinful man, to tremble with fear and he falls upon his face as if to hide. The vision is definitely to be understood *because* it has to do with the time of the end! This should indicate immediately that it is not speaking of the end of *all* time, the Second Advent of Christ, for the N.T. plainly states that "no one knoweth the day nor the hour . . ." and, "in a time that ye think not; the Son of man cometh . . ." Furthermore, there is a specific key to contextual interpretation of this "time of the end" and that is Daniel 8:19, "the latter part of the indignation." It can only refer to the end of time when afflictions or indigation are to be permitted upon Israel. IT IS THE END OF THE O.T. PERIOD AND THE USHERING IN OF THE NEW! This "time of the end" reaches only to *the end* of those special afflictions that are to come on the people of the Jews *before* the Messianic period, and which are made the subject of prophecy because of their importance to the preparation of the convenant people for the coming of the Messiah and the establishment of His kingdom which is gloriously symbolized in the prophets as the time of God's victory over His enemies and the restoring of the fortunes of Judah and Jerusalem. The view that the "time of the end" here has reference to the great tribulation, supposedly to occur during the latter half of the 70th week is utterly without exegetical support from this context or any combination of texts!

QUIZ

1. Why is that "little horn" different from the "little horn" of chapter 7?
2. What is the "glorious land?"
3. How did the horn "wax great" against the stars and the prince?
4. How did it take away the continual burnt-offering?
5. What is the meaning of, "the host was given over to it?"
6. What period of time is indicated by 2300 evenings and mornings?
7. Why is the "time of the end" not the end of time?

c.   GRIEVOUS TIMES AND RETRIBUTION

TEXT: 8:18-27

18 Now as he was speaking with me, I fell into a deep sleep with my face toward the ground; but he touched me, and set me upright.

19 And he said, Behold, I will make thee know what shall be in the latter time of the indigation; for it belongeth to the appointed time of the end.

20 The ram which thou sawest, that had the two horns, they are the kings of Media and Persia.

21 And the rough he-goat is the king of Greece: and the great horn that is between his eyes is the first king.

22 And as for that which was broken, in the place whereof four stood up, four kingdoms shall stand up out of the nation, but not with his power.

23 And in the latter time of their kingdom, when the transgressors are come to the full, a king of fierce countenance, and understanding dark sentences, shall stand up.

24 And his power shall be mighty, but not by his own power; and he shall destroy wonderfully, and shall prosper and do his pleasure; and he shall destroy the mighty ones and the holy people.

25 And through his policy he shall cause craft to prosper in his hand; and he shall magnify himself in his heart, and in their security shall he destroy many; he shall also stand up against the prince of princes; but he shall be broken without hand.

26 And the vision of the evenings and mornings which hath been told is true: but shut thou up the vision; for it belongeth to many days to come.

27 And I, Daniel, fainted, and was sick certain days; then I rose up, and did the king's business: and I wondered at the vision, but none understood it.

QUERIES

a. How shall the "king of fierce countenance" have mighty power, but not by his own power? v. 24

b. How is he to be "broken without hand?" v. 25

c. Why was Daniel told to "shut up the vision?" v. 26

PARAPHRASE

The more the angel spoke to me the more I became upset with my moral sinfulness, until I actually fainted. But the angel simply touched me and I awoke from my faint and had strength to stand up again. Then the angel said to me, Lo, I am revealing to you the things that shall happen in the final period of the Babylonian captivity (the period of God's anger against His covenant-breaking people). Every appointed time of God has an end—and so His anger will end too! The ram which you saw in this vision having two horns represents the two-headed kingdom of Medo-Persia. The shaggy he-goat represents the empire of Greece and the tall horn which grows between its eyes represents its most illustrious emperor, Alexander the Great. When you saw this great horn break off, and four smaller horns replacing it, this indicates that the Grecian empire will break into four sections at the death of this great king with four separate kings, none of them as great as the first king. Toward the end of these four kingdoms, when the apostate Jews, who love the transgressions of paganism, have grown exceedingly wicker, a fierce, wicked and adamant king, who shall also be a master of deceit and cunning, shall arise from this background to rule over the covenant people. His power shall be tremendous, but that is only because God, in His providence, is permitting him to have such power for a season. Prospering wherever he turns, his power to destroy powerful opponents and the saints of God will seem remarkable. And by his cunning he shall be successful in catching many of his opponents off guard as they bask in false security. He will destroy them with craftines; so great will he think himself to be that he will even defy the Almighty God; when his end comes, it will be apparent that he was brought down by Almighty God, and not by mortal men. Now this remarkable and unique vision is true—do not doubt that Daniel. Preserve this revelation safely for, although it has to do with the end times of the Mosaic dispensation, these things are still in the distant future. So overcome was I, that for some days I was sick

315

before I could continue the king's business. And though the contents of the vision and its interpretation remained firmly fixed in my mind, it greatly perplexed me and others to whom I related it.

COMMENT

v. 18-19 . . . I FELL INTO A DEEP SLEEP . . . BUT . . . HE SET ME UPRIGHT . . . KNOW . . . THE LATTER TIME OF THE INDIGNATION . . . Daniel's awareness of the great gulf between the sinfulness of mortals and the perfect holiness of angelic beings was so overcoming that he apparently fainted into unconsciousness. But the supernatural ministration of the angelic being was sufficient to restore Daniel to wakefulness, and strength to stand up and receive the revelation from God the messenger had to relate.

This message had to do with the closing days of the "indignation." Now that term "indignation" (or "wrath") can only refer to the captivities of the covenant people of the O.T. (Israel's captivity by Assyria, and Judah's captivity by Babylon and her successors, Persia, Greece). For scriptural confirmation of this see Isaiah 10:5, 25; 26:20, etc. The term "indignation" is a technical term used by the prophets to designate the wrath of God and His displeasure executed in giving the covenant people over to capitvity, or to oppression by their pagan enemies. So, when the abominations of Antiochus IV occur, it will be a sign that the indignation of God against the covenant people for their idolatry during the Divided Kingdom period is coming to a fierce finality.

This "appointed time of the end" is the *appointed time of the end of the O.T. dispensation,* which would subsequently usher in the Messianic dispensation and the establishment of His kingdom on earth, the church. As is well known from history, when Antiochus IV died (about 165 B.C.), the Maccabean brothers continued their war of Jewish liberation, which was successful, and gave the Jews about 100 years of freedom and self-rule untol about 63 B.C., when Pompey, one of the Roman Triumvirate, occupied Palestine as a part of the Roman empire. "In the fulness of time" God sent forth His Son, the Messiah, to establish His kingdom, the church. The Jews, for the most part, rejected the

Messiah and crucified Him, but God raised Him from the dead, enthroned Him upon David's throne, established His church (Acts 2), and in 70 A.D. permitted the Roman army to destroy the Jewish temple, slay a million Jews and sell another half-million into slavery all over the world. The O.T. dispensation was nailed to the cross at the death of Jesus (cf. Col. 2:8-15). Even the O.T. predicted that its dispensation of God5s law would be supplanted with the new and real (cf. Heb. 8:13; Jer. 31:31-34). Please consult *Minor Prophets*, by Paul T. Butler, pub. College Press, for special studies on Christ now ruling on David's throne.

The point is, God warned the Jews of the divided kingdoms in the earlier prophets (Amos, Hosea, Micah, Isaiah, Zephaniah, Jeremiah) that because of their idolatry (and consequent moral decadance) He was going to bring His "indignation" and "wrath" upon them in the form of captivity and oppression in order to chasten them, preparing them for the glorious blessings that would come to all who believed and accepted the promised Messiah and His kingdom. Now, God reveals through Daniel that this indignation and wrath is going to end some day—every appointed time of God has an end. The end of God's chastening process will be indicated by this fierce, cunning, arrogant, blood-thirsty "little-horn" grown-great, appearing on the scene of history and bringing a terrible onslaught of the world power against God's people. But he will not stand.

v. 20-22 THE RAM WHICH THOU SAWEST . . . AND THE ROUGH HE-GOAT . . . There can be no doubt about this interpretation. God is revealing to Daniel the kingdoms of Persia and Greece (and that which shall grow out of Greece) centuries (about 400-500 years) before they appear on the scene of history. Actually, the entire span of history revealed to Daniel covers the period between Babylonian and Christ, some 600 years! For details on the two kingdoms mentioned here, see comments on 8:1-8 and 7:4-6.

v. 23-25 . . . A KING OF FIERCE COUNTENANCE . . . This is Antiochus (IV) Epiphanes. For details on his reign see comments on 8:9-17 and chapter 11. When the four kingdoms into which Alexander's great empire was divided have about run their course, then this new king will put in his appearance. He is to be a master of deceit and dissimulation, able to conceal his meaning under ambiguous words. One translation has it, "understanding riddles" in place of "understanding dark sentences." This king is not only a master of cunning, but he is also one that can not easily be deceived. The phrase, ". . . he shall be mighty, but not by his own power . . ." indicates plainly that only because God providentially allowed it did he become so great. And this is not foreign to God's providence in the affairs of world rulers, as we have shown in the case of Nebuchadnezzar.

It will seem as if evil and deceit are about to take over the whole world when this king reigns. Whatever he undertakes will prosper (for a while). He will have power and cunning to do as he pleases, especially against his immediate political opponents and against the saints of God in Palestine.

Leupold says: "This is, in fact, a very skillfully condensed account of the checkered career of one of the most remarkable men that strutted across the stage of history. Its very conciseness makes it ambiguous or difficult to understand if one skims over it too readily." One personal characteristic that shall stand out as this man develops his carrer will be his proud, haughty, presumptuous nature. He will be so crafty in destroying any one who opposes him that while opponents think they are perfectly safe he is plotting their destruction, which he also executes craftily and speedily.

His inordinate pride and self-exaltation lead him to blaspheme and challenge the Almighty God ("prince of princes") but God will not allow such evil and rebellion to thwart His Divine purposes. God without hands—by means . . . that appear to be providential or divine—will break this tyrant! His overthrow will come so as to indicate that man himself did not put this arrogant mortal out of the way, but He whose mills grind slowly but exceedingly fine did it. God only allowed this persecutor his day because God was willing that he be given opportunity to repent. When he did not repent, God used his persecutions to purge the people of God in preparation for the coming of the Messiah. The reign of Antiochus IV is chronicled in I Maccabees 1:1—6:16.

v. 26-27 . . . SHUT THOU UP THE VISION . . . Since the prophecy was for a long time hence, Daniel was to **preserve** ("shut up") the prophecy. To "shut up" the prophecy does not mean it is to be kept secret or that it is not yet to be understood. It means quite simply that it is to be permanently preserved by writing it down for posterity's sake (cf. Rev. 22:10). The psychological effect of the vision upon Daniel was exhausting. He was sick for a number of days before he could continue the king's business. The contents of the vision and its interpretation remained for sometime in the immediate consciousness of Daniel and he pondered the vision over and over. But he remained perplexed because what had been told him would never be translated into action in his own lifetime, but was for many years to come.

QUIZ

1. Why did Daniel fall into a deep sleep?
2. When is the time of "indignation?" the time "of the end?"
3. Who is the great horn between the eyes of the he-goat?
4. Who is the king of "fierce countenance?"
5. Why describe him as one with "understanding dark sentences?"
6. Who gave him his power?
7. How did he cause "craft to prosper?"
8. How was he broken?
9. What does "shut up the vision" mean?

SERMON NUMBER EIGHT

LOCKING HORNS

Text: Daniel 8

INTRODUCTION

I. AGAIN, DANIEL TELLS OF A VISION HE HAD DURING HIS DAYS UNDER BELSHAZZAR.
   A. This vision somewhat like the first.
      1. In the form of animal actors

319

2. Deals with future, world-shaping events and empires.

3. These events will have direct bearing on the covenant people of God and their future mission in God's redemptive plan.

4. These events deal with minute details of the far distant future and are important in building an apologetic as well as theistic philosophy of history.

B. Daniel was transported in vision to Susa, capital of the province of Elam.

1. Elam was a country on the east side of Tigris river opposite Babylonia in a mountainous region.

2. Its population a variety of tribes.

Its language—different from Sumerian, Semitic and Indo-European—was written in cuneiform script, and has not yet been deciphered to any extent.

4. Elam was one of the earliest civilizations; in Sumerian inscriptions it was called Numma "high mountain people."

5. The river Ulai runs through the province of Elam, and flows through the city of Susa into the Tigris-Euphrates.

C. Why did Daniel feel it important to mention these places?

1. Because Susa was later to become the summer capital of Persian empire.

2. When the vision came, nothing concerning the future importance of this territory was known.

3. The yet-unknown Susa no doubt needed to be located for many of Daniel's readers. Bears witness to predictive nature of scriptures.

D. Archaeological effort in later 1800's uncovered in Susa the great palace of King Xerxes (486-465 B.C.) in which Queen Esther lived.

1. Many other Jews lived here in the captivities and man stayed here and never returned to the Holy Land when the exiles returned.

DISCUSSION

I. GOAT AND THE RAM, 8:1-8

A. The Ram is Medo-Persia (cf. 8:20)

1. Two horns are two component parts of this empire, Media and Persia
2. The taller horn came up last, and this coincides with the history of this empire where Persia eventually became supreme and assimilated the Medes.
3. The Ram, emblematic of princely power (Ezek. 34:17, etc.) ; and the contrast between ram and he-goat is remarkably close to the contrast between Persia and Greece.
4. Ram likes to butt things, and yet there is something of staid and sober character to it . . . not quite as flambouyant as he-goat.
5. Persia's rapid conquest of world symbolized by butting of Ram west, north and south—did not butt east, because she herself was the easternmost part of the empire.
6. Three points of compass agree with three ribs in mouth of bear.
7. "No beasts could stand before him" compares to imagery of ch. 7, and command to "arise and devour much flesh." There was little resistance to Persia until Philip of Macedon.
8. The Persian conquerors "magnified" themselves; Cyrus, one of history's most significant monarchs, first to dominate the world as an Ayran Persian, brought a veritable millennium for subject peoples; Cyrus' empire lasted 200 years; gave the world the longest peace in history until Rome; great commercial expansion; international language (Aramaic); rapid communications and good roads; international coinage; first world government to attempt to bring different races and nationalities under a central government, assuring to all the rights and privileges of government as well as its burdens; they allowed various subject races and civilizations to go on side by side with their

321

own; interfered as little as possible in local government matters.

9. Persians respect for truth and honor, and their humane and chivalrous character, was the secret of their nation's success; the Persians were the founders of religious freedom on a world basis. Note that the Jews speak well only of the Persian empire. Rome returned to many of the Persian practices. Under Darius the Persian government even helped bear the expense of erecting Israel's new temple.

B. The He-Goat is Greece.

1. Fitting, for it represents ruggedness and power (Zech. 10:3).

2. Sure-footedness and quickness; "He (Alexander) went through the ends of the earth and took spoils of a multitude of nations; and the earth was quiet before him." I Macc. 1:3.

3. He had a horn of conspicuousness (a prominent horn) between the eyes. This represents Alexander the Great

4. River is significant, for it represents the Granicus river, where the Ram and He-goat met in their first Asiatic war.

5. "Great anger" points to the cry for vengeance from the Greek city states after years of assaults across the Aegean by the Persians

6. Alexander won an empire covering more than one and a half million square miles. He mapped unknown territories, built cities, opened trade routes stimulated the exchange of ideas. From the Mediterranean to the Hindu Kush, Greek became the lingua franca of court and commerce.

7. His vast realm survived for only a few years as his successors fought each other for power.

8. Verse 8 and its "four notable horns" coming up in the place of the great horn (Alexander) are parallel to the four heads of the leopard of chapter 7 and represent the four-way division of Alexander's empire between PPtolem, Antigonus, Cassander and Lysimachus.

II. GREAT HORN, AND THE RIGHTEOUS PRINCE; 8:9-17

A. Description here and subsequent verses so definite that "little horn" can be no other than Antiochus IV (Epiphanes), and those who came before him, the Seleucids.

1. Ptolemy I, one of four to get Alexander's empire, appointed Seleucus Nicator (his leading general) to administer Syria for him.

2. There followed a century and a half of war between the Ptolomies and Seleucids for sovereignty in Syria and Palestine.

3. It will be discussed in ch. 11, but here all the Seleucid rulers between Nicator and Antiochus IV are passed over with the phrase "came forth a little horn, which waxed exceeding great, toward the south, etc."

4. Note the little horn is grown great and grows out of one of the four which definitely belong to the Grecian Empire; is not therefore the same little horn of ch. 7 which grew out of the 4th beast.

5. The glorious land can be none other than the Holy Land.

6. The host of heaven and the stars are simply God's covenant people.

7. The terrible, presumptuous deeds of Anticohus IV against the saints of God were in reality arrogant wickednesses against Heaven itself.

B. This Little Horn magnified itself even to the Prince of the Host

1. Arrogated to himself prerogatives of Almighty God

2. Actually considered himself equal to God and commanded that likenesses of himself be placed in the temple of the Jews and worshipped as God.

3. He forbade the Jews to offer their regular sacrifices (I Macc. 1:44-47).

4. He desecrated the temple to such a point, even commanding that swine be slain on the temple altar, so that it was not fit for use.

5. He also substituted an atlar to Jupiter for the altar of burnt offering.
6. Great numbers of the people of Israel consorted with Antiochus and welcomed his Hellenization of their culture. Many were given over to the transgressions of the heathen. God permitted this; He did not cause it (same principle as II Thess. 2:11-12).
7. This pagan ruler cast truth down to the ground, and all descriptions of evil flourished and prospered for a time. Every copy of Jewish scriptures that could be found was burned and many faithful Jews were slain. Read I Macc. 1:56-57.
8. God sent His angel to Daniel so that Daniel might have an authoritative interpretation of these things.
9. 2300 morning-evenings as a Hebrew would understand it would be 2300 days; it points to a period of time to be defined in round numbers and undoubtedly points to the period of Antiochus' abominable treatment of the Jews. His oppression of them began in 171 B.C. (one year before his return from his 2nd expedition to Egypt). The termination would be his death—the 2300 days cover a period of six years and about 4 months. Keil believes the number (being a little short of 7 years) possesses a symbolical meaning, not quite the full duration of a period of divine judgment. The fact it is expressed in days reminds the troubled Israelites that the Lord will not let this period extend a day beyond what they can bear.
10. The phrase "then shall the sanctuary be cleansed" makes it very plain that what is really marked by the 2300 days is the period of the desecration of the sanctuary.

C. How long will it last?
  1. Daniel knows thus far only that it will not last through an entire period of divine judgment.
  2. The presence of perfect holiness before Daniel

causes him to tremble with fear and he falls on his face as if to hide.

3. The vision has to do with the time of the end and is definitely meant to be understood. This should indicate it is not the end of time, for of that day and hour no one knoweth.

4. Furthermore, there is a specific key to contextual interpretation of this "time of the end," and that is Dan. 8:19—"the latter part of the indignation." IT CAN ONLY REFER TO THE END OF TIME WHEN AFFLICTIONS OR INDIGNATION ARE TO BE PERMITTED UPON ISRAEL. IT IS THE END OF THE O.T. PERIOD AND THE USHERING OF THE NEW TESTAMENT (WHICH IS THE END OF THE AGES). This "time of the end" reaches only to the end of those special afflictions that are to come on the people of the Jews BEFORE the Messainic period—the subject of prophecy because of their importance to the preparation of the covenant people for the coming of the Messiah and the establishment of His kingdom which is gloriously symbolized in the prophets as the time of God's victory over His enemies and the restoring of the fortunes of Judah and Jerusalem. THE VIEW THAT THE "TIME OF THE END" HERE HAS REFERENCE TO THE GREAT TRIBULATION, SUPPOSEDLY DURING THE LATTER HALF OF THE 70TH WEEK, IS UTTERLY WITHOUT EXEGETICAL SUPPORT FROM THIS CONTEXT OR ANY OTHER!

III. GRIEVOUS TIMES AND RETRIBUTION, 8:18-27

A. The angel has to revive Daniel in order to make him know.

1. The message has to do with the closing days of the "indignation."

2. The term "indignation" (or wrath) can only refer to the captivities of the covenant people (see Isa. 10:5, 25; 26:20, etc.).

3. It is a technical term used by prophets to designate the wrath of God and His displeasure executed in giving the covenant people over to captivity to their hated enemies

325

4. So, when the abominations of Antiochus occur, it will be a sign that the INDIGNATION of God against the covenant people for their idolatry during the Divided Kingdom period is coming to a fierce finality.

5. This appointed time of the end is the time of the end of the O.T. dispensation. When Antiochus died, the Maccabean brothers continued their war of Jewish liberation, which by its success gave the Jews about 100 years of freedom until about 63 B.C., when Pompey occupied Palestine as a part of the Roman empire.

6. In the fullness of time, God sent forth His Son; the Jews for the most part rejected the Messiah and crucified Him, but God raised Him from the dead. With this the Jewish dispensation came to an end. God mercifully allowed the temple to stand another 40 years, but then allowed the Romans to destroy it and the Jewish commonwealth. YES, EVEN THE O.T. PREDICTED THAT ITS DISPENSATION OF GOD'S GRACE WOULD BE SUPPLANTED WITH THE NEW AND REAL

7. The point is, God warned the Jews earlier (by Amos, Hosea, etc.) that their idolatry would bring this INDIGNATION—Now God reveals through Daniel that this INDIGNATION is going to end some day.

B. Now we have an even more detailed interpretation of who these characters are and when they shall appear.

1. The Ram and He-goat are Persia and Greece.

2. The king of fierce countenance is Antiochus IV.

3. When the 4 kingdoms (divisions of Alexander's) have run their course, then this new king will put in his appearance.

4. He is to be a master of deceit—able to conceal his meaning and deceive his enemies; a master of cunning and cannot easily be deceived himself, except by his own vanity and pride, AND HIS POWER IS PERMITTED ONLY BECAUSE GOD WISHES IT TO BE SO.

5. It will seem as if evil and deceit are about to take over the whole world when this king reigns. Whatever he undertakes will prosper (for a while).

6. Leupold says: "This is . . . a very skillfully condensed account of the checkered career of one of the most remarkable men that strutted across the stage of history. Its very conciseness makes it ambiguous or difficult to understand if one skims over it too readily."

7. One personal characteristic that will stand out will be his proud, haughty, presumptuous nature.

8. His inordinate pride and self-exaltation lead him to blaspheme and challenge the Almighty God, but God will not allow such evil and rebellion to thwart His Divine purposes. God without hand, by means that appear to be providential or divine, will break this tyrant! God only allowed this persecutor his day because God was willing that he be given opportunity to repent. When he did not repent, God used his persecutions to purge the people of God and sift them in preparation for Messiah.

C. Shut Up the Prophecy.

1. Since the prophecy was for a long time hence (about 400 0years from then), Daniel was to *preserve* the prophecy.

2. To shut it up does not mean to keep secret, or that it is not yet to be understood. IT IS TO BE PRESERVED PERMANENTLY SO THAT IT MAY BE READ AND UNDERSTOOD WHEN THE NEED FOR IT ARRIVES!

3. The effect upon the soul and spirit of Daniel was so exhausting that he was ill for a number of days before he could continue the king's business.

CONCLUSION

I. GOD KNOWS THE FUTURE.

A. The names change, the territories change, BUT THE PRINCIPLES REMAIN ETERNAL.

B. Great nations struggle and LOCK HORNS; but out of

all the agony, destruction, apostasy, social improvements, cultural developments, faith, and courage, GOD'S IMMUTABLE PURPOSES ROLL ON, WHILE MAN MAKES MORAL AND MENTAL CHOICES WHICH DETERMINE HIS ETERNAL DESTINY.

C. Men and their wisdom come and go; men and their powers rise and fall. AND GOD'S BOOK HAS PROVEN ONCE FOR ALL THAT GOD KNOWS, SEES, OVERRULES AND USES HISTORY TO HIS OWN GLORY, AND THE GLORY OF ALL WHO ARE FAITHFUL TO HIM!

II. WHEN MEN LOCK HORNS WITH GOD, MEN DESTROY THEMSELVES.

A. Men will have their day.
B. But their day has an appointed end.
C. Oftentimes God permits the tyrants to have sway in order to sift the believers, to purge and purify their lives, and to strengthen their loyalty to Him.
D. BUT THE BELIEVERS CAN REJOICE FOR GOD WILL ALSO HAVE HIS DAY.

Now therefore, O kings, be wise;
be warned, O rulers of the earth.
Serve the Lord with fear,
with trembling kiss the Son
lest he be angry, and you perish in the way;
for his wrath is quickly kindled.
Blessed are all who take refuge in him.

Psa. 2:10-11

EXAMINATION EIGHT

REFUTATIONS

(Answer the following by giving the argument which will correct the statement)

1. The "ram" of chapter 8 represents Russia. Refute!
2. The "little horn" of chapter 8 is the same small "horn" of chapter 7. Refute!
3. The "2300 evenings and mornings" is the millenium. Refute!

ASSOCIATIONS

(Associate the persons or events of column one with the
correct person or event of column two)

1	2
2300 days	saints of God
Greece	Antiochus Epiphanes
the host	the pope
Medo-Persia	Babylon
Shushan	Nebuchadnezzar
Elam	period of desolation
Ulai	millenium
the glorious land	he-goat
holy one	Numma
sanctuary	city
little horn	river
	Palestine
	temple
	angel

MEMORIZATIONS

(Fill in the blanks:)

And through his policy he shall cause _____ to
prosper in his hand; and he shall _____ himself in his
heart, and in their _____ shall he destroy many: he
shall also stand up against the _____ _____ _____;
but he shall be _____ without _____.

EXPLANATIONS

1. Explain the meaning of "the time of the end" in verse
   17.
2. Explain the phrases:
   "the transgression that maketh desolate"
   "the latter time of the indignation"
   "when the transgressors are come to the full"
3. Explain the relationship of the "little horn" to the
   "four notable horns" of the he-goat.
4. Explain the order to "shut up the vision" as it relates
   to "many days to come."

329

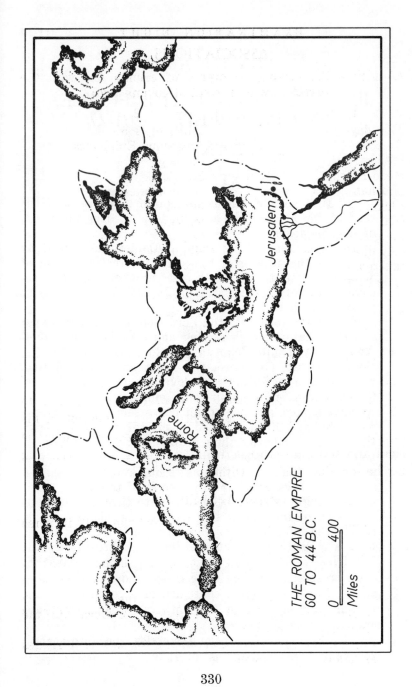

THE ROMAN EMPIRE
60 TO 44 B.C.

0 ———— 400
Miles

Jerusalem

Rome

CHAPTER NINE

III. THE PRAYER, THE PRINCE, AND PROSPERITY—9:1-27

a. REPENTANCE

TEXT: 9:1-14

1 In the first year of Darius the son of Ahasureus, of the seed of the Medes, who was made king over the realm of the Chaldeans,

2 in the first year of his reign I, Daniel, understood by the books the number of the years whereof the word of Jehovah came to Jeremiah the prophet, for the accomplishing of the desolation of Jerusalem, even seventy years.

3 And I set my face unto the Lord God, to seek by prayer and supplications, with fasting and sackcloth and ashes.

4 And I prayed unto Jehovah my God, and made confession, and said, Oh, Lord, the great and dreadful God, who keepeth covenant and lovingkindness with them that love him, and keep his commandments,

5 we have sinned, and have dealt perversely, and have done wickedly, and have rebelled, even turning aside from thy precepts and from thine ordinances;

6 neither have we hearkened unto thy servants the prophets, that spake in thy name to our kings, our princes, and our fathers, and to all the people of the land.

7 O Lord, righteousness belongeth unto thee, but unto us confusion of face, as at this day; to the men of Judah, and to the inhabitants of Jerusalem, and unto all Israel, that are near, and that are far off, through all the countries whither thou hast driven them, because of their trespass that they have trespassed against thee.

8 O Lord, to us belongeth confusion of face, to our kings, to our princes, and to our fathers, because we have sinned against thee.

9 To the Lord our God belong mercies and forgiveness; for we have rebelled against him;

10   neither have we obeyed the voice of Jehovah our God, to
     walk in his laws, which he set before us by his servants
     the prophets.

11   Yea, all Israel have transgressed thy law, even turning
     aside, that they should not obey thy voice: therefore
     hath the curse been poured out upon us, and the oath
     that is written in the law of Moses the servant of God;
     for we have sinned against him.

12   And he hath confirmed his words, which he spake
     against us, and against our judges that judged us, by
     bringing upon us a great evil; for under the whole
     heaven hath not been done as hath been done upon
     Jerusalem.

13   As it is written in the law of Moses, all this evil is
     come upon us: yet have we not entreated the favor of
     Jehovah our God, that we should turn from our iniqui-
     ties, and have discernment in thy truth.

14   Therefore hath Jehovah watched over the evil, and
     brought it upon us; for Jehovah our God is righteous
     in all his works which he doeth, and we have not obeyed
     his voice.

QUERIES

a. Why was Daniel studying the "books" concerning the
   captivity?
b. Why confess sins now after almost 70 years in captivity?
c. Does verse 13 mean they had not prayed to God in the
   captivity?

PARAPHRASE

It was now the first year of the reign of Gubaru (king
Darius, the son of Ahasuerus), 539-538 B.C. (Daruis was a
Mede but was appointed king of the province of Chaldea by
Cyrus). During that first year of his reign I, Daniel, was
studying the scroll of Jeremiah the prophet, and learned
that the time for the captivities of the Jews and the desola-
ion of their land and holy city, Jerusalem, was seventy years,
and thus very near its end. I fasted, donned sackcloth and
ashes, and I pleaded with the Lord concerning the end of our
captivities. I confessed my sins and those of my people,

praying, O Lord, you are a great and awesome God; You
always fulfill Your promises and keep Your covenants, returning love to those who love You and keep Your commandments. But we have sinned against You every way possible.
We have been perverse, stubborn, wicked, rebellious, disobedi-
ent to Your precepts and commandments; we did not even
pay attention to the prophets when You sent them to speak
to our leaders and to us. O Lord, You are altogether
righteous and holy, but we are shame-faced with sin to this
very day. All of Your covenant people—the men of Judah,
Jerusalem and all Israel—scattered all over by Your
righteous judgment for their sins, they are even now shame-
faced with sin. But the Lord our God is merciful, and
pardons even those who have rebelled against Him. O Lord,
our God, we have disobeyed You; we have flouted all the
laws You gave us through Your servants, the prophets.
All Israel has disobeyed; we have deliberately turned away
from You and refused to listen to Your voice. As a consequence the curse of God—pronounced in the law of Moses—
has been poured out upon us. And You have done exactly
as You warned us You would; for never in all history has
there been a disaster like what happened at Jerusalem to
us and our rulers. Every curse against disobedience written
in the law of Moses has come to pass because we have disobeyed Your law. Yet we have not appeased Jehovah our
God by breaking with our sins and turning to the keeping
of Your truth. Therefore God deliberately crushed us with
the calamity He prepared—and He is just and holy in everything He does—because we have not obeyed His Truth.

COMMENT

v. 1-2 IN THE FIRST YEAR OF DARIUS THE SON OF
AHASUREUS . . . We have discussed the identity of Darius
the Mede in chapter 5, verse 31, and concluded that he is the
"Gubaru" of the Nabonidus Chronicle. Mr. Whitcomb,
author of *Darius, The Mede,* says, "The fact that no cuneiform text known to us mentions the name of Gubaru's
father is no evidence that his father could not have been
Ahasuerus." Gubaru (Darius, the Mede) was appointed king
of Chaldea and Babylon in the same year that Cyrus con-

quered it, 539-538 B.C. This then, was the year that Daniel was studying the "books" concerning the duration of the captivities.

The term "books" does *not* mean the entire O.T. canon. Destructive critics would like to have it to mean this in order to claim that the O.T. canon was already complete when the book of Daniel was being written thus making the composition of the book of Daniel as late as 200 B.C. Leupold says, "the article before 'books' according to Hebrew usage, need imply nothing more than the idea of the books requisite for the passage involved (i.e. Jeremiah)." There is a quotation from "Jeremiah" made by Jesus in Matthew 27:9ff. which contains some phrases from the book of Zechariah. This probably indicates that more than one prophet's work was recorded on one scroll—thus one scroll contain two or more "books." As a matter of fact, many ancient Hebrew manuscripts have what is called the book of The Twelve (all of the Minor Prophets on one scroll). It is highly probable that Daniel had a scroll of Jeremiah in his hand which also had other books written on the same scroll, but Daniel was studying Jeremiah. The passage that caught his attention was Jeremiah 25:9-11, "And this whole land shall be a desolation, and an astonishment; and these nations shall serve the king of Babylon seventy-years." The desolation began with the captivity of Daniel in 606 B.C. and the first devastation of Jerusalem by Nebuchadnezzar. So, in the first year of Darius (538 B.C.), the 70 years (536 B.C.) would be almost completed. The above dates are in harmony with II Chronicles 36:21-23 and Ezra 1:1ff which speak of the "first year of Cyrus (which was 539-538 B.C.). Some regard the destruction of Jerusalem in 587 as the point from which the 70 years are to be reckoned. But if this be so, Daniel would hardly feel that now, in the first year of Darius, the 70 years were very soon coming to completion and be in fervent prayer about it.

v. 3-6　AND I SET MY FACE UNTO THE LORD GOD . . . WE HAVE SINNED . . . Daniel knows only too well that the cause for the captivity is the stubborn, deliberate rebellion and sin of the people. He sees that the time appointed by God for the captivity is about complete. He knows that the majority of the people still have not turned to God, so he sets himself in earnest, soul-baring prayer as he confesses his sin and those of his people. His main concern is not to know the precise meaning of the number 70; it is to implore Jehovah God for the complete, full and merciful cleansing and pardon for their sin. *This is very important in understanding the answer the angel gives to Daniel's prayer!* For the answer is not precise in delineating the 70 sevens, calendar-wise, but *the answer emphasizes the fact that complete forgiveness is in the future.*

That Daniel was in earnest is indicated by the fact that he fasted and humbled himself in sackcloth and ashes—the customary attire for a Jew who wished to subdue the flesh in order to concentrate upon the spiritual.

Daniel salutes God as One who by mighty acts of supernatural character chastens and punishes sinful people. Then he praises God for His manifestations of absolute faithfulness in keeping His covenants (Word) to those who love Him. It is in this way God expresses His lovingkindness to those who love Him. Those who love Him keep His commandments (cf. I John).

The prophet uses four-synonyms for sin in order to emphasize the stubborn deliberations of it. Jeremiah 6:16-19 indicates the rebelliousness of their attitude toward God and toward the prophets who spoke God's message. See also Ezekiel, chapter 2 and 3. Their sin was not one of ignorance—it was wilfull disobedience. They loved to have it so! Thus the enormity of the nation's sin! Those who have no love for the truth, but take pleasure in unrighteousness, God will allow them to have deluded minds, if they so desire. This impudent, arrogant, wicked people would not listen to the true prophets who predicted punishment—they listened to false prophets who cried, "Peace, peace, when there was no peace."

v. 7-11 . . . NEITHER HAVE WE OBEYED THE VOICE OF JEHOVAH OUR GOD, TO WALK IN HIS LAWS, WHICH HE SET BEFORE US BY HIS SERVANTS THE PROPHETS . . . THEREFORE HATH THE CURSE BEEN POURED OUT UPON US . . . It is evident from this prayer of Daniel that he thought the time of the captivity was about to be prolonged on account of the sins of his countrymen and he besought the Lord for mercy. It is a prayer of confession. The word confession is in the Greek is *homologeo* which means "to say the same as . . ." In the case of Daniel's confession he is saying the same as God about rebellion against God's will and the conequences of such rebellion. Daniel is admitting (confessing) that God is completely justified in bringing upon the people of Israel this captivity because this was the warning of God when the law was given to Moses (cf. Deut. chaps. 28, 29, 30). The phrase "poured out" is similar to that of the "pouring out" of the vials of wrath which symbolize the wrathful judgments of God depicted in the Book of Revelation (Rev. 16:1-4). What the Jews were enduring in their captivities was what they deserved, and what God, through Moses, warned them would come if they should not hearken to the "prophets" of God.

v. 12-14　AND HE HATH CONFIRMED HIS WORDS . . . YET HAVE WE NOT ENTREATED . . . And now, Daniel is frightened. In spite of the chastening of the captivity for their former sins, they have not, for the most part, "entreated" the favor of God. They have not "mollified" God. The verb translated "entreated" means literally "to make the face sweet." They had not sweetened the face of God toward themselves by turning from their sinful ways in repentance and obeyed the will of God as expressed through His prophets. If they had, God would have removed the evil of captivity from them. They are in the same attitude toward God as before the captivity, so Daniel prays that the captivity not be prolonged.

God confirmed His Word as truly inviolable with the captivities of Israel and Judah. What God promises and warns will surely come to pass! The overthrow of the covenant people (both of Israel and Judah) involved an amount of cruelty and suffering that no other case in history could claim! Just one illustration of such unparalleled degradation is in Deut. 28:53-57 where it is predicted that as a consequence of disobedience to God's law the covenant people will actually be driven to eat the flesh of their own children! It was fulfilled literally in II Kings 6:24-31 for Israel and in Jeremiah 19:9 for Judah! God means what He says!

There is no unfairness or unrighteousness in God's actions. He has done only what He said He would do, and gave ample warning and abundant help in providing a way to escape His judgment. Desipte all this, the covenant people did not, and were not in Daniel's time, hearkening unto Him, so their guilt, therefore, is all the greater.

QUIZ

1. How could Darius the Mede be the son of Ahasuerus?
2. Why would destructive critics like to have the term "books" mean the entire O.T. canon? What does the term mean?
3. When were the 70 years of Israel's captivity to end?
4. What is very important in understanding the answer the angel gives to Daniel's prayer (information concerning the 70 weeks)?
5. Why is Daniel praying about the people's sin in the present tense?
6. How were God's words concerning His judgment confirmed?

b. REQUEST

TEXT: 9:15-19

15 And now O Lord our God, that hast brought thy people forth out of the land of Egypt with a mighty hand, and hast gotten thee renown, as at this day; we have sinned, we have done wickedly.

16 O Lord, according to all thy righteousness, let thine anger and thy wrath, I pray thee, be turned away from thy city Jerusalem, thy holy mountain; because for our sins, and for the iniquities of our fathers, Jerusalem and thy people are become a reproach to all that are round about us.

17 Now therefore, O our God, hearken unto the prayer of thy servant, and to his supplications, and cause thy face to shine upon thy sanctuary that is desolate, for the Lord's sake.

18 O my God, incline thine ear, and hear; open thine eyes, and behold our desolations, and the city which is called

by thy name: for we do not present our supplications before thee for our righteousnesses, but for thy great mercies sake.

19   O Lord, hear; O Lord, forgive; O Lord, hearken and do; defer not, for thine own sake, O my God, because thy city and thy people are called by thy name.

QUERIES

a. Why remind God of His mighty work in delivering Israel from Egypt?

b. Why Daniel's interest in the holy city and the sanctuary?

c. Why pray all this "for thy great mercies sake?"

PARAPHRASE

And now, O Lord our God, my petition for my people. You brought great renown to your name when You delivered Your people from Egypt with a display of miraculous power. And now, though we of the captivity have sinned so terribly and are full of wickedness, have mercy and deliver Your people again as before. O Lord, I beseech You, as is befitting Your absolute righteousness and merciful love, withdraw Your wrath from Your city Jerusalem, the city which You consecrated for Your purposes. All the heathen nations round about us speak derogatory things of us and they reproach Your holy Name because Your city lies in ruins as a result of our sins, and sins of our fathers. We deserve our chastening but, I pray that You will hear Your servant's prayer, Lord, and let Your face radiate in benevolence and good-will upon Your sanctified city, restoring it to its former glory only to establish Your glory, O Lord. O my God, bend down Your ear and listen to my plea. Open Your eyes and direct your gaze upon our wretchedness, and see the desolation of the city which is Yours. We do not ask because we deserve anything but simply in order that Your righteousness and mercifulness may be displayed befort the nations. O Lord, hear me I plead; O Lord forgive your penitent people I pray; O Lord, act on behalf of Your own glory—Your people and Your city bear Your name and our Love for You cannot bear to hear You reproached because of our humiliation.

COMMENT

v. 15-19 . . . WE DO NOT PRESENT OUR SUPPLICATIONS
BEFORE THEE FOR OUR RIGHTEOUSNESS, BUT FOR THY GREAT
MERCIES SAKE . . . This is the key phrase of the entire second
half of Daniel's beautiful prayer. The deep humiliation and
concern for God's glory *must* serve as a model for the attitude in all true prayer!

Daniel begins his petition to the Lord in the attitude
that above all else he wishes the Lord to act to glorify His
Own Holy Name just as He did in His miraculous deliverance of weak, humiliated, sinful Israel from Egypt.

The next concern (vs. 16) is that God withdraw His
desolation of the Holy City and Holy Land and Holy People,
not from any selfish motive on Daniel's part, but in order
that God's righteousness, mercifulnes and power may be
vindicated before the eye of the heathen world which has
taken great delight in mocking Jehovah God and Jehovah's
people because of their seeming powerlessness at the
heathen's hands.

Verses 17, 18 and 19 are emphatic repetitions of Daniel's
concern that only the glory of God be upheld. Daniel is not
concerned that the people be delivered in order to enjoy
physical ease and comfort. Daniel is not interested that the
people be delivered in order that their wounded pride be
avenged. His only interest is that God's holiness and faithfulness be vindicated. After all, sinning man deserves only
judgment. If he is delivered at all, it will be entirely due
to the very nature of God—His mercifulness and lovingkindness.

This is the whole point of prayer! God seeks contrition
and penitence in prayer in order that He may do for man
what He has made up His mind to do for man all along! It
is not the eloquence of man's prayers, nor the quantity of
them that move God to action—if this were so, answer
would come on the basis of merit. It is the attitude!
Prayer does not change things—men are changed, they are
so changed that they are driven to their knees in deep contrition an dependence; and God can then act as He has said
He would act, and wants to act, from the beginning of the
world. God cannot act to bless any man if that man does

not pray, believing, trusting, repenting. It is not God who changes—it is man who changes. Man changes and God acts. God also acts when man does not change to conform to His will, but this action (judgment) is simply in accordance with what God has said He will do when man refuses to repent.

Daniel's prayer that God will act in the interest of His Own Perfect Will is as God wishes. God only wants us to be better than we are, but He knows that this can only come as a result of man's seeking to glorify his Creator and Redeemer. So it is that God acts to glorify His Own Name, not out of selfish egotism, but in order to bless His creation and His creatures. One has only to read such passages as Ezekiel 20:9, 14, 22, and 44 to understand that God acts for the sake of His Own Name. The inevitable result of God acting to glorify His name is that the man who accepts and acts in accordance with God's way is thereby made a partaker of God's glory (cf. II Pet. 1:3-4).

And this is the way Jesus taught us to pray, "Our Father, which art in heaven, Hallowed by thy name, thy kingdom come, thy will be done, on earth, as it is in heaven . . ." Jesus is our divine example in sacrificing oneself wholly to glorify God (cf. Jn. 17).

In answer to his prayer Daniel receives, not just an interpretation of a phrase in Jeremiah's book, but an unfolding of God's program for the ages, which is in effect this: Not only am I, the Lord, going to fulfill this promise of deliverance after 70 years of captivity, but I am going to fulfill all my promises, and this is the pattern after which they shall be fulfilled (as outlined in the succeeding verses 20-27).

QUIZ

1. What is the key phrase of this second part of Daniel's prayer?
2. What historical action of God does Daniel use as the basis of his prayer?
3. What is Daniel's main emphasis in his prayer?
4. Why do we say God does not change but that man must?
5. What other scripture express the idea that God always acts to glorify His Own Name?

6. When man, by faith accepts the above premise and acts in accordance with it, what is the inevitable result?

7. What example do we have to show that glorifying God is our mission?

c. REVELATION

TEXT: 9:20-27

20 And while I was speaking, and praying, and confessing my sin and the sin of my people Israel, and presenting my supplication before Jehovah my God for the holy mountain of my God;

21 yea, while I was speaking in prayer, the man Gabriel, whom I had seen in the vision at the beginning, being caused to fly swiftly, touched me about the time of the evening oblation.

22 And he instructed me, and talked with me, and said, O Daniel, I am now come forth to give thee wisdom and understanding.

23 At the beginning of thy supplications the commandment went forth, and I am come to tell thee; for thou art greatly beloved: therefore consider the matter, and understand the vision.

24 Seventy weeks are decreed upon they people and upon thy holy city, to finish transgression, and to make an end of sins, and to make reconcilation for iniquity, and to bring in everlasting righteousness, and to seal up vision and prophecy, and to anoint the most holy.

25 Know therefore and discern, that from the going forth of the commandment to restore and to build Jerusalem unto the anointed one, the prince, shall be seven weeks, and threescore and two weeks: it shall be built again, with street and moat, even in troublous times.

26 And after the threescore and two weeks shall the anointed one be cut off, and shall have nothing: and the people of the prince that shall come shall destroy the city and the sanctuary; and the end thereof shall be with a flood, and even unto the end shall be war; desolations are determined.

27 And he shall make a firm covenant with many for one week: and in the midst of the week he shall cause the sacrifice and the oblation to cease; and upon the wing of abominations shall come one that maketh desolate; and even unto the full end, and that determined, shall wrath be poured out upon the desolate.

QUERIES

a. What are all the things God intends to complete by the end of "seventy weeks?"
b. Who is the "prince" to be anointed after 69 weeks?
c. Who is the "prince" whose people come to destroy the city?

PARAPHRASE

Even while I was praying and confessing my sin and the sins of my people, and desperately pleading with the Lord my God for Jerusalem, His Holy Mountain, His angel Gabriel appeared to me as a man (this is the messenger of God I had seen in the earlier vision) and flew swiftly to me at the time of the evening sacrifice, and said to me, Daniel, I am here to reveal to you the plans of God for His people and to help you to understand what is to come to pass concerning them. The very moment you began praying, a decree was issued by God concerning all you have prayed and longed for. I am here to tell you what it is—God has greatly honored you for your trust and faith in Him and He desires that you know these things.

The Lord has commanded that, counting from the time of an edict to go forth and rebuild Jerusalem, seventy sevens shall transpire before all the glorious spiritual blessings of the Messianic age are fulfilled. There will be fulfilled at the end of this time such transgressions as will climax all transgressions, killing the Messiah; the power given to overcome sin; the work done of reconciling estranged sinners back to God; the imputation by grace of righteousness to sinful men; the accreditation of God's predictions through His prophets by the fulfillment of their prophecies; and the anointing of a Most Holy Messiah. I want you to know that counting from the year in which the principal incre-

ment of your people return from their captivities to rebuild
and restore Jerusalem, there shall be seven sevens and forty-
two sevens (a total of sixty-nine sevens) before the Messiah
is anointed. During this period Jerusalem will have to suffer
many perilous times while she is rebuilding. Sometime after
the sixty-nine sevens the anointed Messiah will be slain
and buried as a pauper. As a consequence of the Holy City
slaying its anointed One, the people of a foreign emperor
will come and destroy the Holy City and the Holy Sanctuary—this also after the sixty-nine sevens. A flood of destruction shall come upon the Holy City which has slain
its Messiah, and war and desolation shall continue to flood
upon this city until its end. The anointed One shall cause
a strong and everlasting covenant to be established with
many for one seven. And actually it shall be in the middle
of that seventieth seven that the Anointed One shall brong
to an end the sacrifices and oblations of Old Covenant by His
own efficacious death. And the foreign ruler whose people
come to destroy the city, will utterly destroy the Holy Sanctuary of those who killed the Anointed One, because that
Sanctuary has become an abomination in the eyes of God.
And the wrath of God shall pour forth upon this City and
Sanctuary, and their devastation shall continue until God
determines it shall end.

COMMENT

v. 20-23 . . . WHILE I WAS SPEAKING IN PRAYER . .
THE MAN GABRIEL . . . INSTRUCTED ME . . . While he is in
the very midst of his prayer, Daniel is approached by the
angel Gabriel, come in human form, to deliver God's answer
to his prayer. The interesting thing about the answer is
that it came before Daniel was through praying. Furthermore, the angel reported that God's decree to accomplish
what Daniel was praying for went forth at the very moment Daniel opened his mouth and began to pray! God knows
what we have need of before we ask it. But God also knows
that our greatest need is to ask for it! As long as a man is
self-confident and self-dependent, he is in no position morally, intellectually or spiritually to receive. He only demands and spends whatever may come his way in goodness
to confirm himself in his egotism. Repetitious prayers, like

the heathens', are vain and useless, simply because they are used by men to support their own vanity, and are used to seek the blessings of God by meritious repetition of prayers and self-righteousness. Therefore, be assured that the "things" you pray for are no problem with God. He can give you exceeding aboundantly above all you can possibly ask or think (cf. Eph. 3:20), if the power of utter, total, unreserved faith in Him abides in you. The problem is not what you need—the need is you resting on the Everlasting Arms.

v. 24   SEVENTY WEEKS ARE DECREED UPON THY PEOPLE . . . It would be difficult to exaggerate the significance of this passage (v. 24-27) in the teachings of Dispensationalists and Pre-millenialists! It is often appealed to as definite proof that the entire "Church age" is a parenthesis in the prophetic program. The "Church age" is supposed to occur between the events listed in verse 26 and the events listed in verse 27. The twenty-seventh verse of this chapter concerns the "seventieth week" which is supposed to be, according to Dispensationalists, the Millenium (or the 1000 years of Revelation 20).

We have found three excellent discussions of this so-called difficult passage (*Prophecy And The Church,* by Oswald T. Allis; *The King Of Kings,* by E. V. Zollars, a Restoration Reprint from College Press; and *The Prophecy of Daniel,* by Edward J. Young) from which we shall borrow in our comments on this section.

The word translated "weeks" is literally, "sevens." It should be paraphrased, "Sevens—and in fact seventy of them are decreed . . . etc." The correct interpretation, however, in light of other key passages (Ezek. 4:6, etc.) used to form the "year-day theory" is probably, "Seventy weeks-of-years (i.e. 7 years × 70) are decreed, etc. . . ."

Thus these 490 years express in the form of Divine revelation that a definite period of time has been decreed for the accomplishment of all that which is necessary for the "restoration of the fortunes of Judah and Jerusalem," which is a messianic term in itself. Within this definite period of time will be finished all the plan of God's redemption of man which he made known through the prophets to the fathers through divers portions and divers manners, (cf. Heb. 1:1ff).

a. Transgression would be finished: That is, the cup of iniquity of the Jewish people would be filled to the brim. They would reject the Messiah. The full height and depth of their iniquity was yet to be shown but would be shown within the 490 years. In putting the Messiah to death they reached the culmination of all their wickedness. No greater sin was possible. (Matt. 23:32; I Thess. 2:16).

b. In the death of the Messiah God will triumph over man's rebellion and give the power, judicial and experiential, to conquer sin. He will, by a sovereign decree of grace, punish all sin in His Son (II Cor. 5:17ff.), and offer to man a way (faith) to overcome his rebellion. All sin, even that done aforetime, was done away with in the death of Christ (cf. Rom. 3:21-26; Heb. 9:15-28).

c. To reconcile man to God's will and way, God took the initiative and presented His Son as an atonement. Man hardened his heart toward God's goodnes and estranged himself from God. God *so* loved the world that He *gave* His only begotten Son . . . and man's heart is broken and he is drawn to God by the love of the Son. (Col. 1:20-21).

d. The work of the Messiah would also bring in everlasting righteousness. There are two aspects of this righteousness; imputed righteousness, that is, the righteousness which God declares we have which we do not merit; and practiced righteousness, which we are promoted to do by faith and love in God as He reveals to us in His Book the way of righteous living. (Rom. 1:17; I Tim. 6:18).

e. With the accomplishment of the work of the Messiah in fulfilling God's prophesied plan of redemption, prophecy was confirmed, fulfilled, validated and thus sealed up— paid in full! (Acts 3:24; I Pet. 1:10-11).

f. The anointing of the Messiah is to be accomplished during this period of time. The phrase occurs without the definite article and therefore means the anointing of a most holy "thing"—not place. Literally it should read, "the anointing of holiness of holinesses." (Acts 1:38).

Allis, in *Prophecy And The Church*, indicates that there are points of agreement and points of difference between those who interpret the prophecy of the 70 weeks traditionally and those who interpret it dispensationally. Points of agreement are: (1) the 70 weeks represent weeks-of-

years, a total of 490 years; (2) Only one period of weeks
is described, as is proved by the fact that the subdivisions
(7 + 62 + 1) when added together give a total of 70; (3)
the "anointed one, the prince (vs. 25) and the "anointed
one" (vs. 26) are the same person, the Messiah; (4) The first
69 weeks or 483 years had their terminus in the period of
the first advent; their fulfillment is long past. Now the
points of difference revolve around two significant questions:
(1) Have the great events described in vs. 24 been fulfilled,
or is their accomplishment still future?; (2) Is the 70th
week past, or is it still to come?

Now the dispensationalists insist that all the events of
vs. 24 are still in the future. They say, for example, "to
make an end of sins" means to eliminate moral evil completely from this world. The reason the dispensationalists
must insist that vs. 24 refers to the future is quite clear.
If the fulfillment of the prophecy is still incomplete, and if
the predictions relating to the 69 weeks had their fulfillment
centuries ago, then the 70th week must be still future.
Therefore, there must be an interval between the end of the
69th week and the beginning of the 70th week; and the entire Church age can be regarded as forming a "parenthesis"
at this point.

So we must deal with the first difference now. Have the
great events described in vs. 24 been fulfilled, or is their
accomplishment in the future? In the light of plain N.T.
teaching we cannot abide the idea that these events are in
the future! We must resist such an idea with vigor. The
N.T., especially the treatise to the Hebrews, represents all
these transactions (vs. 24) as having been fulfilled at the
first advent—in the great climactic event of the plan of God's
redemption at Calvary. Jesus Christ was the perfect sacrifice, the one and only sacrifice, made for all time which is
able to perfect for all time those who are being sanctified
by it (Heb. 10:12-14). One should read the entire book of
Hebrews, along with the book of Galatians, to understand
that a return to Jewish law and Jewish sacrifices would be
apostasy! Hebrews 9:28—" . . . so Christ, having been offered once to bear the sins of many, will appear a second
time, *not to deal with sin* but to save those who are eagerly
waiting for him." Notice that at Christ's second advent

He is *not* going "to deal with sin" for sin has already been dealt with! Certainly the N.T. teaches that Christ is the end, the fulfillment, the anti-type the confirmation of all prophecy! If Corinthians 1:20, "For all the promises of God find their Yes in him. That is why we utter the Amen through him, to the glory of God." How more specific could it be stated that Christ is the goal of all the promises of God! "For the testimony of Jesus is the spirit of prophecy." (Rev. 19:11). "For our sake he made him to be sin who knew no sin, so that in him we might become the righteousness of God" (II Cor. 5:21).

The "traditional" and in our opinion, the scriptual view is that all these events (vs. 24) were fulfilled and completed in the birth, life, death and resurrection of Christ and the establishment of the church.

v. 25 KNOW THEREFORE . . . THAT FROM THE GOING FORTH OF THE COMMANDMENT . . . UNTO THE ANOINTED ONE . . . SHALL BE SEVEN WEEKS, AND THREESCORE AND TWO . . . We must clearly understand that the fact (based squarely upon N.T. teaching) that all the six items presented in perse 24 are Messianic *settles the terminating point* of the prophecy and the 70 weeks as well! The termination of the 70 sevens coincides then, not with the times of Antiochus, nor with the end of the present age, the second advent of Christ, but with His first advent! When Christ ascended into heaven and the Holy Spirit descended, there remained not one of the six items of Daniel 9:24 that was not fully accomplished.

Now, verse 25, we are told exactly how many years shall intervene between the return of the Jews to rebuild Jerusalem and the coming of the "anointed One," the Messiah. That expiration of time shall total 69 weeks-of-years (69 × 7 = 483 years). This prophecy was fulfilled in a marvellously accurate way.

There are only four events that can be taken as answering to "the commandment to restore and to build Jerusalem." (1) The decree of Cyrus, 536 B.C., Ezra 1:2-4. This was the decree for the building of the temple but did not include the authorization in restore the Jewish commonwealth. (2) The decree of Darius, 518 B.C., a decree for the further prosecution of the work permitted by Cyrus which seems to have been hindered. It was a repetition of the first decree, and did not authorize the re-establishment of the Jewish commonwealth. (3) The decree of Artaxerxes, 457 B.C. The seventh year are Artaxerxes was the year 457 B.C. and is confirmed by concurrent agreement of more than twenty eclipses. An exact copy of this decree is found in the seventh chapter of Ezra. It is written in Aramaic, which was spoken in Babylon at the time. The rest of the Book of Ezra is written in Hebrew. There is something very significant in the preservation of the original form of this decree, and when we see how much depends upon it, we may regard it as providential. By this decree permission was granted to Ezra to go up to Jerusalem, taking as many as he desired that were willing to go. It also was granted him unlimited treasure. It empowered him to ordain laws, set magistrates and judges who had authority to execute punishments—confiscation, banishment and even the infliction of the death penalty were included. In other words, Ezra was authorized to restore the commonwealth, and means were placed at his disposal to enable him to do so. (4) The fourth decree was given to Nehemiah 444 B.C. The purpose of Nehemiah's going was to assist in accomplishing the work undertaken by Ezra which was being retarded. He accomplished his mission in 52 days after arrived at Jerualem (Neh. 6:15).

Now it is evident that the decree given to Ezra in 457 B.C. is the one authorizing the restoring and rebuilding of Jerusalem. Actually the three decrees (Cyrus, Darius and Artaxerxes) may really be regarded as one decree, that of Artaxerxes being the prinicpal one in that his decree authorized the restoration of the Jewish commonwealth. It is so regarded by Ezra (cf. Ezra 6:14). Therefore, the decree of Artaxerxes must be regarded as the one referred to by the angel in the words, "from the going forth of the commanded," and fixes our date from which to reckon.

Reckoning from 457 B.C., the first 7 sevens (7 $\times$ 7, or 49 weeks-of-years) we should arrive at the date of 408 B.C. for the accomplishment of the restoration of the Jewish commonwealth. The date 408 B.C. accords accurately with historic facts. This was the time the work was completed!

This restoration was accomplished in troublous times, as the Biblical record bears out (see Nehemiah, Ezra, Haggai, Zechariah, etc.).

Furthermore, if we reckon from 408 B.C., the next period of time, 62 sevens (62 × 7 weeks-of-years) or 434 years, we come down to the year 26 A.D. as the close of the second period. The close of this second period brings us to the Messiah ("the prince") according to the prophecy. This was the 30th year of Christ's life, since there is an error of four years in the calendar, as is well known. At this time (26 A.D.) Jesus began his public ministry (Lk. 3:23), when he was about 30 years of age. When Jesus was baptized by John in the Jordan, the Spirit of God in the form of a dove descended upon him, and a voice came from heaven, saying, "This is my beloved Son; in whom I am well pleased." Immediately Christ entered upon His work. He was now the Anointed One. Here the second period of the "70 weeks-of-years" (the 434 years) ends.

v. 26-27   AND AFTER THE THREESCORE AND TWO WEEKS SHALL THE ANOINTED ONE BE CUT OFF . . . AND IN THE MIDST OF THE WEEK HE SHALL CAUSE THE SACRIFICE . . . TO CEASE . . . The third period of the "70 weeks-of-years" consists of but one seven (or seven years). This is the long debated 70th week. The "cutting off" of the anointed one and his causing sacrifice and oblation to cease are coincidental—therefore his cutting off is determined to be "in the midst of the week" (in the midst of the 70th week). This settles once for all that the 70th week is not waiting for Christ's second advent!

Dispensationalists are fond of the illustration of a clock. The ticking clock, they tell us, represents Jewish time. The mystery parenthesis is "time out." God only counts time in dealing with Israel, when the people are in the land, according to them. Some add to this the further specification, when "they are governed by God." Neither of these requirements is met by the interval which they find here in the prophecy of the Seventy Weeks. Consequently, the clock ceased to tick at the time of the triumphal entry. It will not tick again until that moment, still future, when God resumes His direct dealings with Israel (the Millenium).

This will be when the Jews are once more in their own land. It will follow the rapture and be marked by the appearance of the (in some interpretations) resurrected Roman prince. So those of us who live now in the so-called "Church age" exist, as far as God's time-clock is concerned, in a sort of "suspended animation," while God's time stands still.

It seems incredible that if the 69 weeks are exactly 483 consecutive years, exact to the very day, as dispensationalists admit, and if the 1 week is to be exactly 7 consecutive years, that an interval (a parenthesis) which is already more than 1900 years, nearly four times as long as the period covered by the prophecy, is to be introduced into this whole prophecy and be allowed to interrupt its fulfillment. It seems very much more plausible that since the 62 weeks are regarded as following directly on the 7, that the last week is to follow immediately on the 62.

There are two very serious objections to the "Jewish time-clock theory." (1) Israel was still in the land for nearly 40 years after the death of Christ. In other words, Israel was still in the land for nearly 40 years (to 70 A.D.) after the clock stopped ticking! (2) And, if the clock could only tick when Israel was "governed by God" can we say this condition was really fulfilled at any time during the period of the 6 9weeks? The "times of the Gentiles" are regarded by Dispensationalists as beginning with Nebuchadnezzar's destruction of Jerusalem. This entire period, then, was distinctly not a period when Israel was "governed by God." If the clock represents "Jewish" time, with Israel in the land and governed by God, how then could it tick at all during the entire period from 606 B.C. to 30 A.D.? What the Dispensationalists really have is a parenthesis ("times of the Gentiles" beginning with Nebuchadnezzar) within which they have placed another parenthesis (the so-called "Church" age). On Dispensational principles the one parenthesis is no more entitled to be called Jewish time than is the other. If the clock could tick during *part* of the "times of the Gentiles", it could tick during the *whole* of it! If the clock stops ticking at 30 A.D., instead of 70 A.D., it does so quite arbitrarily. For Israel continued to be in their land and under foreign rulers during these 40 years (30-70 A.D.), quite as much as from 457 B.C. to 30 A.D.

What then of the 70th week? To sum up so far, the 70th week follows immediately upon the 69th week—there is no parenthesis. In the midst of the 70th week the anointed one is cut off. That much we know. His "cutting off" and His "causing sacrifice and oblation to cease" are one and the same thing. When Jesus was nailed to the cross, the law of Moses in its entirety was nailed to the cross with Him, for He fulfilled its penalty and its purpose (cf. Col. 2:13-15; II Cor. 3:7ff; Eph. 2:13-16, etc.). The very emphatic argument of the whole book of Hebrews is that Christ, by His death, did abolish the sacrifices of the Old Covenant. (cf. Heb. 7:11; 8:13; 9:25-26; 10:8-9).

Christ was actually crucified in the middle of the last prophetic week, (in the midst of the 70th seven) or three and one-half years after the beginning of his public ministry, thus fulfilling this part of the prophecy to the letter.

Only the last half of the 70th seven (3½ years) is left now to be accounted for. It is our opinion that the historic fact that for about three and one-half years after the death of Christ the gospel privileges were confined to the Jews by reason of providence, the prophecy that 490 years would be alloted to the Jews is finally fulfilled completely!

Some think the references in verses 26 and 27 to "the people of the prince that shall come and destroy the city and the sanctuary . . ." and "desolations," and "upon the wing of abominations shall come one that maketh desolate, etc." forces the termination of the 70th seven to be the terrible destruction of Jerusalem by the Roman Emperor Titus Vespasian in 700 A.D. While we believe the statements quoted above from verses 26 and 27 do predict this Roman desolation of Jerusalem, we do not believe that it is necessary to find the termination of the 70th week in this destruction. This destruction of the city and the sanctuary was a consequence of the Jews "cutting off" their Messiah, but its accomplishment extends to a time beyond the strict limits of the 70th week. We quote in full from *Prophecy and The Church*, by Allis, pgs. 114-115 where the difficulty with forcing the destruction of Jerusalem to be the termination of the 70th week is discussed thoroughly:

A difficulty with this interpretation is to be found in the fact that it does not clearly define the terminus of the 70th week. Unless the view is taken that "in the midst of the week" means "in the second half" of it, and even at the end of that half, the end is not definitely fixed. It seems very unlikely that if "in the midst" really meant "at the end," it would have been described in this way. On the other hand if "in the midst" is taken in its natural sense, a half-week, or three and a half years, remains to be accounted for after the crucifixion. Many interpreters regard this as referring to the period of the founding of the Church and the preaching of the gospel exclusively to the Jews, a period ending with or about the time of the martyrdom of Stephen. Others hold that the period of three and a half years was graciously extended to some 35 years, to the date of the destruction of Jerusalem by Titus, a reference to which is found in vs. 26. Both of these explanations may be regarded as possible.

With regard to the claim that the prophecy extends to the date of the destruction of Jerusalem in A.D. 70 it is to be noted that while the language of vs. 26 may seem to favor this, it does not require it. Vs. 26 speaks of events which will come "after the threescore and two weeks." Of these events it mentions first the cutting off of Messiah, which vs. 27 describes as taking place in the midst of the week. Then it speaks of the destruction of the city and sanctuary and finally of an "end" or an "end of war," which is a very indefinite expression. Vs. 27 declares that a covenant is to be made firm for "one week," that "in the midst of the week" someone will cause sacrifice and oblation to cease. Then it goes on to speak of the coming of a "desolator" and of a "full end." None of the predictions of desolation and vengeance contained in these verses can be regarded as so definitely included in the program outlined in vs. 24 that we can assert with confidence that they must be regarded as fulfilled within the compass of the 70 weeks. They are consequences of the cutting off; they may be regarded as involved in it, but their accomplishment may extend, and if this interpretation is correct, clearly does extend beyond the strict limits of the 70 weeks, since the destruction of Jerusalem was much more than three and a half years after the crucifixion. But, in either case, the great climactic event of the last week was the crucifixion which took place "in the midst" of that week. So interpreted there can be no interval between the 69th and the 70th weeks.

There is no doubt that Jesus was predicting the destruction of Jerusalem by Titus in 70 A.D. when He quoted Daniel's "abomination of desolation" in Matthew 24:15-28. This desolation was to pour forth upon this city and its devastation would continue until God determined it was ended. For a graphic account of the destruction of Jerusalem in 70 A.D. read the *Antiquities* of Josephus. Josephus himself interprets the event as a fulfillment of the prophecy of Daniel.

But what is "the firm covenant with many" to be made for one week by the anointed one? It means that during the brief period of His earthly ministry and the infancy of the church (while the gospel was just beginning to be preached to the Jews) Jesus fulfilled the terms of the ancient covenant made with the seed of Abraham (cf. Rom. 15:8), that He secured its benefits to "many," (even the pouring out of the Spirit as prophecied by Joel), for the period up to the stoning of Stephen (or, if you prefer, perhaps in mercy until the time of the distruction of Jerusalem —at which time the "new covenant" which was in fact only the full unfolding of the old covenant and made no distinction between Jew and Gentile, went fully into effect through the destruction of the temple and of Jewish national existence). (Heb. 8:13; 9:15).

Edward J. Young's interpretation of the 70th seven is that the termination of the last week is indefinite. We quote from *The Prophecy of Daniel*, by Edward J. Young, pp. 220-221.

SPECIAL STUDY THREE

ABOMINATION OF DESOLATION

"In response to his prayer, Gabriel announces to Daniel that a period of seventy sevens—the exact length of the seven is not stated—in fact, seventy of them, has been decreed for the purpose of accomplishing the Messianic work. This Messianic work is described both in negative and positive terms; negative—restraining the transgression, completing in and covering iniquity; positive—bringing in everlasting righteousness, sealing vision and prophet and anointing of holy of holies.

Daniel therefore is to know and understand that from going forth of a word to restore and build Jerusalem unto an anointed one, who is also a prince (i.e., a royal priest), is seven sevens, and sixty and two sevens. We are not told when this word went forth from the Lord but the effects of its issuance first appear in the return from bondage during the first year of Cyrus. This period is divided into two. The first period of seven sevens is evidently intended to include the time from the first year of Cyrus to the completion of the work of Ezra and Nehemiah, and the second from the completion of the work of Ezra and Nehemiah unto the first advent of Christ, who alone can be described as an anointed one, a prince. During this entire period the city will be completely rebuilt, although this will be accomplished during times of distress and affliction.

After the expiration of these two periods, two events are to occur. Whether or not these two events fall within the 70th seven is not immediately stated. One of them is the death of the Messiah and the other follows as a consequent, the destruction of Jerusalem and the Temple by the Roman armies of Titus.

For the period of the 70th seven the messiah causes a covenant to prevail for many, and in the half of this seven by His death He causes the Jewish sacrifices and oblation to cease. His death is thus seen to belong within the 70th seven. Consequent upon this causing the sacrifices and oblation to cease is the appearance of a desolator over the pinnacle of the Temple, which has now become an abomination. Upon the ruins a determined full end pours out. This event, the destruction of the city, does not, therefore, take place within the 70 sevens, but follows as a consequent upon the cutting off of the Messiah in the 70th seven.

The question naturally arises, what marks the termination of the 70 sevens? In answer it should be noted that the text does not say a word about the termination. The *terminus ad quem* of the 69 sevens is clearly stated, namely, an anointed one, a prince. No such *terminus ad quem*, however, is given for the 70 sevens themselves. It would seem, therefore, that the *terminums ad quem* was not regarded as possessing particular importance or significance. No important event is singled out as marking the termination. All schools of interpretation, therefore, are faced with the difficulty of determining what marked the close of the 70 sevens. And all schools discover this event upon the basis of considerations other than those presented in the text. The text says nothing upon the subject. Therefore, we may safely follow the text. When the 70 sevens come to a conclusion, we do not know.

For that matter, the text is somewhat vague about the *terminus a quo* of the 70 sevens. It speaks merely of the going forth of a word. It appears that the principal emphasis is not upon the beginning and ending of this remarkable period but upon the mighty events which were to transpire therein, events which have wrought our peace with God. The passage is Messianic through and through. Well will it be for us, if we too, in our study of this supremely important prophecy, place our emphasis, not upon dates and mathematical calculations, but upon that central Figure who was both anointed and a prince, who by being cut off has made reconciliation for iniquity and brought in the only righteousness that is acceptable with God, even His own eternal righteousness."

To clarify a lengthy discussion of this passage concerning the Seventy Weeks, we have chosen to express the three major interpretations of this period alluded to in chart form. The first chart will represent in general, the view of the dispensationalists; the second chart will represent, in general, the view expressed by Edward J. Young; and the third chart will represent, in general, the author's view (which is also that view expressed by E. V. Zollars and Oswald T. Allis, whose works have been referred to in this section).

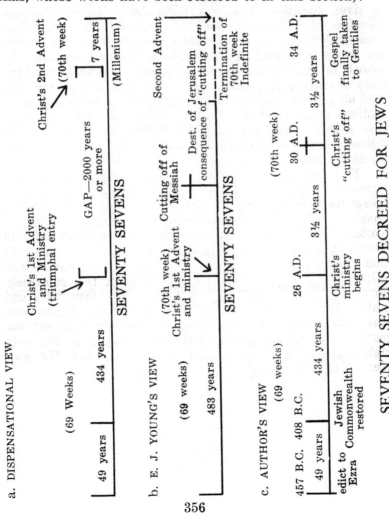

SERMON NUMBER NINE
THE PRAYER, THE PRINCE, AND POSTERITY

Text: Daniel 9

INTRODUCTION

I. WHEN DID THIS PRAYER AND VISION TAKE PLACE?

A. In the first year of Darius the son of Ahasureus.

  1. Already discussed the identity of Darius (ch. 5); he is the Gubaru of the Nabonidus Chronicle. No cuneiform text is known to us today that mentions the name of Gubaru's father, but silence is no evidence that his father could not have been named Ahasuerus.

  2. Gubaru (Darius) was appointed king of Chaldea and Babylon in the same year that Cyrus conquered it, 539-538 B.C.

B. This was an era of many developments which would have far-reaching consequences.

  1. Many of the pagan religions were being founded in this time; Buddhism, Taoism, Janism—these were to hold millions in fear and superstition.

  2. Greek democracy was beginning to reach its peak along with Greek science and philosophy.

  3. But the most important event of the time concerned a nation which had spent more than half a century in captivity, a nation which had lost its structure but not its identity

  4. The Jewish nation was about to be released to return and rebuild its structure in preparation for the Messiah; it had learned one lesson well—idols are not gods.

357

II. HOW DID THE VISION COME ABOUT?

A. Daniel was studying the scroll of Jeremiah.
1. "Books" does not mean the entire O.T. canon (for that had not yet been written).
2. Several "books" might be written on one scroll in those days. Jesus makes a quotation from "Jeremiah" in Mt. 27:9ff which contains some phrases from Zechariah. This probably indicates that more than one prophet's work was recorded on a single scroll.

B. Daniel was studying the "books" and specifically the scroll of Jeremiah.
1. The passage that caught his attention was: "And this whole land shall be a desolation, and an astonishment; and these nations shall serve the king of Babylon seventy-years." (Jer. 25:9-11)
2. The desolation began with the captivity of Daniel in 606 B.C. and the first devastation of Jerusalem by Nebuchadnezzar. So, in the first year of Darius (538 B.C.), the 70 years (to end in 536 B.C.) would be almost completed.
3. Some regard the destruction of Jerusalem in 587 as the point from which the 70 years are to be reckoned. But Daniel would hardly feel that in 538 B.C. the 70 years were very soon coming to completion and be in fervent prayer about it if the 70 years started in 587; for then the completion of the 70-year period would have yet been 20 years in the future from 538 (Darius' first year).

III. WHAT DID DANIEL DO?

A. Exactly what you would expect such a man of God to do—he prayer.
1. And what a prayer!
2. This could be a model prayer for any man.

B. Daniel's prayer was answered.
1. And what an answer!
2. Perhaps not like he expected; maybe not understood by Daniel but certainly meaningful to us, on this side of its completion!

DISCUSSION

I. REPENTANCE, 9:3-14

A. The highest form of prayer or communication with God is that where man pours out a soul of sincere repentance.

   1. Repentance means "change of mind, change of heart."

   2. There are two realizations man must arrive at before God can shower His blessings upon man:

     a. Realize his own impotent condition—sinful, rebellious, lost.

     b. Realize that God and His way is the way of power and victory.

   3. The prayer of penitence is the expression of such realization.

B. Rebellion confessed, 3-6.

   1. Daniel knows for certain that cause for captivity is stubborn, deliberate rebellion of the people.

   2. He sees that time for captivity is about complete.

   3. He knows majority of people still have not turned to God. His main concern is not to know the precise meaning of the number 70 (to come later) BUT TO IMPLORE GOD FOR THE COMPLETE, FULL AND MERCIFUL CLEANSING FOR THEIR SIN.

   4. Important to understand Daniel's desire in order to understand the answer Daniel is given. (THE ANSWER HE IS GIVEN EMPHASIZES THE FACT THAT COMPLETE FORGIVENESS IS IN THE FUTURE IN THE WORK THAT THE "PRINCE" SHALL ACCOMPLISH.)

   5. Daniel is in earnest; he fasts and humbles himself in sackcloth and ashes—to subdue the flesh in order to concentrate on the spiritual.

   6. Daniel uses four synonyms for sin in order to emphasize the stubborn deliberateness of it. Jer. 6:16ff. represents the stubborness of the people: "Thus says the Lord: stand by the roads, and look, and ask for the ancient paths, where the good way is; and walk in it, and find rest for your souls. But they said, We will not walk in it . . . they said, We will not give heed . . ." So

God said He would bring evil upon them . . .
"the fruit of their devices, because they have not
given heed to my words . . ." Ezekiel also hears
God call the people "stubborn, rebellious, hard-
hearted, stone-faced, etc." (Ezek. 2 and 3). THEIR
SIN WAS NOT ONE OF IGNORANCE . . . BUT ONE OF
DELIBERATION . . . THEY LOVED TO HAVE IT SO.

7. Those who have no love for the truth but take
pleasure in unrighteousness will have what they
want. God will allow them to have deluded minds,
if they so desire. This impudent, arrogant, wicked
people would not listen to the true prophets who
predicted punishment — they listened to false
prophets who cried, "Peace, peace, when there was
no peace."

C. Rejection, 7:11.

1. It is evident from Daniel's prayer that he thought
the captivity was about to be prolonged on account
of the sins of the people so he prayed for the
mercy of God.

2. The word confession in Gr. is *homologeo,* which
means "to say the same as . . ." So Daniel, in
his confession, is saying the same as God says
about rebellion against God's will.

3. Daniel admits that God is just in bringing upon
the people this captivity because God pre-warned
them of consequences of rebellion in giving the
law (Deut. 28-30).

D. Refusal, 12-14.

1. Daniel expresses fear for his people; in spite of
the chastening of the captivity, they have not, for
the most part, "entreated" the favor of God.

2. They have refused to appease God by humbling
themselves and offering their hearts to Him.

3. They had not "sweetened their faces toward God
by turning from their sinful ways which would
have sweetened the face of God toward them."

4. God confirmed His Word as truly inviolable with
the captivities of Israel and Judah. WHAT GOD
PROMISES AND WARNS WILL SURELY COME TO PASS!

5. The downfall of the covenant people involved an amount of cruelty and suffering that no other case in history could claim! Even to eating the flesh of their own children (II Kings 6:25-31; Jer. 19:9). GOD MEANS WHAT HE SAYS, AND MAN'S PROPER PRAYER APPROACH IS REPENTANCE AND CONFESSION . . . AGREEING WITH GOD . . . CHANGING THE MIND TO CONFORM TO HIS WILL!

II. REQUEST, 9:15-19.

A. Release, 15-16.

1. Daniel refers to the Lord's mighty supernatural deliverance of Israel from the great Egyptian empire centuries ago.
2. The appeal of Daniel is to the very name or nature of God to have mercy.
3. Daniel's prayer is that for himself and a God-fearing remnant who wish Gods' name to be honored, God will preserve His Holy Name by withdrawing His wrath upon this people and their homeland.
4. They have become a byword among the nations—this, of course, is the arrogant ridicule of the heathen who have no respect for Jehovah—so Daniel prays that first and foremost, God's name will be vindicated by His merciful and mighty deliverance of this holy remnant.

B. Restore, 17.

1. Daniel prays that the Lord's gracious face will shine upon His sanctuary and remove its desolation.
2. Nebuchadnezzar had done such a thorough job that weeds grew up in the courts—it was torn down and burned and left in ruins.
3. Daniel is not interested that the people and their temple be restored in order that their wounded pride be avenged, or that they may enjoy physical comfort and ease.
4. His concern is that God's holiness and faithfulness be vindicated.

361

C. Redound, 18-19.

1. There is an emphatic repetition throughout this passage insisting that God's glory be vindicated in everything He does.

2. Sinning man deserves only judgment. If the Jews are delivered at all it will be entirely due to the very nature of God—His mercifulness.

3. This is the whole point of prayer—God seeks contrition and penitence in prayer in order that He may do for man what He has made up His mind to do for man all along!

4. It is not the eloquence of man's prayers, nor the quantity of them that move God to action—if this were so, answers would be merited. IT IS THE ATTITUDE. PRAYER DOES NOT CHANGE THINGS, MEN ARE CHANGED—THEY ARE SO CHANGED THAT THEY ARE DRIVEN TO THEIR KNEES IN DEEP CONTRITION AND DEPENDENCE, AND GOD CAN THEN ACT AS HE HAS SAID HE WOULD ACT AND WANTS TO ACT FROM THE BEGINNING OF THE WORLD!

5. God cannot act to bless any man if that man does not pray, believing, trusting, repenting. It is not God who changes—it is man who changes. MAN CHANGES—GOD ACTS! GOD ALSO ACTS WHEN MAN DOES NOT CHANGE TO CONFORM TO HIS WILL. BUT AGAIN IT IS IN ACCORDANCE WITH WHAT GOD HAS SAID HE WOULD DO CONDITIONED UPON MAN'S WISHES!

6. Daniel's prayer that God will act in the interest of His Own Perfect Will is as God wishes. GOD ONLY WANTS US TO BE BETTER THAN WE ARE. BUT HE KNOWS THAT THIS CAN ONLY COME AS A RESULT OF MAN'S SEEKING TO GLORIFY HIS CREATOR AND REDEEMER. GOD ACTS TO GLORIFY HIS NAME NOT OUT OF SELFISH EGOTISM, BUT IN ORDER TO BLESS HIS CREATION. Read such passages as Ezek. 20:9, 14, 22, 44, and Isa. 48:9-11 AND SEE THAT THE INEVITABLE RESULT OF GOD ACTING TO GLORIFY HIS OWN NAME IS THAT THE MAN WHO ACCEPTS AND ACTS IN ACCORDANCE WITH THIS IS THEREBY MADE A PARTAKER OF GOD'S GLORY (II Pet. 1:3-3). And

this is the way Jesus taught us to pray, ". . . Hallowed, be thy name . . . Thy will be done . . . etc."

III. REVELATION, 9:20-27.
A. Seraphim, 20-23.
1. Right in the middle of his praying, Daniel is approached by the angel, Gabriel, in human form, to deliver God's answer to his prayer.
2. God knows what His beloved need before they even ask and is able to answer before they get through praying.
3. God also knows that our greatest need is TO ASK!
4. As long as a man is self-confident and self-dependent he is in no position morally, intellectually or spiritually to receive. He only demands and spends whatever may come his way in goodness to confirm himself in his egotism.
5. Repetitious prayers, like the heathens', are vain and useless, simply because they are used by men to support their own vanity and are attempts to earn the blessings of God by meritorius praying and self-righteousness.
6. THEREFORE, BE ASSURED THAT THE "THINGS" YOU PRAY FOR ARE NO PROBLEM TO GOD. HE CAN GIVE YOU EXCEEDING ABUNDANTLY ABOVE ALL YOU CAN POSSIBLY ASK OR THINK, IF YOU UTTERLY, TOTALLY, UNRESERVEDLY TRUST HIM! THE PROBLEM IS NOT WHAT YOU NEED . . . THE PROBLEM IS YOU, RESTING ON THE EVERLASTING ARMS!

B. Seventy, 24-26.
1. Difficult to exaggerate the significance of this passage in teachings of dispensationalists. Often appealed to as definite proof that the entire "Church age" is a parenthesis in the prophetic program.
2. The "church age" is supposed to occur between the events listed in verse 26 and verse 27. Verse 27 concerns the "70th week" which is supposed to be, according to dispensationalists, the Millenium or the 1000 years of Rev. 20.

3. The word translated "weeks" is literally, "sevens." Could be paraphrased, "Sevens — and in fact seventy of them are decreed . . . etc." In light of other key passages (Ezek. 4:6; etc.) we have the "year-day" theory which would make this "Seventy weeks-of-years, that is, 7 years × 70 are decreed, etc." Thus 490 years express in Divine relevation that a definite period of time has been decreed for the accomplishment of all that which is necessary for answering Daniel's prayer.

4. A list of things to be accomplished during these 490 years are given: (a) finish the transgression —the Jews to reach the height of their transgression, crucifixion of the Messiah (b) put an end to sin—in the death of the Messiah God would conquer sin and offer man by faith a way to overcome sin (c) atone for iniquity—reconcile man to God, thus breaking man's heart (d) bring in everlasting righeousness — imputed righteousness and practiced righteousness (e) seal both vision and prophet—God's prophecies and types are confirmed by being fulfilled in Christ (f) anointing a most holy thing (the phrase is without the definite article and refers to a thing, not a place) literally it would read, "annointing of holiness of holiness." Dispensationalists insist that all these events are still in the future.

Of course, if the fulfillment of verse 24 is still future, and if the events of the 69 weeks are already fulfilled, then the 70th week must still be future. Therefore, they think, there must be an interval between the end of the 69th week and the beginning of the 70th week; and the entire Church age can be regarded as a parenthesis.

5. But have these events (v. 25) been fulfilled or not? IN THE LIGHT OF PLAIN N.T. TEACHING IT SEEMS INCREDIBLE THAT ANYONE COULD INSIST THAT THESE THINGS ARE FUTURE! The book of Hebrews represents all these transactions as hav-

ing been fulfilled at Calvary! When Jesus comes the second time He comes NOT to deal with sin (Heb. 9:28).

6. If all items in vs. 24 are Messianic that settles the terminating point of the 70 weeks.

7. In vs. 25 we are told exactly how many years intervene between the return of the Jews to rebuild Jerusalem and the coming of the Messiah— 69 weeks-of-years (483 years). This prophecy was fulfilled in a marvelously accurate way.

8. The 7th year of Artaxerxes (457 B.C.) was the first official decree for the Jews to rebuild their commonwealth (earlier just the temple). Read it in Ezra 7. Reckoning from 457 B.C., counting the first 7, 49 years, we should arrive at 408 B.C. for the restoration of the Jewish commonwealth . . . and this date accords in perfect accuracy with the facts of history. Reckoning from 408 B.C., counting the next 62 (434 years) we come down to the year 26 A.D. as the close of the second period. This is when Christ was baptized (anointed).

C. Seventieth, 27.

1. After the second 62, the Messiah is to be cut off, that is during the 70th week . . . in the midst of it. THIS SHOULD SETTLE ONCE FOR ALL THAT THE 70TH WEEK IS NOT WAITING FOR CHRIST'S SECOND COMING!

2. Dispensationalists are fond of the illustration of a clock. The ticking clock, they say, represents Jewish time. The mystery parenthesis is "time out." God only counts time in dealing with Israel, when the people are in the land. Some add, only when they are governed by God. They say the clock ceased to tick at the triumphal entry and it will not tick again until that moment, still future, when God resumes His direct dealings with Israel (the Millenium).

3. If the 69 weeks are exactly 483 consecutive years, as even dispensationalists admit, and if the 1 week

is to be exactly 7 consecutive years, IT IS INCRED-
IBLE THAT AN INTERVAL WHICH IS ALREADY MORE
THAN 1900 YEARS IS TO BE INTRODUCED INTO THIS
WHOLE PROPHECY. There are also very serious
difficulties with the "Jewish time-clock theory"
(a) Israel was in the land 40 years after Christ
died (2) How could the clock tick anytime during
the 483 years Israel was in its land, since Israel
"governed by God" was not true of all that time.

4. The 70th week follows immediately upon the 69th
   week. In the midst of the 70th the anointed one
   is cut off. His cutting off and causing offering
   and oblation to cease are one and the same.

5. Christ was actually crucified in the middle of the
   last prophetic week or 3½ years after the beginning of His public ministry

6. Only the last 3½ years of the last week is left
   to be accounted for. The historic fact is that for
   about 3½ years after the death of Christ the
   gospel privileges were confined to the Jews by
   reason of prividence—the prophecy that 490 years
   would be allotted to the Jews is finally fulfilled
   completely—for after that 3½ years Paul took
   the gospel to the Gentiles

7. The statements in vs. 26-27 concerning the people
   of the prince who shall make desolate refer to
   the Romans who destroyed the temple and the
   Jewish commonwealth—it is not necessary, how-
   ever, to find the termination of the 70th week
   in this destruction. THIS DESTRUCTION WAS A
   CONSEQUENCE OF THEIR COMPLETE REJECTION OF
   THE MESSIAH BUT THE CONSEQUENCE WAS NOT
   ACCOMPLISHED UNTIL AFTER THE END OF THE 70TH
   WEEK WAS OVER!

8. During the brief period of Jesus' earthly ministry
   and the infancy of the church, Jesus fulfilled the
   terms of the ancient covenant to "many," even in
   the pouring out of the Holy Spirit upon all flesh
   prophecied by Joel, and this is the terminating
   point of the 70th week.

CONCLUSION
I. WHAT DO WE LEARN FROM THIS?

A. When man repents and prays in dependence upon God, when man's primary concern is that God's glory be magnified and His name be exalted, HE PUTS HIMSELF IN A POSITION FOR GOD TO ACT ON HIS BEHALF AS GOD WANTS TO DO.

B. God wants to bless us by spiritual renewal, not by materialistic affluence.

Billy Graham wrote in *Decision*

"Eric Sevareid, the commentator, remarked after the first moon landing: 'There is aftel all another side, a dark side, to the human spirit also. Men have hardly begun to explore these regions, and it is going to be a very great pity if we advance upon the bright side of the moon with the dark side of ourselves; if the cargo in the first rockets to reach there consists of fear and suspicion. Surely we ought to have our credentials in order, our hands very clean, and perhaps a prayer of forgiveness on our lips as we prepare to open the ancient vault of the shining moon.'

"What if we as a people would exert the same effort, the same energy, the same dedication and sacrifice, in setting our individual spiritual houses in order, that the NASA people have done in planning the moon flights? What if each of us would sincerely examine his heart and say with David, 'Search me, O God, and know my heart: try me, and know my thoughts; and see if there be any wicked way in me, and lead me in the way everlasting' (Psalm 139:23-24)? What if we were to pray that prayer and mean it? What if we would exercise the care in our spiritual lives that NASA exercises in keeping a space rocket 'without spot or blemish.'

"Are we assuming by our slipshod faith, our sins, our fears, our failures, that a human soul is less valuable than a rocket made of steel, wire and batteries? Any thinking person should realize that the space hardware will become rusted and corroded by the ravages of time, but our immortal souls will go on living forever.

"No matter how many planets we visit, no matter how advanced our scientific achievements, if we fail to deal with what Mr. Sevareid called "the dark side" of the human spirit, if we fail to conquer "inner space," then the conquest of outer space will have no meaning. The solving of such social problems as inflation, pollution, crime, and a thousand others, will carry little meaning unless we can solve the problems of the human spirit.

"Dr. Wernher von Braun has said: 'The materialists of the nineteenth century and the Marxist heirs of the twentieth tried to tell us that as science yields more knowledge about the creation, it makes us able to live without faith in a Creator. Yet so far, with every new answer we have discovered new questions. The better we understand the intricacies of the atomic structure, the nature of life and the master plan for the galaxies, the more reason we have found to marvel at the wonder of God's creation. But our need for God is not based on awe alone. Man needs faith just as he needs food, water or air. With all the science in the world we need faith in God.'

"To listen to some of our political leaders we might think that all of our problems can be solved without God's help, that all we need is more money. But the Bible teaches that God and man are partners. God created man both for fellowship and as a co-laborer. And man is helpless without God. When Jesus came to do his work in the world, he called 12 men to help him in his ministry. When he left he placed the burden of the work of his Kingdom upon their shoulders, and he said, "Without me ye can do nothing" (John 15:5).

"We Americans have felt that we can build a better world without God. This is what the Communists are trying to do. And wherever they have extended their form of life they have made a mess of it, from Cuba to Czechoslovakia. Their people have a standard of living far below that of the rest of the Western world, and they are robbed of basic freedoms, such as the freedom of the press, freedom of speech and freedom of religion.

"We are in danger of copying the Communists by trying to achieve our goals without reference to God. We are trying to build a perfect society on the cracked foundation of human nature. For example, we are trying to wipe out crime without dealing with the corrupt heart of the criminal. The problem of crime is not just poverty, poor law enforcement and an antiquated judiciary system. It is all of this, but it is more. It is corrupt human nature that needs to be regenerated. This is why Jesus said, "Ye must be born again" (John 3:7).

"When we examine the problems that confront us in our world today, we find that every one of them resolves into a problem of "inner space," a problem of the dark side of the human spirit. We are infected by the disease of sin. The Bible says, "There is none righteous, no, not one" (Romans 3:10). The Bible says, "All have sinned, and come short of the glory of God" (Romans 3:23).

"The Bible gives only one answer, and that is the answer given by Jesus Christ long ago. He said, "Ye shall know the truth, and the truth shall make you free" (John 8:32). We are never going to be free from the binding problems of alienation, loneliness, crime, alcoholism, lust and greed until we know the freedom to be found in a personal relationship with Christ. He said, "I am the way, the truth, and the life: no man cometh unto the Father"—no man will find life's fulfilment—"but by me" (John 14:6).

EXAMINATION NINE

REFUTATIONS

(Answer the following by giving the argument which will correct the statement)

1. Daniel could not have been reading the "books" of the O.T. since the O.T. canon was not complete in his day. Refute!
2. The revelation of the angel to Daniel in the latter part of chapter 9 has nothing to do with Daniel's prayer in the first part of chapter 9. Refute!
3. The seventy weeks are the millenium. Refute!

ASSOCIATIONS

(Associate the persons or events of column one with the correct person or event of column two)

1	2
Jeremiah	angel
seventy weeks	millenium
wing of abominations	Armageddon
anointed one	prophet
Darius	king of Babylon
Ahasuerus	Gubaru
Gabriel	father of Darius
oblation	Messiah
covenant	temple
seventy years	time of Jewish captivity
	meal offering
	the gospel
	time of Jewish history

MEMORIZATIONS

(Fill in the blanks:)

_____ weeks are decreed upon thy people and upon

thy holy _____, to finish _____ and to make an end

of _____, and to make _____ for iniquity, and to

370

bring in everlasting _____, and to seal up _____ and _____, and to anoint the _____ _____.

EXPLANATIONS

1. Explain why Daniel prayed such a prayer of emphatic repentance.
2. Explain why Daniel was studying the "books" to understand the number of years of the Jewish captivity.
3. Explain why the "seventy" weeks are descriptive of the era of Jewish history from Perian release from captivity until the coming of the Messiah.
4. Explain what we know of the "70th week"—its beginning and ending.

CHAPTER TEN

IV. ANGELIC ASSISTANCE—10:1-21

a. ANGELIC APPEARANCE

TEXT: 10:1-9

1 In the third year of Cyrus king of Persia a thing was revealed unto Daniel, whose name was called Belteshazzar; and the thing was true, even a great warfare: and he understood the thing, and had understanding of the vision.

2 In those days I, Daniel, was mourning three whole weeks.

3 I ate no pleasant bread, neither came flesh nor wine into my mouth, neither did I anoint myself at all, till three whole weeks were fulfilled.

4 And in the four and twentieth day of the first month, as I was by the side of the great river, which is Hiddekel,

5 I lifted up mine eyes, and looked, and, behold, a man clothed in linen, whose loins were girded with pure gold of Uphaz:

6 his body also was like the beryl, and his face as the appearance of lightning, and his eyes as flaming torches, and his arms and his feet like unto burnished brass, and the voice of his words like the voice of a multitude.

7 And I, Daniel, alone saw the vision; for the men that
   were with me saw not the vision; but a great quaking
   fell upon them, and they fled to hide themselves.
8 So I was left alone, and saw this great vision, and there
   remained no strength in me; for my comeliness was
   turned in me into corruption, and I retained no strength.
9 Yet heard I the voice of his words; and when I heard
   the voice of his words, then was I fallen into a deep
   sleep on my face, with my face toward the ground.

QUERIES

a. Why was Daniel so upset by this vision?
b. Who was the "man" Daniel saw?
c. What does Daniel mean, "my comeliness was turned in
   me into corruption"?

PARAPHRASE

In the third year of the reign of Cyrus, king of Persia,
Daniel (who had been named Belteshazzar by the Babylonians) had another vision. It was a vision but what was
revealed would certainly come to pass in exact detail. This
vision of future history concerned great suffering which
was to come upon the people of God. Daniel's understanding
of this future history came to him by means of the vision
given to him. In those days I, Daniel, continued in mourning for three full weeks. I ate none of the more pleasant
foods; meat and wine did not cross my lips; I abstained
completely from tending to the ease and comfort of my
body and refrained from anointing myself until three full
weeks were finished. And on the twenty-fourth day of Nisan
(the first Jewish month), when I was standing beside the
great Tigris River, I looked up and suddenly there before
me stood a being in human form robed in pure white linen,
with a wide belt of purest gold around his waist and his skin
glowed like the Tarshish stone; from his face came blinding
flashes like lightning, and his eyes glowed like flaming
torches at night; his arms and feet glistened like polished
brass, and his voice was like the roaring of a multitude of
human voices or like the sea pounding the shore. But I,
Daniel, alone saw this great vision; the men with men saw

nothing; but they sensed that an unusual manifestation of some sort was taking place and they were suddenly filled with unreasoning terror and ran to hide, and I was left alone. When I saw this fearful vision my strength left me; and whatever appearance of health and strength I had left me. Then this being spoke to me, and I fell to the ground unconscious, face downward.

COMMENT

v. 1-3 IN THE THIRD YEAR OF CYRUS KING OF PERSIA . . . Leupold makes an interesting observation: "The last three chapters of the book of Daniel contain the Last Revelation of Things to Come. Chapter ten is introductory; the body of this last revelation is found chiefly in chapter eleven; chapter twelve is a conclusion . . . There is hardly anything in the Bible that is just like these chapters, especially like chapter eleven. Th word, the vision, and minute prediction are combined in a manner that is found nowhere else in the Scripture . . . Everything in chapter ten is preparatory to chapter eleven."

The "Last Revelation of Things to Come" is the last revelation of things to come upon the O.T. covenant people. Daniel recounts, in chapter eleven, in detail, the final centuries of Israel's history as it relates to the Ptolemies and the Seleucids. Chapter ten is an introduction to that prediction of history to come.

"In the third year of Cyrus . . ." indicates that Daniel did not return to Palestine with the first increment of returnees under Zerubbabel, but remained in Babylon. He was now an old man, and God had yet another revelation to give him on behalf of the covenant people. When God revealed such exciting things and such terrible things concerning the future, the prophet was inspired to mark such a momentous revelation in terms of definite time and circumstances. Here the day and the month of the year are marked when the prophet was given this terrifying vision. In order to understand the full significance of this entire revelation concerning the Ptolemies and Seleucids and other enemies (Samaritans) of God's people in the ending era of the O.T. covenant, one must understand that already obstacles (in the third year of Cyrus) had been placed in the way of the first returnees to Palestine. The Samaritans had tried to persuade Cyrus that the Jews he allowed to return to Palestine were plotting treason against his rule. God tells Daniel that much more tribulation and persecution is to come upon the Jews in their restoration before the Messiah comes. The Jews, with carnal mindedness, took Daniel's prophecies in stride, endured the tribulations, but were hoping in a Messiah who would come to avenge all that took place during the abominations of the Seleucids. But Daniel never predicted a carnally-oriented Messiah—he predicted One who would accomplish spiritual victories (Dan. 9:24, etc.) and who Himself would be "cut-off" in the midst of the 70th week. Daniel intended to raise their hopes in God's highest purpose in their lives—but they could not raise their vision above the worldly, so they applied the hopeful tone of Daniel's prophecies to the carnal.

What Daniel saw was so unique he had to emphasize that "the thing was true." The great "warfare" would be better translated the great "suffering." The time of this suffering would be "great" or "long"—in fact it would last nearly 200 years; from the time of Alexander the Great and the division of his empire, to the revolt of the Maccabeans.

The fact that Daniel was able to understand this vision caused him great turmoil of spirit. He mourned three whole weeks. Daniel put his body under subjection to conform to his spiritual penitence and sorrow. This harmony of the outward man with the inner man is most conducive to sincere communication with God. Daniel denied himself all forms of food and drink as well as the customary anointing at this particular time of the year (Passover).

v. 4-6 . . . BEHOLD, A MAN CLOTHED IN LINEN . . . On the 24th day of Nisan (the first month of the Jewish calendar) Daniel received this vision as he was beside the river Iigris (Hiddekel; cf. Gen. 2:14). The Passover feast begins on the 14th day of Nisan, followed by 7 days of unleavened bread. A very appropriate time for Daniel to mourn the coming tribulation of his people.

The being who appeared to Daniel with the revelation of God was dressed in linen (symbolizing purity); girded with pure gold (symbolizing high station); his body was like a rare gem from Tarshish (berly) (symbolizing associa-ation with royalty); his face flashed with startling brilliance like lightning (symbolizing truth); his eyes flamed like torches burning in the night, (symbolizing judgment); his arms and feet glistened like polished brass (symbolizing power); his voice thundered like a roar of the mighty sea (symbolizing power also). This being appeared in the hu-man form of man. Some have taken him to be a pre-incarnate appearance of the Lord Jesus because this man's appearance and the Lord's appearance in Revelation 1:13-15 are so similar. We believe, however, that this man was one of God's mighty angels—one on a par with other mighty angels like Michael. See our discussion of pre-incarnate ap-pearances of the Lord Jesus on Daniel 3:24-25. See also the Special Study on Angels at the end of this chapter.

v. 7-9 . . . AND THERE REMAINED NO STRENGTH IN ME . . . Why his companions could not see the vision we are at a loss to explain. Perhaps it was because of their limited spiritual attainments—more likely it was simply because the Divine being retricted by his own choice and ability his appearance to Daniel only, for Divine reasons. They par-ticipated in the event enough to realize the manifestation was supernatural and enough to cause them to quake with fear and flee to hide from omnipotence. A parallel to this is Paul and his companions on the road to Damascus (Acts 9:3ff).

Daniel was severely affected by what he saw. Any sinner would be so affected, were he to come into contact with a holy being who had come from the presence of the Holiest of Holies. Many saints, both in the O.T. and N.T., expected sudden death when such a manifestation came to them. Such an appearance is not to be taken lightly. The directness of this revelation literally drained every bit of physical strength from Daniel. The prophet had to be re-suscitated frequently to survive this experience. Whatever appearance of health and strength Daniel had disappeared. All the color left his face and when he heard the voice booming forth he fell flat on his face on the ground.

It would be well for those who treat visions from the Lord and visits from angels lightly, claiming many such visions indiscriminately, to note how severely even a saint like Daniel was affected. Some who have claimed such visions speak of them as if they were almost natural, every-day occurrences with no particular effects such as Daniel had. And it may be for this very purpose God moved Daniel to record what seems insignificant details to his own person —the absolute frailty of man in the presence of the holiness and the greatness of God. Isaiah knew it (Isa. 6:1-13); Jeremiah knew it (Jer. 1:4-19); time would fail to speak of those who knew such prostrate uncleanness when faced with the absolute holiness of God—Moses, Jacob, Paul, John, Peter, etc.

QUIZ

1. Why mention the "third year of Cyrus?"
2. What is the "warfare" Daniel saw in his vision?
3. What was the time of year Daniel mourned and saw his vision?
4. Why would the "man" Daniel saw *not* be the Lord Jesus?
5. What portion of N.T. scripture parallels this vision of the heavenly being?
6. How and why did the vision affect Daniel as it did?
7. Why do you suppose the Lord moved Daniel to record his reaction to the vision?

b. ANGELIC ANNOUNCEMENT

TEXT: 10:10-14

10 And, behold, a hand touched me, which set me upon my knees and upon the palms of my hands.

11 And he said unto me, O Daniel, thou man greatly beloved, understand the words that I speak unto thee, and stand upright; for unto thee am I now sent: and when he had spoken this word unto me, I stood trembling.

12 Then said he unto me, Fear not, Daniel; for from the first day that thou didst set thy heart to understand, and to humble thyself before thy God, thy words were heard: and I am come for thy words' sake.

13 But the prince of the kingdom of Persia withstood me one and twenty days; but, lo, Michael, one of the chief

princes, came to help me: and I remained there with
the kings of Persia.

13   Now I am come to make thee understand what shall
befall thy people in the latter days; for the vision is
yet for many days.

QUERIES

a. What power did the "being" exert to restore Daniel
upright?.

b. Who is "the prince of the kingdom of Persia?"

c. What are the "latter days?"

PARAPHRASE

And behold this angelic being touched me, rousing me
and raising me up on my knees and my hands. And he said
to me: Daniel, God has taken great delight in you, so give
all your attention to the words I am telling you, for God
has sent me to you. So I stood up still trembling with fear.
Then he said to me, Do not be frightened, for from the very
first day you humbled yourself and began to fast and pray,
God heard your prayers, and I was sent here to give you
God's answer. However, I was detained for 21 days in
coming to you by the mighty demon who overrules the kingdom of Persia. But Michael, one of God's angels of the
first order, came to assist me overcome this demon, and
Michael left me there to continue my influence with the
kings of Persia until I could safely get leave and come to
you. Now I am here to tell you what will happen to your
people, the Jews, in these latter days of the Mosaic covenant, but these latter days are yet a number of years away.

COMMENT

v. 10-11 . . . A HAND TOUCHED ME . . . The hand of
the divine stranger in some supernatural way imparted
strength to Daniel who was lying unconscious, face down
upon the ground, and roused Him and raised him up in a
crawling position on his knees and the palms of his hands.
"Greatly beloved" is literally, "God has taken great delight"
in Daniel's attitude. The "delight" of God being directed
toward an individual demands a like response, so Daniel is

exhorted to give attention and effort to understand the message the angel has to deliver from God. Next the angel assists Daniel to stand upright, though Daniel was still shaky with his recent unconsciousness.

v. 12 . . . THY WORDS WERE HEARD . . . What a consolation to know that God hears those of humble and contrite heart—hears and is able to answer. When a man willingly arrives at the attitude Daniel had, God is more than willing to act on that man's behalf to that man's ultimate good. Such a man may not always understand the answer God gives or the method God uses to answer, but such a man will accept it in faith and trust.

v. 13-14 . . . THE PRINCE OF THE KINGDOM OF PERSIA WITHSTOOD ME . . . These verses and verses 20-21 of this same chapter form some of the most interesting glimpses of all the Bible on angelology! Daniel's prayer had been concerned with the relation of Persia to God's people and the current slanderous attack upon them by the Samaritans, who seemed to have convinced the Persian court that the few Israelites who had been released to return to Palestine were planning sedition.

The angelic messenger had apparently been sent to forcibly overcome and remove the demonic spirit that was at work against the people of God in its influence upon the Persian monarch. It is intriguing to note that the heavenly helper does not exert his force against the Samaritans or even against the Persian monarch, but against "the prince of the kingdom of Persia." We are afforded here a glimpse behind the scenes of world history to the realm of the supernatural and spiritual, where the unseen but real battle of the ages is transpiring. In the realm of observable history there is more than meets the eye. There are powers at work of which some people never have a conception. This is why Paul exhorts Christians to gird themselves with supernatural armor and arm themselves with supernatural weapons—for "we are not contending against flesh and blood, but against the principalities, against the powers, against the world rulers of this present darkness, against the spiritual hosts of wickedness in the heavenly places." (Eph. 6:10-20). This is the meaning of the second half of the book of Revelation (cf. *More Than Conquerors,* by Wm. Hendriksen). One should also consult such scriptures as Isa. 24.21; Col. 2:15; Heb. 1:14; 13:2 and our Special Study on Angels at the end of this chapter.

Who is this "prince of the kingdom of Persia?" Many have supposed him to be simply the Persian king, himself. But it is not in keeping with biblical teaching to suppose that one mortal king could have so successfully opposed an angel of God for a period of 21 days, if one angel was able to smite 185,000 Assyrians in one night! An angel-prince is the meaning. Demons in the N.T. are, without a doubt referred to here—they are called evil angels in the N.T. It appears that in the downward plunge away from truth and morality the Gentile nations, even as they chose to worship and seek the fellowship of demons (cf. Cor. 10:20ff), came under the powerful influence of Satanic angels. These demon-spirits became the controlling, deceiving, power of decadent, depraved men, and they used whatever powers they had to hamper God's work and thwart His purposes. When Christ came He destroyed Satan's power for all who will believe in Him and "bound" Satan to a much more restricted sphere of influence (cf. Heb. 2:14-16; Col. 2:15; Jn. 12:31; 16:11; Mt. 12:29-30; Rev. 20:1-3).

We get a rare glimpse behind the scenes of world history as it occurred then and even now. There are spiritual forces at work that are far in excess of what men who disregard divine revelation would suppose. They struggle behind the struggles that are written on the pages of history. They explain the Satanic evil that often comes to light under the things that appear on the surface. Since a particular "prince of the kingdom of Persia" is mentioned, it seems to be a valid conclusion that every godless, cruel, tyrannical nation is dominated by some such prince. Whether each evil angel may have but one nation as his domain, or whether there may be broader spheres of activity in which the more powerful among them are active, we cannot decide on the limited information available in Scripture.

There are evidently ranks or orders among the angelic beings. Michael was "of the first order." The name Michael means: "Who is like God?"

Evil angels had held the controlling position at the Persian court. They did not hold it, however, without the consent of the governed. That is, when men becme so bereft of the truth willingly, that they have no love for the truth, but take pleasure in unrigheousness, God will send them a strong delusion, that they may believe a lie (cf. the state to which the Gentiles had fallen in Rom. 1:18ff). Therefore, it must have been the desire of the heart of Cyrus, and perhaps others of his kingdom, to know and be able to live the truth; so God sent His angel Michael to overthrow the rule of the evil angels in the minds and hearts of the Persian court.

It is interesting to note the harmonious cooperation between God's angels in carrying out His work. One helps the other where help is needed. Here is an example of how "God's will is done in heaven." And the fact that certain of these angels of God are great and mighty does not cause any rivalry or opposition among them! What a blessing it would be if God's will were done on earth as it is in heaven!

The angel "stood by the side or remained there with the kings of Persia." After the present king shall have passed from the scene, the same angelic influence from God will remain with his successors. This should be especially comforting for the people of Daniel to know.

Leupold summarizes the teaching of this important passage thus: "The sum of the matter is this: There are powerful forces of evil at work in and through the nations and their rulers to defeat and to overthrow the people of God. This may alarm and cause terror when one considers how powerful these demon potentates are. On the other hand, there are still more powerful agents of good at work who, by harmonious cooperation, will prevail over their wicked opponents. So the cause of the kingdom is in good hands, and its success is assured."

This is one of the great truths of the Bible not often taught in our day and among our people. Yet it sheds light on many a puzzling situation in the course of historical developments and would help God's children to keep a balanced judgment as well as a sure hope in today's mad world.

The *latter days* referred to in verse 14 can be none other than the last days of the O.T. dispensation (from the Persian era to the Roman occupation of Palestine). The certainty of this interpretation is established clearly by the context. In verse 20 of this chapter the angel limits the "latter days" to the era covered by the empires of Persia and Greece. Chapter eleven amplifies that era by predicting in detail the machinations of the Seleucids and Ptolemies. The "latter days" referred to in this chapter, therefore, have nothing to do with the end of all time and the Second Advent of the Lord Jesus Christ. No one is to know that day or hour!

QUIZ

1. Why did the angel touch Daniel?
2. What makes Daniel's attitude exemplary?
3. How does the sending of this angel fit in with the situation in the Persian court at that time?
4. How does his section of scripture give us a revelation of forces behind observable history?
5. Who is this "prince of the kingdom of Persia?"
6. What example do we have of God's will being done in heaven?
7. Should we teach about angels and demons today? Why?

c. ANGELIC ACTIVITY

TEXT: 10:15-21

15 And when he had spoken unto me according to these words, I set my face toward the ground, and was dumb.
16 And, behold, one in the likeness of the sons of men touched my lips: then I opened my mouth, and spake and said unto him that stood before me, O my lord, by reason of the vision my sorrows are turned upon me, and I retain no strength.
17 For how can the servant of this my lord talk with this my lord? For as for me, straightway there remained no strength in me, neither was there breath left in me.
18 Then there touched me again one like the appearance of a man, and he strengthened me.
19 And he said, O man greatly beloved, fear not: peace be unto thee, be strong, yea, be strong. And when he

spake unto me, I was strengthened, and said, Let my lord speak; for thou hast strengthened me.

20 Then said he, knowest thou wherefore I am come unto thee? and now will I return to fight with the prince of Persia: and when I go forth, lo, the prince of Greece shall come .

21 But I will tell thee that which is inscribed in the writing of truth: and there is none that holdeth with me against these, but Michael your prince.

QUERIES

a. Why does Daniel grow weak again?
b. Who is the prince of Greece?
c. What is the "writing of truth?"

PARAPHRASE

All this time I was looking down, being abased in the presence of deity, and unable to speak a word. Then the heavenly being—who looked like a man—touched my lips and I was able to begin speaking again. Then I said to the heavenly being, O my lord, this supernatural visit and your holiness has made me so aware of my unholiness, I haven't even the strength left to stay in your presence. How can such a person as I even dare assume the same level of existence as you? I have no ability in me to even live in your presence, let alone converse with you. Then the same heavenly being touched me again and I felt a superhuman strength in me to sustain me in the presence of this holy one. And the angel said, O man, greatly loved and blessed, do not be afraid, for God's peace is with you. Have the boldness and strength, therefore, which His grace supplies—be strong! And as he was speaking to me, I took courage and said, Then let my lord speak for I am ready now to receive God's awful word. Then the angel said, Do you remember what I told you about my purpose for coming to you? Well, now, I will return to continue my conquest and rule over the demon-angel who influences the king of Persia; and after this I will have to conquer and rule the demon-angel who will be influencing the empire of Greece in order to fulfill God's purpose with the covenant people. But before I go

Daniel and the Ministering Spirit

I will tell you what God has predicted in His history book, the only accurate "writing" of history on record, concerning the last era of history before the coming of the promised Messiah. Do not worry, even though only I and Michael, your prince-angel, are the only two angels protecting the covenant people in the troubled times to come; we shall be sufficient to carry out God's purposes.

COMMENT

v. 15-17 . . . ONE IN THE LIKENESS OF THE SONS OF MEN TOUCHED MY LIPS . . . Daniel was still "dumb-founded." Being in the presence of the divine being, he still found himself in abject abasement, unable to find words in human language to adequately express himself to this glorious one. The angel (undoubtedly the same angel as before) touched his lips (cf. Isa. 6) and enabled him through divine assistance to find boldness to address supernaturalness. It was the unutterable awfulness of the glory of this angelic visitor that intensified Daniel's human limitations. Daniel found there are groanings of the human spirit which have no adequate way of finding expression unless the Divine Spirit helps (cf. Rom. 8:26). This divine appearance took Daniel's breath away! How often we treat the things of glory lightly —we who are so familiar with divine things need to beware for they are not to be taken lightly. If the angels can strike such awe and abasement in sinful man, how much more we ought to be thankful for the gracious blood of Jesus which provides us with bold access to the majestic Throne of God!

v. 18-19 . . . I WAS STRENGTHENED, AND SAID, LET MY LORD SPEAK . . . Daniel, the sinner, realized that there must exist enmity between him and the Holy God and so he was weak with fear. But the angel assured him of God's peace. Daniel's faith appropriated for him the grace of God and thus the message from the throne for Daniel was "peace, be strong, fear not." This knowledge of being approved of and at peace with God brings strength to the weakest sinner. This is the very essence of the message of the New Testament (especially those two great treatises, Romans and Hebrews).

v. 20-21 . . . NOW I WILL RETURN TO FIGHT THE PRINCE
OF PERSIA . . . THE PRINCE OF GREECE . . . The angel's question
is rhetorical, "Do you remember what I told you about my
purpose for coming to you?" The angel expects Daniel to
remember some of what he had been told earlier. Daniel
should remember that the angel had been sent to overcome
the evil-angel who was being allowed to influence the decisions and actions of the rulers of Persia. God's angel
had overcome this evil-spirit and now announces that he is
about to return and continue such overruling. Evidently
God's angelic helper to Persia will not go unchallenged, but
he will have to continue in the spiritual struggle (in the
realm of the unseen spiritual world) just so long as God
deems it necessary to fulfill His work with the covenant
people in preparing them to bring forth the Messiah.

As soon as the one conflict ends with Persia, the angel
will be engaged in the same sort of conflict with another
demon-angel sent from hell to attempt to thwart God's plans
by influencing the rulers of Greece. If God's angel were
not there, demon influence might well meet with success.
So Daniel is apprized of some of the undercover movements
in history and also of the type of checking that God em-
ploys to keep them within proper bounds. One of the interesting revelations of such angelic help for God's people
when God deems necessary is found in II Kings 6:14-19,
where Elisha's servant had his eyes "opened" and was enable to see mountain ". . . full of horses and chariots of
fire round about Elisha." "Fear not; for they that are with
us are more than they that are with them." The same
God is alive today and He can, if He wishes, and will, if
necessary, provide a great host of heavenly beings to minister to those who inherit salvation (cf. Heb. 1:14).

The "writing of truth" is a phrase to inform Daniel that
the history which is about to be revealed (chapter 11) contains events of which God's wisdom alone bears record, and,
as always, infalliably accurate. In other books of prophecy,
future history which God is prepared to unfold before the
eyes of man is represented by a scroll (cf. Ezekiel and
Revelation). And one need only compare Daniel 11 with
profane history to realize that God knows with infinate

accuracy and in minute detail what is to come to pass before it ever passes through the mind of man! (cf. Deut. 32; 34; Rev. 5:1; Psa. 139:16).

QUIZ

1. What would be a good description of Daniel's attitude even after the angel had set him upon his feet?
2. What should be our attitude toward things divine?
3. How was Daniel strengthened?
4. Why did the angel have to be prepared to fight against the "prince of Greece?"
5. Is there a warfare in the unseen realm of the spirit-world?
6. May we expect God to use angels to help Christians today? How?
7. What is the "writing of truth?"

SPECIAL STUDY FOUR

THE MYSTERY AND MINISTRY
OF ANGELS

by Herbert Lockyer

Universal belief in angelic existence became enveloped in a mythological covering, both among Jews and those destitute of Divine Revelation (Col. 2:18). Gradually, the worship of angels prevailed among all people, and became common before the apostolic age, and false teachers, finding this corruption of the true doctrine of angels, adapted it to subserve their ambition, giving it their zealous support. But the prompt reproof John received from the ministering angel testifies to the fact that angel worship was both a mark of folly and a sin (Rev. 22:2-9).

At first men began to worship the sun, moon and stars by whom the clestial hosts were supposed to be inhabited. (cf. Job. 31:26). This was called Zabianism and is believed to have originated among the star-gazers in Chaldea, and brought into Arabia in the days of Job (cf. Deut. 17:2-3).

The Jewish rabbis divided their doctrine of angels thusly:

The Heavens: the residence of seven archangels (neither of the two Biblical archangels are mentioned).

The Heaven of Heavens; divided into 10 departments, each occupied by numerous companies of angels under the command of their respective chiefs.

Another tradition says, "Every man has his angel who speaks for him, and prays for him; as it said, 'O thou that hearest prayer,' Psa. 65:27; that is the prayer of the angel, who is the Marshal or guardian of men."

CREATION OF ANGELS

The angels owe their being to God's creative act, but when this took place belongs to God's secret counsels. As the Sons of God referred to in Job 38:4-7 are generally believed to be angels, they were existing when the foundations of the earth were fastened. (cf. also Psa. 148:2-3; Neh. 9:6).

There are many speculations as to when and how the angels were created, but the creation record was not designed to include a history of celestial beings, but an account of the creation of the earth and man and the scheme of redemption of man. That the angels were created by God and for His glory is undeniable (Heb. 1:1-3).

When created by God, all the angels were good. Some, however, fell from their celestial wisdom and position through the misuse of their liberty. God made nothing evil. The evil spirits were not created demons but became demons when by a free act, they cut themselves off from their Creator.

NATURE OF ANGELS

Angels are spirit-beings. They have no bodies as we understand them, although at times they have assumed human form. As pure spirits, Ps. 104:4; Heb. 1:7, 14, there can be no question of procreation or generation among the angels, of angelic families or relatives. Angels are sexless (Matt. 22:30). Each angel stands apart as a direct creation of God, and complete as an individual. There is a difference of rank among angels, but not of species. All are angels.

The true nature of angels is expressed by the word *Spirit*. It is somewhat hard for us to form any idea of a spirit. We know what it is not, than what it is. (Lk. 24:39).

Being without bodies the angels are *invisible*. Further, being incorporeal and immaterial, they are *immortal*. They have no parts capable of disunion and dissolution. Even the rebellious angels continue and perish not. Psa. 104:4 indicates that they are endowed with wonderful activity, moving with the swiftness of the winds, and operating with the force and energy of flaming fire. Although the angels are invisible through such organs of vision as we possess, it would seem that they will come with Jesus (to bring glory to Him) in a spiritual body (I Cor. 15) which will be recognizable, else how will Jesus be glorified when they come with him.

At His incarnation, our Lord did not take upon Himself the nature—physical constitution or existence—of angels, but the seed of the man Abraham, Heb. 2:16. Had Christ chosen to lay hold of fallen angels, with a view of raising them from their lost estate, He would without doubt have taken upon Himself their nature, and descended into the pit; identifying Himself with their miseries, and paving, by His sufferings, a pathway across the great gulf fixed which intervenes between their lost estate and Paradise. But verily He took not hold of angels, but of the seed of Abraham; and had no alternative, therefore, but to assimilate Himself in all points to the nature of those whom, in infinite mercy and grace, He brothered."

THE ATTRIBUTES OF ANGELS

1. CELESTIAL QUALITIES

As to their nature, angels are Spirits (Heb. 1:7, 14), of windlike velocity, subtle nature, capable of close communion with God, sharers in His truth, purity, love, since they ever behold His face (Matt. 18:10) even as the redeemed shall (I Jn. 3:2); not necessarily incorporeal, (Lk. 20:37; Phil. 3:21; I Cor. 15:44) seemingly but not certainly implying their having bodies. Their glorious appearance (Dan. 10:6) like our Lord's when transfigured and afterwards as the ascended Saviour (Rev. 1:14-16), and their human form (Lk. 24:4) favor the same view.

2. INTELLECTUAL QUALITIES

Angels are the most understanding creatures in heaven or earth and, because of their rationality and knowledge, are likened unto a man, Ezek. 1:5. Angels are the best of philosophers, knowing the principles, causes, effects, life, notions, death, of natural things (Rev. 7:1,12). They are also great statists, knowing the affairs of kingdoms (Dan. 10:13). Gabriel became a courtier, acquainting himself with the affairs of Persia. Angels are never so heavenly minded as to be of no earthly use. The knowledge of angels is limited in that it does not extend to future events (Matt. 24:36) and the mysteries of grace. They desire to look into the wonder of man's redemption and learn of the Church, the manifold wisdom of God (Eph. 3:9-10; I Pet. 1:12; Dan. 10:13).

3. MORAL QUALITIES

The angels as spirits, are superior to men but inferior to God, Psa. 8; 4-5; Heb. 1:7-8. Although spiritual personalities, they cannot create, change, alter the laws of nature, perform miracles of themselves, or search the heart. These prerogatives belong to God and His Word, and the angels act only as He directs.

Along with the highest intelligence, there is the possession of the utmost moral excellence and loveliness of character. Thus the angels are good, gentle, meek, kind and compassionate. Could any creation of the God of love be fashioned without the capacity of love? If the angels can sing and rejoice, then they can love. They exault in victory over the powers of darkness and in the extension of the Redeemer's kingdom and in the salvation of the lost (Lk. 2:14; 15:10).

Dwelling in God, then, the angels dwell in love (I Jn. 4:16). We cannot fully grasp the reach of an angel's mind, or the fervour of one's benevolence and love. They ever hearken to God's voice and obey His will Psa. 103:20. They deem it their chief end to praise and glorify their Creator Psa. 148:2.

4. PHYSICAL QUALITIES

Angels exercise their power in material and spiritual realms (2 Ki. 19:35; 2 Thess. 1:7). They are spoken of as "the sons of the mighty (Psa. 89:6). Their power is superhuman (2 Ki. 6:17; Zech. 12:8; II Pet. 2:11). They "excel in strength," (Ps. 103:20). Angels can "chase," (Ps. 35:5-6) "fight" (Gen. 32:1; 2 Sam. 5:24) "open prison doors" (Acts 5:19—12:7) "liberate the dead" (Matt. 28:2) and "throw great millstones into the sea" (Rev. 18:21) and "shut the mouths of lions" (Dan. 6:22).

THE MISSION OF ANGELS

From first to last, the angels of God are ministering spirits. Worship and ministry are their twofold function—priests in the heavenly temple: messengers on God's errands of love and justice, Isa. 6:1-3; Dan. 7:9, 10; Rev. 5:11. Angelic activity covers all history, ancient and modern, national and personal. THE WORLD IS IN CLOSER TOUCH WITH HEAVENLY FORCES THAN IT DREAMS (and the forces of Hell also, we might add).

As servants of God, Christ and man, the angels have manifold relationship we can summarize in the following way:

1. *Relation of Angels to God*: Brought into being by God, the angels stand ready to do his bidding. His will and theirs are one.

   a. They were created by the wish of God, Neb. 9:6; Col. 1:16
   b. They worship and adore the Triune God, Phil. 2:9-11; Heb. 1:6
   c. They communicate the Will of God, Dan. 8:16, 17; 10:11, etc.
   d. They obey the command of God, Ps. 103:20; Matt. 6:10
   e. They execute the purpose of God in grace and providence, Num. 22:22; Ps. 103:21; Jn. 5:4
   f. They administer the judgments of God, 2 Sam. 24:16; 2 Ki. 19:35; Ps. 35:5-
   g. They celebrate the praise of God, Job. 38:7; Ps. 148:2; Isa. 6:3; Lk. 2:12; Rev. 5:11-12
   h. They minister the law of God, Ps. 68:17; Acts 7:53; Heb. 2:2

2. *Relation of Angels to Christ*: It was personal and intimate.

   a. An angel prophesied the conception and birth of Christ, Lk. 1:26:35 (cf. also Acts 2:29-36)
   b. An angel named the Coming One, Matt. 1:21; the song of redemption is one angels cannot sing, Heb. 2:16. They are happy to surround His throne but will never have the privilege of sitting with Him on His throne, Rev. 3:21; 5:11
   c. Angels announced to the shepherds the birth of Jesus, Lk. 2:8-15
   d. An angel directed Joseph as to the Child's safety, Mat. 1:2-21, 24
   e. Angels ministered to Christ after His temptation, Matt. 4:11; Mk. 1:13
   f. An angel strengthened Christ after His agony in Gethsemane, Lk. 22:43-44
   g. Angels were Witnesses and Heralds of Christ's Resurrection; an angel rolled away the stone, Matt. 28:2-7; they guarded the tomb and witnessed Jn. 20:11-14 (cf. Lk. 24:23)

h. Angels attended Christ at His Ascension, Acts 1:3
i. Angels are to attend Christ at His Second Advent, I Thess. 4:16; II Thess. 1:7-9

Relation of Angels to the Nations

1. Paul speaks of the "world rulers" of the darkness of this world Eph. 2:3; 6:12
2. Christ did not dispute the claim of Satan to the control of the kingdoms of this world (cf. Matt. 12:26) where a kingdom of Satan is taught)
3. In Dan. 10:21; 12:1 we discover that demon-angels have power to connect themselves with different nations. An important angelic personage is Satanic angel (demon) "the prince of the kingdom of Persia," Dan. 10:13. A second demonic personality is mentioned as "the prince of Grecia," Dan. 10:20
4. The devil has angels (Rev. 12:7). They are the instruments of his will. Satan enthroned himself as the unseen ruler of the nations and, at different times in the history of the world, has expressed through rulers his own character in opposition to God's character.
5. Under Satan's leadership Tyre became one of the leading powers of the world and leaders in wickedness (Ezek. 28)
6. Babylon became the seat of Satanic influence. At another critical period in the Church's history Satan's throne was in Pergamos Rev. 2:13
7. Unseen forces are presently active as "the rulers of the darkness of this world."
8. It is distressing to think of these mighty potentates of evil being the invisible rulers of this world . . . Yet how comforting to know that no existing power, seen or unseen, can tear the believer from the love of God

Relation of Angels to the Jewish Nation

1. The law was ordained of angels; Gal. 3:19; Heb. 2:2; Acts 7:53; Ps. 68:17
2. Note:
   An angel commissioned Moses to redeem Israel, Ex. 3:2
   An angel led the nation in the wilderness, Es. 14:19; 23:20-23
   An angel rebuked the nation for its idolatry, Judges 2:1-5

An angel called Gideon to deliver the nation, J. 6:11-40
An angel smote the nation with pestilence, 2 Sam. 24:16-17
An angel smote the nation's foes, 2 Ki. 19:35
An angel encamped round about the nation, Ps. 34:7; 91:11

3. The Sadducees denied angels' existence

Relation of Angels to the Church and believers

1. Angels are present when the church gathers for worship I Cor. 11:10
2. Angels watch over the affairs of the church, I Cor. 4:9; Heb. 12:22; I Tim. 5:21
3. Angels present the Church's worship before God, Rev. 8:3-4, 5; I Pet. 1:12; I Cor. 4:9; I Cor. 6:2-3
4. God does not now speak to men through angels, Gal. 1:8-12; Acts 9:5
5. Angels are employed to Guard and Preserve the saints, Matt. 4:11; Lk. 22:43; Jn. 5:4; Acts 27:21-35; Ps. 91:11; Heb. 1:14; Acts 12:7; 27:23; Acts 5:19
6. Angels care for the young in faith, Matt. 18:10; 18:16; Ps. 34:7; 91:11; Heb. 1:14; Lk. 1:19
7. Angels assist in answering the prayers of saints, Rev. 8:3; 5:8; Dan. 10:12-14
8. Angels afford evidence of God's love and care for saints, Gen. 28:12-13; Jn. 1:51
9. Angels convey to heaven the souls of saints, Lk. 6:22; Mk. 13:27; Heb. 12:22-23
10. Angels minister at the resurrection of saints, I Thess. 4; Matt. 24

SERMON NUMBER TEN

THE MYSTERY AND MINISTRY
OF ANGELS

Text: Daniel 10

INTRODUCTION

I. WHERE DO ANGELS COME FROM?
  A. God created them
   1. When this took place belongs to God's secret counsels.
   2. They were existing when the foundations of the earth were fastened (cf. Job 38:4-7; Psa. 148:2-3; Neh. 9:6).
   3. The scriptures were not designed to include a history of celestial beings, but mainly the scheme of redemption of man: "For surely it is not with angels that he is concerned but with the descendants of Abraham . . ." Heb. 2:16.
   4. When created by God, all the angels were good. Some, however fell from their celestial wisdom and position through the misuse of their liberty. God made nothing evil. The evil spirits were not created demons but became demons when by a free act, they cut themselves off from their Creator.
  B. Universal belief in angelic existence became enveloped in a mythological covering, both among Jews and pagants (Col. 2:18).
   1. The worship of angels prevailed among all people, and became common before the apostolic age.
   2. False teachers exploited this superstition.
   3. Angel worship is both a follow and a sin (Rev. 22:2-9).
   4. Jewish rabbis divided their doctrine of angels thusly:

394

a. The Heavens: residence of 7 archangels (neither of the two biblical archangels are mentioned).

b. The Heaven of Heavens: divided into 10 apartments, each occupied by numerous companies of angels under the command of their respective chiefs.

c. Another tradition says: "Every man has his angel who speaks for him, and prays for him; as it is said, 'O thou that hearest prayer,' (Psa. 65:2; that is the prayer of the angel, who is the Marshal of guardian of men.")

DISCUSSION

I. ANGELIC APPEARANCE, 10:1-9

A. In the form of a man; dressed so gloriously Daniel grew ill with awe.

1. Angels are spirit-beings. They have no bodies as we understand them, although at times they have assumed human form.

2. Angels are sexless (Mt. 22:30), so each angel stands apart as a direct creation of God, and complete as an individual.

3. The true nature of angels is expressed by the word *Spirit*. It is somewhat hard for us to form any idea of a spirit. We know better what it is not, that what it is (Lk. 24:39).

4. Being without bodies, the angels are invisible unless they manifest themselves visibly); being spirits and without corruptible bodies they are immortal. Even the rebellious angels continue and perish not.

5. Psa. 104:4 indicates they are endowed with wonderful activity, moving with the swiftness of the winds, and operating with the force and energy of flaming fire.

6. It seems they will come with Jesus (I Cor. 15) in a spiritual body which will be recognizable . . . they are to glorify Him when they come.

B. Attributes of Angels
1. Celestial qualities
   a. They are spirits (Heb. 1:7, 14) of windlike velocity, subtle nature, capable of close communion with God, sharers in His truth, purity, love, since they every behold His face, Mt. 18:10).
   b. The glorious appearance here to Daniel shows that they reflect the overwhelming glory of God in whose presence they dwell.
2. Intellectual qualities
   a. They are the most understanding creatures in heaven or earth and because of their rationality and knowledge are likened unto a man (Ezek. 1:5).
   b. They are the best of philosophers knowing the principles, causes, effects, life, notions, death, of natural things (Rev. 7:1, 12).
   c. They are also great statesmen, knowing the affairs of kingdoms (Dan. 10:13).
   d. Their knowledge is limited, however, and does not extend to things which God reserves in His secret counsels (Mt. 24:36). They desire to look into the wonder of man's redemption and learn of such things, but they are incapable (Eph. 3:9-10; I Pet. 1:12; Dan. 10:13).
3. Moral qualities
   a. Although spiritual beings, they cannot create, change, alter the laws of nature, perform miracles of themselves, or search the heart of man. These prerogatives belong to God and the angels act only as He directs and empowers them.
   b. They possess the utmost moral excellence and loveliness of character. They are good, gentle, meek, kind and compassionate.
   c. They sing and rejoice over one sinner when he repents . . . they can love; they rejoice over victories of light over darkness.
   d. They ever harken to God's voice and obey His will (Psa. 103:20).

      e. They deem it their chief end to praise and glorify their Creator (Psa. 148:2).

   4. Physical qualities

      a. They exercise their power in material and spiritual realms (2 Ki. 19:35; 2 Thess. 1:7).

      b. They are "sons of the mighty" (Psa. 89:6); their power is super-human (2 Ki. 6:17; Zech. 12:8; II Pet. 2:11).

      c. They excel in strength (Psa. 103:20).

      d. They can chase, fight, open prison doors, liberate the dead, and throw great millstones into the sea, shut the mouths of lions (Psa. 35:5-6; Ge. 32:1; 2 Sam. 5:24; Acts 5:19; 12:7; Mt. 28:2; Dan. 6:22).

C. Is it any wonder then that Daniel fainted flat on his face when such a being appeared to him?

   1. Do we treat the fact that God has spoken to us in these last days in His Son too flippantly (Heb. 1:1ff)?

   2. If an angelic appearance should cause such vexation of soul in sinful man, is it any wonder that Peter cried, "Depart from me, for I am a sinful man!" when Jesus walked on the water?

   3. Since God has appeared in the flesh in Jesus Christ our only proper response is adoration, thankfulness and obedience.

II. ANGELIC ANNOUNCEMENT, 10:10-14

A. "Now I am come to make thee understand what shall befall thy people in the latter days; for the vision is yet for many days." v. 14

   1. Angels are the messengers of God.

   2. They announced the law to Moses; Gal. 3:19; Heb. 2:2; Acts 7:53; Psa. 68:17.

   3. They announced the birth of the Messiah (Lk. 1:26-35; Mt. 1:21; Lk. 2:8-15).

   4. They directed Joseph to Egypt for the Child's safety, Mt. 1:2-21, 24.

   5. They ministered to Christ after His temptation, Mt. 4:11.

6. They ministered to Him after His Gethsemane agony, Mt. 22:43-44.
7. They were witnesses and heralds of Christ's resurrection; an angel rolled away the stone (Mt. 28:2-7; Jn. 20:11-14; Lk. 24:23).
8. They attended His Ascension, Acts 1:3.
9. They will attend and announce His Second Advent, I Thess. 4:16; II Thess. 1:7-9.

B. What the angel has to announce to Daniel follows in chapter 11.
1. In verse 20 the angel limits the "latter days" to the era of history covered by the empires of Persia and Greece.
2. These are the "latter days" of the O.T. dispensation, just preceding the coming of the Messiah.
3. Chapter eleven deals in detail with the life and death struggles between the Seleucids and the Ptolemies (two of Alexander's generals who inherited these two segments of his divided kingdom).
4. And it concerns this great struggle because poor little Palestine, the glorious land and the glorious people through whom the Redeemer the King, the Messiah is to come, is caught up in this life and death struggle, and it will appear as if God has forgotten His promise, and as if evil is soon to overcome good and the Messiah will never come.
5. The angel shows in graphic detail, event by event, how even though evil personified in Antiochus IV appears to have won the battle, eventually God will overthrow evil and fulfill His promise.

C. Angels have been sent often with such messages to comfort and strengthen God's saints in the midst of trials.
1. One is reminded of the time when Elisha's servant thought all was lost but had his eyes opened and was enabled to see the mountain "full of horses and chariots of fire round about Elisha" . . . and hear . . . "Fear not; for they that are with us are more than they that are with them." II Ki. 6:14-19.

III. ANGELIC ACTIVITY, 10:15-21

A. "Knowest thou wherefore I come unto thee? and now will I return to fight with the prince of Persia: and when I go forth, lo, the prince of Greece shall come." v. 20.

1. The angel's question, we believe, is rhetorical, "Do you remember what I told you about my purpose for coming to you?"

   a. That he (the angel) had been sent to overcome the evil-angel who was being allowed to influence the decisions and actions of the rulers of Persia.

   b. The angel says he had overcome this evil-spirit and now announces that he is about to return and continue such work of overruling in order that God's purposes may be carried out.

2. As soon as the one conflict ends with Persia, the angel will be engaged in the same sort of conflict with another demon-angel sent from hell to attempt to thwart God's plans by influencing the rulers of Greece.

B. Angels not only announce, they are active in affairs that go on in the world.

1. Here in Dan. 10 we are afforded a glimpse behind the scenes of world history to the realm of the supernatural where the unseen but very real battle of the ages is transpiring.

   a. In the realm of observable history there is more than meets the eye!

   b. There are powers at work of which some people never have conceived.

   c. The Christian warfare is one of supernatural elements (Eph. 6:10-20 . . . we wrestle not against flesh and blood; II Cor. 10:3-5).

2. These "princes of the kingdoms of Persia . . . and of Greece . . ." are not simply the mortal kings of these empires only. No mortal king could have so successfully opposed an angel of God for a period of 21 days (one angel was able to smite 185,000 Assyrians in one night)

    a. He is a demon-prince straight from Hell sent to gain some influence with sinful, pagan rulers, to attempt the thwarting of God's plan to redeem man!

    b. It appears that in the downward plunge away from truth and righteousness the Gentile nations, even as they chose to worship and seek the fellowship of demons (1 Cor. 10:20ff), came under the powerful influence of Satanic angels.

    c. These demon-spirits became the controlling, deceiving, power of decadent, depraved men, and they used whatever powers they had to hamper God's work. They even deceived those who delighted in being deceived with lying wonders and signs

3. Paul has much to say about "the world rulers" of the darkness of this world (Eph. 2:3; 6:12; Col. 2:15; I Cor. 10, etc.)

4. Christ did not dispute the claim of Satan to the control of the kingdoms of this world (cf. Mt. 12:26—a kingdom of Satan is mentioned).

5. The devil has angels (Rev. 12:7). They are the instruments of his will. Satan enthroned himself as the unseen ruler of the nations and, at different times in the history of the world, has expressed through rulers his own character in opposition to God's character. HE IS A BEAST (ROARING LION) HIS HELPERS ARE BEASTS.

6. Under Satan's leadership Tyre became one of the leading powers of the world and leaders in wickedness (and personified Satan in the ruler of Tyre), Ezek. 28.

7. Babylon became the seat of Satanic influence. At another critical period in the church's history Satan's throne was in Pergamos, Rev. 2:13.

8. Unseen forces are presently active as "the rulers of the darkness of this world."

C. There are spiritual forces at work that are far in excess of what men who disregard divine revelation would suppose.

1. They struggle behind the struggles that are written on the pages of history.
2. They explain the Satanic evil that often comes to light under the things that appear on the surface.
3. Since a particular "prince of the kingdom of Persia" is mentioned, it seems valid to conclude that every godless, cruel, tyrannical nation is dominated by some such prince.
4. Whether each evil angel may have but one nation as his domain, or whether there may be broader spheres of activity in which the more powerful among them are active, we cannot decide on the limited information available in Scripture.
5. Evil angels had held the controlling position at the Persian court. They did not hold it, however, without the consent of the governed. That is, when men become so willing opposed to the truth, when they have no love for the truth, but rather take pleasure in unrighteousness, God will send them a strong delusion that they may believe a lie (cf. Rom. 1:18ff) . . . God gives them up to their own ungodly passions. It must have been the desire of the heart of Cyrus, and perhaps others of his kingdom, to turn from their wickedness and the powerful influences Hell had over them. . . . SO GOD SENT HIS ANGEL MICHAEL TO OVERTHROW THE RULE OF THE EVIL ANGELS AND CYRUS' HEART WAS STIRRED TO LET THE ISRAELITES RETURN TO THEIR PROMISED LAND!
6. It is distressing to think of these mighty potentates of evil being the invisible rulers of this world . . . YET HOW COMFORTING TO KNOW THAT NO EXISTING POWER, SEEN OR UNSEEN, CAN TEAR THE BELIEVER FROM THE LOVE AND POWER OF GOD

CONCLUSION

I. CHRIST CONQUERED THE FORCES OF HELL IN HIS REDEMPTIVE WORK

A. When Christ came He destroyed Satan's power for all who will believe and trust Jesus Christ.

1. Christ bound the strong man by entering his abode and plundering his goods (Mt. 12:29-30).
2. Christ destroyed the power of the devil, the fear of death, by dying and rising from the dead (Heb. 2:14-16).
3. Christ judged the ruler of this world and cast him down (Jn. 12:31; 16:11).
4. Christ took captivity captive (Eph. 4:8).
5. Christ disarmed the principalities and powers and made a public example of them, triumphing over them, (Col. 2:15).
6. Any one born of God is kept by God and the evil one does not touch him, I Jn. 5:18).
7. Although the whole world is in the power of the evil one (I Jn. 5:19), our faith is the victory that overcomes the world (I Jn. 5:4-5), FOR HE WHO IS IN YOU IS GREATER THAN HE WHO IS IN THE WORLD.
8. If the word of God abides in us we will overcome the evil one (I Jn. 2:12-17).
9. I WOULD SAY THIS, ANY MAN WHO REFUSES THE LIGHT OF GOD'S TRUTH . . . WHO REFUSES WHAT HE KNOWS TO BE PURE, TRUE AND RIGHTEOUS, AND EXCHANGES TRUTH FOR LIE, DELIBERATELY, IS DEFINITELY IN DANGER OF HAVING HIS MIND AND SOUL INHABITED, DIRECTED AND EXPLOITED BY A MESSENGER OF HELL.

II. THE SCRIPTURES SHED SOME LIGHT ON ANGELIC FORCES FROM THE THRONE OF GOD SENT TO DO SERVICE FOR THOSE WHO SHALL INHERIT SALVATION
A. Our present text in Daniel is a good starting place.
   1. It is interesting to note the harmonious cooperation between God's angels (Michael and Gabriel) in carrying out His work.
   2. One helps the other where help is needed . . . AN EXAMPLE OF HOW GOD'S WILL IS DONE IN HEAVEN.
   3. And the fact that certain of these angels of God are great and mighty does not cause any rivalry

or opposition among them! WHAT A BLESSING IT WOULD BE IF GOD'S WILL WERE DONE ON EARTH AS IT IS IN HEAVEN!

    4. Leupold summarizes the teaching of this important passage thus: "The sum of the matter is this: There are powerful forces of evil at work in and through the nations and their rulers to defeat and to overthrow the people of God. This may alarm and cause terror when one considers how powerful these demon potentates are. On the other hand, there are still more powerful agents of good at work who, by harmonious cooperation, will prevail over their wicked opponents. So the cause of the kingdom is in good hands, and its success is assured."

B. Angels are present when the church gathers for worship, I Cor. 11:10.

C. Angels watch over the affairs of the church, I Cor. 4:9; Heb. 12:22; I Tim. 5:21.

D. Angels present the church's worship before God, Rev. 8:3-5; I Pet. 1:12; I Cor. 4:9; 6:2-3.

E. God does *not* have any further revelation to make to man through angels, Gal. 1:8-12; Acts 9:5.

F. Angels are employed to guard and preserve the saints, Mt. 4:11; Lk. 22:43; Jn. 5:4; Acts 27:21-35; Psa. 917:11; Heb. 1:14; Acts 12:7; 27:23; 5:19.

G. Angels care for the young in faith, Mt. 18:10; 18:1-6; Psa. 34:7; 91:11; Lk. 1:19.

H. Angels assist in answering the prayers of saints, Rev. 8:3; 5:8; Dan. 10:12-15.

I. Angels afford evidence of God's love and care for saints, Gen. 28-12-13; Jn. 1:51.

J. Angels convey to heaven the souls of saints, Lk. 16:22; Mk. 13:27; Heb. 12:22-23.

K. Angels minister to the resurrection of the saints, I Thess. 4; Mt. 24.

III. FROM FIRST TO LAST THE ANGELS OF GOD ARE MINISTERING SPIRITS.

A. Worship and ministry are their twofold function—

priests in the heavenly temple; messengers on God's errands of love and justice.

B. Angelic activity covers all history, ancient and modern, national and personal.

C. THE WORLD IS IN CLOSER TOUCH WITH HEAVENLY FORCES THAN IT DREAMS (and with Hellish forces, we might add).

THANK GOD FOR ANGELS. DO NOT NEGLECT TO SHOW HOSPITALITY TO STRANGERS, FOR SOME HAVE ENTERTAINED ANGELS UNAWARES, BUT DO NOT WORSHIP THEM . . . WORSHIP CHRIST.

EXAMINATION TEN

REFUTATIONS

(Answer the following by giving the argument which will correct the statement)

1. The "latter days" explained to Daniel in chapter 10 are the latter days before the close of the Christian age. Refute!

2. The angelic appearance to Daniel was so common to him at this point it had little effect upon him. Refute!

ASSOCIATIONS

(Associate the persons or events of column one with the correct person or event of column two)

1	2
Belteshazzar	king of Babylon
Cyrus	demon power in ruler of Greece
Hiddekel	archangel
Nisan	Abed-nego
prince of Persia	Daniel
Michael	demon power in ruler of Persia
prince of Greece	king of Persia
	Tigris river
	first month
	Feast of the Jews

MEMORIZATIONS
(Fill in the blanks:)

Fear not, _____; for from the first day that thou didst set thy heart to _____, and to _____ thyself before thy God, thy words were _____: and I am come for thy words' sake. But the _____ of the kingdom of _____ withstood me one and twenty days; but, lo, _____ one of the chief _____, came to help me: and I remained there with the kings of Persia.

EXPLANATIONS

1. Explain the relationship of chapter 10 to chapters 9, 11 and 12.
2. Explain the struggle between Michael and the "prince of Persia" and the "prince of Greece."
3. Explain the meaning of "the great warfare" in 10:1
4. Explain what implications chapter 10 and the angelic "fighting" has for Christians today.

CHAPTER ELEVEN

V. THE CONTEMPTIBLE ONE— 11:1-45

a. PROGENITORS

(1) PERSIA AND GREECE

TEXT: 11:1-4

1 And as for me, in the first year of Darius the Mede, I stood up to conform and strengthen him.
2 And now I show thee the truth. Behold, there shall stand up yet three kings in Persia; and the fourth shall be far richer than they all; and when he is waxed strong through his riches, he shall stir up all against the realm of Greece.

3 And a mighty king shall stand up, that shall rule with
   great dominion, and do according to his will.
4 And when he shall stand up, his kingdom shall be broken,
   and shall be divided toward the four winds of heaven,
   but not to his posterity, nor according to his dominion
   wherewith he ruled; for his kingdom shall be plucked
   up, even for others besides these.

QUERIES

a. Who are the "three kings of Persia" yet to stand?
b. Who is the "mighty king" to rule with great dominion?
c. What are the "four divisions of his kingdom?

PARAPHRASE

And I, in the first year of Darius the Mede, I stood up
to be a supporter and a stronghold unto Michael. And now
I will show you the truth as to what the future holds for
God's people. Three more Persian kings will reign after the
present one. These three will be succeeded by a fourth, far
richer than the others. Using his wealth for political advantage, he will plan total war against Greece. Then a
mighty king will rise in Greece, a king who will rule a vast
kingdom and accomplish everything he sets out to do. But
at the zenith of his power, his kingdom will fall to pieces
and be divided into four kingdoms, which will be much
weaker than his former powerful one. Not one of these
four kingdoms will be ruled over by this great king's children. His empire will be torn apart and given to those not
of his family.

COMMENT

v. 1 AND AS FOR ME . . . This verse really belongs to
chapter 10 and should be the closing sentence of 10:20. The
angelic speaker is relating how he had previously helped
Michael, the archangel, as Michael had to overcome great
obstacles at the Persian court in the first year of Gubaru
(Darius). See our coments on 10:30 and 10:20.

v. 2 . . . YET THREE KINGS IN PERSIA; AND THE FOURTH
. . . We take this to mean there would be three kings of

Persia to follow Cyrus. And after the three following Cyrus there would be a fourth, richer by far than any of the others. Edward J. Young tabulates the prophecy thus:

1.			Cyrus
2.	1	YET	Cambyses
3.	2	TO	Smerdis
4.	3	STAND	Darius Hystaspis
5.	The 4th		Xerxes

For an excellently detailed account of the history of these Persian monarchs, see *Between The Testaments*, by Charles F. Pfeiffer, pub. by Baker, pages 11-43. Cambyses, son of Cyrus, while returning home from a protracted campaign in Egypt and Ethiopia, died of a wound accidently self-inflicted when mounting his horse. The Persian record of his death suggests suicide. We know that he suffered from epileptic fits. Cyrus had at least two sons, Cambyses and his brother, Bardiya. Cambyses is reported to have murdered Bardiya. Before his death, a revolt in the homeland had been initiated by one Gaumata. The news of this revolt was what precipitated Cambyses' hasty return from Egypt. Gaumata claimed to be Bardiya, the brother of Cambyses, and heir to the throne. After Cambyses died, the army remained loyal to the government which he represented. Two months later the pretender (known as Pseudo-Smerdis) Gaumata was taken prisoner and executed.

Legend states that, after the death of Cambyses, seven Persian nobles, under the leadership of Darius, conspired againt the false Bardiya. They agreed to choose as king the one whose horse neighed first after sunrise. Through the ruse of his groom, the throne was won for Darius. Darius claimed to be the legitimate successor of Cambyses. In the eyes of many of his contemporaries he was a usurper. The Behistun inscription shows the pains which Darius Hystaspis took to prove that he was the scion of the house of Achemenes.

Darius Hystaspis is the emperor who protected the Jews from their Samaritan enemies, who were trying to thwart the rebuilding of the walls of Jerusalem and the temple. Darius found in the royal archives at Ecbatana the decree of Cyrus that the Jews be permitted to re-occupy and rebuild their commonwealth. Darius determined that the decree must be honored. His royal order is found in Ezra 6:7-8.

Darius attempted to conquer the Scythians (originating in the vast plains of western Russia and settling north of the Black Sea, and west and south as far as the Danube) but they only retreated. Their "scorched earth" policy compelled Darius to give up pursuing them. He conquered Asia Minor and its coastal cities of commerce. He conquered large portions of India and Egypt and turned his attention to Greece. When Darius landed at Marathon, he was met by the Athenian army. Before reinforcements could arrive from Sparta, the Athenians met the Persians and won a resounding victory. Seven Persian ships were captured by the Greeks, and the remainder withdrew. Troubles in Egypt demanded the attention of Darius, and he gave up his plans for resuming his operations against Greece.

Shortly after Marathon, Egypt was in open revolt against Darius. The heavily garrisoned troops living off the land, and the heavy tribute and taxes demanded by Darius, proved too much for the Egyptians. The Greeks had probably encouraged revolting in Egypt and other trouble spots in the Persian Empire.

Before the Egyptian revolt was ended, Darius had died. As an organizer of the civil government, he has seldom been equaled. The royal palace which he built at Persepolis was one of the great structures of antiquity. Darius could be cruel. He ruled as an absolute monarch. Organizationally, the Persian Empire reached its peak of efficiency under Darius, but decay had already begun to set in.

Xerxes was the son of Darius by Atossa, a daughter of Cyrus. For twelve years he served under his father as viceroy of Babylon before succeeding to the throne at the death of Darius. The Persian form of the name Xerxes is Khshayarsha, which, in Hebrew, is rendered Ahasuerus (cf. Ezra 4:6 and the Book of Esther). Under Xerxes the Persians were soundly defeated by the Greeks at Salamis, 480 B.C. He lived 14 years after the loss of Greece, but little is known about him in that time. He was murdered by a usurper, Artabanus, who is said to have reigned seven months before being killed by Artaxerxes, the third son and legitimate heir of Xerxes. Xerxes was about 55 years old when he was assassinated. He was reported to be very rich and indulgent and to act habitually like a spoilt child. The Esther episode agrees well with this description. He was given to ostentation and loved display, and appears to have been susceptible to the flattery and intrigue of fawning courtiers.

From this time on the strength of the Persian empire began to wane and it was finally overwhelmed by Alexander the Great (whose history we have recorded in connection with chapters 7 and 8.

v. 3-4   AND A MIGHTY KING SHALL STAND UP . . . HIS KINGDOM SHALL BE BROKEN, AND SHALL BE DIVIDED TOWARD THE FOUR WINDS OF HEAVEN, BUT NOT TO HIS POSTERITY . . . When Alexander died in 323 B.C., he left no heir. A son was posthumously born to Roxana, Alexander's Bactrian wife, but the *diadochoi,* or "successors" of Alexander, seized power before he could reach maturity. One of the *diadochoi,* Cassander, murdered Roxana and her son.

Alexander had had many able generals, but there was not one that arose as his logical successor. By 315 B.C., after seven years of struggle, four outstanding leaders appeared: Antigonus who occupied the country from the Mediterranean to central Asia; Cassander, who ruled Macedonia; Ptolemy Lagi who ruled Egypt and Southern Syria; and Lysimachus, ruler of Thrace. Ptolemy's foremost general was Seleucus who occupied an important role in the subsequent history of Palestine.

In 315 B.C., Ptolemy, Cassander, and Lysimachus formed an alliance to check Antigonus, who aspired in his own right to be a second Alexander. After much fighting within the alliance it came to a head in 301 B.C. when Lysimachus, Seleucus (now almost independent of Ptolemy) and Cassander with their combined forces met and overcome the forces of the empire-conscious Antigonus at Ipsus, in Phrygia. Antigonus died on the battlefield, and his Asiatic empire came to an end. Ptolemy had remained on the sidelines during the fighting at Ipsus. It had been agreed that Syria and Palestine would be assigned to Ptolemy in the event of victory over Antigonus. Since Ptolemy had not taken an active part in the fighting the other three allies decided that the territories of Syria and Palestine should be assigned to Seleucus.

It is nothing short of supernatural and miraculous to observe how the actual history of this period and this part of the world and these people confirms in minute detail the prophecies here made by Daniel some 300 years before it transpired! The minuteness and detail of this eleventh chapter, and its actual fulfillment to the letter is the one factor motivating the destructive critics of the Bible to place the Book of Daniel as late as the 2nd century B.C. For if the Book of Daniel was written near 600-500 B.C. his prediction of these details of history which can only have happened to the Ptolemies and Seleucids is proof-positive of supernatural revelation! The history unfolds in even more detail in the succeeding verses of this eleventh chapter.

QUIZ

1. Where does verse 1 belong in the text?
2. Who is the angelic being "strengthening?"
3. Name the four kings to succeed Cyrus in Persia and tell of their exploits.
4. Who is the "mighty king?"
5. Why was his kingdom not given to his posterity?
6. Who did obtain rule of his kingdom after his death and how?

(2)   PTOLEMIES AND SELEUCIDS, I

TEXT: 11: 5-9

5 And the king of the south shall be strong, and one of his princes; and he shall be strong above him, and have dominion; his dominion shall be a great dominion.

6 And at the end of years they shall join themselves together; and the daughter of the king of the south shall come to the king of the north to make an agreement: but she shall not retain the strength of her arm; neither shall he stand, nor his arm; but she shall be given up, and they that brought her, and he that begat her, and he that strengthened her in those times.

THE KINGS OF THE NORTH AND SOUTH
Daniel 11 and 12

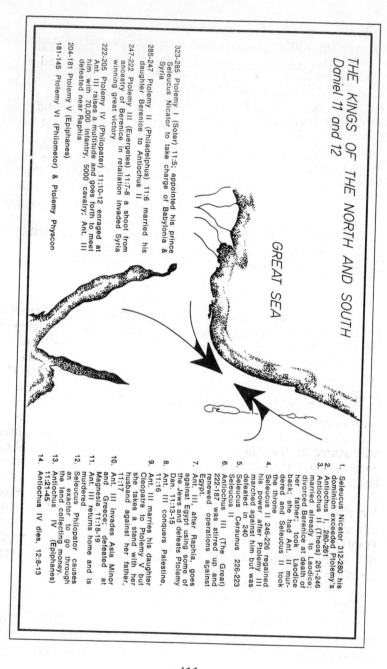

GREAT SEA

323-285 Ptolemy I (Soter) 11:5; appointed his prince Seleucus Nicator to take charge of Babylonia & Syria

285-247 Ptolemy II (Philadelphus), 11:6 married his daughter Berenice to Antiochus II

247-222 Ptolemy III (Euergetes) 11:7-8 a shoot from ancestry of Berenice in retaliation invaded Syria winning great victory

222-205 Ptolemy IV (Philopater) 11:10-12 enraged at Ant. III raises a multitude and goes forth to meet him with 70,000 infantry, 5000 cavalry; Ant. III defeated near Raphia

204-181 Ptolemy V (Epiphanes)

181-145 Ptolemy VI (Philometor) & Ptolemy Physcon

1. Seleucus Nicator 312-280 his dominion exceeded Ptolemy's
2. Antiochus I, 280-261
3. Antiochus II (Theos) 261-246 married already to Laodice; divorced Berenice at death of her father; took Laodice back; she had Ant. II murdered and Seleucus II took the throne
4. Seleucus II 246-226 regained his power after Ptolemy III marched against him but was defeated in 240
5. Seleucus II Ceraunus 226-223
6. Antiochus III (The Great) 222-187 was stirred up and renewed operations against Egypt.
7. Ant. III, after Raphia, goes against Egypt using some of the Jews and defeats Ptolemy Dan. 11:13-15
8. Ant. III conquers Palestine, 11:16
9. Ant. III marries his daughter Cleopatra to Ptolemy V but she takes a stand with her husband against her father, 11:17
10. Ant. III invades Asia Minor and Greece; defeated at Magnesia 11:18-19
11. Ant. III returns home and is murdered
12. Seleucus Philopator causes an exactor to go through the land collecting money.
13. Antiochus IV (Epiphanes) 11:21-45
14. Antiochus IV dies, 12:8-13

411

7　But out of a shoot from her roots shall one stand up in his place, who shall come unto the army, and shall enter into the fortress of the king of the north, and shall deal against them, and shall prevail:

8　and also their gods, with their molten images, and with their goodly vessels of silver and of gold, shall he carry captive into Egypt; and he shall refrain some years from the king of the north.

9　And he shall come into the realm of the king of the south, but he shall return into his own land.

QUERIES

a. Who is the "king of the south" and his "strong prince?"
b. How did the two "join themselves together?"
c. What does the "daughter" have to do with it all?

PARAPHRASE

And the king of Egypt shall be strong, and his favorite general shall be stronger than he is, and shall reign over a larger dominion. And after the expiration of a course of years alliances will be formed between the successors of these two. To carry out the terms of the agreements the daughter of the king of Egypt will go to the king of Syria as his wife. The king of Syria himself shall not last long as a consequence of his promiscuous actions toward his wives. One of the blood relatives of the king of Egypt's daughter will stand in the place of the king of Egypt and he shall come against the army of the king of Syria. He shall even enter the fortified territories of the king of Syria. He will do according to his will and deal with those who murdered his sister. He will rob their temples and carry their gods of silver and gold back to Egypt. He shall refrain some years from attacking the king of Syria. But the king of Syria will march against the king of Egypt but he shall be completely defeated and retreat to his own land.

COMMENT

v. 5 . . . THE KING OF THE SOUTH . . . AND ONE OF HIS PRINCES . . . SHALL BE STRONG ABOVE HIM . . . This prophecy concerns Ptolemy I and Seleucus Nicator (Ptolemy's general). See our comments on verses 3-4 above. When Antigonus was defeated, since Ptolemy sat on the sidelines and let Seleucus do his fighting, the other three generals of Alexander decided Seleucus should be sovereign over Syria-Palestine. As a matter of actual historical fact, the dominion of the Seleucids did greatly exceed that of the Ptolemies. It reached from Phrygia in the west to the Indus river in India on the east. And Daniel had this revealed to him hundreds of years before it took place!

v. 6 AND AT THE END OF YEARS THEY SHALL JOIN THEMSELVES TOGETHER . . . Ptolemy I (Soter, or Lagi) was succeeded by his son Ptolemy II (Philadelphus) in 283 B.C. Seleucus Nicator was murdered in 281 B.C. and succeeded by his son Antiochus I. In 275 B.C. Ptolemy II invaded Syria and was repulsed by the Seleucid forces. Ptolemy's naval power, however, enabled him to prolong the war. Hostilities ceased in 272 or 271 B.C. without a decisive victory for either side. When Antiochus II (Theos) (261-246 B.C.) succeeded his father to the Syrian throne in 261 B.C., war broke out again. The results were indecisive, and peace was concluded in 252 B.C. At this time Berenice, the daughter of Ptolemy II, was married to Antiochus II, for political purposes. But Antiochus was already married to Laodice, who had given him two sons, Seleucus Callinicus and Antiochus. Berenice was brought to Antiochus in great pomp. Two years later Ptolemy II died, and Antiochus divorced Berenice, taking back Laodice, from whom he had been separated. Laodice, fearing lest her husband might again turn to Berenice, had him poisoned and encouraged her son Seleucus to murder both Berenice and her infant, thus obtaining the throne for himself (Seleucus II [Callinicus]). Again, in minute detail, Daniel knows the intrigues of political marriages between two powerful enemies of God's covenant land centures in advance! Only the God who knows the beginning from the end of all history could have dictated this to Daniel—to assume that Daniel could have guessed such detail is foolish.

v. 7 BUT OUT OF A SHOOT FROM HER ROOTS . . . In 246 B.C. Antiochus II was murdered and his son Seleucus II (Callinicus) succeeded him. In 245 B.C., the following year,

Ptolemy II died and was succeeded by Ptolemy III (Euergetes). Ptolemy III (Euergetes) was the brother of Berenice. Thus is fulfilled the prophecy of this verse that "one of the shoots from her roots" (i.e., from her ancestry) will stand in the place of Ptolemy Philadelphus. How could Daniel have guessed this correctly? He might just as well have guessed that a usurper would stand in the place of Ptolemy II—for all Daniel knew. He did not guess! God revealed it to him!

War broke out between the Seleucids and the Ptolemies again when it was learned that Berenice had been murdered, with her infant son, through the intrigue of Laotice, half sister and wife of Antiochus II. The murder of the daughter and grandson of Ptolemy II was an outrage to the honor of the Ptolemies and resulted in the "Laodicean War." After a series of brilliant victories in which northern Syria was completely subjugated, and the murderess Laodice was put to death, Ptolemy III was called back to Egypt to care for a local problem.

v. 9   AND HE SHALL COME INTO THE REALM OF THE KING OF THE SOUTH . . . The "he" undoubtedly refers to the king of the "north" (Seleucus II) who, after two years (about 240 B.C.) succeeded in regaining lost territories as far south as Damascus. He then proceeded to march against Ptolemy and was soundly defeated. Peace was concluded in 240 B.C., and no further attacks were made on Syria during Ptolemy III's reign. He died in 221 B.C. and was succeeded by Ptolemy IV (Philopater), one of the worst of the house of Ptolemy. Seleucus II (Callinicus) was succeeded, in 226, by Seleucus III, who died by poison, and he in turn was succeeded by his younger brother who is known as Antiochus III, the Great.

QUIZ

1. Who is the "king of the south"?
2. Who is the "prince" of the king of the south? and how was his dominion greater than the king's?
3. Who is Berenice? Who is Laodice?
4. Who avenged the murder of Berenice?
5. Who is Euergetes?

6. What happened to Seleucus II when he marched against Euergetes?
7. How long before these events transpired did Daniel predict them?
8. How well do the actual events fit the predictions?

(3) PTOLEMIES AND SELEUCIDS, II

TEXT: 11:10-20

10 And his sons shall war, and shall assemble a multitude of great forces, which shall come on, and overflow, and pass through; and they shall return and war, even to his fortress.

11 And the king of the south shall be moved with anger, and shall come forth and fight with him, even with the king of the north; and he shall set forth a great multitude, and the multitudes shall be given into his hand.

12 And the multitude shall be lifted up, and his heart shall be exalted; and he shall cast down tens of thousands, but he shall not prevail.

13 And the king of the north shall return, and shall set forth a multitude greater than the former; and he shall come on at the end of the times, even of years, with a great army and with much substance.

14 And in those times there shall many stand up against the king of the south: also the children of the violent among thy people shall lift themselves up to establish the vision; but they shall fall.

15 So the king of the north shall come, and cast up a mound, and take a well-fortified city: and the forces of the south shall not stand, neither shall there be any strength to stand.

16 But he that cometh against him shall do according to his own will, and none shall stand before him; and he shall stand in the glorious land, and in his land shall be destruction.

17 And he shall set his face to come with the strength of his whole kingdom, and with him equitable conditions; and he shall perform them: and he shall give him the

415

daughter of women, to corrupt her; but she shall not stand, neither be for him.

18 After this shall he turn his face unto the isles, and shall take many: but a prince shall cause the reproach offered by him to cease; yea, moreover, he shall cause his reproach to turn upon him.

19 Then he shall turn his face toward the fortresses of his own land; but he shall stumble and fall, and shall not be found.

20 Then shall stand up in his place one that shall cause an exactor to pass through the glory of the kingdom; but within few days he shall be destroyed, neither in anger, nor in battle.

QUERIES

a. What does "north" and "south" mean in this context?
b. Who is the "daughter of women" in verse 17?
c. What are the "isles" of verse 18?

PARAPHRASE

The sons of the king of Syria will assemble a mighty army that will overflow across Israel into Egypt, to war against the fortifications of the king of Egypt. Then the king of Egypt, in great anger, will rally against the vast forces of the king of Syria and defeat them. And the multitudes of Syria, having been disposed of, the king of Egypt will be filled with pride. But due to a dissolute life his success will be short lived. The king of Syria, after great successes in the East, will return when some thirteen or fourteen year have elapsed. He will return with a larger army and better equipment than he ever had before. Other nations will join him. Even some Jewish insurgents will join him against Egypt. These violent revolutionaries among the Jews will bring great trouble on their fellow countrymen as a consequence of their playing into the hand of the Syrians. This will confirm the prediction made to you in the vision of the "seventy weeks." The king of Syria, after some bitter fighting against the Egyptians in the land of Palestine, will besiege the Egyptian forces. The king of Syria

will so decisively defeat the Egyptian army it will be forced
to surrender, leaving the whole of Syria in the hands of the
king of Syria. He will march on toward Egypt unopposed;
none will be able to stop him. And he will also march into
Israel, the land of God's Glory, and it shall be entirely in
his hand. This will be his plot for conquering all Egypt: he
will make an agreement or treaty with the king of Egypt
and confirm it by betrothing his daughter to the king of
Egypt. But she will constantly side with her husband
against her father and his stratagem will fail. The king of
Syria will then turn his attention to the islands and coasts
of Asia Minor and Greece. But a great general and noble-
man will defeat and humiliate him. The king of Syria will
return to Syria in abject defeat, his power gone, he will
come to an ignominious end. Another king shall follow him,
one of his sons, who will be forced to send a tax-collector
through the land of Palestine exacting taxes. But within a
short time this king will be destroyed, methodically and in
cold blood, not in a fit of anger or in a battle.

COMMENT

v. 10-11 . . . HIS SONS SHALL WAR . . . THE KING OF
THE SOUTH SHALL BE MOVED WITH ANGER . . . The "sons"
are sons of Seleucus II, Seleucus III (Ceraunus) (226-223
B.C.) who died in battle in Asia Minor, and Antiochus III
(The Great) (223-187), who became king only 18 years
of age. Antiochus III, however, had experience in government, having served as ruler of Babylonia under his older
brother, Seleucus III. Young points out that grammatically
the "they" of vs. 10 should read "he." The prediction therefore, is that one of the two sons will campaign against the
king of the South (Ptolemy IV (Philopator), 221-204 B.C.).
History actually records that Antiochus III, after crushing a
revolt in the eastern part of his empire, attempted an invasion of Palestine in the summer of 221 B.C. He did not
get very far (the Marsysas valley in Lebanon) until he was
forced to withdraw by Theodotus, the commander-in-chief
of the Egyptian forces in Syria. Antiochus invaded Palestine again in 219 B.C. and Theodotus deserted Ptolemy and
joined Antiochus' ranks delivering to his new sovereign the

417

cities of Ptolemais (Acre) and Tyre. There were more skirmishes until Antiochus in the spring of 217 B.C. had conquered all of Palestine and had reached in his conquests the Egyptian frontier town of Raphia. An Egyptian army under the personal command of Ptolemy Philopater met the Syrians south of Raphia. Here the armies of Antiochus met a disastrous defeat. Historians record that Ptolemy went forth to fight with 70,000 infantry, 5,000 cavalry and 73 elephants.

v. 12　. . . HIS HEART SHALL BE EXALTED . . . HE SHALL CAST DOWN TENS OF THOUSANDS . . . The Syrians are reported to have lost 10,000 infantry, 300 cavalry, 5 elephants dead plus 4,000 lost as prisoners. Ptolemy IV, however, was too much of a "playboy" to utilize his success to the fullest. He resumed his life of luxury and dissolutions and died in 203 B.C., without building up or strengthening his imperial fortifications.

v. 13　AND THE KING OF THE NORTH SHALL RETURN . . . AT THE END OF THE TIMES . . . Meanwhile, Antiochus was busy in the East. All during the years Ptolemy IV was "living-it-up" and letting his defenses deteriorate, Antiochus was making plans to annex Palestine. He gathered a vast army and better equipment than before, and launched an attack. Ptolemy Philopator was dead, his son and heir-apparent was only a child of four, and Egypt was rent with turmoil and rebellion. After some bitter battles without much success, Antiochus finally won a decisive victory at the Battle of Panion. The phrase "he shall come on at the end of the times, even of years . . ." does not refer to the Antichrist coming at the end of the world but simply describes the years intervening between Antiochus' defeat by Ptolemy IV and Antiochus' victory at Panion.

v. 14-15　. . . MANY STAND . . . AGAINST THE KING OF THE SOUTH . . . THE VIOLENT AMONG THY PEOPLE . . . THE KING OF THE NORTH SHALL COME . . . AND TAKE A WELL-FORTIFIED CITY . . . Antiochus III made a league with Philip of Macedon and probably had the help of some rebel forces or malcontents in Egypt against their own government. Antiochus also had the support of certain violent and factious Jews whose "aid and comfort to their enemy" eventually brought trouble upon their country. This confirms the prediction of the vision of Daniel in 9:25 about the "troublous times" of this era. After the Battle of Panion, near the sources of the Jordan, Scopas, the Egyptian general, fled to Sidon where Antiochus besieged him by land and sea. In the spring of 198 B.C. Scopas was forced to surrender, leaving the whole of Syria in the hands of Antiochus.

v. 16 . . . AND HE SHALL STAND IN THE GLORIOUS LAND . . . In passing through his newly acquired territories, Antiochus came to Jerusalem where, according to Josephus, the inhabitants gave him a cordial welcome. The "glorious land" refers, of course, to Palestine. The phrase, "in his hand shall be destruction," should be according to Leupold, and the RSV, "all of it shall be in his power." In other words, Antiochus II does not devastate the land of Palestine, but he had complete control of the land and its people. Historians report of Antiochus that "he released Jerusalem from all taxes for three years, and afterwards from one-third of the taxes. He also sent a large sum of money for the service of the Temple and released the elders, priests, scribes and singing men from all taxes for the future." When a king remits taxes and has such control over the influential men of the nation, it is evident that he controls even the minute details of their society.

v. 17 . . . WITH . . . EQUITABLE CONDITIONS . . . HE SHALL GIVE . . . THE DAUGHTER OF WOMEN TO CORRUPT . . . Antiochus plots ("sets his face") to throw all the power and cunning of his whole kingdom at Egypt in order to conquer her. It is nothing short of amazing that God knows not only historical events before they happen but also the schemes of men before they are even thought! Antiochus The Great (III) plots that he will give his daughter to Egypt to corrupt her. History again confirms in absolute perfection the omniscience of God. In a treaty (198 B.C.) with Ptolemy V (Epiphanes), who was then only seven years of age, Antiochus III betrothed his daughter Cleopatra to Ptolemy V. (204-181 B.C.) The marriage, however, was not consummated until five years later. Antiochus hoped by

419

this stratagem to gain in advantage over the king of Egypt by trusting that his daughter would be her father's ally rather than her husband's. But, as history records, Cleopatra constantly sided with her husband over against her father—fulfilling the words, "she shall not stand, neither be for him."

v. 18-19 . . . TURN HIS FACE UNTO THE ISLES . . . BUT A PRINCE . . . SHALL CAUSE HIS REPROACH TO TURN UPON HIM . . . AND SHALL NOT BE FOUND . . . When the Carthaginian, Hannibal, was defeated by the Romans at Zama (202 B.C.), bringing to an end the Punic War, he fled eastward and took refuge in the court of Antiochus III. Interested in stirring up trouble for Rome, Hannibal encouraged Antiochus to invade Greece. Rome thereupon declared war on Antiochus. The Roman forces moved into Greece, where Antiochus had come in his move to conquer Macedonia, defeated Antiochus, and forced him to retreat to Asia Minor. There at Magnesia, between Sardis and Smyrna, the Romans under the brilliant Cornelius Scipio defeated Antiochus (190 B.C.). He had to pay an enormous indemnity (15,000 talents or more), surrender his war elephants and his navy. His younger son, later to rule as Antiochus IV (Epiphanes), was taken to Rome as hostage for the payment of the indemnity. Antiochus marched against the revolted Armenians in 187 B.C. In order to replenish his exhausted treasury, he attempted to plunder a temple and both he and his soldiers were slain by the Elamites. So he died in disgrace and violence. "He that liveth by the sword shall die by the sword."

v. 20 . . . IN HIS PLACE ONE THAT SHALL CAUSE AN EXACTOR TO PASS . . . The next to rule was Selecus IV (Philopator) (187-175 B.C.), son of Antiochus III (The Great) and brother of Antiochus IV (who was away in Rome as a hostage). Rome had so thoroughly defeated Syria that she was now able to demand and get an enormous tribute annually—a thousand talents. Syria was forced to exact heavy taxes from its tributary nations which included Palestine. A special tax collector by the name of Heliodorus (cf. II Macc. 7) was sent to appropriate the rich treasures

of the Temple at Jerusalem. A divine apparition is supposed
to have frustrated him. Montgomery shows that the position of Heliodorus as prime minister has been supported by
archaeological evidence. The text here is historically accurate, for after a short time upon the throne Seleucus IV
was suddenly and mysteriously removed, possibly through
poisoning administered, according to Appian, by Heliodorus.
More of the "troublous times" predicted in 9:25, that is to
come upon the Jews between the time they are released
from captivity and the coming of the "anointed one." But
these troublous times are mild compared with what is to come
under the Contemptible One, Antiochus IV (Epiphanes), who
is next on the scene.

It very nearly overwhelms the finite mind of man to
realize that Daniel is being told by the angel in detail 200
years of history before it happens. And this 200 years of
history is being predicted some 300 years before it *begins* to
happen! Detail such as partitioning of kingdoms, wars,
victories and defeats, treaties, marriages, deaths, taxations—
all before the people are born and the battles fought—all predicted centuries in advance! Make no mistake dear reader,
this, or nothing, is a sign of supernatural revelation! The
Bible is the word of God! And this word reveals that God
not only knows history before it happens, but He is also
active in and directing history to serve His glorious purpose
to "redeem . . . from all iniquity and purify for himself a
people of His own who are zealous for good works." His immediate purpose was to reveal to Daniel, and subsequently
to the Jews, all that they must endure as a purifying process
preparing them for their presentation of the Messiah ("the
anointed one") to the world.

QUIZ

1. Whose "sons" are spoken of in verse 10? What are their
   names?
2. What victory is predicted for the king of the south in vs.
   11?
3. What victory is predicted for the king of the north in vs.
   13?
4. Who are the "children of the violent among thy people?"

5. Which king of the north is prominent in this whole section?
6. What historical event is the fulfillment of the prediction that the king of the north shall "give him the daughter of women?"
7. What was the end of Antiochus III?
8. Who caused the exactor to pass through Israel—who was the exactor—and what did he exact—and why?

b.   PROSPERITY

TEXT: 11:21-28

21 And in his place shall stand up a contemptible person, to whom they had not given the honor of the kingdom: but he shall come in time of security, and shall obtain the kingdom by flatteries.

22 And the overwhemling forces shall be overwhelmed from before him, and shall be broken; yea, also the prince of the covenant.

23 And after the league made with him he shall work deceitfully; for he shall become strong, with a strong people.

24 In time of security shall he come even upon the fattest places of the province; and he shall do that which his fathers have not done, nor his fathers' fathers; he shall scatter among them prey, and spoil, and substance: yea, he shall devise his devices against the stronghold, even for a time.

25 And he shall stir up his power and his courage against the king of the south with a great army; and the king of the south shall war in battle with an exceeding great and mighty army; but he shall not stand; for they shall devise devices against him.

26 Yea, they that eat of his dainties shall destroy him, and his army shall overflow; and many shall fall down slain.

27 And as for both these kings, their hearts shall be to do mischief, and they shall speak lies at one table: but it shall not prosper; for yet the end shall be at the time appointed.

422

28 Then shall he return into his land with great substance;
and his heart shall be against the holy convenant; and
he shall do his pleasure, and return to his own land.

QUERIES

a. Why call the next king of the north "contemptible?"
b. When was the "time of security?"
c. When did both kings "speak lies at one table?"

PARAPHRASE

And in the place of the murdered king of Syria will come
one to the throne who is held in contempt and despised. He
will not be legal heir to the throne but will gain it by stealth
and intrigue in a time when men think all is safe and secure.
And it shall be a time when armies shall surge back and
forth through the land. This despised king of Syria will
finally sweep away all opposition and in these troublous
times also the high priest of the covenant people shall lose
his life. From the very first when he makes alliances his
method will be deceit, and with a mere handful of followers
he will become strong. He will enter the richest areas of
the land when people are unaware and do what none of his
predecessors before him did; he will plunder and extort the
properties of the people and *distribute it lavishly* to buy
influence among men. By such devices he will capture
powerful strongholds throughout his dominion, but this will
last for only a short time. Then this contemptible one will
stir up his courage and raise a great army against Egypt:
and Egypt, too, will raise a mighty army, but to no avail,
for treachery will be used against the king of Egypt. Those
of his own court, who eat at his table, will bring his downfall; his army will desert, and many will be killed. Both
these kings will plot deception against each other while they
pretend to gather around a conference table to talk of peace.
But it will not matter for there is an appointed time, sure
and certain, decreed by the will of God when their end shall
come. The despised Syrian king will return home with great
riches. But his antagonism against the people of God will
move him to malevolently ravage their land as he passes
through on his way home to Syria. When he has satisfied
his brutish rage he will return to his own land.

COMMENT

v. 21 . . . A CONTEMPTIBLE PERSON . . . This is the notorious Antiochus (IV) Epiphanes (175-164 B.C.). Epiphanes means "illustrious one." Antiochus gave himself this name. The Jews called him, "Epimanes" which means "mad-man." The term "contemptible one" probably has reference to his non-royal lineage and illegal usurpation of the Syrian throne. When he assumed rule of Syria there were three aspirants to the throne: Demetrius I (Soter), son of Seleucus IV—sent as a boy to Rome, by his father, to serve as a hostage, he remained there quietly during his father's life and was detained there aslo during the reign of his uncle, Antiochus Epiphanes; a younger brother of Demetrius I, named Antiochus, a baby in Syria; and Antiochus IV (Epiphanes), brother of the late king Seleucus IV. Antiochus IV had also served as a hostage to Rome for fourteen years. He happened to be at Athens when the death of his brother, Seleucus IV, came.

The way Antiochus IV came to rule is indicated by the phrase, "to whom they had not given the honor of the kingdom." The kingdom was not given to him by right of succession; he took it! His manner of taking it was catching people unawares in times when they thought things were safe and secure and by intrigue and deceit. He began by posing as the guardian of the boy-king Antiochus; and later, when the boy-king was murdered by Antronicus, Antiochus promptly put Andronicus to death. By flattery he won over the kings of Pergamus to his cause, and the Syrians gave in peaceably. He was a master of intrigue.

v. 22 . . . THE OVERWHELMING FORCES SHALL BE OVERWHELMED . . . A graphic description of the troublous times (9:25) when armies of the Syrians and Ptolemies shall surge back and forth through the land. This could very well be a generalizing of Antiochus' first campaign against Egypt. He attempted three such expeditions against Egypt. The second campaign (170 B.C.) is probably that indicated in 11:25 and the third (168 B.C.) indicated in 11:30.

In these troublous times also the high priest shall lose his rule predicted by the statement that the "prince of the covenant" shall be broken. In the early days of the reign of

Antiochus IV, Jerusalem was ruled by the High Priest, Onias III, a descendant of Simon the Just, and a strictly orthodox Jew. The Jews who looked favorably (and there were large numbers of them) on Greek culture opposed Onias and espoused the cause of his brother, Jason. By promising larger tribute to Antiochus, Jason succeeded in having himself appointed High Priest and Onias was slain by command of Antiochus in 172 B.C. Jason (who had changed his name from the Hebrew Joshua to the Greek Jason) encouraged the Hellenizing of Palestine. A gymnasium was built in Jerusalem. Jewish lads exercised there in the nude. Greek names were adopted in place of the Jewish names by people and for cities. Hebrew ways and doctrines were looked upon as "behind the times."

In opposition to this paganizing of their culture there arose a resistance movement so zealous it became fanatical. The Hasidim (the "separated ones") swore to follow the ways of their fathers, even welcoming death to do so. This caused consternation in the Syrian court and Antiochus sought a means of solving the unrest in Palestine. The opportunity came for a change in Palestine when a dispute arose between Jason and one of his closest associates. Menelaus, of the tribe of Benjamin, could make no legal claim to the office of high priest, but by offering higher tribute to Antiochus than that being paid by Jason, he was nominated to the office of High Priest. A Syrian garrison was stationed in the citadel in Jerusalem to insure order and respect for the new High Priest. This infuriated the Hasidim, and Jason began plotting ways and means to regain his office.

v. 23 . . . AFTER THE LEAGUE . . . HE SHALL BECOME STRONG . . . Meanwhile, Antiochus was on campaign against Egypt. By many devices of intrigue, flattery and deceit, and with a comparatively small army, he won a significant victory at Pelusium and captured Memphis and generally all of lower and central Egypt. He penetrated into the heart of their country before the Egyptians were fully aware of the fact or had made arrangements to resist. Antiochus cagily made it a point to establish as friendly a relation with a defeated opponent as possible. Even while the battle raged at Pelusium, Antiochus displayed great kindness toward the Egyptians, everywhere interfering to check the slaughter by his soldiers, and thus won the hearts of his foes. He also pretended to espouse the cause of Ptolemy Philometor, his one nephew, against that of Ptolemy Physcon (Euergetes II) his other nephew—pretending that it was only his nephew's interests that he had at heart. The nephews themselves finally saw that their uncle was "practicing deceit," and that he was "becoming strong with but a few people by stealth."

v. 24 . . . HE SHALL DO THAT WHICH HIS FATHERS HAVE NOT DONE . . . Lower Egypt (which is really the northern part of Egypt) was well known for its fertility and richness. These are the provinces Antiochus captured. Another device of the crafty Antiochus was to lavish upon his troops a distribution of the plunder taken in conquest. Not even his forefathers did this. By this squandering he purchased influence and loyalty. But, as usual, such crass mercenary dealings accomplished only superficial loyalties and his advantages were only for a short time.

While Antiochus was busy fighting in Egypt, Jason raised an army in Transjordan and raided Jerusalem. Menelaus beat off the attack, but it became obvious to Antiochus that large segments of Judaism were still opposed to Hellenism and Syrian control in Palestine. On the return of Antiochus from Egypt Menelaus welcomed him in Jerusalem. What was left of the Temple treasure was placed at his disposal. Since Menelaus was unpopular with many of the Jews, he found it all the more expedient to court the favor of Antiochus.

v. 25 . . . HE SHALL STIR UP HIS POWER . . . AGAINST THE KING OF THE SOUTH . . . Antiochus was forced to return to Syria to quell a revolt of the Tarsians and the Mallotes in Cilicia. The prophet Daniel then predicts that Antiochus will raise a great army and go against the king of Egypt again—this is the second campaign. In this expedition Antiochus came as close as he ever came to subduing the empire of the Ptolemies. Although the king of Egypt would also make elaborate plans for defense, he would be defeated by

intrigue and treason on the part of those of his own court.
History confirms in exact detail this prophecy.

v. 26 . . . THEY THAT EAT OF HIS DAINTIES SHALL DE-
STROY HIM . . . Probably means Lennaeus and Eulaeus, the
guardians and state ministers of the young Ptolemy Physcon,
who were betraying him to his enemies. Ptolemy Physcon
and Cleopatra had allied themselves against Ptolemy Philo-
meter, their brother, to defend Physcon's rule of Alexandria.

v. 27 . . . AS FOR BOTH THESE KINGS, THEIR HEARTS
SHALL BE TO DO MISCHIEF, AND THEY SHALL SPEAK LIES AT
ONE TABLE . . . The prediction undoubtedly has reference to
Antiochus and Ptolemy Philometor. Antiochus called a truce
and met Philometor at the conference table. Antiochus "pretended" to be conducting his campaign against Egypt in
order to help Philometor regain total control of Egypt.
Philometor "pretended" to believe him. The decisive victory
of this second Egyptian campaign was the victory of Antiochus over Physcon and Cleopatra in a massive naval action
near Pelusium. Their lying deals with one another to overthrow Physcon did not "prosper." Physcon, to the contrary retained possession of Alexandria and Philometor had
to be content with half the kingdom to rule.

The phrase, "for yet the end shall be at the time appointed," is very significant. Although Antiochus and Philometor would "pretend" an alliance to conquer Egypt, it
failed *because* "in the appointed time" of Almighty God it
was not "yet" time for the end of the wars between Syria
and Egypt, which in turn were bringing such "troublous
times" upon the covenant people. God knows exactly when
and how the troubled times of His covenant people shall be
ended. Their troubles shall come to an end after "sixty-nine
sevens!" (cf. 9:24-27). The "seventieth seven" shall be the
era in which their troubles shall cease, and the "cutting off
of a prince" shall be how it is accomplished. Thus the peace
predicted for the troubled saints was to be the peace found
in the Messiah (Jesus) and in His kingdom (the church).
Physical circumstances were to have no bearing upon the
end of "troublous times" except to mark the point in history
(the end of the Syrian and Egyptian struggles and the end

of the Maccabean era) where the Messiah would be ushered in. The end of the saints troubles will come exactly when God has appointed and predicted through Daniel—in the days of the fourth world empire.

v. 28 THEN SHALL HE RETURN INTO HIS LAND WITH GREAT SUBSTANCE . . . After apparent success (which, as later prediction and history confirm, was only temporary) and laden with the spoils of war, Antiochus returned to his own land to attend to its affairs. A part of that land was the Holy Land, and he had to pass through it in order to get to Syria proper. The phrase, ". . . his heart shall be against the holy covenant; and he shall do his pleasure . . ." it appears, that there was a burning hatred in Antiochus' heart against the Jews. I Maccabees 1:20-28 is a record of his plundering of the Holy Land. The prophecy here made by Daniel was intended to strengthen the Jews in that future time when it would appear as if evil were prospering under Antiochus—they were to understand that it was only temporary and that in the appointed time of God it would come to an end.

QUIZ

1. How did Antiochus IV obtain the throne of Syria?
2. What is the "league" made with him?
3. What did he do that his fathers had not done?
4. Who was the king of the south and how was he destroyed by those who ate of his "dainties?"
5. What time is predicted by "the end shall be at the appointed time?"

c. PERVERSITY

TEXT: 11:29-39

29 At the time appointed he shall return, and come into the south; but it shall not be in the latter time as it was in the former.

30 For ships of Kittim shall come against him; therefore he shall be grieved, and shall return, and have indignation against the holy covenant, and shall do his pleasure:

he shall even return, and have regard unto them that forsake the holy covenant.

31 And forces shall stand on his part, and they shall profane the sanctuary, even the fortress, and shall take away the continued burnt-offering, and they shall set up the abomination that maketh desolate.

32 And such as do wickedly against the covenant shall be pervert by flatteries; but the people that know their God shall be strong, and do exploits.

33 And they that are wise among the people shall instruct many; yet they shall fall by the sword and by flame, captivity and by spoil, many days.

34 Now when they shall fall, they shall be helped with a little help; but many shall join themselves unto them with flatteries.

35 And some of them that are wise shall fall, to refine them, and to purify, and to make them white, even to the time of the end; because it is yet for the time appointed.

36 And the king shall do according to his will; and he shall exalt himself, and magnify himself above every god, and shall speak marvellous things against the God of gods; and he shall prosper till the indignation be accomplished; for that which is determined shall be done.

37 Neither shall he regard the gods of his fathers, nor the desire of women, nor regard any god; for he shall magnify himself above all.

38 But in his place shall he honor the god of fortresses; and a god whom his fathers knew not shall he honor with gold, and silver, and with precious stones and pleasant things.

39 And he shall deal with the strongest fortresses by the help of a foreign god: whosoever acknowledgeth him he will increase with glory; and he shall cause them to rule over many, and shall divide the land for a price.

QUERIES

a. What is the "time appointed?"

b. Who are those who "do wickedly against the covenant?"

c. When and what is the "indignation" that shall be accomplished?

PARAPHRASE

At the time appointed in the providence of Almighty God, the king of Syria will make a third military expedition against the kingdom of Egypt. But he will not have success on this expedition, because a fleet of warships shall come against him from the West. This will cause the king of Syria great vexation and on his return to Syria he will vent his rage on the covenant people and there will be no one in Palestine able to resist him. He will make influential associations with apostate Jews and use them to his advantage while at the ame time he will station a garrison of Syrian troops in the citadel. They will defile the Holy Sanctuary of the Jews by forbidding all the temple services and by erecting an abominable idol inside the temple. And by deceit and flattery the king of Syria will encourage the wicked Jews to commit even more wickedness and apostasy. But those who believe in Jehovah and remain loyal to Him will show themselves to be people of courage accomplishing many valiant deeds in His name. The spiritually wise and understanding leaders of the covenant people will also cause many others of the people to appreciate and understand spiritual things of God. But many of these valiant ones will lose their lives in terrible persecution and slavery which shall continue for a long time. They will have very little help in these terrible times; as a matter of fact, many of those who appear to be of their number will be false loyalists. The terrible suffering of the faithful shall serve to purify God's people and purge them of the ungodly among them. This painful, purifying process will continue to the end of the "troublous times" of the Jewish dispensation, just as God has appointed and predicted it before. During this time the king of Syria will appear to be able to do whatever he wishes to do. He will be so audacious as to elevate himself above every man-made god and will viciously and blatantly blaspheme the God of heaven and he will not be hindered until God's righteous indignation against His covenant-breaking people is fulfilled, for it will be fulfilled even as it was prophesied long before. This egotistical maniac will renounce the gods of his ancestors, the favorite gods of other nations, and will exalt himself above everything, whether divine or human. He will give allegiance to no god but war and to that he will devote great treasures of gold, silver, jewels, and other treasures. The strongest fortresses will call forth his most ardent love for warfare. He will confer honor on those who, like himself, love warfare and elevate such to rule over territories which he shall apportion to them for their loyalties.

COMMENT

v. 29 AT THE TIME APPOINTED HE SHALL RETURN . . . INTO THE SOUTH . . . There is no question among exegetes that from vs. 29 through 35 Daniel is predicting the future of Antiochus IV. At verse 36, however, some would have Daniel begin to predict the "Antichrist" to come supposedly at the end of the Christian age. We shall deal with this problem later.

Daniel means "at the time appointed" within the providential schedule of God. God knows the future of all history and whatever happens God uses to serve His purposes. This third expedition of Antiochus IV against Egypt in the spring of 168 B.C. ultimately served the Divine purpose toward the Jews. Antiochus' efforts against Egypt did not fare as well on this third campaign as before. In fact, he was humiliated. In Egypt the two brothers, Ptolemy Philometor and Ptolemy Physcon, were no longer at odds with one another. Their sister, Cleopatra, had succeeded in persuading them that their interests lay along the same lines, and that any efforts to allow Antiochus to control the situation for them was pure folly. Besides these brothers had sought the support of the Romans. Because of this Antiochus decided to attack.

v. 30 FOR SHIPS OF KITTIM SHALL COME AGAINST HIM; . . . Kittim is Cyprus but to those of Palestine Cyprus (Kittim) referred not only to the island but to all the regions that lay beyond it to the west—therefore Rome. Those who translated the LXX understood this so well that they rendered his verse, "And the Romans will come, etc."

What happened is a famous historical episode that has often been retold. C. Popillius Laenas headed the Roman embassy at the time when it encountered Antiochus, who was beseiging Alexandria. The Roman appraised him of the de-

431

mand of the senate that he quit the land. Antiochus hesitated and sought to gain time. With his staff the Roman drew a circle about the king and curtly told him that his decision must be reached before he stepped outside of the circle, or else he would have to meet the Romans in war. Antiochus, having lived in Rome as a young man for many years, well knew the strength of the Romans and, above all things, wanted to keep them appeased, and so, though thoroughly vexed and agitated, he had to give his word that he would withdraw from Egypt immediately.

The rage he was unable to vent on Egypt is now turned against the people of Palestine. If Egypt was to remain unconquered by him and a rival power, Antiochus found it more necessary than ever to retain his hold on Palestine. He dispatched Appolonius, his general, to occupy the city of Jerusalem. In a Sabbath attack, when he knew that the orthodox Jews would not fight, he slaughtered large numbers of the Jews. The city walls were destroyed, and a new fortress, the Akra, was built on the site of the citadel. Antiochus' forces were assisted by Menelaus and his apostate followers. Antiochus "had regard" unto these that had forsaken the holy covenant.

v. 31   AND FORCES SHALL STAND ON HIS PART . . . The Akra was garrisoned by a large force of Syrian soldiers which was expected to keep the Jews in submission to the policies of Antiochus. One of Israel's darkest periods began. A systematic attempt was made to Hellenize the country by force. An edict demanded the fusion of all the nationalities of the Seleucid empire into one people. Greek deities were to be worshipped by all. An elderly Athenian philosopher was sent to Jerusalem to supervise the enforcement of the order. He identified the God of Israel with Jupiter, and ordered a bearded image of the pagan deity, perhaps in the likeness of Antiochus, set up upon the Temple altar. The Jews spoke of this as "the Abomination of Desolation." Syrian soldiers and their paramours performed licentious heathen rites in the very Temple courts. Swine were sacrificed on the altar. The drunken orgy associated with the worship of Bacchus was made compulsory. Conversely, Jews were forbidden to practice circumcision, Sabbath observance, or the observance of the feasts of the Jewish year, upon penalty of death. Copies of the Hebrew Scriptures were ordered destroyed. All of this can be obtained from the historical record of I Maccabees.

v. 32 . . . BUT THE PEOPLE THAT KNOW THEIR GOD SHALL BE STRONG, AND DO EXPLOITS . . . Those Jews who had followed Menelaus in welcoming the paganization of their religion and society were encouraged by the deceit and flattery of Antiochus' representatives to become even more degenerate and apostate. On the other hand, the pious Jews suffered extreme tortures but they left examples of courage and faith in their wake. The laws of Antiochus promulgating Hellenism and proscribing Judaism were enforced with the utmost cruelty. An aged scribe, Eleazar, was flogged to death because he refused to eat swine's flesh. A mother and her seven children were successively butchered, in the presence of the governor, for refusing to pay homage to an image. Two mothers who had circumcised their new-born sons were driven through the city and cast headlong from the wall. But such loyalty to God's laws in the face of suffering only served to fan the spark of freedom in the hearts of the pious Jews. This spark would later ignite and burn into a flame in the Maccabean family.

v. 33-35 AND THEY THAT ARE WISE AMONG THE PEOPLE . . . It is now revealed to the prophet that in the midst of all the paganizing of the covenant people in the centuries to come there will be a "faithful remnant"—the wise ones. In the book of Maccabees they are called "the godly ones— Hasidim," (cf. I Macc. 2:42). These godly ones will teach others the faithful way of God, but many of them shall suffer much for their faith. It is possible that Hebrews 11:32-40 may have reference to these times.

The "little help" they receive probably refers to Judas Maccabees whose efforts were valiant enough but he was never able to put an end to all the distresses of the people (cf. I Macc. 3:1ff; 4:14ff). Many Jews who did not really believe in the Maccabean cause played the hypocrite and joined it for fear of being classified as an apostate.

The suffering this remnant had to endure for its faith, however, would have a purging, purifying effect. It did not take long to separate the hypocrites from the true "godly ones." And this purging process was to last until "the end, because it is yet for the time appointed." God has appointed the exact time within which these troublous times shall occur. They will end! We believe their end will come with the end of the Syrian domination and the occupation of Palestine by Rome. In other words near the end of the Jewish dispensation and the coming of the Messiah. This would parallel the predictions concerning the 70 weeks of chapter 9 where the beginning and end of the "troublous times" are shown to be, respectively, the restoration under the Persians and the coming of the Messiah. Chapters 10 and 11 are, after all, simply amplifications of chapters 8 and 9.

v. 36 . . . THE KING SHALL DO ACCORDING TO HIS WILL . . . There are numerous speculations as to who "the king" is here: (a) Constantine the Great; (b) Omar ibn El-Khattab; (c) The Roman empire; (d) the little horn of Dan. 7, who is an apostate from Christianity—he establishes his palace in Jerusalem, from which time runs the Great Tribulation, the last 3½ years of Daniel's 70th week (SRB); (e) the Antichrist, a Jew who in the midst of the Jewish people will assume kingly honors, being recognized by the Jewish postate as the Messiah-King, and by the Christian apostates as the Antichrist. In the middle of the 70th week he will come and take his seat in the Jerusalem temple and will claim divine worship (Gaebelein); (f) The pope of Rome and the Papal System; (g) Herod the Great; (h) The Antichrist of the so-called traditional interpretation of the Christian Church.

We believe "the king" is none other than Antiochus Epiphanes. (a) It is contrary to all sound principles of contextual exegesis to suppose that, in a continuous description, with no indication whatever of a change of subject, part should refer to one person, and part to another, and that "the king" of v. 36, should be a different king from the one whose doings are described in vv. 21-35; (b) There would be no purpose served for Daniel to predict for the Jews of the captivity the machinations of some Antichrist whose deeds 2500 years hence would have no relationship whatsoever to their present predicament or their future hope for a Messianic deliverance; (c) "the king" cannot

be the "little horn" of Daniel 7 which grew out of the fourth
world empire (Rome) because this king very evidently
grew out of the "he-goat" (Greece); (d) this king is the
same as the "little horn grown great" out of the "four
notable horns" from the he-goat of Daniel 8. Lange writes,
"The king can be no other than the one hitherto represented, the antitheistic persecutor of Israel, the king of the
north, Antiochus Epiphanes. It is therefore not . . . the N.T.
antichrist . . . all of which interpretations contradict the
context, and arbitrarily interpose a hiatus of centuries
between v. 35 and the closing verses of the chapter."

Antiochus, in his proud imagination, conceived of himself as the only god. He caused to be inscribed the following
words: "Of King Antiochus, God. Manifest, Victory-bearer."
Antiochus "magnified himself above every god" plundering
temples at Jerusalem, Elymais and other places. He commanded that all national religious systems under his power
should be united in one which he himself had decreed. He
blasphemed the name of Jehovah in word and action.

One other scriptural parallel which ties "the king" of
verse 36 to Antiochus IV is the phrase "the indignation."
One need only refer to Daneil 8:19 to see that "the indignation" belongs contextually to the time of the successors of
the he-goat (Greece). Thus, "the king" of v. 36 is none
other than Antiochus IV. The power of the king to "do according to his will" shall continue until the God-determined
end of the period of "indignation," which is the end of the
"troublous times" of 9:25.

v. 37 NEITHER SHALL HE REGARD THE GODS OF HIS
FATHERS . . . Antiochus, who had lived some years at Rome,
had learned to despise the Syrian gods, and to prefer Jupiter
Olympius and Xenias of the Romans and Greeks. But secretly he had contempt for all religion except a religion of
military power as vv. 38-39 show.

"The desire of woman" is a title applied to one of the
pagan goddesses such as the goddess of nature, Astarte,
Artemis and Nanaea. It is expressly reported of Antiochus
that he inflicted a gross indignity on the worship of the
great goddess by attempting to plunder a temple of Artemis
or Aphrodite in Elymais.

435

v. 38-39 . . . IN HIS PLACE SHALL HE HONOR THE GOD OF FORTRESSES . . . It is not so much a particular god whom Antiochus honors as it is his tendency to trust in and worship fortifications and war in general. He will regard no god, but only war; the taking of fortresses he will make his god. To this end he will devote great treasures, gold, silver, jewels and all sorts of treasurers—even people.

All strong fortresses and strategems of war shall receive his adoration and worship. All who worship warfare and fortification will receive his support and he will elevate all such to positions of rule.

Antiochus IV was, without doubt, a mad man (Epimanes). He arrogantly defied every god known and unknown, except military power (Rome). He blatantly blasphemed even Jehovah-God of the Jews. He worshipped war. He attempted paganization of the world. He was crafty, deceitful, and capable of any treachery to serve his own purposes. There were many such haters of God and lovers of self before him. There have been many like him since (Hitler, Lenin, Stalin, etc., just to name a few in our own century). But this section is no more a prophecy of "The Antichrist" than any other such person in the Bible or subsequent history like him is. The apostle John plainly indicates that there is no *one* individual who is "The" antichrist, but there are *many* antichrists. In fact, "Who is the liar but he that denieth that Jesus is the Christ? This is the anticrist, even he that denieth the Father and the Son," and "even now have there arisen many antichrists;" (cf. I Jn. 2:18-23). Antiochus, like the great image, the four beasts, the ram and the he-goat, is simply a personification of the enemy of God, the devil, as chapter 10 indicates when it speaks of supernatural powers at work in these world powers.

QUIZ

1. What were the ships of "Kittim" and how did they stop Antiochus?
2. Which campaign against Egypt is this for Antiochus?
3. What did he do to the Holy Land on his way back to Syria from Egypt?

4. How did the terrible things which came upon the Jews serve to purify them?
5. What evidence is there that verse 36ff is not speaking of The Antichrist?
6. What god did Antiochus revere the most?
7. What relationship does Antiochus have to other ungodly men who have come upon the world since him?

d. PROSTRATION

TEXT: 11:40-45

40 And at the time of the end shall the king of the south contend with him; and the king of the north shall come against him like a whirlwind, with chariots, and with horsemen, and with many ships; and he shall enter into the countries, and shall overflow and pass through.
41 He shall enter also into the glorious land, and many countries shall be overthrown; but these shall be delivered out of his hand: Edom, and Moab, and the chief of the children of Ammon.
42 He shall stretch forth his hand also upon the countries; and the land of Egypt shall not escape.
43 But he shall have power over the treasures of gold and silver, and over all the precious things of Egypt; and the Libyans and the Ethiopians shall be at his steps.
44 But tidings out of the east and out of the north shall trouble him; and he shall go forth with great fury to destroy and utterly to sweep away many.
45 And he shall plant the tents of his palace between the sea and the glorious holy mountain; yet he shall come to his end, and none shall help him.

QUERIES

a. Why did the king of the south "contend" with the king of the north?
b. How was he able to make such extensive advances into Egypt?
c. What were the "tidings" which distrubed him?

PARAPHRASE

Yes, to summarize, the end of the troublous times for God's people will be during the wars between the king of Egypt and the king of Syria. The king of Syria will be the most powerful and he will react with the strength and fury of a whirlwind; his vast army and navy will flood through many lands. He will invade and conquer many lands, including the Holy Land; however, Moab, Edom, and most of Ammon will escape his ravages. On the other hand Egypt and many other lands will be occupied by the king of Syria. In fact, he will capture great amounts of gold and silver and other treasurers of Egypt—the people of Libya and Ethiopia will also be enslaved by him. But all this will not last forever, for alarming news shall come to him from the eastern and nothern reaches of his empire and he will be forced to return. This will make him very angry and as he proceeds toward the trouble in his empire he will destroy as he goes. Even though he may pitch his war-tents between the Holy City and the sea, and appear invincible, yet he will eventually come to his end and there will be no one to help him when his end comes.

COMMENT

v. 40-43 . . . AT THE TIME OF THE END . . . We believe these verses to be a general summarization of the whole war-like career of Antiochus Epiphanes especially against Egypt and Israel. There are no historical records of a fourth Syrian campaign against Egypt with details to fit this context. This, however, does not necessarily mean such a campaign did not actually take place. The careful Bible-believer has learned that the silence of history does not necessarily prove biblical prophecy contradictory. The silence of history only proves the silence of history! When more history is uncovered by the archaeologist's spade, we may find more of biblical prophecy confirmed (cf. our comments on Belshazzar, chapter 5). For present purposes, however, we prefer to regard this section as a recapitulation of the life of The Contemptible One (Antiochus) who is to appear at the end-time of the Jew's "indignation." This is, in our opinion, preferable to "The Antichrist" theory which is unsound contextually and historically. The careful reader will have noted that much of what has already been said of Antiochus Epiphanes fits this summary.

This recapitulation of the overwhelming and devastating decade of Antiochus' reign would also make the prophecy (v. 44-45) of his end more emphatic. It would say, in other words, "Yes, even though this king of the north may do his worst, he too shall pass away."

v. 44-45 . . . TIDINGS . . . SHALL TROUBLE HIM . . . HE SHALL COME TO HIS END . . . Antiochus had his armies in the field in Judea attempting to put down the Maccabean revolt when he received alarming news from Parthia and Armenia. Insurrection was spreading in the east and north of his empire also and so Antiochus was obliged to set out upon expedition to Parthia and Armenia to quell this revolt. He left Lysias behind, as regent and guardian of his young son, Antiochus V, with orders to depopulate Judea. Lysias at once dispatched a large body of troops under the command of Ptolemy, Nicanor, and Gorgias; and with them came merchants to purchase the expected Jewish slaves. At Emmaus, Judas Maccabeaus inflicted so singular a defeat upon Gorgias that the Syrian troops fled out of the country. In 165 B.C. Lysias in person led a still larger army against Judas, but was completely defeated at Bethzur. Judas regained possession of the entire country and on the 25th of Chislev (December) entered the Temple and removed all the signs of paganism which had been installed there. The altar dedicated to Jupiter was taken down and a new altar was erected to the God of Israel. The statue of Zeus-Antiochus was ground to dust. Beginning with the 25th of Chislev they observed an eight-day Feast of Dedication, known as Hanukkah, or the Festival of Lights. In this way they celebrated the end of the three-year period during which the Temple had been desecrated.

Meanwhile Antiochus had been baffled in an attempt to plunder in Elymais the temple of Nanaea. He retired to Babylon, and moved from there to Tabae in Persia, where he became mad and died 164 B.C.

The heroic Maccabean struggle lasted another 29-30 years. Much blood was shed. Eventually an uneasy peace came to the Holy Land in 134 B.C. when Hasmonean dynasty began to rule. For some 60 years, filled with hate, intrigue and murder within the Hasmonean family, the land of the Jews knew no foreign occupancy. Following the death of Alexandra, her sons Aristobulus II and Hyrcanus II were fighting for the right of succession. The news of the choas in Palestine reached Rome. Pompey, the Roman general who had been so successful in bringing Roman power to the East, determined to intervene. Palestine was then occupied by the Romans, the fourth world empire, during whose reign the kingdom of God was to be established by the coming of the "anointed one" (the Messiah).

So Daniel has, in fine detail, painted a panorama of predicted history from the release of the captive Jews from Persia by edict of Cyrus, through troublous times, to the end of the indigantion and the death of Antiochus IV, all in preparation for the coming of the anointed one. His message in all this: God will not desert His people and His holy covenant in any of the storms and changing events of the history of the nations, but He will send deliverance in the precise moment when their need has reached its highest point.

QUIZ

1. Why is it preferable to regard this section as a recapitulation of the career of Antiochus IV?
2. Why does the absence of historical data regarding this section not necessarily invalidate it?
4. What is the overall message of Daniel in this eleventh chapter?

SPECIAL STUDY FIVE

WHY ETERNITY MUST FOLLOW
THE SECOND ADVENT

From March 9 "Christian News"
by Wick Broomall, A.M., Th. M.
Atlanta, Georgia

INTRODUCTION

Perhaps the chief point of difference among students of prophecy is the question regarding the event or events that follow the second coming of Christ. The question in its simplest form is this: Will Christ's return usher in eternity or the millennium? Those who hold to the view that eternity follows the second event are generally called amillennialists; those who teach that the millennium must follow Christ's return are usually referred to as premillennialists or dispensationalists.

The present paper addresses itself to the thesis that the second coming of Christ terminates human history and introduces eternity. If this view is the correct interpretation of the biblical data, then it logically follows that no millennial age as taught by premillennialists will come into existence when Jesus Christ returns. This vital question must be answered in the light of a careful examination of the teachings of Scripture. The objective authority of God's infallible Word must outweigh any contrary view that we may have arrived at or inherited from others.

The author of this paper is so certain that eternity follows the second coming that he feels that this question must now be taken out of the realm of debate and controversy among prophetic students. The reasons presented below will sustain this conclusion.

WHY ETERNITY MUST FOLLOW
THE SECOND ADVENT

The following propositions are not stated in any necessary order or importance. Nor can it be said that they are all equally conclusive. Taken together, they constitute a chain of evidence that amounts to absolute certainty.

I. THE BIBLICAL TEACHING REGARDING "THE LAST DAYS."
This teaching mainly relates to two passages of Scripture: Acts 2:17 and Hebrews 1:1. The following points
will help to clarify these and related passages:

A. The word "last" (eschatos) indicates the last in a
series. The Greek word indicates that which is final
or ultimate whether in degree (Mt. 12:45; 27:64),
space (Acts 1:8; 13:47), or time (Jn. 6:39-40, 44, 54;
11:24; I Pet. 1:5).

B. In Hebrews 1:1 the present gospel age is unmistak-
ably contrasted with the O.T. dispensation. The N.T.
period is called "the last days" (more literally, "upon
the last of these days." Acts 2:17 also equates the
gospel age with "the last days" of Joel's prophecy
(2:28-32). Peter very definitely states that the
phenomenon of Pentecost is "that which hath been
spoken" by Joel.

C. However, some premillennialists, in order to avoid
the implications of the passages cited above, make a
distinction between "the last days" as they relate to
Israel and as they relate to the Church. It is af-
firmed that Joel's prophecy (Acts 2:28-32) really
refers to Israel's millennial blessings, not to the
events of Pentecost (except by way of what is called
a double fulfillment of prophecy). But there is no
justification for this distinction. The N.T. plainly
shows that "the last days" of O.T. prophecy (e.g.,
Isa. 2:2-4; Joel 2:28-32; Mic. 4:1-5) are the "days"
of the present gospel age introduced by Christ.

D. Thus it is logically worthy of our acceptation that
the age begun at Pentecost and climaxed at the second coming is the last period of human history. We
cannot expect another age after the second advent;
the Bible knows of no such age at that time. The
gospel age of grace definitely fulfills the O.T. "last
days."

II. THE BIBLICAL TEACHING REGARDING THE TWO AGES. This
teaching is very important in deciding the question that
is before us. The details will be set forth thus:

442

A. The N.T. speaks of "this age" and "the age to come." This contrast is found in the following passages: Mt. 12:32; Mk. 10:30; Lk. 20:34-37; Eph. 1:21. In some passages "this age" is referred to without any specific contrast to "the age to come" (Lk. 16:8; Rom. 12:2; I Cor. 1:20; 2:6, 8; 3:18; II Cor. 4:4; I Tim. 6:17; II Tim. 4:10; Tit. 2:12). Nevertheless, in all these places the period of time from creation to the second advent is undoubtedly meant; and there is an implied contrast to "the age to come." Sometimes an equivalent expression "in this time" is used to indicate a contrast to "the age to come." (Mk. 10:30; Lk. 18:30). Sometimes "the age to come" is referred to absolutely (Eph. 2:7; Heb. 6:5; cf. Rom. 8:18).

B. That "the age to come" designates eternity (and not the millennium) is proved by the facts that the in-inhabitants of that age are: 1) resurrected ones (Lk. 20:34-36; cf. I Cor. 15:35-58; I Thess. 4:13-18); 2) incapable of marriage (Lk. 20:34-36); 3) beyond the power of death (Lk. 20:36; cf. Jn. 5:24; 11:25-26); 4) recipients of eternal life (Mt. 10:30; Lk. 18:30); 5) beneficiaries of eternal blessings (Eph. 2:7).

C. Two facts are certain: 1) "this age" designates all of human history; 2) "the age to come" represents eternity. The unpardonable sin is described as "an eternal sin" because it cannot be forgiven either in "this age" or in "the age to come" (Mt. 12:31-32; Mk. 3:29). The conclusion from these facts is that there is no place in God's plan for an interval of time called the millennium between "this age" and "the age to come." Therefore, the premillennial view lacks biblical support.

III. THE BIBLICAL TEACHING REGARDING "THE END." This teaching is of paramount importance in arriving at the truth regarding what the Bible teaching is regarding what will follow Christ's return. The following details should be noted:

443

A. The word "end" (telos) is used in the following places to designate the terminal point of human history: Mt. 24:6, 13-14; Mk. 13:7, 13; Lk. 21:9; I Cor. 1:8; 15:24; Heb. 3:6, 14; 6:11; I Pet. 4:7. The word "consummation" (sunteleia) is used eschatologically in the following passages: Mt. 13:39, 40, 49; 24:3; 28:30; Heb. 9:26.

B. Two of the passages cited above are worthy of special note. One of these (Heb. 9:26) definitely states that Christ's first advent was "at the end (consummation) of the ages"—which surely teaches that the gospel age of grace is the final age or period of human history. The other of these passages (I Cor. 15:23-24) certainly teaches that the second coming of Christ is co-terminous with "the end" (telos).

C. The Parable of the Tares (Mt. 13:36-43) teaches conclusively that "the harvest is the end (consummation) of the world (age)" (13:39). All minkind is included in the division made at the time of the harvest. The Parable envisions no other harvest after the one here depicted at the terminal point of human history (cf. Rev. 14:14-20).

D. The conclusion to which we are brought by the foregoing facts is that the return of Christ signalizes the termination of human history. It is inconceivable that there is another "end" (telos) and another "consummation" (sunteleia) after the second advent. Thus the only "end" and the only "consummation" known to the Bible is that which terminates human history at the second coming. Consequently, there is no place in biblical teaching for the view that a millennial age must follow the return of Christ.

IV. THE BIBLICAL TEACHING REGARDING THE FINALITY OF THE PRESENT AGE OF GRACE. There is hardly any truth more evident in the N.T. than that truth that tells all mankind that God is now dealing with humanity in His final display of grace in this present age. The following points will make this truth quite clear:

A. The N.T. age fulfills the prophecies of the O.T. age. This is obvious from the many quotations of the O.T. found in the N.T. Christ fulfilled these prophecies completely. (Lk. 24:25-27, 44-49).

B. The N.T. age is the exact period of time anticipated in the O.T. and for which the O.T. saints hoped (Mt. 13:17; Jn. 8:56; Acts 3:24; 26:22-23; I Pet. 1:9-12). The only age that they anticipated beyond the present age of grace is the same eternal age for which we also wait; the new earth, the New Jerusalem (Heb. 11:10, 16; 12:22; 13:14).

C. The N.T. age is the final opportunity for man to be saved. Now is the day of salvation (II Cor. 6:2). Now is the time when God's longsuffering is extending to men to allow them time to be saved (II Pet. 3:9, 15).

D. The N.T. age is the time of Satan's decisive defeat. Christ announced his defeat parabolically (Mk. 3:27), anticipatively (Lk. 10:18) and dramatically (Jn. 12:31; 16:11). This defeat is stated as a major reason for Christ's incarnation (Heb. 2:14-15; I Jn. 3:8).

E. The N.T. age is the time when Christ is reigning from the throne of David. His kingship upon this throne was announced at His nativity (Lk. 1:32-33). He took his seat upon this throne when He sat down at God's right hand (Acts 2:29-36; Heb. 1:3; 8:1). This mediatorial reign of Christ will be terminated at the second advent. (I Cor. 15:23-28).

F. The N.T. age is the time when the entire body of the saved will be gathered together in one body, the body of Christ, the true Israel of God (Mt. 8:11; Eph. 2:11-22; Heb. 11:39-40; cf. Gal. 6:16).

G. The N.T. age is the time when evil will reach its final climax and when all evil forces will be finally overthrown. These evil forces head up in the Antichrist who shall arise shortly before Christ's second coming and be overthrown by His coming in glory (II Thess. 1:5-10; 2:1-12; Rev. 13:19).

All the facts presented above lead us to the obvious conclusion that there is no need of another period of time after the second advent to complete any of God's plans or purposes. The second coming of Christ will bring to their consummation all the purposes and plans that God has set forth in His Word as objectives to be accomplished in the span of human history. There is no place for a millennium in God's announced program.

V. THE BIBLICAL TEACHING REGARDING THE DESTRUCTION OF THE PRESENT WORLD. The basic passage here is II Peter 3. Other passages where this destruction is alluded to include the following: Mt. 5:18; 24:35; Lk. 21:33; II Thess. 1:7-8; Heb. 1:11-12. II Peter 3 is of fundamental importance in our study of eschatology. This passage of Scripture completely repudiates the view that a millennium must follow the second advent. Let us look at this passage more in detail.

A. Peter answers the claim of the scoffers that the second coming will never take place (vs. 3-4) by pointing to the following realities: 1) God's previous destruction of the world in the time of Noah (vv. 5-7); 2) God's statement of time (v. 8); 3) God's purpose in delaying His judgment (v. 9); 4) God's final and definitive judgment in the destruction of the present world (vv. 10-12); 5) God's purpose to establish a "new earth wherein dwells righteousness" after His destruction of the present world (v. 13).

B. It is quite obvious that Peter is giving us a succinct and simple outline of the things to come in his closing chapter. It is also quite evident that there is no place at all for a millennial age anywhere in this outline. Peter does not mention such an age before the final destruction; and it is certain that "the new earth wherein dwells righteousness" (v. 13), does not refer to the millennial age. In fact, it can be positively asserted that Peter's eschatology absolutely excludes a millennium before or after the destruction of the present world. If there is to be a millennium after the second advent, then Peter's eschatology needs some serious revision, for Peter

446

knew nothing about a millennium after the second advent.

VI. THE BIBLICAL TEACHING REGARDING THE CHRISTIAN'S HOPE. This is an important aspect of the subject that we are dealing with. It is one that needs renewed emphasis. The following points will bring this hope before us more clearly:

A. In II Peter 3:13 we are instructed to "look for new heavens and a new earth wherein dwells righteousness." The verb "look" (prosdokao) is found three times in II Peter 3 (vv. 12, 13, 14). This verb indicates a strong expectation or hope. It is used also of those who were awaiting the arrival of Christ at His nativity and later (Mt. 11:3; Lk. 3:15; 7:19-20). It is also used of those waiting for Christ's second advent (Mt. 24:50; II Pet. 3:12, 13, 14).

B. The anticipation indicated by the word "look" in II Peter 3:13 corresponds to what the patriarchs looked forward to in "the city which hath foundations, whose builder and maker is God" (Heb. 11:10). It is said that these ancient worthies of the faith "desire a better country, that is, a heavenly; wherefore God is not ashamed of them, to be called their God; for he hath prepared for them a city" (Heb. 11:16). No one could possibly maintain that Abraham and his spiritual descendants were expecting God to bless them with an earthly kingdom wherein sin still dwells. God promised them something far better—a heavenly country, the New Jerusalem. And this hope of the patriarchs of the O.T. dispensation is still our hope in the N.T. age of grace (Heb. 12:22-23; 13:14).

C. The anticipation set forth in II Peter 3:13 and in Heb. 11:10, 16 also corresponds to the "earnest expectation" described in Rom. 8:18-25. The verb "wait" (apekdechomai) is used three times in this passage (vv. 19, 23, 25). This verb expresses the waiting of creation and of believers for creation's new birth at the second advent of Christ. The same verb is used to set forth the believer's waiting for his Savior (Phil. 3:20; Heb. 9:28). Thus it can be said that all creation joins in the anticipation of that final deliverance that will come at the second advent of Christ.

D. The passages cited above can be summed up in the statement, expressed negatively, that nowhere in the Bible is the believer urged to look forward to the establishment of a millennial kingdom upon this present earth. The saints of the O.T., as we have seen above, surely did not anticipate such a dream, nor do the N.T. saints differ from them regarding their hope. We look for a "new earth wherein dwells righteousness." And this "new earth" can only be the "heavenly country" which Abraham looked forward to (Heb. 11:10, 16). Put in a positive fashion, our hope is the "abiding city . . . which is to come" (Heb. 13:14).

CONCLUSION

The purpose of our thesis has been satisfied. Sufficient evidence has been presented in this paper to prove two points: 1) that this present age of grace is the final age in God's dealings with the human race; 2) that eternity, not a millennial age, will follow the second advent of Christ.

We must not end this paper without calling attention to the gravity and importance of the truth we have been trying to set forth. There is something more required of us than an intellectual reception of this truth. We must remember that the final destruction of this present world is delayed because God is still seeking the salvation of lost souls (II Pet. 3:9). And the impact of this truth upon our lives should be profound (II Pet. 3:11, 14-18).

CHAPTER TWELVE

VI. EPILOGUE—12:1-13

a. TRIBULATION

TEXT: 12:1-4

1 And at that time shall Michael stand up, the great prince who standeth for the children of thy people; and there shall be a time of trouble, such as never was since there was a nation even to that same time: and at that time thy people shall be delivered, every one that shall be found written in the book.

2 And many of them that sleep in the dust of the earth shall awake, some to everlasting life, and some to shame and everlasting contempt.

3 And they that are wise shall shine as the brightness of the firmament; and they that turn many to righteousness as the stars for ever and ever.

4 But thou, O Daniel, shut up the words, and seal the book, even to the time of the end: many shall run to and fro, and knowledge shall be increased.

QUERIES

a. What is "that time" when Michael shall stand up?
b. What is the "time of trouble, such as never was . . . ?"
c. Why order Daniel to "seal the book?"

PARAPHRASE

But take courage for during those troublous times of which I have just spoken, Michael, the prince guarding over God's people shall interpose on their behalf. Now when the troubles of the faithful shall have reached unprecedented intensity, then shall be the time for God's great deliverance to appear for all who are, in God's book, truly of Israel. And many of them that sleep in the dust of the earth shall awake, some to everlasting life, and some to shame and everlasting contempt. Those who are wise and believe God in these matters and who turn many of their brethren to righteous living will glorify God and shine like the stars forever and

449

ever. As for you, Daniel, your job is about finished, so
complete your prophetic writing and see that its authority
concerning the things of the end of the troublous times is
corroborated, for many shall search it through, and the understanding shall become great.

COMMENT

v. 1   AND AT THAT TIME SHALL MICHAEL STAND UP . . .
Once again it is apparent to the careful exegete that this
is contextually connected to the whole vision which was begun in chaper 10! If the reader would disregard, momen-
tarily, the imposed chapter and verse divisions, and read
chapters 10 through 12 as one unit, he would readily observe
the continuity of purpose. It is also apparent from the
phrase, "the great prince who standeth for the children of
thy people," that the same subject, namely, God's providential protection of His people in a time of exceeding affliction by heavenly warriors, is still under consideration from
chapter 10.

The holocaust of human suffering under Antiochus IV
and its termination is still the primary revelation being
made to Daniel, for in the termination of this convulsion
shall be the sign that the age of the Messiah or the eternal
kingdom of God (ch. 2, etc.) is beginning to rise on the
horizon.

That "there shall be a time of trouble, such as never
was . . ." is no exaggeration! The troubles that came upon
the Hebrew people under the persecutions of Antiochus IV
probably surpassed any that the Hebrew nation, or any
other nation for that matter, had ever experienced. The
Lord Jesus spoke of the Roman tribulation of 70 A.D. in the
same terms, and that later prophecy was no exaggeration,
either!

Further, at this time of the end of their tribulations
which shall signal the time for establishing the predicted
eternal kingdom of God (ch. 2, etc.), all those who were true
Israelites, enrolled in God's "book" would be delivered.
In other words, the predicted "deliverance" of 9:24-27 would
be accomplished. It does not mean, necessarily, that certain pious Jews in the days of Antiochus IV would be saved
from death by the Maccabean heroes. There were many

faithful written in "the book" long before Antiochus's time
(cf. Moses, Ex. 32:32; Heb. 11:4-40), who were *delivered*
by that which was accomplished in fulfillment of Dan. 9:
24-27;! as well as all the millions of christians since the
substitutionary death of Christ who have been delivered by
it.   The death of Christ was efficacious for all men of God
who, by their faith, either looked forward to God's unde-
served grace or look backward toward it (cf. Rom. 3:21-26;
Heb. 9:15).   Even Abraham saw the Messiah's day, by faith,
and rejoiced (cf. John 8:56)!

v. 2 . . . AND MANY OF THEM THAT SLEEP IN THE
DUST OF THE EARTH SHALL AWAKE . . . There are two interpretations of this passage, both of which would be acceptable in our opinion.   (a) It was primarily to refer to
events that would occur in the time of Antiochus—to the
arousing of many to defend their country, as if called from
the dust of the earth, or to their being summoned by Judas
Maccabeus from caves and fastnesses, and to the honor to
which many of them might be raised, and the shame and contempt which would await others.   This primary, figurative
meaning, at the same time, was intended, typically and pro-
phetically, to teach the literal and final resurrection from the
dead.   Perhaps it was the angels intention to bring this final
resurrection into view, even though secondarily, in order to
focus the thoughts of the pious onward, far beyond the
troubles and the triumphs in the days of the Maccabees, to
the time when the dead should arise, and when the retribu-
tions of eternity should occur.   There are a few places in the
O.T. prophets where a "resurrection" is spoken of in figurative terms with a possible double reference (Isa. 25:6-12; 66:
18-24; Hosea 6:2, etc.)   (b) Or, what seems more likely to
us, the angel, passing in rapid succession from the "time of
trouble" in the days of Antiochus (v. 1), to the end of that
time and "deliverance" as predicted of the Messiah in 9:24-27
(v. 1), to the final resurrection of the dead (v. 2), has done
what we call "shortened perspective" (see our comments in
Minor Prophets, College Press, pg. 32). Widely separated
events (often times separated by many centuries) are spoken
of in unseparated succession in the text.   Two successive
verses in the same chapter may be divided by 700 unspoken
centuries (such as between Joel 2:27 and 2:28)!   It is evi-

dent that the O.T. clearly teaches a doctrine of the resurrection of the just and the unjust, literally and bodily! Granted it is veiled and sparse—life and immortality was not brought to light until the Word became flesh and dwelt among us. The reason for unspoken centuries between the days of the prophets and the final consummation is spiritual immaturity. And this is no surprise for the apostles found spiritual immaturity a hindrance to apprehension of the profound things of God even in N.T. times!

We believe, therefore, the angel is referring directly and literally to the final resurrection of the just and the unjust at the consummation of all things—that the angel "skipped over" untold centuries of time between the Messiah's accomplishment of deliverance (Dan. 9:24-27) and His Second Advent. The aim of the angelic revelation is the birth of hope in the hearts of the people of God when they should be undergoing the persecution predicted. There was no need to explain in detail all of history that should transpire between the Christ and the consummation (any more than there is a need for such detail today).

v. 3   AND THEY THAT ARE WISE . . . This reminds one of the closing verses of Hosea (14:4-9, esp, v. 9). The wise, those who fear the Lord (Psa. 111:10), will understand what the angel has revealed to Daniel—that those who remain faithful unto death in the midst of persecution for the sake of God's glory will be "delivered" at the final judgment. They will "shine" with the glory of God which they have inherited. They will be precious jewels in the treasury of God! Their wisdom will also include an urgency in turning others to righteousness in those troublous times as well as turning many succeeding generations of believers to righteousness by their example.

v. 4   . . . SHUT UP THE WORDS, AND SEAL THE BOOK . . . As is evident from our paraphrase of this verse, we believe it does not command Daniel to "hide" the prophecy. The angel has disclosed all that God wishes to be revealed. Daniel is commanded to discontinue writing and to insure that what has been thus far revealed is confirmed or authenticated as a revelation from God. In spite of the fact that nothing more is to be revealed, those of future generations, when these prophecies are being fulfilled or after their fulfillment, much more (knowledge shall be increased) will be understood about their place and their message as it relates to the entire scheme of God's redemptive work on the earth. Lange comments, "many shall search it through, and the understanding shall become great." Barnes comments, "by diffusing information, and by careful inquiry, those of coming ages would obtain much clearer views on these points; or, in other words, that time, and the intercourse of individuals and nations, would clear up the obscurities of prophecy." It may mean that in future times when the apostles and all christians ever after "run to and fro" as missionaries in all the earth preaching the gospel of Christ, the fulfillment of these predictions of Daniel would be understood; or as the prophecies of Daniel were used to confirm the truth of the gospel, more power would be given its proclamation and "knowledge" of the Father and His Son would be increased. One is reminded of the "magi from the East" who came to worship the king of the Jews!

The "time of the end" has been thoroughly discussed in this section. It is the same time "of the end" referred to throughout Daniel 9 through 12—the end of the troublous times and the nearing end of the O.T. dispensation and the nearing establishment of the eternal kingdom of God. It is **not** the end of all time—the Second Advent of Jesus Christ. Daniel did not mean that the prophecies of his book were to be "hidden" all through the Christian dispensation and reserved for fulfillment and understanding in some far distant future millenium (see Rom. 15:4; I Cor. 10:6; Lk. 24: 26-27; 24-44, etc.).

QUIZ

1. Who is Michael and where is he mentioned otherwise in Daniel's book?
2. When shall the people of Daniel "be delivered?" (v. 1)
3. What is the meaning of the prediction about the resurrection in vs. 2 and how does it relate to circumstances in the time of Antiochus IV?
4. Who are the "wise?"
5. How is Daniel to "shut" the book and "seal" it?
6. How is "knowledge to increase" in relation to Daniel's prophecies?

b. TERMINATION

TEXT: 12:5-7

5 Then I, Daniel, looked, and, behold, there stood other two, the one on the brink of the river on this side, and the other on the brink of the river on that side.

6 And one said to the man clothed in linen, who was above the waters of the river, How long shall it be to the end of these wonders?

7 And I heard the man clothed in linen, who was above the waters of the river, when he held up his hand and his left hand unto heaven, and sware by him that liveth for ever that it shall be for a time, times, and a half; and when they have made an end of breaking in pieces the power of the holy people, all these things shall be finished.

QUERIES

a. Why the other two angelic beings?
b. Why did one hold up both hands to heaven and swear?
c. What are the "time, times and a half?"

PARAPHRASE

Then I, Daniel, looked and saw two other angels, besides the one in linen, one on each bank of the Tigris River. And one of them asked the one who was clothed in linen and now hovered above the waters of the river, How long will it be until all these extraordinary terrors end? This great angel then lifted both his hands toward heaven, swearing by Him who lives forever and ever, and declared that they would end in three and one-half years; in other words, when the scattering of a part of the holy people shall have ceased, then all these extraordinary terrors will have come to their end.

COMMENT

v. 5 . . . THERE STOOD TWO . . . Why the appearance of two other angels? Most likely as witnesses of the oath to be taken by the angel dressed in linen and to confirm the

454

very significant announcement about the end of the troublous times this angel was to make. The river is the Tigris.

v. 6 . . . HOW LONG SHALL IT BE TO THE END OF THESE WONDERS? Lange says the angel "hovering" above the river "serves to designate the mighty and swiftly flowing stream of the Tigris . . . as a symbol of the surging world of nations over which the good spirit of the world-power exercises sway as a beneficient and guiding principle of order." The "wonders" are the *extraordinary* sufferings which Antiochus IV was to bring upon the holy people.

v. 7 . . . IT SHALL BE FOR A TIME, TIMES, AND A HALF . . . That the angel swears by the name of the Almighty God is indication of the solemn significance of the announcement about to come.

What must necessarily guide us in the determination of the 3½ times is the question, "How long shall it be to the end of these wonders?" We believe this question, in the present context, can only have reference to the extraordinary terrors of the reign of Antiochus IV—not to some New Testament "Antichrist" removed by at least some 2000 years from those O.T. saints for whom Daniel's revelation was given. We have discussed earlier (Dan. 7:23-25) the meaning of "time, times and half a time." It symbolizes a definite period of time in "round numbers" which God knows exactly but man does not need to know. Further, 3½ being half of 7 (the perfect number), symbolizes a time that shall not be complete or last forever. Now it happens that from the time that Antiochus IV first removed the daily sacrifice from the Temple until Judas Maccabeus purified the Temple it was a little over 3½ years. So the angel dressed in linen has answered the angel who asked that the time of extraordinary terror for the holy people will be, in round numbers, 3½ years.

The angel adds a qualifying, clarifying remark. When the dispersing of the power of the Hebrew people comes to an end—when their being scattered ceases—this will signal the end of the extraordinary terrors of the Contemptible One. It is interesting to observe that when the scattered Jews were finally rallied under the Maccabees (I Macc. 8), the purifying of the Temple takes place and the subsequent

455

death of Antiochus IV is announced (I Macc. 9 and 10). A more exact time to denote the beginning and ending of this extraordinary trouble is declared in the next section.

QUIZ

1. What does the word "wonders" mean in v. 6?
2. How long is "time, times and a half?"
3. Why is it improper to apply these 3½ times to a N.T. "Antichrist?"
4. How does 3½ years coincide with the most terrible times of Antiochus IV?
5. How does the phrase, ". . . an end of breaking in pieces the power of the holy people" clarify the 3½ years?

c. TRIUMPH

TEXT: 12:8-13

8 And I heard, but I understood not: then said I, O my Lord, what shall be the issue of these things?

9 And he said, Go thy way, Daniel; for the words are shut up and sealed till the time of the end.

10 Many shall purify themselves, and make themselves white, and be refined; but the wicked shall do wickedly: and none of the wicked shall understand; but they that are wise shall understand.

11 And from the time that the continual burnt-offering shall be taken away, and the abomination that maketh desolate set up, there shall be a thousand two hundred and ninety days.

12 Blessed is he that waiteth, and cometh to the thousand three hundred and five and thirty days.

13 But go thou thy way till the end be; for thou shalt rest, and shalt stand in thy lot, at the end of the days.

QUERIES

a. What did Daniel "not understand?"
b. When was the "continual burnt-offering" taken away?
c. How would Daniel "stand in his lot?"

PARAPHRASE

I heard what he said but I did not understand when and what it all meant. So I said, Sir, please explain to me in more detail exactly when and how all these things shall finally issue forth! But the angel replies, Daniel, it is now time for you to return to your earthly labors, so go in peace and trust in your God. I have revealed all that God wills shall be revealed and what I have told you will surely come to pass and when they do the words will have the seal of God stamped upon them and be better understood. Those who are wise by faith in God will understand when these predictions begin to come to pass. They will know that God is about to send The Redeemer, The anointed One, and they will prepare for Him by purifying and sanctifying themselves. But none of the impenitent apostates shall understand. They will continue on in the paganism they have adopted from the Contemptible One. But know this Daniel, these terrible times will be coming to an end 1290 days after the desecration of the Temple by the Contemptible One—1290 days after he stops the holy people from offering the continual burnt-offering and sets up in their Temple the pagan altar. The man who, during this era, endures it through faith in God will receive further blessed assurance after 1335 days, or after 45 days additional to the 1290, that the terrible times of the Contemptible One are ended. As for you, Daniel, you have a job to do so be at it diligently and do not let what has been revealed to you cause you to lose faith. Be faithful in your appointed labor for the Lord until the end of your life and you shall find the eternal rest and receive your portion of the inheritance which is what will be accomplished for you by the Anointed One at the end of these terrible days predicted.

COMMENT

v. 8 . . . I UNDERSTOOD NOT . . . Daniel stood almost 400 years removed from the events being predicted to him. The temple had not even yet been rebuilt—the Jews were still in Persian captivity—how difficult it would be for him to contemplate the things he heard from these angels!

History Is God's Word in the Hand of Time

How extremely anxious he would be to know every detail of time and manner about the things revealed to him! A vast amount of symbolism and facts had already taxed his powers of comprehension—his head must have been swimming with facts and dazed with the struggle to understand.

v. 9 . . . GO THY WAY . . . THE WORDS ARE . . . SEALED TILL THE TIME OF THE END . . . Perhaps Daniel even entertained some fears that he might have to very soon experience the terrible times just predicted to him by the angel. This verse and vs. 13 seems to indicate this. But the answer to Daniel's perplexity is, Go on in the job you now have to do in Persia—these terrible times are reserved or sealed for the future at the end of the time of preparation for the eternal kingdom of God. It should not be strange to a believing, discerning Jew that the Mosiac administration of the covenant would come to an end—the O.T. itself predicted its own fulfillment (cf. Jer. 31:31ff, etc.).

v. 10 MANY SHALL PURIFY THEMSELVES . . . THEY THAT ARE WISE SHALL UNDERSTAND . . . This is similar to verse 3. The god-fearing Jews will, by faith, wisely endure and profit spiritually by the terrible experiences to come upon them during the days of the Contemptible one. They will, because they believe that Daniel's record of this angelic revelation is the will and word of God, understand that God's redemption in the Anointed One is drawing nigh. They will therefore sanctify and purify themselves and teach others to do so. They will pass it on to their children and their grandchildren (two generations removed from the Maccabeans would make one an adult at the birth of Jesus) their grandchildren would be anticipating eagerly some stupendous Messianic era to commence (cf. Simeon, righteous and devout, looking for the "consolation of Israel" in Luke 2:25-35; Anna, of great age, who gave thanks for the baby Jesus and spoke of him to all who were looking for the "redemption" of Jerusalem; and other such references). Now the wicked, apostate Jews who eagerly adopted the life of the pagan Hellenists, both in the Maccabean era and that of Jesus (the Herods, etc.), would not understand that the terrible times of Antiochus IV were preparatory to ushering in the Messianic age. They would go on in their wickedness hoping for a carnal Messiah who would nationalize and free them from foreign control in order to indulge them in paganism. Or perhaps they would not even want or look for a Messiah, content with the pagan sensuality they had learned from Antiochus.

v. 11 . . . FROM THE TIME . . . SHALL BE A THOUSAND TWO HUNDRED AND NINETY DAYS . . . How is it possible for the "continual burnt-offering" to be taken away in the Christian dispensation? The only possibility that this prediction is future to the time of Antiochus IV is that it refers to some "millenial" age when a Jewish system of sacrifices has been reinstituted. In our opinion, such an assumption violates the plain teaching of the N.T. Book of Hebrews. Therefore, we must suppose that the *terminus a quo*, "from the time that continual burnt-offering shall be taken away, and the abomination that maketh desolate set up," is the time in (end of May or beginning of June) 168 B.C. when Antiochus IV forced the cessation of Temple services and commanded Appolonius to erect an altar to Jupiter in the Temple. From this time until Judas Maccabeus removed this abomination and purified the temple, December 25th, 165 B.C., the time is 1290 days. We quote Stuart here: "The 1290 days are more specific than the phrase 'time, times and a half,' in ver. 7, and also in 7:25. The latter ('time,' etc.) is, as it were, a round number, three and a half first equalling the one half of the sacred number seven, and the fractional part equalling the half of one year. In such a case minute exactness of course is not to be expected. But the thirty additional days here (over 1260 days = forty-two months = three and a half years) are doubtless designed as an exact account of time during which the detestable (desolating) abomination continued in the temple. The *terminus a quo* is the time when Antiochus first removed the daily sacrifice, which probably was near the end of May or at the beginning of June in B.C. 168. Judas Maccabeus removed this . . . and purified the temple, Dec. 25th of B.C. 165, making the time in question, i.e., three and a half years, as nearly as history will enable us to compute it. There can hardly be room for doubt that the statement in our text is minutely correct. The work of Judas here is the *terminus ad quem* of the period in question." In other words, the abomination of desolation is to last, first, in round numbers "time, times and a half," or $3\frac{1}{2}$ years (equal to 1260 days or 42 months). Add to this 30 more days, in order to be more exact, and you have 1290 days, the exact time between the time when Antiochus IV desecrated the Temple and Judas Maccabeus purified it.

v. 12 . . . COMETH TO THE THOUSAND THREE HUNDRED AND FIVE AND THIRTY DAYS . . . Now, add to the 1290 days 45 more days, and one has 1335 days, the time from the abomination that maketh desolate until the time of Antiochus' death! Lange writes, ". . . the meaning (of this verse) . . . can only be as follows: 'After 1290 days have expired, the tribulation shall end; it shall not be completely ended, however, until forty-five additional days . . . have elapsed, hence, until a total of 1335 days has been reached."

In I Maccabees 2:26-37 we have an account of the situation of Antiochus while in the glorious land. His treasury was empty. He had already robbed the Temple of everything valuable in it so he was forced to look to some other source for booty. He left half of his army with Lysias, one of his favorite officers, and marched over the Euphrates in order to plunder the countries of the East. First he subdued Armenia, and then turned off to rob the temple at Elymais, where he met with disgrace, and eventually death.

Not long after the departure of Antiochus, Lysias began the contest in Palestine in serious earnest; but Judas Maccabeus came off victorious in every encounter and so decisive was one such victory, Judas proceeded to purify the Temple and restore its worship. This took place December 25th, 165 B.C. as already noted. The Feast of Dedication of the Jews commemorates this. This would have occupied some months. Of course Antiochus had had sufficient time for his conquest in Armenia and his advance to Elymais before the winter had far advanced. It was in early spring that he undertook the robbery of the temple in Elymais. After disgrace here and during his retreat from Elymais, news came to him of total defeat in Palestine . This contributed emotionally and physically to the sickness already decimating him. In I Mac. 6:1ff we have an account of the close of the life of Antiochus and of his disgrace at Elymais. If we now count onward, from the consecration of the Temple by Judas to the time when Antiochus died, we shall see at once that the period of 1335 days is in all probability the period of Antiochus' death. From the time that the daily burnt-offering was removed by Apollonius, at the command of Antiochus, to the time of the reconsecration, is 1290 days. From the same *terminus a quo* to the death of Antiochus is 1335 days, i.e., 45 days more than is included in the 1290 days of vs. 11. History has not anywhere recorded the precise day of Antiochus' death, so we cannot compare the passage before us with that. But we are certain as to the order of events, and as to the season of the year, as well as the year itself, in which the death of Antiochus took place. Of the general accuracy there can be no doubt.

Abomination of desolation set up	First of June, 168 B.C.
Purification of Temple by Judas	December 25th, 165 B.C.
Time expired:	Three and one-half years plus one month, or, 1260 days plus 30 = 1290 days
Death of Antiochus IV	Early spring, 164 B.C. 1335 days after abomination of desolation set up, or 45 days after the 1290 days

We believe this interpretation of the meaning of the time periods in this section is historically and contextually sound. In our opinion it does not present the serious hermeneutical and practical irregularities that other interpretations involve. It seems very clear to us that Daniel's primary mission in recording this angelic revelation was to comfort and strengthen those people of God contemporary with Daniel enduring the captivity and those Jews of succeeding generations as they endured such terrible times as

to make it appear the covenant people were about to be ex-
terminated. It might appear to those of Antiochus' day that
God's purpose to bring redemption and the fulfillment of the
covenant made with Abraham would fail. They would need
to know *that* the terrible days would end and to know very
nearly *when* they would end! Now what consolation would
it be to those enduring the terrors of Antiochus to have a
prediction of the eventual overthrow of some unknown
"Antichrist" in some unknown age many centuries future to
them? This, then, is why Daniel is told that those Jews
who wait with endurance and faith will be "blessed" — because they will see definite proof that Divine providence
is fulfilling its promises to bring an end to the great
persecutions.

v. 13   BUT GO THOU THY WAY TILL THE END BE . . . The
idea is that Daniel should not let all these awesome predictions paralyze him with fear and anxiety. He is to go
on in his labors for the Lord until his labors shall end.
Even he shall some day realize the fulfillment of what he
has predicted and has heard here from the angel. He will
receive the redemption accomplished by the Anointed One
(9:24-27) which will be accomplished after the "end" of the
terrible things the angel predicted (10:1—12:12). Daniel
will be raised from the dust of the earth with all the other
children of God to receive their inheritance.

QUIZ

1. What did the angel mean when he commanded Daniel,
   "Go thy way?"
2. How were the words "shut up and sealed until the time
   of the end?"
3. How does the predicted purification of many relate to
   the "time of the end?"
4. What are the 1290 days—when do they begin and when
   do they end?
5. What are the 1335 days—when begin and when end?
6. Why are they blessed who wait for the 1335 days?
7. What practical value does all this have for Daniel's
   future?

SERMON NUMBER ELEVEN
DEITY OR DEMON?

Text: Daniel 11-12

INTRODUCTION

I. MAN MAKING HIS OWN GODS

A. Montaigne once said, "Man is certainly stark mad; he cannot make a flea, and yet he will be making gods by dozens."

B. Men will accept anything or anybody for a god— all the way from a piece of wood to a man—rather than surrender to dependence upon the One True God (cf. Rom. 1:18ff.).

C. Man must have a god! If he will not allow his Creator to have sovereignty over him, then man will stupidly enslave himself to a god of his own making.

D. And when man does, he degrades himself and depraves himself, ". . . they came to Baal-peor, and consecrated themselves to Baal, and became detestable like the things they loved." (Hosea 9:10; cf. also Psa. 115).

II. MAN CLAIMING TO BE GOD

A. Equally as tragic and portending consequences even more terrifying are moments in history when men have declared themselves gods.

B. History is replete with monstrous men and movements such as this.

C. The ages of enlightenment and science were supposed to usher in a Utopia where peace and harmony and understanding would prevail and governments would be paternalistic and benevolent. J. Wallace Hamilton wrote, "Nobody is talking now about automatic progress, about every day in every way, getting better and better. Who is saying that now? Nobody! What if the sons of evil come? What if animal men, brain men and brawn men with no God in their hearts, with all humanity bleached out, should hold these powerful forces (atomic power, etc.) in their hands? We have had some glimpses of that. We saw it in the Nazis, in their scientific savagery; they were monster men with powerful forces—Dachau, Buchenwald. It sickened us; it frightened us. . . . What if the sons of evil come? We cannot shrug this off or talk glibly about being emancipated from divine authority or from the old ethical rules by which civilization has emerged from the darkness. The problem of man is still that downward bent in his heart, by whatever name you want to call it."

III. DEITY OR DEMON?

A. Indeed we have seen glimpses of "the sons of evil" come upon our world; men claiming to be gods, but acting like demons.

B. Here in Daniel 11 and 12 we have a brief history of such a "contemptible one," Antoichus IV (Epiphanes)

C. There are many infamous demagogues in history whose histories parallel that of Antiochus; one such is Adolph Hitler.

D. We do not believe Antiochus IV is prophetic or typical of any ONE such demagogue (such as "The Antichrist" so-called—since *many* antichrists are predicted).

E. He is just one, in a long line, of many "beasts" who shall oppose all that The Holy God and His Kingdom shall stand for until the final overthrow of the Dragon and the Beasts and The Harlot.

DISCUSSION

I. ENVIROMENT, 11:1-20

A. Ancestry

1. The ancestry of Antiochus IV was a history of despots devoted to ruthless exploitation of friends and foreigners to serve their own lusts for power.

465

      a. Seleucus Nicator progenitor of the Seleucid dynasty, Antiochus' ancestor, betrayed his king (Ptolemy I), and usurped his rule over Syria.

      b. Another of his ancestors, Antiochus II, committed bigamy and adultery, marrying two wives, for political purposes.

      c. Seleucus II murdered women and children to obtain the throne.

      d. Antiochus III called himself Theos (God).

      e. Robbery, murder, adultery, deceit all were the way of life for the Seleucids, ancestors of Antiochus IV.

  2. The ancestry of Adolf Hitler, as much as we know, is fraught with pseudo-despots.

      a. Alois, father of Adolf, was the illegitimate son of Maria Anna Schickelgruber, who married three times.

      b. Adolf's mother was a bride of Alois, 23 years younger than her husband, former maid in his first wife's home.

      c. Adolf's father put on all the airs of a petty customs official, bitterly opposed Adolf's ambition to become an artist. Adolf came to hate his father.

      d. Encyclopedia Britannica (from which this information on Hitler is excerpted) says: "It may indeed be doubted whether at any time in his life he ever truly loved, or was loved by, any normal man or woman."

B. Training

  1. Antiochus IV spent most of his youth as a hostage in Rome's royal courts.

      a. There he learned the Roman ways of pragmatism to serve the ends of the empire.

      b. He learned to worship power.

      c. He learned to practice deceit.

      d. He learned rutslessness.

  2. Adolf Hitler was an orphan at 15 years of age.

      a. He went to Vienna where his mind was saturated with the humanism and hatemognering of a generation of youthful malcontents and rabble-rousers.

b. He became a failure, academically, artistically and economically; he couldn't get in school or get a job of any value.

c. He began a reaction mechanism of hate for trade unions, socialists, and Jews.

d. He wrote in Mein Kampf, "Gradually I began to hate them (Jews). I was transformed from a weakly world-citizen into a fanatic anti-Semite."

e. He joined the army and at the coming of WW I he fell on his knees and thanked Providence that he was privileged to live in "heroic" times and to participate in "noble" deeds of pan-Germanic, Wagnerian splendor.

3. His mind was poisoned by the evil-producing theory of evolution.

a. A few quotations from him will show what effect evolution had upon his thinking.

b. "Thus there results the subjection of a number of people under the will, often of only a few persons, a subjection based simply upon the right of the stronger, a right which, as we see it in Nature, can be regarded as the sole conceivable right, because it is founded on reason." at a speech at Nuremberg in 1933.

c. His hatred of the Jews was rationalized by using evolution. The Germans were the higher race, destined for a glorious evolutionary future. For this reason it was essential that the Jews should be segregated, otherwise mixed marriages would take place. Were this to happen, all nature's efforts "to establish an evolutionary higher stage of being may thus be rendered futile" (Mein Kampf).

d. ". . . the whole world of Nature is a mighty struggle between strength and weakness—an eternal victory of the strong over the weak . . ." speech at Munich, 1923.

e. "He who would live must fight. He who does not wish to fight in this world where permanent struggle is the law of life, has not the right to exist. To thing otherwise is to insult nature. Distress, misery and disease are her rejoinders" (Mein Kampf).

C. As the twig is bent, so grows the tree! DIETY OR DEMON.

1. Ancestors or parents are not totally responsible for the demonical behavior of their offspring, but their influence goes a long way in determining whether they will partake of the nature of the Divine or the nature of the devil.

   a. "Children obey your parents in the Lord, for this is right. Honor your father and mother (this is the first commandment with promise), that it may be well with you and that you may live long on the earth. Fathers, do not provoke your children to anger, but bring them up in the discipline and instruction of the Lord" Eph. 6:1-4.

   b. ". . . that through these (his precious and very great promises) you may escape from the corruption that is in the world because of passion, and become partakers of the divine nature." II Pet. 1:4.

   c. It is possible for parents to direct their children so that they may become partakers of the divine nature!

2. Training has a tremendous influence upon children.

   a. The evolutionary indoctrination they get in public schools, news media, entertainment, literature, turns them into demons.

   b. *Life* magazine, May 25, 1962, editorial entitled, "The Nego" interview of a reported surveying a broad cross-section of America's most prestigious pre-schools heard them say to him: "I have no values because there is no basis for them . . . Nothing's solid; there are no values

468

to depend upon . . . Everything's gray; there aren't any values . . ." WHERE DID THEY GET THESE PHILOSOPHIES AND STANDARDS? LISTEN TO THEIR OWN ACCUSATION! "They bring us here and feed us full of Charles Darwin, Sigmund Freud, Sartre, Camus, Arthur Miller, J. D. Sallinger."

3. Parents BE ALERT, YOU HAVE IT IN YOUR POWER TO DIRECT THE DESTINIES OF YOUR CHILDREN. . . . WILL THEY BE DIVINE OR DEMONICAL?

II. ENORMITY, 11:21-43

A. Blasphemous
1. Antiouchous IV was irreligious, irreverent and blasphemous of any deity except himself called himself God 11:36-37.
2. He profaned the sacred temple of the Jews as well as temples of the gods of other nations . . . he did not even pay homage to the gods of his ancestors. In the Jewish temple he put up a statue of Jupiter (probably in his own likeness); he sacrificed a pig on the sacred altar.
3. Hermann Goering said of Hitler, "We love Adolf Hitler because we believe deeply and unswervingly that God has sent him to save Germany." Hans Franck said, "Hitler is like God."
4. Hitler preached anti-Christian, antiwestern and anti-Semitic hate and followed the blasphemous teachings of Nietzsche.
5. There have been other blasphemers equally as precocious and audacious. Herod (Acts 12); Nebuchadnezzar; Pharoah, etc.
6. Antiochus' "heart was set against the holy covenant." 11:28 He hated the holy people and their God. Hitler hated godfearing people and their God. There will always be haters of God as long as the world stands unconverted.

B. Deceitfulness
1. Antiochus was a "flatterer; one who acted deceitfully; seducer; liar;" 11:21, 23, 27, 32, 34, 36.

469

2. He made alliances and dishonored them by attacking his allies.
3. He deliberately lied about his intentions.
4. He tricked, flattered, seduced and deceived for his own ends.
5. Adolf Hitler: "The tale of how he and his aides destroyed the German republic by treachery and deceit, built a totalitarian tyranny upon foundations of intolerance and terrorism, rearmed the reich and ultimately enslaved Europe is the tale of what Konard Heiden, perhaps Hitler's most accurate biographer, 'The Epoch of Irresponsibility.' Hitler became Caesar over Europe because of prodigious power of self-deception which most influential Europeans displayed in the face of a menace which they failed to understand and in some cases even mistook for salvation. The man who fled from reality into fantasy and became a devil thereby was able to turn his fantasies into realities because his victims in all lands were blinded by their own insecurities of the old and simple distinctions between what is actual and what is illusory, what is true and what is false, what is good and what is evil." Encyclopedia Britannica
6. Hitler lied, made treaties and broke them, flattered, deceived, attacked his own allies, betrayed and murdered his friends.
7. Communist demons (Stalin, Khrushchev, Mao, Castro) have all followed the pattern of the "contemptible" Antiochus. As long as there are unbelievers in the world willing to let the devil enslave their minds, we will have DEMON POSSESSED TYRANTS.

C. Violence, Brutality
    1. Antiochus was brutal and cold-blooded. One has only to read I Maccabees to read of the atrocities committed by him and his representatives.

2. Antiochus plundered, scattered, killed, enslaved 11:24, 33.
3. Antiochus was a warmonger — he defied and worshipped war and power.
4. Josef Goebbels, Hitler's homosexual minister of propaganda, said: Hitler's opportunity was to "unchain volcanic passions, to arouse outbreaks of fury, to set masses of men on the march, to organize hate and suspicion with ice-cold calculation."
5. On Dec. 11, 1941, Hitler declared, "A historic revenge has been entrusted to us by the Creator."
6. In his last anniversary speech on Jan. 30, 1945, he declared, "The life that is left to us should serve only one task—namely, to make up for all the wrongs done by the international Jewish criminals and their henchmen to our nation . . ."
7. Things ordered to be done by him and his demon-possessed cohorts almost defy description.
   a. 8,000,000 Jews slain in gas chambers, shot, buried alive, starved to death, frozen to death, burned alive.
   b. Aged and infirm methodically slaughtered to prevent them from bearing unfit children.
   c. Human beings used as laboratory animals for experimentation by surgeons.
   d. Rape, tortures, enslavement, the skins of human beings used in one prison camp as lamp shades in the concentration camp commandant's office
   e. Cultural rape of conquered nations.
8. IS IT ANY WONDER WHY DEPRAVED, UNGODLY HUMAN GOVERNMENT AND RULERS ARE SYMBOLIZED AS "BEASTS" IN THE BIBLE?!
   a. Actually, depraved human beings are worse than the brutes.
   b. Some demon-possessed human beings will fall lower than the brutish instincts of beasts . . . THE BEAST ACTS BY INSTINCT. . . . THE DEPRAVED HUMAN ACTS DELIBERATELY AGAINST HIS CREATOR!

471

D. When human beings are taught by precept and example that they are animals—when human beings are robbed of Divine fellowship through atheism or polytheism—they will act like animals.

1. The center of the person is the will; the center of the will is attention; therefore we will be what we give our attention to (Hosea 9:10).

2. In Romans, chapter one, we see what happens to people who worship animal gods or human gods —they act like animals.

3. When men saturate their demonical wisdom (cf. James 3:13—4:10), they act like demons. BUT THANKS BE TO GOD, THROUGH A KNOWLEDGE OF HIS SON JESUS CHRIST (a knowledge both empirical and experiential) WE CAN BECOME PARTAKERS OF THE DIVINE NATURE. . . . THERE IS A WAY TO BE TRANSLATED FROM THE KINGDOM OF DEMONS TO THE DIVINE KINGDOM!

III. END

A. Despised

1. Antiochus was hated and despised by everyone except a few followers.

2. The Jews nicknamed him "Epimanes" (mad-man)

3. He was called "the contemptible one" and betrayed by his own officers.

4. He was hated by most of his own family and every other nation in the world.

5. He was contemptuously despised by the Romans.

6. Adolf Hitler was despised by most of the world.

a. Joseph Stalin described Hitler as a "cannibal."

b. Neville Chamberlain said, "In all history no other man has been responsible for such a hideous total of human suffering and misery as he."

c. Winston Churchill said he was "a bloodthirsty guttersnipe, a monster of wickedness, insatiable in his lust for blood and plunder."

d. Henry Wallace said of Hitler, "Satan has turned loose upon us the insane."

B. Cowardly

 1. Such people are usually compensating for cowardice to face up to what they think are inadequacies by their ambitions to power and by their cruelty when they have the upper hand.

 2. Antiochus was a coward when it came to facing up to the superior mettle of the Roman legate when confronted in Egypt (see our comments on 11:30).

 3. Antiochus made a sniveling death-bed attempt to confess and repent and begged the Jews to be good to his successor-son since Antiochus had been so good to the Jews.

 4. Goebbels wrote in his diary in December, 1932, "Four hours on end, the Fuehrer walks up and down in his hotel room. Once he stops and says: 'If the Party should ever break up, I'll make an end of things in three minutes with a revolver.'"

 5. Sometime in May, 1945, as Berlin's death agony approached its end, Hitler, paralyzed from a former attempt on his life and raging insanely in his bunker, carried out a death pact he had made with his mistress, Eva Braun.

C. Evaluation of these demons

 1. Antiochus IV: ". . . one of the most extraordinary characters exhibited on the pages of history. He was both avaricious and prodigal, excessive in his indulgences and prone to violent passions, a compound of the veriest folly and weakness in some respects, and of great cunning and dexterity in some others, especially in regard to flattery . . ." Stuart.

 2. Adolf Hitler: "In death, as in life, he man from Braunau remained the most sinister symbol and the most appalling incarnation of the desperate sickness of western culture in the 20th century . . . Shockingly incredible was the revelation that men, thus stripped of human attributes by their inner conflicts, can become devils, driven toward deeds of insane criminality and sadistic cruelty which

stagger the imagination and reveal depths of depravity in the human psyche hitherto unsuspected save by psychoanalysts." Encyclopedia Britannica.

CONCLUSION

WHAT IS TO BE THE REACTION OR RELATIONSHIP OF THE GODLY MAN TO DEMONIC RULERS or, HOW ARE GOD'S PEOPLE TO ACT IN TIMES WHEN DEMONS RULE?

I. PRAY FOR THEM AND PREACH TO THEM AND LIVE SO AS TO CONVERT THEM. Some have seen this come to pass; Daniel, Paul (Caesar's household).

II. TRUST IN THE LIVING GOD AND HIS PROVIDENTIAL JUSTICE AND GOODNESS TO BRING ABOUT THEIR DEMISE IN GOD'S OWN GOOD TIME.

III. UPHOLD GOOD CIVIL GOVERNMENT AND STRUCTURES OF SOCIETY WHICH ARE INSTITUTED TO BRING RESTRAINT UPON EVIL AND JUSTICE UPON THE UNCONTROLLABLE.

EXAMINATION ELEVEN AND TWELVE

REFUTATIONS

(Answer the following by giving the argument which will correct the statement)

1. The "kings of the north and of the south" are prophecies of the battles to take place in the Middle East during the millenium. Refute!

2. The "king" of 11:36ff is a prophecy of "The Antichrist" to come at the end of the N.T. age. Refute!

3. The 3½ times, the 1290 days and the 1335 days in Daniel 12 are predictions of the terrible times during a millenium age or just preceeding it near the final judgment. Refute!

ASSOCIATIONS

(Associate the persons or events of column one with the correct person or event of column two)

1	2
Cambyses	The Great
Antiochus IV	Alexander's generals
Seleucus Nicator	Ptolemly I
Smerdis	Cyrus' son
Popillius Laenas	Carthaginian
Marathon	Epiphanes
Heliodorus	mad-man
Hystaspis	city in Persia
Xerxes	Babylonian king
Ptolemy Lagi	Ptolemy's general
diadochoi	usurper to Persian throne
Antiochus III	Roman legate
Hannibal	capital of Elam
Epimanes	tax-collector
Cleopatra	Darius
Judah Maccabeus	Persian king of Esther
Kittim	Antichrist
Indignation	battle of Persians and Greeks
1290 days	millenium
1335 days	Feast of Dedication
Hanukkah	sister of Ptolemy Philometor
	prophet
	captivity of Jews
	abomination of desolation
	death of Antiochus IV

MEMORIZATIONS

(Fill in the blanks:)

And many of those who _____ in the _____ of the earth shall _____, some to _____ _____, and some to _____ and _____ _____. And those who are _____ shall _____ like the brightness of the _____; and those who _____ many to _____, like the stars for ever and ever.

475

EXPLANATIONS

1. Explain how the Seleucids came to rule over Syria and Palestine.
2. Explain the relationship of the Seleucids to the Ptolemies.
3. Explain why Antiochus IV was not the legal heir to the throne of Syria.
4. Explain why some of the Jews joined in with Antiochus Epiphanes' Hellenization of Palestine.
5. Explain how Antiochus IV was thwarted in his ambition to conquer Egypt.
6. Explain what it means when describing Antiochus IV as "honoring the god of fortresses."
7. Explain how Antiochus IV came to his end.
8. Explain the contextual meaning of the periods of time in chapter 12 entitled "time, times and half a time," "1290 days" "1335 days".

SPECIAL STUDY SIX

OUTLINE OF MATTHEW 24:1-51

by Seth Wilson

(Cf. Mark 13 and Luke 21)

I. vv. 1-3—THE OCCASION AND THE QUESTIONS. (Mk. 13:1-4; Lk. 21:5-7).

1. Observing the magnificent buildings of Jerusalem. v. 1.
2. Jesus' dire prediction: "There shall not be left here one stone upon another, that shall not be thrown down" v. 2.
3. The disciples' questions:
   (1) *"When shall these things be?"* (Destruction of Jerusalem).
   (2) *"What shall be the sign of thy coming,* and of the end of the world?" v. 3

II. vv. 4-31—ANSWERS TO THE QUESTIONS.

1. *Answers to first question,* concerning Jerusalem. (Matthew 24:4-28; Mark 13:5-23; Luke 21:8-24).

DON'T EXPECT IT TOO EARLY!

   a. Warning of preliminary troubles—"the beginning of travail." (4-14; 5-13; 8-19)
      (1) False Christs, wars, rumors of wars, famines and earthquakes do not indicate the end: be not troubled.
      (2) Persecutions, apostasies, false prophets, shall afflict the church: "take heed to yourselves", endure to the end; trust God for help; the gospel testimony shall go into all the world. (9-14; 9-13; 12-19) cf. Col. 1:6, 23; Rom. 1:8; 10:18; 16:19.

WHEN YOU DO SEE THE SIGN, EXPECT IT IMMEDIATELY!

   b. The sign of Jerusalem's end, and how to escape the woes of that terrible time. (15-28; 14-23; 20-24)
      (1) "The abomination of desolation standing in a holy place" is "Jerusalem compassed with

477

armies"; then know that her desolation is at hand."

(2) Let those in Judea flee to the mountains without delay. Pray that the hardships of flight may be lessened; but the unprecedented afflictions of the city must be escaped at all costs. Believe no false prophets, signs or promises; I have forewarned you; the Christ will not return at this time, or at any time without being seen from east to west.

EVEN THEN DON'T EXPECT THE PERSONAL
COMING OF THE LORD!

(3) The tribulation shall be excessive, shall threaten extinction of the Jewish people, shall take them captive to other nations, shall leave Jerusalem to the Gentiles, "until the times of the Gentiles be fulfilled."

2. Answer to the second question, concerning Christ's coming. (29-31; 24-27; 25-28)

a. The time is purposely indefinite; but the event is to be watched for at all times ("immediately"— Matt. 24:29), after a terrible and extended (see Luke 21:24) tribulation.

b. The event itself shall be unmistakable; accompanied by tremendous sights and sounds in all earth and heaven, the Lord Himself shall be seen by everyone, coming in the clouds with power and great glory.

c. The angels shall gather the elect from everywhere: look up, your redemption draws near. (31; 27; 28)

III. vv. 32-36—THE ANSWERS REVIEWED IN CONTRASTING SUMMARY.

1. Parable of the fig tree: signs are easily recognized. Watch for ALL THESE THINGS—wars, persecutions, false Messiahs, the desolation of Jerusalem, and great tribulation, to come to pass in this generation. (32-34; 28-30; 29-32).

2. Solemn affirmation of unfailing certainty of His words. (35; 31; 33).

478

3. But of THAT DAY, Jesus' coming, no one knows. The time cannot be told, even by the Son of God. (Matt. 24:36; Mark 13:32).

IV. vv. 37-51—PARABLES AND EXHORTATIONS TO BE READY AT ALL TIMES.

1. As in the days of Noah the flood came suddenly upon those who had been warned but believed not, so shall the coming of the Son of man be without any immediate forewarning signs. (Matt. 24:37-39)

2. In the midst of daily work, suddenly one shall be taken and another left; WATCH for you know not the day. (Matt. 24:40-42; cf. v. 31; I Thess. 4:16, 17; I Cor. 15:52.)

3. Parable of a householder unprepared for a thief who came when he was not expected. Be ready, for when you think not, the Son of man comes. (43, 44)

4. The servants of the absent Lord have each one his own work (Mark 13:34) to be faithful until He comes. He may not come as soon as they imagine; but if they think that He tarries and they can take advantage of His delay to indulge in sin, He will come when they least expect it and will punish them. (45-51; 33-37; 34-36). "WATCH AT EVERY SEASON" —Luke 21:36.

(Christ continued the same lessons in the 25th chapter —1. in the parable of the ten virgins waiting for the bridegroom, 2. in the parable of the talents committed to servants until the Lord's return, and 3. in the scene of judgment that shall take place when the Son of man shall come in His glory.)

(In these additional prophetic pictures, He emphasizes that the servants must be prepared to wait patiently and to serve faithfully even though the Master may not come for "a long time" [see v. 19]; also that His coming will bring strict judgment and swift vengeance upon all who have not used the intervening time in His service.)

479

IN CONCLUSION

"For this prophecy and similar ones were not written that we might (beforehand exactly) know history and the troubles of the future, so as to feed our curiosity as with an item of news; but that the pious might comfort themselves and rejoice over them, and that they should strengthen their faith and hope in patience, as those that see and hear that their wretchedness shall have an end, and that they, delivered from sin, death, the devil, and every evil, shall come to Christ in heaven, in his blessed eternal kingdom."

—Martin Luther

"He said to them, It is not for you to know times or seasons which the Father has fixed by his own authority. But you . . . shall be my witness in Jerusalem and in all Judea and Samaria and to the end of the earth."

—Jesus Christ (Acts 1:7-8)

"The prophets who prophesied of the grace that was to be yours searched and inquired about this salvation; they inquired what person or time was indicated by the Spirit of Christ within them when predicting the sufferings of Christ and the subsequent glory. It was revealed to them that they were serving not themselves but you, in the things which have now been announced to you by those who preached the good news to you through the Holy Spirit sent from heaven, things into which angels long to look."

—I Peter 1:10-12

BIBLIOGRAPHY

1. Lange, *Ezekiel & Daniel*, commentary, Zondervan
2. Ed. J. Young, *The Prophecy of Daniel*, Eerdmans
3. Albert Barnes, *Daniel, Vol. I & II*, Baker
4. Leupold, *Exposition of Daniel*, Baker
5. Pfeiffer, *Between The Testaments*, Baker
6. Boutflower, *In And Around the Book of Daniel*, Zondervan
7. John C. Whitcomb, *Darius The Mede*, Eerdmans
8. Robert Dick Wilson, *Studies In The Book of Daniel*, Putnam
9. J. S. Exell, *The Biblical Illustrator, Daniel*, Revell
10. Orr, *International Standard Bible Encyclopedia*, Eerdmans
11. Ed. J. Young, *An Introduction To The Old Testament*, Eerdmans
12. Butler, *Minor Prophets*, College Press
13. Hastings, *Dictionary of The Bible*, Scribners
14. Hendriksen, *More Than Conquerors*, Baker
15. Summers, *Worthy Is The Lamb*, Broadman
16. Halley, *Pocket Bible Handbook*, Zondervan
17. Keil and Delitzsch, *Daniel*, Eerdmans
18. Allis, *Prophecy and The Church*, Presbyterian & Refored
19. Josephus, *Antiquities and Wars of the Jews*, Kregel
20. Tenny, *Pictorial Bible Dictionary*, Zondervan
21. *Everyday Life in Bible Times*, National Geographic Society
22. *Greece and Rome*, National Geographic Society
23. The American Standard Version of the Bible
24. The Revised Standard Version of the Bible
25. Living Prophecies, The Minor Prophets Paraphrased with Daniel and Revelation, by Kenneth N. Taylor
26. The Berkeley Version of the Bible
27. The Douay Version of the Bible, I and II Maccabees